MW00807936

A WORLD OF ENEMIES

A
WORLD
OF
ENEMIES

AMERICA'S WARS AT
HOME AND ABROAD FROM
KENNEDY TO BIDEN

· OSAMAH F. KHALIL ·

HARVARD UNIVERSITY PRESS

CAMBRIDGE, MASSACHUSETTS
LONDON, ENGLAND

2024

Publication of this book has been supported through the generous
provisions of the Maurice and Lula Bradley Smith Memorial Fund.

Cataloging-in-Publication Data available from the Library of Congress

Names: Khalil, Osamah F., 1971– author.
Title: A world of enemies : America's wars at home and abroad from
Kennedy to Biden / Osamah F. Khalil.
Other titles: America's wars at home and abroad from Kennedy to Biden
Description: Cambridge, Massachusetts ; London, England : Harvard
University Press, 2024. | Includes bibliographical references and index.
Identifiers: LCCN 2023036132 | ISBN 9780674244221 (cloth)
Subjects: LCSH: War on Terrorism, 2001–2009. | Drug control—History—
20th century. | Drug control—History—21st century. | United States—
Foreign relations—20th century. | United States—Foreign relations—
21st century. | United States—Military policy. | United States—Politics and
government—20th century. | United States—Politics and government—
21st century.
Classification: LCC E744 .K453 2024 | DDC 327.10973—dc23/
eng/20230810
LC record available at https://lccn.loc.gov/2023036132

For Dalal and Laila

Contents

List of Maps   *ix*

Prologue   *1*

I. THE FIREMEN   *7*

1. Vietnam's Long Shadow   *11*

2. Nixon's Wars and the Long 1970s   *52*

3. Civilization's Thin Line and the Fear of Decline   *98*

II. BADLANDS   *141*

4. The Limits of Primacy   *145*

5. Constructing Global Terrorism and the Long War for Civilization   *185*

6. Dark Lands and the Geography of Empire   *233*

Epilogue   *278*

Archival Sources   307

Notes   311

Acknowledgments   377

Index   381

List of Maps

Map 1. North Vietnam and South Vietnam, 1954–1975   *15*

Map 2. Israel and the Occupied Territories, 1967–2023   *41*

Map 3. The Golden Triangle of Southeast Asia, 1968–1975   *66*

Map 4. PLO Para-state in Lebanon   *90*

Map 5. The Horn of Africa   *94*

Map 6. Southern Africa, 1969–1989   *127*

Map 7. Philadelphia's Badlands   *142*

Map 8. Colombia and the FARC   *177*

Map 9. Iraq, 2003–2020   *206*

Map 10. Afghanistan and Pakistan   *228*

Map 11. Map of International Heroin Trafficking   *235*

Map 12. Mexico and Leading Drug Trafficking Organizations, 2010–2017   *262*

Map 13. Kurdish Para-states   *284*

A WORLD OF ENEMIES

Prologue

Invocation of Vietnam as quagmire, syndrome, and war speaks neither to Vietnamese reality nor to current difficulties in Iraq and Afghanistan. It speaks to American fear. Americans think that defeat
in these wars is the worst thing, when winning in Iraq and Afghanistan today only means more of the same tomorrow: Somalia, Pakistan, Yemen, and so on. This is the most important reason for Americans to remember what they call the Vietnam War, the fact that it
was one conflict in a long line of horrific wars that came before it
and after it. This war's identity—and, indeed, any war's identity—
cannot be extricated from the identity of war itself.

—VIET THANH NGUYEN

THE STEALTH BLACK HAWK helicopters crossed the night sky into Pakistan.
They carried two teams of the elite SEAL Team Six Special Forces unit, a
translator, and a dog. Three Chinook transport helicopters with reserve
forces, as well as jet fighters and other combat aircraft, were ready to provide support. High above the quiet neighborhood, an advanced drone
transmitted live video of the target. Admiral William McRaven of Special
Forces Command communicated with the teams from a base in Jalal-
abad, Afghanistan. In Washington, President Barack Obama and his
national security team watched the assault in a White House conference
room. After forty tense minutes, the mission was complete. The SEAL
Team leader confirmed, "For God and country, I pass Geronimo," he
said, "Geronimo E KIA." The long search for the most wanted man in the
world, Osama bin Laden, was over.[1]

Code-named Operation Neptune's Spear, the mission reflected the might and technological advantage of the US military. The latest military hardware was deployed and augmented with advanced geospatial maps and imagery. Yet bin Laden's death was not the final devastating blow against his al-Qaʻida network. Indeed, President Obama cautioned that it "does not mark the end of our effort." More than a decade later, the battlefields of the Global War on Terror have expanded. It has also persisted in pervasive surveillance and law enforcement programs that have blurred the lines between the domestic and foreign arenas.[2]

As Obama addressed the nation and the world about the successful operation, cheering crowds filled New York City's Times Square, and Lafayette Square near the White House. Operation Neptune's Spear framed Obama's reelection campaign a year later. At the Democratic Party's convention in Charlotte, North Carolina, Vice President Joe Biden reassured the crowd and viewers watching at home with the campaign's unofficial slogan: "Osama bin Laden is dead and General Motors is alive." More than a decade after the September 11 attacks and four years after the 2008 financial crisis that nearly crippled the global economy, it was an intentional marriage of domestic and foreign policies infused with triumphal militarism.[3]

The mission also reproduced the engrained use of Native American names and imagery by the US military. It was evident in the helicopters deployed ("Black Hawks" and "Chinooks") to the ceremonial hatchets adopted by Special Forces units and the tattoos that adorned their arms. Bin Laden was code-named "Geronimo," after the Chiricahua Apache chief who eluded the US and Mexican armies for more than two decades until his final surrender in 1886. The cultural appropriation disguised as honoring the "warrior ethos" of Native American tribes is not limited to military equipment and weaponry. Indeed, embedded within the military's discourse about operations in hostile territory is the metaphor of "Indian country." Usage of the phrase from Vietnam in the 1960s to Iraq and Afghanistan four decades later demonstrates the persistence of racialized rhetoric that dehumanizes entire populations. This book examines how the notion of "Indian country" was extended not just overseas but at home, as well. In the geographical imagination of policymakers, the perception of lawless "badlands" that described urban neighborhoods during the Prohibition era was later applied to disparate areas from South Asia to the southwest United States.[4]

This book traverses the contested terrains and intersecting trajectories of the Wars on Crime, Drugs, and Terror. From the streets of major American cities to the sites of US military interventions, it explores the implications of the policies developed and implemented to manage these constructed spaces across the globe. In manufacturing these hostile territories, the United States presented the conflicts as part of a larger War for Civilization that was fought at home and abroad. The expanding map of American military operations reified these areas as chronic sources of instability and violence that were best mitigated by force. Yet Washington's inability to impose its will reflected and reinforced the perception of American weakness and decline.[5]

America's status as the preeminent world power has been sustained by the geographical imagination of policymakers and national security experts. This imaginary draws on the United States' history of racial and religious supremacy. It informs how Americans interact with the rest of the world. The imaginary is also influenced by and reproduces constructed notions of ethnic, religious, and sectarian identities. American policymakers drew on and employed social science expertise that reified the biased perceptions of domestic minorities as well as populations overseas. Often cloaked in the language of cultural and religious differences, these perceptions reinforced a manufactured civilizational divide.[6]

Defining civilization necessitates an opposite. Notions of the "other" accompany constructed geographies and are intrinsic to civilizational discourse. During the colonial period, Native Americans were depicted as the primitive savage to be tamed. After independence, westward expansion was justified as a messianic mission for progress. Official and unofficial perceptions of natives were transported to America's overseas territories and beyond. As in the American West, the civilizing mission was imposed by force and opposition was equated with barbarism. By the early twentieth century, civilizational rhetoric was invoked to justify American police powers in the Western hemisphere and then globally. During the Cold War, Washington invariably viewed native populations under European colonial rule as unfit for independence and sought to manage their transition to self-rule. Even when national liberation movements did not espouse Marxist-Leninist ideology, American policymakers viewed them with suspicion. After the Cold War, the specters of savagery and chaos hung over the deliberations and the policies that were implemented across the Global South.[7]

At home, the War for Civilization was initially embodied in the narratives accompanying anti-crime and anti-drug policies. Crime and drugs were depicted as existential threats to society. The dire warnings evidenced a paternalism and notions of racial and religious inferiority toward minorities similar to those employed for populations across the Global South. Like drug trafficking, terrorism bridged the domestic and foreign arenas. America's wars at home and abroad have been mutually reinforcing and the line between domestic policing and military occupations has diminished. In both spheres, policymakers and national security experts deemed the inhabitants to be uncivilized and validated the use of excessive force. Barbarism and the badlands justified even more interventions and greater force.[8]

This is a story about policy failures across six decades. But rarely have these failures been acknowledged. As will be demonstrated, policies were introduced with great fanfare and outlandish goals, and frequently touted as successes for export to other areas. Historical amnesia accompanied by often deliberate manipulation and falsification of history ensured that these failed policies were adapted and applied to new conflicts. As will be seen in the pages that follow, the replication of those failures has had a profound influence on America's standing in the world and constrains, rather than benefits, US domestic and foreign policies.

To demonstrate the implications of these policy failures, this book examines three converging trends. The first is America's increasing involvement in the developing world. This has been evidenced in overt and covert interventions and proxy conflicts over the past six decades. It was not limited to the Cold War competition with the Soviet Union as the War for Civilization continued into the twenty-first century. Both the War on Drugs and the Global War on Terror have become institutionalized.[9]

A World of Enemies unifies these conflicts and their associated literatures to explore intersecting case studies from Southeast Asia to South America. These were the sites of covert and overt interventions that occupied significant attention from American policymakers and had implications for domestic politics. The policies that were implemented and their underlying perceptions were mutually reinforcing. The case studies demonstrate the geographic imaginary of American policymakers as Cold War conflict zones were transformed into global badlands in the post–Cold War era. These were the battlefields of America's War for Civilization.

The second trend is the influence of domestic politics and policies on US foreign policy. This has been evidenced in obvious and subtle ways. Policy development and implementation are often reactive, and this is particularly true in foreign affairs. American presidents and presidential candidates rarely center their campaigns on foreign policy issues. Their presidencies, however, have often been dominated by crises overseas. During the Cold War, US containment policies had bipartisan support. In the post–Cold War era, aggressive hyperpower has become a bipartisan project. Domestic policies have also been exported in overt and latent ways. As will be explored in the following pages, this is apparent in counternarcotics and counterterrorism policies.[10]

Aligned with the domestic sphere is American popular culture and its global influence. *A World of Enemies* demonstrates how popular culture provided a reference point for American policymakers, national security experts, journalists, and law enforcement officials, as well as the general public. Washington also recognized the "soft power" of popular culture and sought to influence domestic and foreign audiences with subtle and overt messages that aligned with US interests.[11]

The final intersecting trend is the evolution of notions of American primacy and decline. Even as they sought to achieve and maintain primacy, American policymakers and national security experts were also preoccupied with the implications of decline. Domestic and foreign threats were amplified after the Vietnam War as the preponderance of American power was no longer presumed. Failure in Vietnam contributed to an existential angst about America's future and the implications for the postwar order. In the post–Vietnam War era, the effort to reassert American dominance was limited by an economic contraction. The societal and generational ruptures that accompanied the Vietnam War and the anti-war movement exacerbated the perception that the American dream was no longer unbounded. Post-Vietnam fears of decline contributed to the 1980 election of Ronald Reagan and conservative dominance. Notions of decline were present in the post–Cold War triumphalism, the post–September 11 hyper-militarism, the 2008 financial collapse and ensuing "Great Recession," and Donald Trump's presidency. This was compounded by the depiction of threats everywhere. American politicians and policymakers saw a world of enemies at home and abroad.[12]

Crime and narcotics have been portrayed as symptoms of American decline. They have also served to bridge domestic and foreign policies. During and after the Vietnam War era, crime and narcotics were racialized and portrayed in the starkest terms as a threat to the American way of life. From Johnson to Trump, these portrayals were effective for politicians and their advisors. The Wars on Crime and Drugs provided an opportunity for successive administrations to unleash America's military might inside and outside the United States, establishing precedents for the Global War on Terror. They were depicted as struggles to secure the homeland and save civilization, and their conflation and institutionalization has had intended and unintended consequences.[13]

This is not a book about the Vietnam War. It is about the world that conflict helped to shape. The war served as a reference point for influential diplomats, soldiers, and experts, although they did not always draw the same lessons. It was an experience they frequently returned to for better and worse. In Vietnam, the United States adapted some of its tactics and practices from prior conflicts, including in the Philippines and Korea, but the war had its own important impact on popular memory and culture. American militarism has not been limited to foreign battlefields. Politicians and policymakers have insisted that Americans are engaged in an existential struggle against foes seen and unseen, foreign and domestic. Thus, militarism has seeped into everyday American life as the United States has not settled for defeat or victory but for war as a permanent state.[14]

This is a story that begins with a young senator from Massachusetts and an insurgency in South Vietnam and continues to this day.

PART I

THE FIREMEN

LESS THAN FOUR YEARS after becoming a United States Senator, John F. Kennedy was already a rising star in the Democratic Party. With the 1956 presidential election only six months away, Kennedy spoke before a new organization, the American Friends of Vietnam (AFV). The AFV was led by General William "Will Bill" Donovan. During the Second World War, Donovan had been the head of the Office of Strategic Services (OSS), the United States' wartime intelligence service. Donovan remained active with the intelligence community until his death in 1959. The goal of the AFV, founded in 1955, was to maintain support for Vietnam as a broader symbol of freedom in the Cold War competition with Moscow. Toward that end, it boasted bipartisan membership of Democratic and Republican politicians, as well as the leading publishers and editors of major media outlets—most prominently, Time-Life's Henry Luce. Donovan and the AFV's leadership did not favor implementing the 1954 Geneva Accords that brought French colonial rule in Vietnam to an end. In opposing the agreement's provision for national elections, the AFV found like minds in the Eisenhower administration.[1]

Kennedy, who was the keynote speaker at the AFV's conference held in Washington, had become increasingly hawkish on Vietnam and this was reflected in his speech. "Vietnam represents the cornerstone of the Free World in Southeast Asia, the keystone in the arch, the finger in the dike," he declared, and it was a "test of American responsibility and determination." Reviewing American efforts in Southeast Asia and globally, Kennedy found them haphazard and wanting. "Our neglect of Vietnam is the result of one of the most serious weaknesses that has hampered the long-range effectiveness of American foreign policy over the past several years," he said, "and that is the over emphasis upon our role as 'volunteer fire department' for the world. Whenever and wherever fire breaks out—in Indo-China, in the Middle East, in Guatemala, in Cyprus, in the Formosan Straits—our firemen rush in, wheeling up all their heavy equipment, and resorting to every known method of containing and extinguishing the blaze. The crowd gathers—the usually successful efforts of our able volunteers are heartily applauded—and then the firemen rush off to the next conflagration, leaving the grateful but still stunned inhabitants to clean up the rubble, pick up the pieces and rebuild their homes with whatever resources are available."[2]

One still-classified study produced a few months after Kennedy's speech suggested that America's intelligence agencies were setting the fires, rather than extinguishing them. The 1956 report, produced by two veterans of the intelligence community, David Bruce and Robert Lovett, was critical of the CIA. Bruce and Lovett argued that the agency's emphasis on "King Making" in the Third World and reliance on covert action and psychological warfare operations detracted from its intelligence-gathering capabilities. But those warnings were ignored.[3]

Instead, the CIA was emboldened by the success of the coup that had overthrown the Iranian prime minister, Muhammad Mossadeq, in August 1953. Less than a year later, President Eisenhower had approved National Security Council Directive 5412, in May 1954. The directive authorized global covert operations. Director of Central Intelligence Allen Dulles later described it as "one of the most secret documents in the US government." For the next five years, NSC 5412 was the lodestar. Covert operations were launched across the Third World and were overseen by Dulles and the 5412 Group, which included senior administration officials selected by President Eisenhower. Washington attempted to undermine

Egypt's Gamal Abdel Nasser, Indonesia's Sukarno, and Shukri al-Quwatli in Syria, among others. Operations to destabilize North Vietnam also continued. That these failed to achieve their goals did not deter more adventures.[4]

The Cuban revolution created a new rationale for American intervention in the Western Hemisphere. Although CIA planning to overthrow Fidel Castro's government had begun before the 1960 election, it had repeatedly been delayed. During the campaign, Kennedy criticized his opponent, Vice President Richard Nixon, and the Eisenhower administration over the "loss" of Cuba. After Kennedy took office, he oversaw planning for an expanded operation.

In April 1961, Operation JMATE was launched. It was a debacle. In the aftermath, President Kennedy requested that his brother, Attorney General Robert F. Kennedy, and former Army Chief of Staff General Maxwell Taylor convene a study of the operation. They were joined by Allen Dulles and Chief of Naval Operations Admiral Arleigh Burke. The review placed the blame on the Eisenhower administration for not recognizing that the situation in Cuba made a covert operation difficult. Dulles stepped down as CIA director and General Taylor was appointed chair of the Joint Chiefs of Staff a year later. But the Bay of Pigs review did not lead to a substantial change in covert operations or Washington's culture of intervention.[5]

Instead, RFK and Taylor led Operation Mongoose, the secret initiative to assassinate Castro. They were joined by General Edward Lansdale, recently returned from South Vietnam and already a living legend in the world of covert operations. President Kennedy briefly considered naming Lansdale his ambassador to South Vietnam. In place of Saigon, Lansdale focused on Havana with RFK, Taylor, Cuban expatriate groups, and unsavory characters from the intelligence community and American organized crime. But their efforts to kill Castro had the unintended consequence of bringing Havana and Moscow closer together and culminated in the Cuban Missile Crisis.[6]

Well before Soviet Premier Nikita Khrushchev declared that national liberation movements were sacred, Washington was working to subvert them. Nearly fifteen years earlier, in his famous "Long Telegram," George Kennan had warned that "toward colonial areas and backward or dependent peoples" Moscow would attempt to weaken the European colonial powers. Soviet Premier Joseph Stalin had evidenced little interest, however, in the colonial territories or their potential for extending Moscow's influence. NSC 5412 was authorized a year after Stalin's death and reflected a combination of American power and anxiety. This continued for the remainder of the Cold War and beyond.[7]

In a soaring inaugural address that captured the imaginations of youthful baby boomers, Kennedy also harked back to his AFV speech. The world needed American leadership and he pledged the nation would "pay any price, bear any burden, meet any hardship, support any friend, oppose any foe in order to assure the survival and the success of liberty." As Kennedy spoke, South Vietnam was already afire. Part I tells the story of how, in their attempts to contain the blaze, America's firefighters ensured its spread.[8]

CHAPTER ONE

Vietnam's Long Shadow

The war in Vietnam is but a symptom of a far deeper malady within
the American spirit.

—REVEREND MARTIN LUTHER KING JR., 1967

IN EARLY APRIL 1965, President Lyndon B. Johnson traveled to the leafy
campus of Johns Hopkins University in Baltimore. A month earlier, he
had ordered the first US ground troops into South Vietnam. Their stated
mission was to protect American bases in support of the punishing air
campaign against North Vietnam known as Operation Rolling Thunder.
Johnson and his advisors had no intention, however, of limiting ground
troops to just two Marine battalions. In his speech, Johnson portrayed
the intervention as a noble and necessary sacrifice. He evoked memories
of his political hero, President Franklin Delano Roosevelt, and the Second
World War. "Why must this Nation hazard its ease, and its interest, and
its power for the sake of a people so far away? We fight because we must
fight," he intoned, "if we are to live in a world where every country can
shape its own destiny. And only in such a world will our own freedom be
finally secure." In short, he concluded, "we must deal with the world as it
is, if it is ever to be as we wish."[1]

Yet over the next three years, Johnson ignored the realities of Vietnam
and the larger world as it was. Instead, Vietnam was a conflict his

administration chose and shaped, with implications that resonated far beyond Southeast Asia and Johnson's term in office. This chapter argues that the Kennedy, Johnson, and Nixon administrations adopted policies at home and abroad to contain the impact of the Vietnam War. They employed methods and tactics that would become persistent features of counterinsurgency operations—and later, counterterrorism efforts—that entrenched conflicts from Southeast Asia to South America. Domestically, the same methods were applied in the overt War on Crime and in covert surveillance to squelch dissent. The Vietnam War experience had a profound impact on a generation of American diplomats, intelligence, and military officers as they formed their perspectives on American power and policy in future conflicts.

BEAR ANY BURDEN

Three days before John F. Kennedy took the oath of office, General Edward Lansdale drafted a lengthy report for Thomas Gates Jr., the outgoing secretary of defense. Lansdale warned that 1961 would be a fateful year in Vietnam as the "Communist Viet Cong" sought to capture all of South Vietnam. "A Communist victory also would be a major blow to US prestige and influence, not only in Asia but throughout the world," Lansdale wrote, "since the world believes that Vietnam has remained free only through US help." Washington needed to recognize that South Vietnam was in "critical condition and should treat it as a combat area of the cold war, as an area requiring emergency treatment," he added. The United States should pick the "best people" with experience in "dealing with this precise type of emergency, and send them to the spot with orders to remedy the situation."[2]

Although Lansdale discussed the opposition within Vietnam to President Ngo Dinh Diem, missing from his report was any analysis of its size and composition. Rather than address the very real and growing animosity toward Diem's government, Washington and Saigon dismissed the opposition as "Viet Cong" or Vietnamese communists. Less than two years before Lansdale's report, Diem had effectively outlawed all opposition to his government under Law 10/59. In December 1960, only a few weeks before Lansdale submitted his report, the National Liberation Front (NLF) had been formed as a coalition of political parties, ranging from nationalists to communists, united in opposition to Diem. The NLF's popularity and demands were ignored by the Kennedy and Johnson administrations. Instead, Washington emphasized Hanoi's influence over the insurgency and framed it as an invasion rather than a civil war. Evidence to the contrary was ignored or dismissed. References to the "Viet Cong," whether communist or not, became part of the daily vernacular of American political and military officials.[3]

Eight days after he was inaugurated, Kennedy met with General Lansdale in the Oval Office, and Lansdale's report on the situation stunned the new president. Afterwards he spoke with Deputy National Security Advisor Walt Whitman Rostow. "This is the worst one we've got, isn't it?" Kennedy said. "You know, Eisenhower never uttered the word Vietnam." An economic historian by training, Rostow was based at the Massachusetts Institute of Technology's Center for International Studies and was very influential in the development of modernization theory. His 1960 book *The Stages of Economic Growth* was one of that field's seminal texts. In the Kennedy and Johnson administrations, he had the rare opportunity to put theory into practice. Rostow believed that modernization theory and counterinsurgency efforts were entwined, and Vietnam was the ideal test case.[4]

Lansdale, meanwhile, had developed a reputation as a counterinsurgency expert in the Philippines prior to his deployment in Vietnam. A veteran of the OSS and a successful advertising executive, he was the inspiration for the protagonists of two 1950s novels, Graham Greene's *The Quiet American* and William Lederer and Eugene Burdick's *The Ugly American*. Both works were critical examinations of America's burgeoning role in Southeast Asia and they added to Lansdale's carefully cultivated mythology.

In the Philippines in the early 1950s, Lansdale had applied a combination of espionage, marketing, self-promotion, and grift to defeating the Huk insurgency. Like the Viet Minh in Japanese-occupied French Indochina, the Hukbo ng Bayan Laban Sa Hapon (People's Anti-Japanese Liberation Army) had been natural wartime allies of the United States. But their adoption of Marxist philosophy was a liability in the emerging Cold War competition between Washington and Moscow. The Philippines had declared independence in 1946 and its fledgling government had been unable or unwilling to address the grievances of peasants for fundamental reforms.[5]

Launched a year later, the Huk insurgency had amassed a large base of support in Central Luzon, the largest and most populous of the Philippines' two thousand inhabited islands. But even as the insurgency's fifteen thousand fighters enjoyed early successes against the overmatched Filipino military and police, the United States was finalizing treaties with Manila that promised a direct American military presence for the next century. This was reaffirmed by the Truman administration's August 1948 determination that the Philippines were of the same strategic importance as Western Europe, the Eastern Mediterranean and Middle East, and Japan. Washington was determined to keep these areas from falling into hostile hands. Two years later, during the Korean War, the Philippines became part of the United States' defense perimeter.[6]

Lansdale had arrived in Manila three years into the insurgency. He launched an integrated intelligence gathering, counterinsurgency, psychological warfare, and propaganda operation to defeat the Huks. Lansdale also promoted Ramon Magsaysay, a former Filipino congressman who was appointed secretary of national defense. With American military assistance and Lansdale's advice, Filipino forces made rapid gains against the Huks. Defeating the insurgency and maintaining close ties to Washington ensured Magsaysay's victory in the November 1953 Filipino presidential election. By the time those votes were cast, Lansdale was already in Saigon.[7]

The Eisenhower administration sought to apply the lessons of the Philippines to Vietnam. To undermine the 1954 Geneva Accords, Lansdale was tasked by CIA Director Allen Dulles and his brother, Secretary of State John Foster Dulles, to "do what you did in the Philippines." Just as he had for Magsaysay, Lansdale was able to strengthen Diem's image and promote him to eager supporters in Washington and the American press. Diem consolidated his rule during the Eisenhower administration, but he was unable to secure a broad base of support in the fledgling Republic of Vietnam. His policies, rather than suppressing a brewing insurgency, contributed to its emergence. The Lansdale approach to the Philippines was just one of several that Washington applied to Vietnam in vain.[8]

With Washington eagerly seeking counterinsurgency models to adopt, the Pentagon embraced and promoted Malaya as another successful example. The situation there, however, had not been similar to the one in South Vietnam. Britain's initial postwar attempts to maintain its Malayan

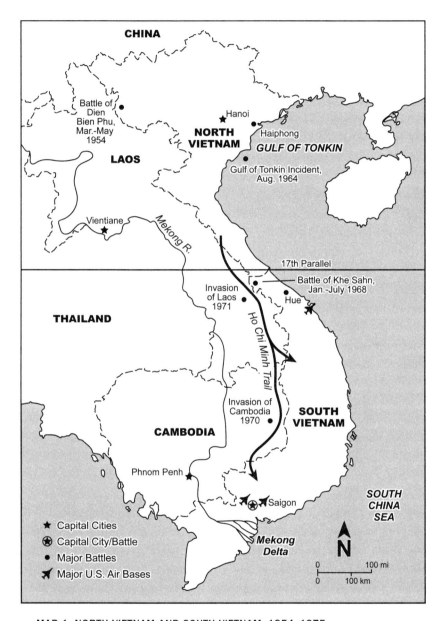

MAP 1. NORTH VIETNAM AND SOUTH VIETNAM, 1954–1975

colony had engendered resistance from local leaders and an emerging Communist Party. The communist-led insurgency had provided British officials with the opportunity to implement reforms and counterinsurgency strategies while developing alliances with conservative religious and ethnic groups. Still, the idea that Britain's successful counterinsurgency approach was exportable to the rest of Asia found a keen audience in the Kennedy White House and the Pentagon. American political and military planners relied on the advice of Malaya veterans—in particular, Robert Thompson, leader of the British Advisory Mission to Vietnam. He was consulted, for example, on the "Strategic Hamlet Program," which was launched in 1962 to eliminate rural support for the insurgency. As would become the habit over the next six decades, the differences between Malaya and South Vietnam were overlooked as policies were adapted and ultimately failed.[9]

French colonial rule in North Africa yielded yet another counterinsurgency model. Inspired in part by the Viet Minh's 1954 victory over French forces at Dien Bien Phu, the Algerian revolution had followed a similar trajectory. As in Vietnam, Algerian resistance to French colonial rule dated from its inception in 1830. But French colonial and military authorities had succeeded in suppressing Algerians through a combination of brute force, racist laws, and divide-and-conquer politics. The emergence of the Algerian National Liberation Front, or Front de Libération Nationale (FLN), was partially due to the successful disruption of existing nationalist parties by French authorities.

Less than four months after the Geneva Accords were signed in 1954, simultaneous attacks across Algeria heralded a new challenge to the French empire. Over the next three years, violence escalated in Algeria as French security services attempted to quell the uprising, and internecine fighting between the FLN and rival movements contributed to the rising death toll. Hoping to crush the revolution, French forces hijacked an airliner carrying the FLN's external leadership on October 22, 1956, and held them prisoner for the remainder of the conflict. A week later, after months of secret planning, France joined Britain and Israel in the 1956 Suez War. That conflict failed, however, to remove the FLN's main supporter, Egypt's Gamal Abdel Nasser, from power. These actions, coupled with increasing repression by French security forces and harsh sentences (including liberal application of the death penalty), further tarnished France's international reputation.[10]

With international awareness of the Algerian struggle heightened by France's tactics, the FLN attempted to seize the advantage. In early 1957, the United Nations scheduled a session on Algeria's future. Leading up to the UN debate, the FLN launched an eight-day general strike accompanied by attacks on targets across Algiers. The French military, determined to break the Algiers cell, relied on sweeping arrests, torture, and summary executions. France's military victory in what became known as the Battle of Algiers proved to be a political failure at home and in Algeria. The Eisenhower administration attempted to convince Paris of the need to reach a negotiated settlement, and Senator John F. Kennedy publicly endorsed Algerian independence in a speech on the Senate floor. Over the next two years, revelations of France's tactics undermined popular support for the war. Algeria finally declared independence on July 5, 1962.[11]

Four years later, Gillo Pontecorvo's now classic film *The Battle of Algiers* was released to widespread acclaim, winning the prestigious Golden Lion award at the Venice Film Festival, over French protests, and the top prize at the London Film Festival. American viewers saw in it reflections of their own escalating war in Southeast Asia and urban unrest at home. The film was chosen as the opener for the New York Film Festival in September 1967. "Viewers with partisan feelings and historical sympathies," observed *New York Times* film critic Bosley Crowther, "can readily see in the endeavors of the Algerians to free themselves (at least, from French domination) a parallel to what is happening in Vietnam or to events that have transpired this past summer in the cities of the United States." The latter reference was to unrest in Detroit and Newark in the summer of 1967—which had broader implications for US domestic politics and foreign policy.[12]

The Battle of Algiers was embraced in radical circles in the United States and overseas. Writing in the *New Yorker* three years after its release, Pauline Kael reflected that it had "become known as the black militants training film." The Black Panthers may have been embraced as darlings of New York's "radical chic" crowd, but across the country they were subjected by federal, state, and local authorities to surveillance, harassment, arrest, and assassination. Two of the group's leaders, Donald L. Cox and Eldridge Cleaver, fled the United States for Algeria, home of the party's international headquarters. Although Algeria's internal politics were increasingly author-itarian, the country had become a magnet for national liberation move-ments across the Third World. Over the next four decades, *The Battle of Algiers* continued to influence filmmakers, and in the aftermath of September 11, 2001, it would find a new audience at the Pentagon.[13]

Among the counterinsurgency measures employed by the French in Vietnam and Algeria and later adapted by the Kennedy administration was the practice of establishing "secure zones" for the relocation of Vietnamese peasants, similar to the concentration camp policy employed in Algeria. The secure zones were initially established by Diem's government through its "agroville" program. Although neither the secure zones nor the agrovilles managed to reduce the insurgency, their lack of success was ig-nored by the Kennedy administration. Kennedy and Johnson forged ahead, both also disregarding warnings from French President Charles de Gaulle about deepening involvement in Vietnam.[14]

By 1962, the Kennedy administration began implementing its own ver-sion of a counterinsurgency policy. First proposed by a staff member of the National Security Council (NSC), Robert Komer, the policy had its roots in both Vietnam and the April 1961 Bay of Pigs attempt to over-throw Cuba's Fidel Castro. On January 18, 1962, Kennedy authorized Na-tional Security Action Memorandum (NSAM) 124, which established a senior-level interdepartmental committee called the "Special Group (Coun-terinsurgency)." NSAM 124 states that one function of the Special Group is to ensure proper recognition across government that "subversive insur-gency ('wars of liberation') is a major form of politico-military conflict equal in importance to conventional warfare." Drawing on support from a range of government agencies, the policy focused on the insurgencies in Laos, South Vietnam, and Thailand.[15]

Six months later, Kennedy also approved NSAM 162, authorizing the development of internal defense plans for countries facing insurgencies and drawing on prior experiences in the Philippines, Malaya, and Algeria. In addition to identifying appropriate counterinsurgency personnel, NSAM 162 called for increased reliance on third-country personnel, the "exploita-tion" of minorities for use in paramilitary groups, improved indigenous intelligence capabilities, and enhanced research and development on coun-terinsurgency. All these measures were adopted in part or in full in South-east Asia and globally during and after Kennedy's presidency.[16]

Although Kennedy's presidency was cut short, his policies in Vietnam had profound implications. Perhaps the most consequential was the decision to overthrow Ngo Dinh Diem. This coup differed from those authorized during the Eisenhower administration and the Bay of Pigs invasion, in that Diem was a US ally. There was evidence, however, that he was preparing to negotiate a cease-fire with Hanoi that would have embarrassed Kennedy in the midst of a reelection campaign. The assassination of Diem, along with his brother Ngo Dinh Nhu, did not bring stability to South Vietnam, improve the performance of the South Vietnamese military, or shorten the war. Instead, it had the unintended consequence of galvanizing the insurgency. It also limited Johnson's options, as Diem was replaced by a series of hapless and corrupt generals. While it is unlikely that Kennedy would have pursued the large-scale conflict that Johnson later embraced, it is unclear what he would have done if counterinsurgency efforts had continued to falter and the South Vietnamese military had remained ineffective. In any case, after that fateful day in Dallas, Vietnam became Lyndon Johnson's war.[17]

PACIFICATION

"In 1964 we will be better prepared than ever before to defend the cause of freedom," President Johnson wrote, "whether it is threatened by outright aggression or by the infiltration practiced by those in Hanoi and Havana, who ship arms across international frontiers to foment insurrection." The recipient of Johnson's missive was Rostow. For over two years as deputy national security advisor Rostow had advocated an increasingly hard line toward North Vietnam, but had been effectively sidelined within the Kennedy administration. A month after Kennedy's assassination, Rostow recommended that Johnson include a message to Hanoi in his first State of the Union Address, warning against any infiltration of guerrillas into South Vietnam. Johnson's positive response showed Rostow he had found a kindred spirit. The new president shared his perspective on countering insurgencies and the countries and individuals responsible for them. Policies they would go on to institute would come with extraordinary body counts and other consequences persisting long after they left Washington.[18]

One of Rostow's vehicles to achieve modernization and defeat the insurgency in South Vietnam was the Strategic Hamlet Program. Rostow oversaw its development and implementation. In practice, the program amounted to a massive rural relocation program, with over sixteen thousand villages being migrated into heavily fortified and guarded compounds. Within the hamlets, corrupt local government officials oversaw the surveillance of relocated villagers. Despite the significant resources Washington devoted to the program, it did not have the intended result. Instead of shrinking, the ranks of the insurgents swelled—and the popularity of Diem's government was further diminished. In part, this was due to a fundamental flaw in the program, as the opposition it engendered among the South Vietnamese was difficult for Rostow and others to comprehend. Rostow focused on the open border areas with Laos that allowed for infiltration of guerrillas and supplies into South Vietnam. This also conveniently reinforced his support for an approach that would couple a more aggressive military campaign against North Vietnam with an active counterinsurgency program in the south.[19]

Over the course of the Johnson administration, the United States introduced, modified, and abandoned a range of aggressive counterinsurgency measures and escalating bombing campaigns. Although American forces inflicted massive casualties, the insurgency remained potent. Yet there was consistent pressure on the US military and the CIA to report progress from the highest levels of the Johnson administration. In March 1966, nearly two years after introducing ground troops into South Vietnam, President Johnson tasked Robert Komer with leading civilian pacification there. Known as "Blowtorch Bob," either because of his volatile temperament or his preferred interrogation method, Komer was the man Johnson saw as right for the job. He reported directly to Johnson on pacification matters and participated in Tuesday lunch discussions on Vietnam with the president and his key advisors.[20]

Yet Komer's presidential access and frequent trips to South Vietnam did not translate to improved pacification on the ground or enhanced coordination with the US embassy in Saigon. Writing to Johnson in July 1966, after his second visit to South Vietnam, Komer reported there had been some military success against the insurgency, but it was "not yet matched by our pacification and civil side operations." The "weak link in the chain," he wrote, was the South Vietnamese government (GVN) and armed forces (ARVN): "We must get a greater return out of them—and it would be cheap at the price." Although the ARVN had a force of seven hundred thousand men, they were "not pulling their weight. Nor is the GVN civil side. The US is bearing the brunt of the effort—which is neither necessary nor desirable."[21]

Among his recommendations, which were supported by Secretary of Defense McNamara, were suggestions to improve on South Vietnam's "Civic Action Cadre" program and expand its rural police field force. The cadre program dispatched young administrators to oversee development projects in rural areas. Although Komer noted the inconsistency of their training and supervision, he still saw the potential benefit. "The cadre program is promising," he reported, "but it is just one of many pacification instruments and will take time to achieve significant impact." With regard to the police field force, Komer argued that it should be expanded to fifteen thousand officers by 1967. As demonstrated by Komer's memorandums and recommendations, Washington placed increasing emphasis on counterinsurgency in South Vietnam's countryside, while also calling for greater efforts by Saigon and the ARVN. These goals were not achieved, and accurate reporting to Washington that reflected this reality remained an issue.[22]

Hanging over the attempts to determine if the pacification efforts were successful was the history of the US military's optimistic reporting during the Kennedy years. McNamara's solution was to roll out, in 1967, a Hamlet Evaluation System based on objectively observable and quantifiable measures. Although it was designed to prevent manipulation of data in the field, key figures in the Johnson administration were more difficult to manage. Even as Rostow pushed for this improved reporting on pacification efforts to be expanded nationwide, he applied political pressure on the military commanders to demonstrate that operations were successful.[23]

On July 12, 1967, McNamara briefed President Johnson on his recent visit to South Vietnam. "There is not a military stalemate," the defense secretary reported, and his assessment was confirmed by General Earle Wheeler, chair of the Joint Chiefs of Staff. While progress on pacification was still slow, McNamara claimed it was exceeding his expectations. "Pacification is a serious problem because it is difficult to detect who is a Viet Cong and who is not," McNamara emphasized, and the means used to determine the identities of insurgents were "sloppy."[24]

Hearings held by the House Select Committee on Intelligence nearly nine years after McNamara's briefing exposed the tensions that had

existed between the US military and the CIA over reporting on the Vietnamese insurgency. Former CIA Director William Colby related to the
Pike Committee (chaired by Democratic Representative Otis Pike of New
York) that, four months before the January 1968 Tet Offensive, a conference had been held in Saigon between the CIA and the US Military Assistance Command in Vietnam (MACV) to resolve their different views
of the Vietnamese insurgency. While MACV had viewed the insurgency
in the "classic military sense" of standing forces, the CIA had argued that
this severely underestimated the size and support of a "much broader people's war." It had been MACV's approach that successfully influenced the
description and classification of the insurgency in a subsequently produced National Intelligence Estimate. Thus, on the eve of the Tet Offensive, the intelligence community discounted the total size of the insurgency by nearly two hundred thousand—all the Vietnamese who were
associated with irregular and self-defense forces and youth cadres. The
State Department had challenged this narrower definition in part because
it raised the question of how to classify Vietnamese casualties when those
killed were not described as insurgents. Meanwhile, analysts at the Pentagon had asserted that the new classification system indicated that the
previous estimates of the insurgency's size were too low. In short, the understanding of the insurgency had been distorted by bureaucratic and domestic politics.[25]

Underlying the fight over how to define the insurgency was what was
done with the data. Although the objective of gathering information was
to make policymakers aware of the reality of a situation, Colby testified in
1975 that the State Department and the Pentagon had routinely relied on
more optimistic figures to demonstrate success. This was to meet an expectation set by the Johnson White House. The Pike Committee found
that "considerable pressure was placed on the intelligence community to
generate numbers, less out of tactical necessity than for political purposes."
It reported that the Johnson administration had needed support for its
"contention that there was light at the end of the tunnel, that the pacification program was working, and generally that American involvement in
Vietnam was not only correct, but effective."[26]

Further undermining the accuracy of reporting were the actions of the
US and South Vietnamese forces. In the midst of pacification and "search

and destroy" missions, US forces repeatedly conflated civilian casualties with those of insurgents.

From their basic training to their deployment, American soldiers were habituated to the dehumanization of the Vietnamese. Racial epithets were adopted widely and civilians were seen as active supporters of the Vietnamese insurgency. Even children were perceived as "possible foes or outright enemies." This perception was embodied in the acronym "MGR" for "mere gook rule," which justified a range of actions and abuses against civilians and insurgents. Studies conducted by the US military during the war found that a majority of officers-in-training and officers admitted that they would abuse or torture prisoners of war to obtain information during an interrogation. As will be seen, this behavior persisted in the War on Terror.[27]

Reporting was also warped by the pressure to produce corpses, real or manufactured. From the Pentagon to officers in the field, the emphasis on "body counts" drove the actions of the US military. Two of McNamara's "whiz kids," Assistant Secretary of Defense Alain Enthoven and NSC program analyst K. Wayne Smith, would later bemoan the "extreme emphasis on body count as *the* measure of success" in the Pentagon. It also influenced promotions and the awarding of rest passes and citations. Thus, the military's incentive system rewarded the deaths of insurgents and civilians as well as their broad categorization as killed combatants. This also contributed to the inflation of statistics and incorrect reporting—the exact opposite of what McNamara hoped to achieve. Nick Turse writes that "one of the most common phrases of the war was: 'If it's dead and Vietnamese, it's VC.'"[28]

Adding to the unwarranted deaths of civilians were deliberate assassinations during the war, carried out under the now infamous Civil Operations and Revolutionary Development Support (CORDS) program, also known as the Phoenix Program and as Project Phung Hoang. Its announced goal was to reduce and ultimately eliminate the "Viet Cong infrastructure" (VCI). One issue with achieving this target was how the VCI was defined. The CIA asserted that it was made up of those native South Vietnamese who had received training in North Vietnam in 1954 and then been reinfiltrated—a group assessed to be roughly seventy-five thousand strong. This was the figure that became the baseline for CORDS operations.

The program's target for 1968 was to "neutralize" twelve thousand members of the VCI. In the first six months of that year, the program reported 711 killed, over 4,700 captured, and 588 known to have abandoned the insurgency. Most of the insurgents successfully targeted by the program were at the hamlet and village level and few were from the leadership ranks in the provinces or districts. In his detailed history of the failure, journalist Douglas Valentine reports that South Vietnamese officials empowered by the Phoenix Program often threatened assassination or arrest purely for purposes of extortion. The program was ripe for abuse and corruption.[29]

As the Phoenix Program was implemented in early 1968, Hanoi and the NLF launched a massive uprising on the Vietnamese lunar holiday of Tet. In the past, the US military had generally observed a cease-fire during the Tet holiday. The Pentagon's attention was focused, moreover, on attacks by the North Vietnamese Army on US military bases near the demilitarized zone between North and South Vietnam—in particular, the Marine base at Khe Sahn. But the attacks had been a diversion to enable a more broad-based uprising across South Vietnam including symbolically powerful assaults by Vietnamese insurgents on the US embassy and the Presidential Palace. The Tet Offensive put the lie to the Johnson administration's claims about progress in the war effort.[30]

Nevertheless, the inflated reports of the Phoenix Program's success continued into the Nixon administration. In a March 1969 report to President Nixon, Secretary of Defense Melvin Laird recounted his discussion with William Colby, at that time the deputy responsible for CORDS. According to Colby, the Phoenix Program had already eliminated sixteen thousand members of a Viet Cong infrastructure numbering eighty-three thousand. Yet Colby had conceded that "these losses have probably been replaced." Laird explained that "a successful anti-infrastructure effort will thus require a substantially higher rate of attrition than has yet been realized."[31]

As would be observed in later counterinsurgency initiatives, one issue driving the implementation of CORDS was the ineffectiveness and corruption of the Vietnamese National Police. Although its size increased dramatically while CORDS was in operation, eventually reaching some 120,000 by 1972, the National Police proved unable to conduct effective counterinsurgency operations. Instead, the Phoenix Program served as the counterinsurgency force, while the National Police were trained to eventually assume responsibility for the effort. By 1971, the CIA had trained 8,500 South Vietnamese in interrogation techniques.[32]

Even though the death toll climbed significantly during its course, the Phoenix Program never achieved its goal. In Congressional testimony, Colby claimed that over twenty thousand Vietnamese were killed. The actual number was significantly higher, however, and continued to climb after the program was transferred to South Vietnamese intelligence. By 1972, more than 81,000 Vietnamese identified as insurgents had met their deaths and over 26,300 had been imprisoned through the Phoenix Program. The March 1968 My Lai massacre has received significant attention, both because of the large number of civilians deliberately killed by US forces in a single operation and thanks to the subsequent war crimes investigations and political interference by the Nixon administration, but the Vietnamese claim this was only one of many similar incidents during the war. This assertion is supported by the Phoenix Program and other counterinsurgency efforts. Part II of this book will return to the Phoenix Program, as the perception that it had been successful in Vietnam led to its replication in other counterinsurgency campaigns.[33]

THE CRUCIBLE

Vietnam was a proving ground for a generation of diplomats, soldiers, and intelligence officers. Over the next several decades, many drew on the experience to inform their perspectives on the potential for resolution or to encourage military action in other conflicts. Among these figures, Philip Habib, Richard Holbrooke, and Anthony Lake were particularly influential.

Philip Habib had an unlikely path to the State Department. Born in Brooklyn, he was the son of an immigrant; his father had come to the United States from Sidon in present-day Lebanon as a teenager in the 1880s. After serving in the Army during World War II, including overseeing a prisoner of war camp, Habib enrolled in a PhD program in agricultural economics at the University of California, Berkeley. He joined the foreign service a year later and developed a reputation for hard work, pragmatism, and brusque candor.

In 1965, Habib was recruited by William Bundy, then assistant secretary of state for Asian affairs, to serve as chief political officer at the US embassy in Saigon. Bundy's brother, McGeorge, was national security advisor to Presidents Kennedy and Johnson. He was also one of the architects of the war, with McNamara and Rostow. Habib supported the war effort and viewed America's commitment in South Vietnam within the broader perspective of US containment policy. Although he apparently disagreed with the United States' military strategy, Habib did not voice his opposition publicly. Throughout the war, the Saigon embassy attracted a number of ambitious young foreign service officers. Along with their superiors in Washington, they formed the core of what journalist David Halberstam ironically dubbed "the best and the brightest" due to their involvement in Vietnam. Habib mentored several individuals who had long careers in the State Department and intelligence community, including Holbrooke, Lake, John Negroponte, Peter Tarnoff, and Frank Wisner.[34]

Two years later, Habib returned to Washington to serve as deputy assistant secretary for East Asian and Pacific affairs. His main focus, however, was Vietnam. Habib established and oversaw an interagency working group which, although it was informal, was also secret, with its key members having previously been stationed in Vietnam. Habib's main counterparts were veteran CIA analyst George Carver and Major General William DePuy. After the 1968 Tet Offensive, the three men were sent to Saigon to assess the situation. Their subsequent advice to Dean Acheson (the former secretary of state and Cold War "wise man") and Clark Clifford (Johnson's new secretary of defense) was that Washington should pursue negotiations with Hanoi.[35]

Unlike Habib, Richard Holbrooke was a junior Foreign Service officer, and Vietnam was his first assignment. Holbrooke was raised in the affluent suburb of Scarsdale, New York, where his best friend was a son of Dean Rusk, president of the Rockefeller Foundation and a veteran of the Truman administration's State Department. By the time Holbrooke joined the State Department and was assigned to South Vietnam, Rusk was already secretary of state in the Kennedy administration, a position in which he would continue through the Johnson presidency. Before his posting, Holbrooke learned some Vietnamese. When he arrived in Saigon in May 1963, Holbrooke was assigned to work on the civilian aspect of the Strategic Hamlet Program in the Mekong Delta. He initially served under Rufus Phillips, a former army and intelligence officer mentored by Lansdale. In Ba Xuyen province, Holbrooke became part of a "triumvirate" that included an ARVN officer and a US military advisor. He dispensed money and supplies directly to South Vietnamese peasants, and also trained and armed strategic hamlet militias.[36]

The experience was formative. Holbrooke learned that many areas identified on provincial maps as controlled by the government were actually held by insurgents. Government forces entered the towns and hamlets only in large contingents. "The fact that the military was reporting most of these areas as under control puzzled me at first, and later it disturbed me deeply," Holbrooke later wrote. "We were deceiving ourselves, which would make formulating the right policy all the harder."[37]

While Holbrooke was visiting Washington in May 1965, he met briefly with Secretary of State Rusk for an "out of channels" conversation. Holbrooke would, some twenty years later, describe this "discouraging conversation." His experience on the ground had convinced him that "some of the things in Vietnam were not being accurately reported in Washington," and that the "reporting chain of command was distorting information." He described his mentor and one-time father figure as "disappointed" in the discussion. Rusk attempted to convince Holbrooke of the need to stop infiltration from North Vietnam. Holbrooke argued, however, that even if the United States were successful in halting infiltration it would not be able to pacify South Vietnam. Rusk countered that the North Vietnamese were not "Supermen." Holbrooke was frustrated by the exchange and Rusk was not pleased with his protégé. Their relationship would become increasingly tense over the next two years, as Rusk became convinced, with good reason, that Holbrooke was leaking information to the press.[38]

When Holbrooke returned to Washington, in 1966, he worked on Komer's pacification staff. His attempts to temper Komer's optimism about the progress of pacification were unsuccessful. Where Holbrooke failed in exposing the false claims and illusions of victory, the January 1968 Tet Offensive succeeded. Holbrooke was eventually assigned to the Vietnam Task Force convened by the office of the secretary of defense, where he worked to produce what later became known as "the Pentagon Papers." When Daniel Ellsberg leaked the Pentagon Papers in June 1971, the documents confirmed decades of duplicity by successive administrations, from Truman to Johnson.[39]

Like the Pentagon Papers project, Holbrooke himself attempted to find lessons in the Vietnam experience. Writing a year after the fall of Saigon, he examined the tensions between presidents and the foreign service bureaucracy. He pointed to the problematic role of presidential aides who, as he saw under Kennedy and Johnson, "reduced the information flow upward to the President, narrowed potential understanding of the problems, and simply served their President badly." Holbrooke also blamed the presidents themselves, noting that each of them "had ample warning signals that things might be off-course, and each chose to ignore or minimize them." As he put it, "Presidents get the advice and advisers they want—and ultimately deserve." Holbrooke argued that even though the "system worked" in Vietnam, "within it men failed, made serious errors of judgment, and contributed greatly to our long agony." In a prescient conclusion, Holbrooke asserted that the "myth—'no more Vietnams' or 'next time we'll do it right'—will carry more force than elusive facts." Indeed, as will be demonstrated, it was the latter myth that was the most seductive over the next half-century, as veterans of Vietnam either ignored their experience in Southeast Asia or presented it in the most favorable light to be replicated.[40]

Anthony Lake also arrived in Saigon as a young foreign service officer in early 1963. While Holbrooke was based in the Mekong Delta, Lake remained in Saigon and worked at the US embassy. Five months later, he was named assistant to Henry Cabot Lodge Jr., the newly appointed US ambassador to South Vietnam. The ambitious scion of a prominent Boston political family, Lodge had lost his Senate seat to John Kennedy in 1952. He had served as Eisenhower's UN ambassador and been Nixon's running mate in the 1960 presidential election. After the narrow loss, Lodge was expected to be a presidential candidate in 1964. Fate and domestic politics intervened when Kennedy asked Lodge to serve as ambassador. Shortly after arriving in Saigon, Lodge reported that elements of the South Vietnamese military were proposing a coup to overthrow President Diem. Less than three months later, Diem was deposed and assassinated. Living near the Presidential Palace, Lake watched the coup unfold. He would later interpret this fateful decision as the United States sending a "message to the Vietnamese that we were the ones who really controlled their country, which meant that we had become responsible for fighting their war."[41]

Like Holbrooke, Lake returned to Washington and the State Department. He eventually secured a staff position with Under Secretary of State

Nicholas Katzenbach, which provided him with insight into the weekly, senior-level discussions on the war. He later recalled that, unlike the young soldiers in the field, administration officials were removed from the realities of the conflict and the implications of their decisions. After President Nixon took office, Lake was approached by Henry Kissinger to serve on the National Security Council staff. Lake agreed because he believed the national security advisor wanted to end the war—little suspecting that Kissinger would proceed to order a wiretap on his phone. Nixon's decision to invade Cambodia in April 1970 after conducting a secret bombing campaign, and Kissinger's support for that decision, led to a rift in the NSC. Lake, Roger Morris, and William Watts resigned. Halperin and Lake later sued Kissinger over the wiretaps. The case was eventually settled in 1992 after Kissinger apologized.[42]

Lake's experiences in Vietnam and Washington influenced his perceptions of official decision-making. Six years after resigning, Lake warned that US foreign policy going forward would always wrestle with the very different imperatives learned from Munich and Vietnam. The former—a reference to the appeasement of Adolf Hitler by Britain and France prior to the Second World War—had given rise to a broad consensus that aggression required a firm response. Although "many of the cold war lessons of Munich may still have force," Lake wrote, "they are likely to be contradicted by some of the emerging lessons of Vietnam," which cautioned against embroiling the US military in faraway conflicts. While Munich provided a rationale for a greater American role in the world, Vietnam offered "vague, negative injunctions against American sacrifice and expenditures abroad." In its aftermath, Lake expected a greater tendency to "conclude that the United States should avoid foreign wars not by nipping them in the bud, but simply by staying out of them." As it turned out, Lake's prediction of a less interventionist impulse would prove optimistic.[43]

PREVENTIVE MEDICINE

The Johnson administration attempted to offset failure in Vietnam with victories elsewhere. For the CIA, perhaps no figure other than Fidel Castro loomed larger than Ernesto "Che" Guevara. After the Cuban Missile Crisis, the Argentinian doctor traveled the globe as a revolutionary emissary.[44] In December 1964, Guevara addressed the United Nations General Assembly.

Using the forum to chastise the United States for its domestic and foreign policies, he broadly criticized Washington's stance toward Cuba and Latin America, and more specifically pointed to US actions in the Congo.

Four years earlier, Belgium and the United States had worked together to bring about the overthrow and assassination of Prime Minister Patrice Lumumba. The series of civil wars known as the Congo Crisis, initiated as a struggle to end colonial rule, had quickly turned the country into a Cold War battleground. Guevara underscored that, at the same time that the United States and Belgium were coordinating an imperialist campaign in the Congo, South African apartheid was allowed to thrive and America's own system of segregation endured. Soon after his UN speech, in early 1965, Guevara embarked for the Congo with an ambitious plan: he believed that, after it was liberated, the country could serve as a base for launching and supporting other movements across Africa. He found few supporters for his vision, however, and his failure in the Congo led him to Bolivia.[45]

At the beginning of the decade, the State Department had described Bolivia as a test case for the Kennedy administration's policies in the Western Hemisphere. It received more US aid per capita than any other Latin American country and was the second-highest recipient in the world after South Vietnam. As Americans went to the polls in November 1964 to elect Johnson by a landslide, the Bolivian military launched a coup.[46]

Two years after that coup, Guevara believed that conditions in Bolivia made it ripe for revolution. All it needed was the spark. He was mistaken, however. Guevara arrived in La Paz in November 1966 disguised as a Uruguayan economist and envoy for the Organization of American States. As in the Congo, Guevara had a grand vision for the future that began in Bolivia. The country would serve as a base to launch revolutions in neighboring countries. He hoped the United States would be drawn in to fight the insurgencies and replicate the conflict in Southeast Asia. While Guevara's core guerrilla force had less than fifty members (including twenty-nine Bolivians and sixteen Cubans), he thought it would be sufficient to recreate the conditions which had led to victory in Cuba, and could catalyze a movement to defeat American imperialism in the hemisphere and globally. But Washington had other plans.[47]

A joint task force composed of the Bolivian Army's Second Ranger Battalion and CIA paramilitaries advanced with orders to kill or capture

Guevara. Felix Rodriguez, a Cuban American and veteran of the agency's anti-Castro operations, was one of several operatives dispatched to Bolivia. As Rodriguez later recalled, the CIA mistakenly believed that Guevara's operation was not his own initiative but managed by Havana. Analysts in the United States were also concerned about a call to action Guevara had published, in April 1967, in the magazine of the "Tricontinental" (more formally, the Organization of Solidarity with the Peoples of Asia, Africa, and Latin America), which portrayed the Vietnam insurgency in a heroic light. "How close we could look into a bright future," Guevara proclaimed, "should two, three, many Vietnams flourish throughout the world with their share of death and their immense tragedies, their everyday heroism and their repeated blows against imperialism, impelled to disperse its forces under the sudden attack and the increasing hatred of all the peoples of the world!" Guevara's message was echoed by official Cuban proclamations promoting "various Vietnams" across the Western Hemisphere.[48]

By the fall of 1967, Guevara's guerrillas had successfully engaged with Bolivian forces a number of times, but at a heavy price. The group was running short on supplies and was unable to garner additional support in the countryside or more broadly. On October 8, Guevara was wounded and captured after a skirmish with the joint CIA-Bolivian task force. Hoping to interrogate him, Rodriguez traveled from La Paz, posing as a Bolivian interior ministry officer, as CIA Station Chief John Tilton and Douglas Henderson, the US ambassador to Bolivia, lobbied Bolivian President General René Barrientos to keep Guevara alive for questioning. For Barrientos, however, the fear of Guevara's potential influence and symbolism outweighed the value of any intelligence that could be obtained through continued interrogation. Barrientos ordered Guevara's execution and Rodriguez relayed the command to the task force. In eagerness to claim victory, pictures of Guevara's dead body were circulated to the press.[49]

Guevara's death was welcomed in Washington. A pleased Rostow informed President Johnson that it marked "the passing of another of the aggressive, romantic revolutionaries like Sukarno, [Ghana's Kwame] Nkrumah, [Algeria's] Ben Bella—and reinforces this trend. It shows the soundness of our 'preventive medicine' assistance to countries facing incipient insurgency."[50]

After overseeing the operation to capture and assassinate Guevara, CIA Station Chief Tilton was eventually transferred to South Vietnam. In

Saigon, Tilton was the last director of the Phoenix Program. Rodriguez continued serving in the CIA's Latin American division in the Reagan administration and sought to counter or eliminate Guevara's successors.[51]

Washington also sought a more aggressive containment of communism in Southeast Asia. At its height, Indonesia's Communist Party (PKI) was the largest and best organized in insular Southeast Asia. Increased tensions between Indonesia and the United States were reproduced within domestic Indonesian politics and in the relationship between President Sukarno and the military. As one of the covert operations authorized under NSC 5421, the Eisenhower administration had supported an armed insurrection in Indonesia that ultimately failed. But over the following seven years, the Pentagon had strengthened its ties to the Indonesian military.[52]

September 1965 proved to be a critical moment in Indonesia, with implications for the broader region. Elements of the PKI attempted a purge of the Indonesian military's leadership, killing six top generals for insufficient loyalty to Sukarno. The reprisal was swift and bloody. Over the next three months, the Indonesian Army led a mass murder campaign against the PKI. The US embassy in Jakarta closely monitored the situation and reported on the Army's efforts to unite conservative religious parties with elements of Sukarno's Indonesian Nationalist Party. By the end of the year, at least a hundred thousand were already dead. Over the next year, at least three hundred thousand and perhaps as many as five hundred thousand Indonesians were killed by the Army and paramilitary groups. The PKI and other leftist groups were erased. Sukarno remained in power for another year, but eventually stepped down and was replaced by General Suharto.[53]

While America's difficulties in Vietnam were already clear by the end of 1965, Indonesia offered a sharp contrast of what a military campaign of eradication could achieve. Writing to President Johnson in March 1966, then Acting National Security Advisor Robert Komer reveled in the Indonesian military's success in preventing "another expansionist Communist state" from emerging in Southeast Asia that would have threatened the position of the United States and its allies in the region. Johnson's new ambassador to South Vietnam, Henry Cabot Lodge Jr., also praised the Indonesian military. Lodge had overseen the coup that deposed and killed Diem two years earlier. Now in his second stint as ambassador to South Vietnam, he saw the Indonesian military's actions as "a direct result of our

having taken a stand in Vietnam." Less than three years later, President
Suharto would reassure Washington that the war in Vietnam had assisted
the overthrow of Sukarno and his rise to power. The implications of taking a stand were also felt at home.[54]

THE WAR ON CRIME

As President Johnson chose war in Vietnam, he also launched his ambitious plan to reshape America. Johnson gave his "Great Society" speech at
the University of Michigan only a few months before the Gulf of Tonkin
incident. Written by Richard Goodwin, the speech was long on rhetorical
flourishes and short on specifics. But the Great Society, Vietnam, and Johnson's support for civil rights were intertwined.

Elizabeth Hinton explains that the 1965 Law Enforcement Assistance
Act was directly linked to President Lyndon Johnson's civil rights agenda.
Johnson's War on Crime became inextricable from his previously declared
War on Poverty. The Law Enforcement Assistance Act—and three years later,
the creation of an administrative agency to administer it—represented an
unprecedented shift in the federal government's involvement in local police operations, the courts, and state prisons. It also contributed to the expansion of the American carceral state and the racialization of crime in
the United States.[55]

As in Vietnam, underlying these efforts and the federal policies was
flawed data. In the 1960s and 1970s, the Uniform Crime Report (UCR)
produced by the Federal Bureau of Investigation (FBI) showed increasing
rates of crime. In particular, it appeared to demonstrate that crime among
Black Americans was on the rise. Yet the UCR recorded numbers of arrests, not actual convictions, and while Blacks had the highest rates of arrest
for the crimes of murder, rape, and robbery, these were the categories of
crime in which the lowest percentage of arrested suspects wound up being
prosecuted or brought to trial. Missing from the UCR data was whether
an individual was eventually released and not charged.[56]

With flawed data like this informing crime policies formulated in Washington and implemented at the local level, one strategy that took hold was
the deliberate arrest and incarceration of young Black men to prevent "future crime." One of the most prominent experts influencing policy makers
was James Q. Wilson, a political scientist at UCLA and Harvard. Writing

in the Fall 1966 edition of the conservative journal *The Public Interest*, Wilson offered sweeping assertions to explain increased crime in urban areas. He acknowledged that crime statistics were misleading and there was a tendency to exaggerate its prevalence. Wilson drew on a recent study to argue that socioeconomic status, race, and age were key factors across the country based on arrest records. He claimed that crime rates were always higher among youth, but allowed that "what appears to be a crime explosion may in fact be a population explosion." He offered the wry observations that "the only sure way we know of fighting crime is birth control" and "short of locking up everyone under the age of thirty," not much could be done about increasing crime. Wilson recommended a range of measures to make the "scene of the prospective crime" more secure by, for example, making doors and windows harder to breach and adding lighting to streets and doorways. rather than attempting to identify potential criminals. Yet the reliance on flawed data and suspect analyses would continue to inform policy. Wilson concluded his essay with the warning that a future presidential candidate on the right could make crime a major issue. As Chapter 2 discusses, Richard Nixon seized the opportunity as urban unrest and the failing war in Vietnam tested the nation.[57]

Although civil rights leaders were hesitant to break with Johnson over Vietnam, fearing they would lose their most powerful advocate, the increasing violence at home and in Southeast Asia made their continuing support untenable. The young John Lewis, for example, as chair of the Student Nonviolent Coordinating Committee (SNCC), was moved to issue a fierce statement of opposition to the war in the midst of the January 1966 uproar over the murder of Black civil rights activist Sammy Younge Jr. The backlash against one part of SNCC's statement in particular—its declaration of support for all those who had defied the draft—was intense, even including a threat by Alabama's selective service director to review Lewis's own draft status.[58]

Almost sixteen months later, Martin Luther King Jr. publicly split from Johnson in a speech at Riverside Church in New York City's Morningside Heights neighborhood. King emphasized the devastating impact the war was having on poor Americans and the disproportionate number of Black soldiers dying in combat. He referred to the United States as "the greatest purveyor of violence in the world today." This damning indictment of the Johnson administration and the war, coming from the nation's most

prominent civil rights leader, was a watershed moment. King's speech angered civil rights supporters and drew criticism in the editorial pages of
the *Washington Post* and the *New York Times*—both of which condemned
his attempt to link the struggle for equality with the war. Inside the Johnson
White House, the anger was mixed with concern that King's speech would
embolden other antiwar voices. FBI Director J. Edgar Hoover saw it as justifying his continued campaign against King. "It is clear," Hoover wrote
in a memorandum to President Johnson, "that he is an instrument in the
hands of subversive forces seeking to undermine our nation." Yet in the
months that followed, King's sentiments would only grow more strident.[59]

The summer of 1967 brought the collision of two movements that in
some ways were polar opposites but equally challenged the prevailing social order—and were both fueled by opposition to the war raging in Vietnam. Beginning with the Monterey Pop Festival in mid-June and concluding in San Francisco's Golden Gate Park, the Bay Area became a magnet
for the emerging counterculture. Promising peace, love, and drugs, the
"Summer of Love" brought together the growing antiwar movement and
the free-spirited ethos of the "hippies."[60]

Less than a month later, a riot broke out on the other side of the country,
in Newark, New Jersey. The unrest was triggered by rumors that Newark
police had killed an unarmed Black motorist. Although the driver had
been severely beaten after his arrest, he had not died. However, the riots
left twenty-three dead and over a thousand injured. The violence radiated
not only to five other New Jersey cities but across the country, from Erie,
Pennsylvania, to West Fresno, California—setting the stage for even more
tragic conflict in Detroit a week later.[61]

The Detroit riot began after a police raid on an illegal after-hours club
selling alcohol, commonly referred to as a "blind pig." Among the eighty-
five people arrested in the wee hours of Sunday July 23 were two Black
veterans who had just returned from Vietnam. Police violence was not the
immediate catalyst, as it had been in Newark, but as the officers left the
scene, the crowd of roughly two hundred people gathered outside the club
began tossing bricks, then looting, then setting fires. The ensuing riot was
fueled by rumors of police killing protestors. This was compounded by the
introduction of the Michigan National Guard, which was not prepared to
contain a riot. "I'm going to shoot anything that moves and is Black," one
guardsman told a *Newsweek* reporter. When the two weeks of rioting were

over, the US Army and National Guardsman patrolled the city. Over forty were dead, including children, and twenty-five hundred buildings were burned. Unrest followed in other cities in Michigan and across the country for the rest of July. The strife of the "long, hot summer" reflected the anger, frustration, and impact of institutionalized racism in America. As Elisabeth Hinton explains, the categorization of community violence was racialized. Rather than *unrest*, in which whites participated, often with the support of law enforcement, public disturbances involving Black residents were labeled, and criminalized, as *riots*.[62]

In the wake of the Detroit riot, President Johnson addressed the nation on July 27. He lamented the tragic events of the previous week and sought to distinguish the violence from the civil rights movement. Johnson announced the creation of the National Advisory Commission on Civil Disorders, better known as the Kerner Commission, after its chairman, Governor Otto Kerner of Illinois, to determine the origins of the urban unrest. Its report, released in February 1968, came as a surprise to Johnson. Unlike previous assessments and studies, including by the McCone Commission after the 1965 Watts riots in Los Angeles, it did not, as Johnson hoped, identify specific agitators or find that the summer's violence had been instigated by communist agents. Instead, the Kerner Report argued that institutional and systemic racism in American society was at fault.[63]

Among the findings were criticisms of the police and National Guard units deployed to Detroit. The report argued that "there is a grave danger that some communities may resort to the indiscriminate and excessive use of force." It used striking language to discuss efforts to expand the arsenal of city police. "The Commission condemns moves to equip police departments with mass destruction weapons, such as automatic rifles, machine guns, and tanks. Weapons which are designed to destroy, not to control, have no place in densely populated urban communities."[64]

The report assessed the capabilities of police, National Guard, and US Army forces to control major riots and offered recommendations for improvement—among them, ways in which the federal government could assist cities preparing for riots in the future. It also advocated federal research into the use of riot control equipment and alternatives to lethal force. This latter recommendation served to connect counterinsurgency tactics used in the Vietnam War with those aimed at urban American unrest. It led, for example, to the approval in 1968 of the use of CS gas by domestic law enforcement—after, as Stuart Schrader notes, this new and faster-acting aerosol tear gas had been deployed in massive quantities in Vietnam for purposes of "riot control."[65]

Even before the Kerner Commission report was issued, National Security Advisor Rostow sought to connect the domestic and foreign spheres. Rostow wrote to President Johnson after his July 27 televised address announcing the Kerner Commission, but his analysis was rooted in Vietnam. He noted the parallels between the administration's "deterrence of aggression" abroad and its "law and order" policies at home, each trying to create conditions for "a future of economic and social progress." Extending the comparison, Rostow likened Washington's role in regional organizations to the federal government's partnership with states. He explained that "the equivalent of domestic law and order on the world scene is that nations forego the use of violence across international borders." Johnson and his successors adopted the idea that similar responses might be effective in fighting foreign and domestic sources of strife.[66]

As part of Johnson's War on Crime and in response to the urban unrest, Congress passed the Omnibus Crime Control and Safe Streets Act in June 1968, authorizing $400 million in federal funding over two years to state and local law enforcement agencies. As he signed the bill, Johnson heralded it as a response to "one of the most urgent problems in America today." Taking a swipe at Republican critics and presidential candidates, Johnson said that "crime will never yield to demagogic lament—only to action." But his own campaign against crime was hardly short of demagoguery. And within two years, the Safe Streets Act spurred the transfer of $40 million of military hardware to local law enforcement agencies, a major contribution to the militarization of police.[67]

Efforts to racialize crime in the years that followed were accompanied by an increasing criminalization of dissent. Johnson turned to the CIA to counter both the growing antiwar movement and simmering urban unrest. Convinced that communists were influencing the antiwar activists, he found a willing partner in CIA Director Richard Helms. When Helms tasked counterintelligence head James Jesus Angleton, along with Thomas Karamessines, the agency's deputy director for plans, to investigate, Operation CHAOS was born. A sweeping program to monitor antiwar activists, CHAOS by its conclusion had put roughly 300,000 Americans under some level of surveillance. Actual files were kept, and shared with the FBI, on over seven thousand of these individuals, plus a hundred organizations. Yet even before CHAOS, the CIA had predecessor efforts underway, including its monitoring of *Ramparts* following the magazine's critical reporting on the agency and the Vietnam War.[68]

The CIA coordinated with the Justice Department and with a special operation through the US Army called Continental United States Intelligence, designed to gather personal and political information on Americans suspected of being radicals, Black militants, or dissenters against the war in Vietnam. "Conus Intel," as the latter operation was known, placed Army intelligence agents inside antiwar groups and supplemented their reports with information gleaned from wiretaps and mail interceptions. The joint efforts of the three organizations were later augmented by intelligence units within state police departments.[69]

Accompanying CHAOS was the NSA's Operation Minaret. Although it was not dubbed Operation Minaret until 1969, the program's origins date to the interwar period. In a declassified account of the NSA's Cold War intelligence activities, the agency's historian prefaces his description of Minaret with a general observation: "There is no stark line between 'foreign intelligence' and domestic law enforcement. The phrases, which appear to be watertight, actually leak into each other at many points. But this never became an issue until the Watergate period." Since the 1930s, the FBI had regularly received information pertaining to American citizens obtained through foreign intelligence surveillance. This continued after the NSA was created in 1952. Following the Cuban Missile Crisis, domestic surveillance grew when President Kennedy requested information on Americans traveling to Cuba.[70]

Kennedy's "watch list" of Americans visiting Cuba became Johnson's Operation Minaret. The program expanded in accordance with new priorities and real and perceived threats. After Kennedy's assassination, the Secret Service asked the NSA to monitor and report on Americans that could potentially threaten the president. During the 1960s, individuals involved in narcotics trafficking dominated the watch list, as they would again during the Global War on Terror. Other targets included prominent activists like Martin Luther King Jr., Malcolm X, certain journalists, and even elected politicians from both parties. In 1967, the watch list expanded to include "domestic terrorists" and "foreign radical suspects" based on names provided by the FBI. This new set of targets grew out of

Johnson's request to monitor the antiwar movement. The NSA coordinated with the Army and the FBI to monitor sixteen hundred individuals. Its reports did not identify the agency of origin, however, and the sources were deliberately masked to appear as if the information were gleaned from individual sources ("human intelligence") rather than through communications monitoring ("signals intelligence"). This obfuscation would years later cause an NSA lawyer to say that "the people involved seemed to understand that the operation was disreputable if not outright illegal."[71]

Like Minaret, the FBI's counterintelligence programs, referred to as COINTELPROs, had earlier roots. The COINTELPROs began in the 1950s with the monitoring of suspected communists. They expanded dramatically during the 1960s to encompass the Ku Klux Klan and other white hate groups, the New Left, the antiwar movement, and Black Liberation organizations. The materials the FBI collected in its monitoring of the New Left were often mundane, considering the politics of the time, and were related to Constitutionally protected speech and political organizing and assembly. Among a group of leaflets collected by agents prior to the August 1968 Democratic National Convention in Chicago were some outlining how the Vietnam War, civil rights, and the War on Crime intersected. One flyer produced by the National Mobilization Committee to End the War in Vietnam (or the Mobe) called for demonstrators in the "tens of thousands for: Stopping the Bombing, Immediate withdrawal of US Troops from Vietnam, Liberation and self-determination for black people, and An end to poverty and exploitation." Far from fading away after Johnson left office, the COINTELPROs only expanded to inform the Nixon administration's policies at home and abroad, from Southeast Asia to the Middle East.[72]

FEDAYEEN

Although Vietnam dominated the Johnson administration, the Arab-Israeli conflict also loomed, with its potential for broader escalation. The simmering tensions reflected unresolved issues dating back to Israel's creation. Disputes over the Palestinian refugee crisis, borders, and water-sharing rights combined with a buildup of conventional arms to create a volatile mix. The Palestinian refugees from the 1948 Palestine War were the major impediment to a comprehensive resolution to the conflict. The destruction and erasure of Palestinian society that accompanied the creation of the state of Israel in 1948 resulted in the creation of over 750,000 Palestinian refugees, scattered across the region and under varying legal and political regimes. Washington chose to address this as a humanitarian problem rather than a political one.[73]

Meanwhile, Palestinians unwilling to wait for Washington to revise its approach to the situation became increasingly committed to armed struggle, in line with the larger global trend of decolonization and postwar national liberation movements. As Palestinian armed groups emerged, they were not unified geographically or politically, and were monitored by the military and intelligence services of different Arab states. In the two countries where the largest refugee populations were located, Lebanon and Jordan, Palestinian political organizing was actively suppressed. In Egyptian-controlled Gaza and Syria, Palestinians had more legal and political rights. Thus, there was more military and intelligence coordination by Palestinian armed groups with Egypt and Syria. Indeed, infiltration and attacks by armed groups in Syria and Egyptian-controlled Gaza contributed directly or indirectly to the 1956 Suez War and the June 1967 war.[74]

Following the 1956 Suez conflict, new armed groups emerged that were inspired by Egyptian President Gamal Abdel Nasser, the Algerian revolution, and Pan Arabism. Known collectively as the *fedayeen*, or those who sacrifice themselves, their ranks were filled by Palestinian refugees from across the region. Most prominent was Fatah, formed in Kuwait by 1958. Fatah's core leadership was drawn from the Palestinian refugee and exile communities—among them, its eventual longtime leader, Yasir Arafat. In its first official statement almost seven years later, Fatah hailed the success of an operation on New Year's Day 1965. Those attacks did not have the impact that the movement's propaganda claimed, but the goal was recruitment, not veracity.[75]

Fatah's emergence contributed to a broader conflagration with lasting implications. Following a January 1967 cross-border raid by Fatah fedayeen, sharp exchanges between Syria and Israel appeared to portend a growing crisis. Although Washington and Moscow sought to defuse the situation, it escalated further after an erroneous Soviet intelligence report indicated that an Israeli attack on Syria was imminent.[76]

As the crisis heightened over the next five months, the Johnson administration hoped a conflict could be avoided. In a series of miscalculations

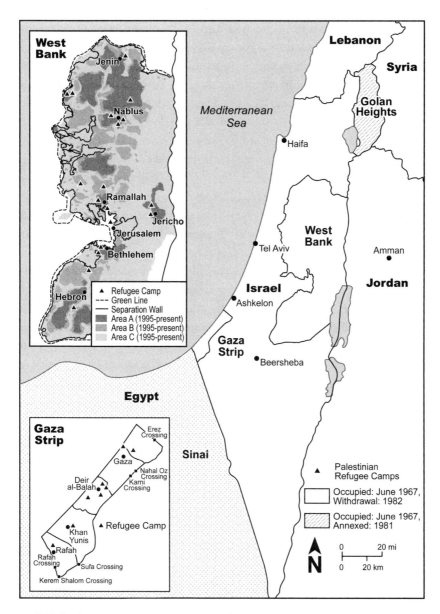

MAP 2. ISRAEL AND THE OCCUPIED TERRITORIES, 1967–2023

that contributed to the eventual debacle, Egypt and Syria activated a mutual defense pact. This was compounded by Cairo's request to withdraw UN peacekeeping troops from the Sinai Peninsula. Nasser hoped that heightening tensions would force the superpowers to help deescalate the situation, but his gamble did not pay off. Instead, his decision to close the Straits of Tiran to Israeli shipping was a fateful error. Although Egypt indicated that ships escorted by American naval vessels would be permitted into the waterway, closing the Straits activated an understanding between Israel and the United States that dated to the end of the 1956 Suez War.[77]

President Johnson's perceptions of Egypt and the Suez crisis over a decade earlier also played a role. As Senate majority leader during the 1956 Suez War, Johnson had criticized Eisenhower's pressure on Israel to withdraw from the Sinai Peninsula after a cease-fire was declared. Johnson had also been deeply critical of Egypt's Nasser, and the antagonistic relationship his administration had with Cairo had only deteriorated further.[78]

Vietnam hung over the Johnson administration's internal discussions, as did US domestic politics. The Israelis were convinced that Vietnam was distracting the Johnson White House and preventing a more forceful response. Bill Moyers, a former White House spokesman and publisher of *Newsday*, shared his opinion with Johnson that supporting Israel provided "a real opportunity to make some points on Vietnam," and also "a chance to silence some of the carping criticism from the Jewish press." While public statements from Washington indicated caution and a desire to avoid conflict, privately the Israelis were reassured that they had American support.[79]

Although he was initially angered by Israel's surprise attack to begin the June 1967 War, Johnson was pleased by the swift victory. He believed that it chastened Egypt and the Soviet Union and thus might assist America's efforts in Vietnam. Israel's occupation of the West Bank, including East Jerusalem, the Gaza Strip, Syria's Golan Heights, and Egypt's Sinai Peninsula, was also influenced by America's experience in Vietnam. After visiting Saigon, Israeli Defense Minister Moshe Dayan was not impressed by America's military might and its inability to defeat the insurgency. Dayan was also unwilling to adopt the American style of occupation in the newly captured territories. Dayan was also unwilling to adopt the American-style of occupation in the newly captured territories.[80]

Israel's occupation of the West Bank after the June 1967 War created a new wave of Palestinian refugees. Although the conflict was brief, its repercussions continue to be felt. Over 150,000 Palestinians were expelled or fled into Jordan during the war, adding to that country's large Palestinian majority. The war also dealt a political blow to Egypt's Nasser and his call for Pan Arabism while discrediting the regimes in Syria and Jordan. Stepping into the leadership breach were the fedayeen.

After the June 1967 War, King Hussein of Jordan struck a tenuous balance with the fedayeen. Although King Hussein engaged in secret talks with Israel to regain the West Bank, the negotiations were fruitless. Meanwhile some elements of his government and army were sympathetic to the fedayeen. This situation escalated ten months after the June War, with the Battle of Karameh. On March 21, 1968, a large Israeli force crossed into Jordan to attack the village of Karameh. What should have been a quick victory against the lightly armed fedayeen turned into a fiasco after Jordan's Arab Legion intervened to confront the Israelis. Arafat's Fatah turned Karameh, which means "honor" in Arabic, into a rallying cry and recruiting bonanza. The success there allowed Fatah and other armed groups to wrestle the Palestine Liberation Organization (PLO) away from an older generation of Palestinian leaders beholden to Egypt's Nasser. A year after Karameh, Fatah seized control of the PLO and, with several other prominent Palestinian armed groups, transformed it from a tool of Nasser's government to an internationally recognized nonstate actor that was respected in some quarters and reviled in others.[81]

The emergence of a Palestinian-led PLO challenged Washington's attempts to resolve the Arab-Israeli conflict without Palestinian participation. The PLO's declared goal was a "democratic, secular state" that encompassed all of historic Palestine (that is, Israel and the occupied West Bank and Gaza Strip). Based on the Vietnamese, Algerian, and Cuban examples, the organization sought an active base for its political and military operations. In establishing para-states in Jordan and Lebanon, the PLO challenged the regional and international orders while also testing a new American presidential doctrine.

VIETNAMIZATION

While the Vietnamese insurgency inspired national liberation movements across the Third World, it was a political embarrassment for Washington and Saigon. The 1968 Tet Offensive exposed the ARVN's leadership and capabilities and undermined the Johnson administration's claims of progress. In a late March 1968 meeting, President Johnson was briefed by Wheeler, as chair of the Joint Chiefs of Staff, and General Creighton Abrams, deputy commander of MACV. Abrams allowed that some ARVN divisions, despite extensive training, performed poorly and had high desertion rates, but he still expressed confidence that the South Vietnamese forces could step up to carrying a larger part of the fighting.[82] By the time Johnson left office ten months later, South Vietnam's military and paramilitary forces numbered more than a million men and women. Over 20 percent had been added in 1968 alone. There were also more than a million men and women in civil defense groups. Abrams had succeeded General Westmoreland as the commander of MACV in June 1968, and continued to revamp the ARVN.[83]

In early March 1969, Secretary of Defense Melvin Laird reported to President Richard Nixon on his weeklong trip to Vietnam. His assessment was that, despite their size, South Vietnam's armed forces and police organizations would not be able to defend and keep peace in the country if US forces were withdrawn. Laird recommended enhancing and expanding training efforts, but also argued that it was time to move on from the focus on counterinsurgency operations. Instead, he advised, the emphasis should be "shifted to measures through which South Vietnam can achieve a self-defense capability that will strengthen our joint hand in [negotiations with North Vietnam in] Paris and prevent ultimate military defeat if political settlement proves impossible."[84]

By the summer, the Joint Chiefs of Staff had developed a plan for "Vietnamizing" the war along the lines Laird described. Detailed in national security study memorandum (NSSM) 36, the new plan called for a withdrawal of fifty thousand US troops in 1969 in two increments. The withdrawal of the second increment of twenty-five thousand troops was contingent on the situation on the ground and the reactions of adversaries, allies, and the US public. The number of US military personnel in Vietnam was, at its peak in 1969, 543,000. NSSM 36 also mapped out larger reductions that might be made over the following forty-two months. Laird cautioned Nixon, however, that troop reductions would undermine ongoing counterinsurgency efforts and that the larger troop withdrawals, if not matched by the North Vietnamese, would have a negative impact on the South Vietnamese government and military. By that fall, National Security

Advisor Henry Kissinger was warning Nixon about the flawed assumptions he perceived in the Vietnamization plan. South Vietnamese forces were not close to being prepared to replace the US military, he cautioned, and President Nguyen Van Thieu's government, already lacking broad support, could not be expected to "gain solid political benefit from its current pacification progress."[85]

Nevertheless, on November 3, President Nixon addressed the American public on his Vietnamization policy. Nixon dismissed calls for an immediate withdrawal and asserted that it "would be a disaster not only for South Vietnam but for the United States and for the cause of peace." The issue, moreover, was not just ending the war. Nixon was committed to securing an American victory because the implications of a defeat were profound: "For the United States, this first defeat in our Nation's history would result in a collapse of confidence in American leadership, not only in Asia but throughout the world."[86]

Vietnamization was presented as the centerpiece of "the Nixon Doctrine," a major policy shift which would not only help end the war but endure as "an essential element of our program to prevent future Vietnams." Nixon reassured America's allies and partners that Washington would maintain its treaty commitments and continue supplying military equipment as well as economic assistance. But it would not directly participate in future combat operations. Meanwhile, the withdrawal of US combat ground forces from Vietnam would have to take place on a protracted timetable. "A nation cannot remain great if it betrays its allies and lets down its friends," Nixon argued. Again raising the specter of "defeat and humiliation" in Vietnam, he warned that a hastier withdrawal would also embolden America's enemies elsewhere, and "spark violence wherever our commitments help maintain the peace—in the Middle East, in Berlin, eventually even in the Western Hemisphere."[87]

Over the next three years, the Nixon administration steadily withdrew American forces. The final combat troops left in March 1973 after the Paris Peace Accords were signed. Vietnamization was a qualified success in that American forces no longer carried the burden of fighting. But critics of the Nixon administration's approach argued that Vietnamization did not lead more directly to peace or to better terms in the eventual accord. Instead, the outcomes were greater casualties, especially among the Vietnamese, and deepened political rifts in the United States. As David Anderson recounts, the capability-building aspect of Vietnamization was never fully implemented. Although the expedited training of the South Vietnamese security forces was completed, they did not become capable enough to win, as the final, humiliating collapse of the ARVN in April 1975 revealed. As will be discussed in Part II, the most important lessons from the Vietnam experience, and especially their applications to domestic political concerns, were willfully ignored. Meanwhile, it was the Nixon Doctrine and Washington's attempts to contain the defeat in Vietnam that would "spark violence," with decades of ramifications.[88]

BLACK SEPTEMBER

In August of 1969, Yasir Arafat declared that "Amman shall be the Hanoi of the revolution." It was eighteen months after the Battle of Karameh, and the PLO was attempting to replicate the Algerian and Vietnamese revolutions. As it established a para-state in Jordan, King Hussein faced a difficult choice. One option, to support the PLO, was compelling since Palestinian refugees made up the majority of the country, but doing so would undermine his rule and make him a figurehead. Hussein's precarious position—being either unwilling or unable to prevent attacks by Palestinian groups against Israel, and further embarrassed by Israel's harsh reprisals—was further imperiled by the PLO's growing regional and international stature. As the organization's actions inside Jordan grew more brazen, the Nixon administration believed that a clash there was likely, and could even amount to civil war. The PLO's attempt to turn Amman into a Palestinian Hanoi or Havana made Jordan an early test case of the Nixon Doctrine.[89]

The tensions between the PLO and King Hussein came to a head in the summer of 1970. June brought not only clashes between the Palestinian fedayeen and the Jordanian Army, but a purported assassination attempt against the king himself. Even though the PLO denied any involvement in the latter, the situation was untenable. A cease-fire was reached between the Jordanian Army and the PLO, but it did not hold for long.[90]

In early September of 1970, the Popular Front for the Liberation of Palestine (PFLP), a Marxist-Leninist faction of the PLO and rival to Fatah, successfully hijacked four commercial aircraft from different international airlines. Israeli security foiled the hijacking of a fifth plane. Three of the hijacked planes were brought to Jordan's Dawson Field near Amman. Over three hundred passengers were held hostage as the PFLP demanded the release of Palestinians held in jails in Israel and Western European countries. While the International Committee of the Red Cross handled the negotiations, Washington closely monitored the ensuing hostage crisis and coordinated with European allies as well as Israel, Jordan, and Iraq.[91]

Behind the scenes, the Nixon administration urged a showdown between King Hussein and the fedayeen. Almost a week into the crisis, Kissinger had good news for President Nixon. The PFLP had just released nearly seventy hostages, forty of which were Americans, without conditions. While there were internal tensions within the PLO and criticism of the PFLP over the hijackings, Kissinger instead emphasized the benefits of threatening military action. "We will not play a soft game in the future," Nixon stated. "And every time we use the hard line, it works," Kissinger added.[92] Yet some observers advocated for a harder response.

In an editorial, *New York Times* executive editor James Reston placed the hostage-takers within a broader set of small-scale actors menacing America with increasing impunity. He contrasted the challenge the hijackings presented to Nixon with the situation Thomas Jefferson faced in the eighteenth century when the Barbary Pirates demanded "tribute" payments to allow commercial ships to pass. Unlike Jefferson, "Mr. Nixon, who has apocalyptic power, cannot handle the Arab pirates without risking the lives of the Americans he wants to rescue." While Reston agreed it was "undoubtedly right" for Nixon not to react with force, he worried that such behavior could "easily spread into an infectious disorder" if it generally went unchecked, "and not only in the Middle East." For that matter, "probably the most spectacular example of the weak over the strong" had come from the communist guerillas in Southeast Asia who had, despite far inferior arsenals, succeeded against the militaries of first France and then the United States. More terrifying for *Times* readers, Reston envisioned such threats coming soon to their own neighborhoods: "We have not yet had to face organized guerrilla war in the urban centers of America, but the skyjackers, the wreckers in the universities, and even the unorganized hoodlums have given us some idea of what can be done by tyrannical minorities." He urged any skeptics to open their eyes: "All you have to do is take a long walk through almost any American city these days to realize how many angry and demented people there are wandering around loose—many of them willing to risk their lives to remove some real or imagined grievance."[93]

Reston was joined by C. L. "Cy" Sulzberger, a former *Times* foreign correspondent and nephew of the paper's former publisher. Sulzberger echoed Reston's sentiments and added his own assessment. Although the "philosophical genesis" of the hijackings was in the Arab-Israeli conflict and "the noisome slum villages in which Palestinian refugees have festered for a generation," he wrote, "it is dramatized by the jet age's implicit dangers and television's instant facilities which favor revolutionists by stressing tension and emotion." Like Reston, Sulzberger found an analogy in the Barbary Pirates crisis, and saw the same irony that possession of nuclear weapons limited the possible response: "Today's byword is that one must not use a sledgehammer to smash gnats. No substitute has yet been found and as a result the gnats feel free to sting." He concluded that "compassion and sentimental dictates caution against recourse to the discarded gunboats of Jefferson and cudgels of Roosevelt. But if the gnats are allowed to pester the sledge unhampered, more disasters will come." Even as the United States was experiencing the limits of its military power in Vietnam, neither Reston nor Sulzberger appeared ready to apply the lessons of the conflict and advocate for negotiations to address the root causes and underlying issues that contributed to the hostage situation. Instead, the United States was depicted as a hapless giant, unable or unwilling to use force and sliding into decline.[94]

Henry Kissinger, in a lengthy September 16 memo to Nixon, assessed the situation. He outlined how Jordan's political base could evolve, the implications for King Hussein's rule, the prospects of a negotiated settlement with Israel, and the stableness of the broader region. Although a decisive defeat of the Palestinian groups was ideal, he warned that it was unlikely. In the worst case, "some combination of fedayeen elements could demonstrate the King's impotence and force on him a weak civilian government that would do its bidding." In addition to cutting off prospects for a solution "on terms Israel could consider," this would produce "one more radical state in the Middle East where the US is barred. A radical fedayeen base there would strengthen the movement against Saudi Arabia, Kuwait and the Persian Gulf states." As will be seen, six years later, Kissinger would voice the same concerns about the PLO in Lebanon.[95]

Also on September 16, 1970, the newly appointed US ambassador to Jordan, Dean Brown, reported that King Hussein wanted "his hand held." Assigned to Jordan in the middle of the hostage crisis, Brown would become increasingly associated with the crackdown on the Palestinian groups. He recommended that Washington encourage King Hussein to confront the fedayeen. Secretary of State William Rogers concurred. "You should not discourage [the] King from taking stern measures against fedayeen," Rogers said, "One cannot help but feel at this juncture, that unless he asserts his authority more effectively the chances of his regime surviving are worse than if he were to continue to cater to [the] fedayeen."[96]

In a bloody, ten-day campaign, King Hussein followed Washington's advice. The Jordanian Army attacked the PLO and Palestinian refugee camps inside Amman and several other cities. Behind the scenes, Hussein coordinated with the United States and Israel. A cease-fire was brokered by Egypt's Nasser on September 27. Nasser died the next day of a heart attack, but the agreement for the withdrawal of the Jordanian Army and Palestinian guerrillas from major population centers held. Hussein later informed the Israelis that the operation had effectively dismantled the emerging PLO para-state in Jordan. But the PLO's expulsion from Jordan contributed to the formation of the organization's para-state in Lebanon. As in Jordan, it was a contested process. Chapter 2 demonstrates that it also intersected with America's domestic politics and foreign policy.[97]

CONCLUSION

On April 3, 1970, five months before Jordan's "Black September" civil war, President Nixon addressed the American public on the topic of Cambodia. Although Vietnamization was progressing and he had recently announced the withdrawal of an additional 150,000 American troops, Nixon said that "increased enemy activity" in Laos, Cambodia, and South Vietnam threatened the remaining US troops. The ARVN, Nixon explained, would have "major responsibility" for the intervention, and be supported by US forces. He denied that this constituted an "invasion" and said the United States did not intend to occupy Cambodia; the US-ARVN forces would be withdrawn once enemy forces were driven from their sanctuary and weapons caches were destroyed. Nixon laid the blame squarely on North

Vietnam and insisted that Washington respected Cambodian sovereignty, eliding any mention of the secret bombing campaign he had authorized over the previous year. The secret bombings of Cambodia were part of Nixon's "Madman Strategy," intended to convince Moscow and Hanoi that his virulent anti-communism would influence a more aggressive war footing, but neither was intimidated. The invasion of Cambodia was another desperate gamble that failed to achieve its goals.[98]

There were nonetheless consequences for this action, both immediate and long-term. The antiwar movement was energized by the invasion and the subsequent killing of two students at Jackson State University in Mississippi and four students at Kent State University in Ohio. Three NSC staff members resigned over the invasion. Cambodia was another of the many implications, domestic and international, of America's continued challenges in Vietnam. From Indonesia to Bolivia, Washington adapted and employed many of the same tactics it utilized against the Vietnamese insurgency. At home, it did the same in the open War on Crime and the secret war on dissent.

The final death toll in Vietnam from the "American War" was staggering. Over fifty-eight thousand Americans and at least three million Vietnamese were killed. The number of wounded was far higher. There were also hundreds of thousands of Vietnamese refugees, displaced persons, and war orphans. The United States dropped far more bombs on North Vietnam than it did in the Second World War or the Korean conflict. Remarkably, even more tonnage was dropped in South Vietnam than in the North. Laos and Cambodia were also sites of heavy US bombing campaigns that eclipsed previous conflicts. The use of the Agent Orange defoliant caused widespread health defects and environmental damage, and continues to do so. Yet one of the legacies of the Vietnam War was also a substantial number of American policymakers, military and intelligence officials, and national security experts who insisted that the United States could have done more to achieve victory.

From Eisenhower to Nixon, persistent warnings from the White House about the dangers of defeat in Vietnam contributed to America's deepening involvement in Southeast Asia and globally. Failure in Vietnam fueled an existential angst among American officials and elites, accompanied by perceptions of decline. In his reflection on the lessons of Vietnam, Anthony Lake presciently observed that, torn between the historical examples of Munich and Vietnam, "presidents may be buffeted between continued public expectations of foreign 'success' and widespread doubt about the actions necessary to achieve it." Specifically, he worried that "political leaders could find more enticing than ever the unfortunate twin temptations to disguise the scope of American foreign activities from the public eye and also to overstate the present and future successes of American diplomacy." As will be seen in chapters to come, these twin temptations would shape the next four decades of America's wars, at home and abroad.[99]

CHAPTER TWO

Nixon's Wars and the Long 1970s

> If when the chips are down, the world's most powerful nation—the United States of America—acts like a pitiful, helpless giant, the forces of totalitarianism and anarchy will threaten free nations and free institutions throughout the world.
>
> —PRESIDENT RICHARD M. NIXON, 1970

SURROUNDED BY COASTAL REDWOODS on the shores of a small, private lake in California, Richard Nixon unofficially launched his second bid for the White House on July 29, 1967. Located seventy-five miles north of San Francisco on 2,700 wooded acres, the Bohemian Grove belonged to the exclusive, all-male Bohemian Club, whose wealthy members included executives from some of America's leading corporations. There, between two and three thousand men, spread across dozens of camps, spent sixteen days every summer socializing, communing with nature, and listening to talks, some of them by prominent guests invited by members. Nixon, an honorary member himself, had recently returned from a trip abroad and crafted his lakeside talk to demonstrate that he was a legitimate contender for the presidency. He had failed in his 1960 presidential and 1962 California Gubernatorial campaigns, giving Republican party leaders reason to view his candidacy with skepticism. Nixon later wrote that the speech "marked the first milestone on my road to the presidency" as it provided "an unparalleled opportunity to reach some of the most important and influential men, not just from California but from across the country."[1]

Honoring the memory of a mentor and the camp's most renowned member, former president Herbert Hoover, Nixon offered a big-picture perspective on US foreign policy. He decided not "to dwell on current issues" such as the failing war in Vietnam and the Arab-Israeli War fought just seven weeks earlier. Instead, he took a long view of America's challenges abroad—and could not resist alluding to troubles at home. "Twenty years ago, after our great World War II victory, we were respected throughout the world. Today, hardly a day goes by when our flag is not spit upon, a library burned, an embassy stoned some place in the world," Nixon claimed. "In fact, you don't have to leave the United States to find examples."[2]

Turning to the "much brighter side," Nixon outlined the broad themes that would become prominent in his 1968 campaign and eventual presidency: "Never has a nation had more advantages to lead. Our economic superiority is enormous; our military superiority can be whatever we choose to make it. Most important, it happens that we are on the right side—the side of freedom and peace and progress against the forces of totalitarianism, reaction and war. There is only one area where there is any question—that is whether America has the national character and moral stamina to see us through this long and difficult struggle."[3]

Nixon found reason to worry about the national character in the riot that had been raging in Detroit just a few days before this speech, quieted only by the deployment of the National Guard and US Army paratroopers to the city. In his eyes, it was evidence that judges, opinion-makers, teachers, and community leaders had "gone too far" with a tendency to, "when a law is broken, blame society, not the criminal." America was "reaping the whirlwind for a decade of growing disrespect for law, decency and principle in America." Nixon's platform of restoring law and order at home and reasserting American leadership abroad would propel him to the White House.[4]

This chapter examines the intersection of Nixon's domestic and foreign policies. It argues that Nixon and National Security Advisor (later also Secretary of State) Henry Kissinger implemented policies based on an inaccurate assessment of America's global standing, and the political, military, and legal influence of these policies had serious consequences both intended and unintended. As America passed aggressive drug laws and encouraged proxy conflicts in the developing world, its "wars" at home became increasingly institutionalized, and the effects only multiplied as Nixon's successors embraced the same political strategies.

CONSTRUCTING LAW AND ORDER

Nixon entered the White House in January 1969 with the outlines of a foreign policy strategy that built on his Bohemian Club address. During the campaign, Nixon promised an "honorable end to the war in Vietnam" and it was central to his plans. Over the next three years, Nixon authorized punishing air campaigns and extended the war into Cambodia and Laos. At his side was Henry Kissinger. Nixon and Kissinger were convinced that America's international influence had diminished due to Vietnam, but rather than substantially reevaluating America's losing war, Nixon expanded the conflict and attempted to intimidate Hanoi and Moscow. Kissinger justified the policy by arguing that the United States "could not simply walk away." But, seemingly unchastened by the Vietnam experience, he sought to reassert American primacy and deterrence across the Third World, with long-term consequences.[5]

Famously, Nixon and Kissinger reframed US foreign policy efforts with a "grand strategy" approach—the idea that America's actions on the world stage should proceed from a strategic blueprint and not simply be reactive to discrete events. As their big-picture view of US interests and others' goals drove foreign policy initiatives, Nixon focused on law and order at home. This unfolded in two separate but related policies. The first was aimed at the antiwar movement and campus protestors. The second targeted street crime—in particular, narcotics dealing. Nixon's campaign against the antiwar movement was partially inherited from Lyndon Johnson, but it was also popular with the Republican Party's base. During the 1966 California gubernatorial campaign, Ronald Reagan's unconcealed contempt for the student protestors at Berkeley had been an important factor in his victory over two-term incumbent Pat Brown.[6]

Two years later, Reagan and Nixon found common cause on crime at the Republican National Convention, with Reagan linking campus protests with urban crime and unrest, and Nixon describing the "right to be free from domestic violence" as "the forgotten civil right." Nixon echoed the point in his speech accepting the party's nomination, declaring that

"the first civil right of every American is to be free from domestic violence, and that right must be guaranteed in this country." Explicitly re-
butting "those who say that law and order is the code word for racism," he
made this reply: "Our goal is justice for every American." Whoever won
the election, he observed, would face an unprecedented challenge: "For
the first time in our nation's history, an American president will face not
only the problem of restoring peace abroad but of restoring peace at home."
And in a rhetorical flourish perhaps crafted to appeal to disaffected Democrats he borrowed a phrase from Franklin Delano Roosevelt: "We shall
reestablish freedom from fear in America so that America can take the
lead in reestablishing freedom from fear in the world."[7]

Nixon's campaign ran television advertisements building on his acceptance speech. In two of the ads, "The First Civil Right" and "Crime,"
ominous soundtracks and disturbing images accompanied Nixon's stark
narration, concluding with a promise to restore order and rebuild respect
for the law.[8]

The campus protestors who drew the ire of Nixon, Reagan, and their
conservative supporters came from a broad coalition of organizations.
One of them was the socialist group Students for a Democratic Society
(SDS), which had issued its "Port Huron Statement" in August 1962, when
Kennedy was president and Nixon was running for governor of California. Presented as "an agenda for a generation," the statement criticized
segregation at home and Cold War policies abroad. The SDS was part of
the global New Left movement and was, in its American form, fueled by
the civil rights struggle. It had national chapters whose members were active in the antiwar movement on and off university campuses.[9]

Less than a year after Nixon was elected, key figures in the SDS's national leadership left the organization and formed the Weather Underground. While the SDS and other groups continued to challenge the war,
and the size and ferocity of protests increased, the Weathermen had the
more aggressive goal to spark a revolution and overthrow the US government. Inspired by the examples of the Cuban and Vietnamese revolutions, the Weathermen believed they were the vanguard of a violent insurrection in the United States. In 1970, however, the group's bomb-making
operation in a Greenwich Village townhouse caused a massive explosion,
killing some of its leaders and discrediting its organization—and, to some
extent, the broader antiwar movement.[10]

Shortly after taking office, Nixon had visited CIA headquarters in McLean, Virginia. In remarks to its staff and new director, Richard Helms, the president alluded to recent protests against the CIA but said he viewed the agency not as an organization "necessary for the conduct of conflict or war . . . but in the final analysis as one of the great instruments of our Government for the preservation of peace, for the avoidance of war, and for the development of a society in which this kind of activity would not be as necessary, if necessary at all." It was a hint that, like Johnson, Nixon would use the CIA and other agencies to target perceived domestic enemies. Fifteen months later he asked the CIA, FBI, and NSA to expand their surveillance of antiwar protestors. According to Seymour Hersh, with midterm elections less than six months away, "Nixon summoned the intelligence chiefs and demanded that they prove what he insisted was the case: that the antiwar demonstrations were the result of outside communist agitators carrying out the policies of America's enemies." Presumably any revelations of communist influence would benefit Republican candidates.[11]

Nixon had inherited two domestic spying programs from President Johnson, and an ongoing FBI crackdown on the Black Panther Party (BPP). J. Edgar Hoover's FBI had coordinated since the fall of 1968 with state and local law enforcement agencies and helped to bring about, according to Michelle Alexander, the incarceration of roughly a thousand BPP members. Over forty Black Panthers were killed, she reports, some by police and others by fellow members—with a portion of the latter deaths likely instigated by the authorities' infiltration of informants into the party and efforts to sow internal discord. Other key members fled the country to avoid indictment, imprisonment, or assassination.[12]

Four months after the 1970 midterm elections, a group of eight antiwar activists broke into the office of the US Army's Continental US Intelligence Program in Media, Pennsylvania, and stole over a thousand files. Calling themselves the Citizens' Commission to Investigate the FBI, the group sent copies of COINTELPRO documents anonymously to Democratic Senator George McGovern of South Dakota, Maryland Democrat Representative Parren Mitchell, and journalists at three leading newspapers. The embarrassing articles that followed in the *Washington Post* and *New York Times* put a damper on the FBI's activities.[13] At the CIA and NSA, however, the work continued. The Watergate investigations would later reveal that the spying programs grew beyond the antiwar movement to include members of the president's cabinet and National Security Council staff. Kissinger relied on the claim of national security to justify the wiretaps but, according to Hersh, also used the information to undermine rivals within the administration and staffers he perceived to be disloyal.[14]

The CIA's program, Operation CHAOS, was run by James Jesus Angleton and the agency's Counterintelligence Bureau. Initiated in early 1967 at the behest of President Johnson, CHAOS grew in size and scope over the next seven years, eventually intersecting with the NSA's Operation Minaret. Minaret continued until September 1973, when, in the midst of the Watergate scandal and a court case involving the Weather Underground, the threat of revealing the program and ensuing embarrassment (and potentially, criminal charges) led to its abrupt cancellation.[15]

Nixon's decision to expand surveillance had a palpable effect on student protestors and contributed to paranoia and schisms within the ranks of the antiwar movement. Despite the intrusive monitoring, however, campus protests grew as the conflict in Vietnam escalated. Even though the intelligence community failed to identify foreign influencers of the antiwar movement, Nixon insisted they were incorrect. But Nixon was unable to defeat the insurgency in South Vietnam or the protest movement at home. Meanwhile, the application of the Nixon Doctrine in the Middle East contributed to the expansion of domestic spying programs.

OPERATION BOULDER

The Nixon Doctrine—by which the new president pledged that, under his leadership, America would support its allies facing military threats with economic and military aid but not by putting US troops on the ground—was first tested during the September 1970 Jordanian Civil War. Fourteen months later, Jordanian Prime Minister Wasfi al-Tal was assassinated in Cairo. The previously unknown Black September Organization (BSO) claimed responsibility for assassinating the "traitor" and said it was a warning to other Arab leaders not to make concessions at the expense of those living under occupation. Although it was a new organization with an unclear leadership and number of members, the BSO was formed by top Fatah officials and aides to Yasir Arafat.[16]

Nine months later, the BSO was responsible for an even more brazen attack, at the 1972 Summer Olympics in Munich. The BSO's attempt to raise awareness and generate sympathy for the Palestinian cause had the opposite effect. With international attention focused on the games, the BSO's attack killing two Israeli athletes and holding nine others hostage unfolded on live television over twenty hours. The BSO demanded the release of two hundred and thirty-four Palestinians imprisoned in Israel as well as members of the West German leftist Baader-Meinhof group. Horrified viewers learned that the hostages were killed in a botched rescue attempt at Fürstenfeldbruck Air Base. Five of the BSO assailants and one West German police officer were also slain in the firefight. Early in the crisis, Nixon had expressed confidence to reporters that American athletes were safe, but added that, "since we are dealing with international outlaws who are unpredictable, we have to take extra security measures to protect those who might be the targets of this kind of activity in the future."[17]

The next morning, with the shocking outcome having transpired, Nixon and Kissinger sought to balance geopolitical interests with domestic political concerns. Nixon expressed to Kissinger his eagerness to assure the Israeli government—and the American Jewish community—that Washington would not be silent. They agreed that the United States should publicly call on the UN Security Council to set international rules against harboring guerillas. Privately, Nixon and Kissinger feared that an Israeli invasion of Lebanon to kill or capture the PLO's leadership would instigate a broader regional conflict, with the 1972 Presidential election only two months away. "We've got an election campaign. Now, I got a promise out of Golda Meir two months ago, when you asked me to, that they wouldn't take military action [before the election]," Kissinger said. "But this is an enormous provocation. And they are emotional. And I don't want them to think that they've got you in their hip pocket." Although Israel launched airstrikes and an incursion into southern Lebanon, Kissinger was able to convince Meir not to order a larger invasion. Israel targeted the BSO's leadership over the next five years. Meanwhile, the CIA began more robust reporting on Palestinian political factions, especially the BSO, and stepped up its intelligence sharing with Israel and European allies.[18]

One quick response to Munich was the program called Operation Boulder. Launched in early October 1972 to "screen more closely visa applications of potential terrorists" from the Middle East and North Africa, it also subjected visa holders from these regions already in the country to extra scrutiny. This was the first "special measure" enacted through a new, cabinet-level advisory committee that Nixon had created in the aftermath of the BSO attack. The Cabinet Committee to Combat Terrorism, under the leadership of Secretary of State William Rogers, was made up of the heads of at least eight federal departments and agencies. Its mission: to "consider the most effective means by which to prevent terrorism here and abroad, and . . . take the lead in establishing procedures to ensure that our government can take appropriate action in response to acts of terrorism swiftly and effectively." As well as flagging visa applications of "potential terrorists," the committee directed an effort to monitor any student groups who maintained relations with Arab or Iranian organizations known to practice or advocate political violence. Thus, Operation Boulder intersected with COINTELPRO and contained elements of Operation CHAOS.[19]

Unlike most other intelligence activities, Operation Boulder was not secret but disclosed to and discussed by the media. In an October 5 article, the *New York Times* reported that, according to an Immigration and Naturalization Service official in New York, individuals were being surveilled only if the government had reason to believe they might be planning terrorist acts. The piece quoted Palestinians from the Arab League and its affiliated Arab Information Center in New York complaining that in the past ten days they had been openly trailed and threatened by FBI agents. It was said, the article reported, that interrogation and surveillance was intended to discover the activities and membership of Fatah, the BSO, the Popular Front for the Liberation of Palestine, and their sympathizers. Although the INS official assured the reporter that the intention was not to harass the "Arab community in general," this was precisely what occurred over the next three years. Later it would be revealed that the FBI broke into the Arab Information Center in Dallas and rummaged through files, looking for connections to Palestinian militant organizations.[20]

Undeterred by the enhanced scrutiny, the BSO did go on to target the United States directly. In March 1973, a BSO team attacked a celebration at the Saudi embassy in Khartoum, and took ten hostages, among them the US ambassador and deputy chief of mission to Sudan. Within twelve hours, the gunmen killed these two along with the Belgian chargé d'affaires. US intelligence produced evidence that Arafat himself had given the order for the murders, indicating it was an official action. Kissinger, through a CIA back channel, attempted to reach an understanding with Arafat to prevent the future targeting of American officials. Soon enough, the Arab-Israeli War that erupted in October 1973 forced the issue of what relations Washington would maintain with the organization.[21]

Less than five months after the assassinations in Khartoum, an October 1973 attack by Egypt and Syria on Israeli positions in the occupied Golan Heights and Sinai Peninsula shattered the tense Arab-Israeli conflict on two fronts. The crisis could have been avoided; UN Security Council Resolution 242, unanimously passed after the June 1967 War, had offered a "land for peace" framework by which the Arab states could regain the territories lost in that conflict in return for peace with Israel. Secretary of State Rogers had initiated discussions with the belligerents, but the negotiations were undermined by Nixon and Kissinger's insistence that Cairo and Damascus cut ties with Moscow as a precondition for Washington's deeper involvement. Nixon and Kissinger wanted to reinforce Israel's superior position while also preventing the Soviet Union from participating in future negotiations and break the unified Arab negotiating stance. The frustrated presidents of Egypt and Syria, Anwar al-Sadat and Hafiz al-Asad, launched their secretly planned attack on October 6, 1973, the Yom Kippur holiday.

Even as the war waged across the next nineteen days created a real threat of superpower confrontation, it also offered an opportunity for a diplomatic breakthrough. Kissinger's high-profile efforts resulted in a joint proposal by the USSR and United States to the UN Security Council, which was promptly adopted as Resolution 338 establishing a cease-fire as of October 25. Before the cease-fire went into effect, Kissinger encouraged Israel to continue pressing its counteroffensive against Egyptian forces, which led to a near nuclear showdown with Moscow. The United States' overt support for Israel also provoked the imposition of a six-month oil embargo by some Arab member states of the Organization of the Petroleum Exporting Countries. The political impact of the ensuing domestic energy crisis would hang over the remainder of Kissinger's tenure at the State Department and continue to influence his approach to the Arab-Israeli peace process.[22]

With the cease-fire in effect, Kissinger initiated contact with the PLO by sending General Vernon Walters, deputy director of the CIA, to meet with two of Arafat's deputies in Morocco. In dialogue with Khalid

al-Hassan and his brother Hani al-Hassan, both founding members of
Fatah, Walters reached an understanding: Fatah would agree not to attack
Americans as long as a communications channel remained open between
it and Washington, through the CIA. Highly aware that Sadat wanted
the United States to develop relations with the PLO, Kissinger saw a chance
to placate the Egyptian president and thereby encourage the fledgling peace
process between Egypt and Israel. At the same time, recognizing the PLO's
desire to participate in negotiations and any planned peace conference, he
found a way to prevent the organization from disrupting negotiations by
hinting that the PLO might get that chance to establish relations with
Washington. As the 1976 presidential election approached, and the PLO
remained on the sidelines of the peace process, Kissinger's hope was to
weaken, if not eliminate, the organization.[23]

THE CRIME CAPITAL

As he had for foreign policy, Nixon telegraphed his intentions for domestic policy before taking office, emphasizing a focus on law and order.
In strategy meetings before and just after the election, Nixon met with
members of his incoming team—Attorney General nominee John Mitchell,
and domestic advisors John Ehrlichman, Egil (Bud) Krogh Jr., Daniel
Patrick Moynihan, John Dean, and Donald Santarelli—to debate what
types of crime might best be targeted by initiatives at the federal level. The
decision reached, that the focus should be on narcotics, was at least as
practical as it was political; although the rise of armed robbery and bur-
glary was more top-of-mind for the public, those crimes were strictly the
purview of local enforcement. Meanwhile, it was already the federal government's responsibility to interdict any narcotics traffic traversing state
and national borders, so it could more easily extend its crime fighting to
the domestic level in that realm. There was also a political opportunity in
targeting narcotics. As Radley Balko writes, drug use "was the common
denominator among the groups—low-income blacks, the counterculture,
and the antiwar movement—against whom Nixon had unified 'ignored
America.'"[24]

Another practical decision was to focus on crime reduction in the District of Columbia, because it was the one city where Congress did have
jurisdiction over local laws. Egil Krogh recognized how the city could

serve as a "laboratory" and showcase for federally designed law-and-order policies that other locales might choose to emulate. Krogh led the administration's crime efforts and coordinated with congressional allies. A recent law school graduate, he had briefly worked at the law firm of John Ehrlichman, a family friend in Seattle. Ehrlichman recruited his protégé to join the Nixon administration shortly after the 1968 election. Krogh later recalled that Nixon "had singled out Washington, DC, as the crime capital of the country," which was an especially unfortunate distinction given that, for workers in foreign embassies and consulates and millions of visitors annually, it represented America. Krogh and his colleagues felt "a special obligation to see if we could really improve it, by reducing crime in the District of Columbia. And we felt that programs that could work in the district could then be used in other cities."[25]

The Nixon administration deliberately linked its anti-crime proposals for the district with the anti-drug actions it was taking nationally. In a July 1969 message to Congress, Nixon declared that "society has few judgments too severe, few penalties too harsh for the men who make their livelihood in the narcotics traffic." He noted that narcotics "have been cited as a primary cause of the enormous increase in street crimes over the last decade." Nixon pointed to an 800 percent increase in juvenile drug-related arrests from 1960 to 1967 and claimed that "New York City alone has records of some 40,000 heroin addicts, and the number rises between 7,000 and 9,000 a year."[26]

Meanwhile, in the district laboratory, the Nixon administration implemented several policies that would also be applied nationally. When the District of Columbia Court Reform and Criminal Procedure Act of 1970 went into effect, judges could for the first time deny pretrial release to criminal defendants based not just on flight risk considerations but also on their perceived dangerousness to the community. The new law also provided for "no knock" warrants to be issued in situations where it was deemed likely that an announced search or arrest would prompt escape efforts, destruction of evidence, or injury to police officers. Both practices would subsequently be copied by many other jurisdictions and become cornerstones of law enforcement across America and in foreign territories under US military occupation during the Global War on Terror. Preventive detentions were employed in DC to imprison criminal defendants without bail for sixty days. This was coupled with a thousand new district

police officers. Meanwhile, at the national level, the administration increased the funding of two existing agencies—the Bureau of Narcotics
and Dangerous Drugs (BNDD) and the Law Enforcement Assistance Administration—and expanded the ranks of federal drug agents.[27]

While Nixon escalated the war in Vietnam with the invasion of Cambodia, Congress passed legislation on drugs and crime in advance of the
1970 midterm elections. Although both parties sought to capitalize on the
public's fear of rising crime, Nixon and the Republicans scored more
political points from the legislation. In late October, Nixon signed the
Comprehensive Drug Abuse Prevention and Control Act at the Narcotics
Bureau's office in the Justice Department. Known as the Controlled Substances Act, the law mirrored at the national level some of the changes
introduced in the district, including allowing federal enforcement officers
to obtain "no knock" warrants. In contrast to later anti-drug legislation,
not all of this act's provisions involved harsher penalties. Possession and
use were reduced to misdemeanors, and judges were given autonomy in
sentencing first-time offenders. The legislation did, however, increase the
mandatory sentences for first-time and repeat sellers of narcotics and major traffickers. Even though the legislation drew on the Nixon administration's policies in the District of Columbia, increased crime in the city undermined their attempts to make it a showcase.[28]

The Controlled Substances Act classified drugs into five schedules.
Schedule I drugs were defined as those with "high potential for abuse"
and "no currently accepted medical use" and included heroin and other
opium derivatives as well as marijuana and lysergic acid diethylamide
(LSD). Even though the medical community has objected to the classification, marijuana remains on the Schedule I list.[29]

The Organized Crime Control Act of 1970 also had a significant impact over the next half-century, especially through its provisions raising the
penalties for state and federal crimes committed by "racketeer-influenced
and corrupt organizations." The RICO provisions were not actually limited to organized crime organizations but could be applied broadly in civil
and criminal cases, and, over time, Congress expanded the list of crimes
subject to these penalties to include narcotics trafficking, terrorism, and
narco-terrorism. One form of penalty in particular, asset forfeiture, would
become a key feature of narcotics cases prosecuted nationally, and was
eventually used overseas.[30]

Less than a year after the acts were passed, Nixon declared that drug abuse had "assumed the dimensions of a national emergency." Invoking an already familiar refrain, Nixon said that drugs were "public enemy number one." He called for an "all-out offensive" and declared, "if we cannot destroy the drug menace in America, then it will surely in time destroy us." His proposal allocated significant funds for community-based treatment programs and to create a Special Action Office for Drug Abuse Prevention at the White House. Nixon also linked the rise in domestic drug abuse to soldiers coming home from Vietnam, and instituted mandatory testing of returning military personnel. Although the issue received significant attention at the time, Jeremy Kuzmarov demonstrates that the association between addiction and military defeat was a convenient political myth propagated by the Nixon administration.[31]

THE GOLDEN TRIANGLE

New York City's Harlem neighborhood was one of the domestic arenas where the Vietnam War and Nixon's new War on Drugs intersected. Frank Lucas, a Harlem transplant originally from rural North Carolina, established a direct connection for high-grade heroin from Southeast Asia's "Golden Triangle." Later he would boast that the heroin was cleverly stashed in the coffins of dead American servicemen being shipped home from Vietnam. What is more certain is that Lucas acted as a stateside partner to Leslie "Ike" Atkinson, a former master sergeant who ran a Bangkok bar frequented by American soldiers, and was able, through contacts, to make his shipments through the military postal system.[32]

At the time, Italian-American organized crime syndicates working with a network of corrupt narcotics police officers were New York City's main source of heroin. One of the highest-profile scandals to hit the New York City Police Department (NYPD) in that era was the theft, reported in December 1972, of heroin and 120 pounds of cocaine from a department vault in Lower Manhattan. The heroin was decade-old evidence related to the famed, and still open, "French Connection" case immortalized by the 1971 William Friedkin film by that name. Originating in Turkey, the heroin was of inferior quality, and made even worse as officers controlling the supply diluted it. No one was ever charged in connection with the theft, but in 1974 twelve members of the NYPD narcotics division were arrested on corruption charges. By that time, Golden Triangle heroin had already supplanted the NYPD-Mafia supply and triggered a legislative backlash that reverberated for decades.[33]

The Golden Triangle is the borderlands where present-day Myanmar (formerly Burma), Thailand, and Laos meet. For heroin shipped from there, Frank Lucas claimed he was able to pay just $4,200 per kilogram for the 132 kilograms he bought, while his competitors paid $35,000 per kilo from the NYPD-Mafia cabal. The suppliers of Golden Triangle heroin had first come to the region as soldiers of the Kuomintang (KMT)—the Chinese Nationalist Party defeated in 1949 by the Communists in mainland China. Fleeing what was now the People's Republic of China, some 1,700 members of the Ninety-Third and Twenty-Sixth Divisions of the KMT's Eighth Army had settled in Burma's Kengtung state, near the border with Thailand. Given the group's initial strategy of using the area to launch an invasion and guerrilla raids against the Communist forces, Washington and Taipei provided the KMT forces with weapons and supplies and expanded a World War II–era airstrip into a military base with the capacity for large supply aircraft. Within three years, however, the KMT's cross-border invasions had repeatedly failed, and the organization, now settled in the Golden Triangle, had seized control of the opium trade, establishing a mini narco-state in northern Burma.[34]

The opium trade in the Golden Triangle predated the British colonial period, when it was legal but restricted. In Burma, it was largely under the control of the ethnic Shan minority. Although the Burmese government objected to the KMT's presence, its army was unable to dislodge their forces. Negotiations brokered by the Eisenhower and Kennedy administrations led to tensions with Jiang Jieshi in Taipei. Although some KMT forces were publicly withdrawn from northern Burma, they were reintroduced through Thailand from Taiwan or reinforced by new recruits fleeing the People's Republic of China. For more than a decade, the KMT's secret army created difficulties for relations between Washington and Taipei, and was a source of frustration for Rangoon.[35]

The Vietnam War contributed to a new rationale for the KMT's secret army. In coordination with the CIA, the secret army conducted counterinsurgency operations against the Pathet Lao in Laos and the Vietnamese NLF. By 1967, the KMT had secured its hold on the opium trade in the Golden Triangle. It began producing the highest-grade heroin, known as

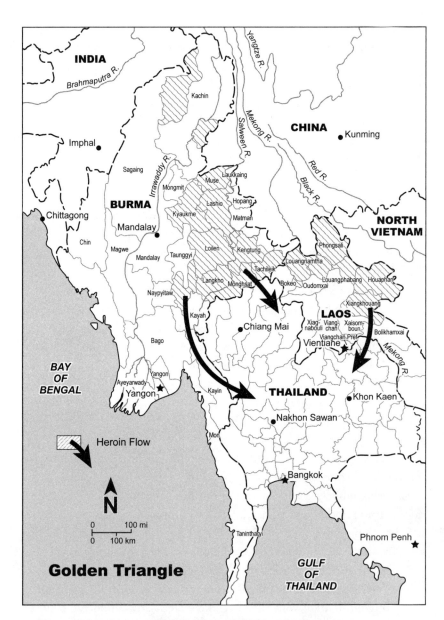

MAP 3. THE GOLDEN TRIANGLE OF SOUTHEAST ASIA, 1968–1975

heroin no. 4, which was 90 to 99 percent pure, initially selling it to a market of American servicemen. Soon enough, heroin no. 4 was being exported to the United States, including to Frank Lucas and his Country Boys Gang in Harlem. Unlike other narco-para-states, the KMT maintained its rule with covert and, at times, overt American assistance. If American support wavered, the opium trade provided a mechanism for the KMT to continue funding its crusade against the People's Republic of China and its real or perceived allies. "We have to continue to fight the evil of communism and to fight you must have an army, and an army must have guns, and to buy guns you must have money," explained Tuan Shi-wen, a KMT general. "In these mountains the only money is opium."[36]

Frank Lucas agreed with this sentiment. Years later, reflecting on his rise and the impact of the heroin trade on Harlem in the 1970s, Lucas said he had not had much choice. After a teenage cousin was murdered by the Ku Klux Klan, Lucas began engaging in low-level theft and eventually left North Carolina. By the time he was a teenager, Lucas had already spent time in prison in Tennessee. He was only sixteen when he arrived in Harlem and started stealing from other criminals. Lucas was eventually adopted and employed by famed gangster Ellsworth "Bumpy" Johnson. "Kind of son-of-a-bitch I saw myself being, money I wanted to make, I'd have to be on Wall Street. On Wall Street, from the giddy-up," Lucas explained, "But I couldn't have even gotten a job being a fucking janitor on Wall Street." Although Lucas never became a Wall Street "master of the universe," he did achieve another American dream. Aspects of his story were portrayed in the 2007 Ridley Scott film *American Gangster*, where he was played by Denzel Washington. As Lucas's aspirations intersected with the ambitions of a wealthy and prominent politician, both men influenced the domestic and international legal regimes to curtail narcotics trafficking.[37]

THE ROCKEFELLER DRUG LAWS

Nelson Rockefeller was born to be president and he came agonizingly close. The grandson of the founder of Standard Oil, John D. Rockefeller, his family name was synonymous with affluence and privilege. Born on the same day as his grandfather, great things were expected of Nelson and he aspired for them as well. "Rocky," as he became known in his first run for Governor of New York in 1958, was the standard bearer for a certain wing of his party: northerners who were friendly to big business but also labor, and generally more progressive on social issues than western Republicans or southern Democrats. The shifting political currents of the 1960s, however, left Rockefeller as a Republican party outsider. Although he immediately set his sights on the White House, he was unable to overcome Vice President Richard Nixon's entrenched support within the party. Rockefeller's subsequent bids in the 1964 and 1968 campaigns fell embarrassingly short. By 1972, as Nixon appeared to be coasting for reelection, Rockefeller was preparing for the future. He planned to win a fifth term as governor in 1974 and attempt another presidential bid two years later. With narcotics, Rockefeller found an issue that appealed to conservatives and aligned with Nixon's messaging, both on law and order and on the nascent War on Drugs.[38]

In February 1970, Rockefeller called for a "total war" on juvenile drug abuse. Two years later, President Nixon visited New York City to discuss anti-narcotics efforts. Nixon joined Rockefeller in a meeting with the official representatives of federal, state, and local law enforcement agencies. Nixon's speech at John F. Kennedy Airport demonstrated the shared perspective and language on the issue. "We must wage what I have called total war," Nixon declared, "against public enemy number one in the United States: the problem of dangerous drugs." Afterward, Nixon and Rockefeller met state and local judges for a discussion of proposed narcotics courts. Within two months, the New York State legislature passed a law approving a hundred new judges to focus primarily on narcotics cases. The law portended Rockefeller's aggressive new strategy.[39]

Meeting with his advisors in autumn 1972, Rockefeller proposed a penalty that shocked the room. "On drugs, anyone who pushes gets life in prison. And I mean life—no matter what amount. No more of this plea bargaining, parole, probation." Rockefeller rebuffed attempts to soften the plan and presented it to the New York State Legislature. "I have one goal and one objective," he stressed in a boisterous January 1973 speech, "and that is to stop the pushing of drugs and to protect the innocent victim." He acknowledged that he was proposing "drastic measures," but claimed that, "after trying everything else, there is nothing less we can do." Although the final legislation was less restrictive than Rockefeller's intent, the penalties were still severe. The crimes of selling narcotics and possessing narcotics with intent to sell were now subject to three classes of felony conviction with mandatory terms ranging from one to twenty-five years in prison, including for first offenders. Class A felonies, the most serious, carried the possibility of life imprisonment. If parole were granted, it would also be for life. Restrictions were placed on plea bargaining, as well.[40]

After passing the law, Rockefeller defended his choice of a more aggressive approach that abandoned rehabilitation. New York's existing programs, he claimed, were clearly not achieving their goals. In Nixonian fashion, he focused on the impact of the drug trade on broader society and stoked public safety fears. As he put it to a *New York Times* reporter, "I got to feel maybe we've got to focus on the public who is being mugged, mobbed, robbed, murdered, raped and so forth—so how to restore civil liberties to our citizens." Support for these policies did not come only from White suburban and rural New York. As documented by Michael Javen Fortner, middle- and working-class Blacks lobbied for and embraced more punitive measures to curtail the influx of high-quality heroin across New York City's boroughs. Hoping for a reversal of the damage their communities were sustaining from the burgeoning narcotics trade, they requested greater police protection and enforcement. The law received bipartisan support, including from influential Black politicians at the state and local levels and in the US Congress.[41]

Media coverage emphasized the probable downsides of the nation's toughest laws. The combination of mandatory minimum sentences and felony charges for even small amounts threatened to overwhelm the already overburdened New York court system. As part of the legislation, funding was allocated for special judges, courtrooms, and staff. For their part, state officials seemed eager to exaggerate the legislation's positive impact, even before its first day in effect. "There have already been indications that some drug dealers are holding last-minute going-out-of-business sales," the counsel for New York's Drug Abuse Control Commission claimed. As it would turn out, critics of the new policy underestimated its detrimental impact.[42]

The 1973 New York State Substance Control Act, also known as the Rockefeller drug laws, contributed to mass incarceration and the greater institutionalization of the drug war.[43] Rockefeller and law enforcement officials had claimed the goal was to target major distributors and "kingpins," but later analysis showed that those arrested and incarcerated were overwhelmingly low-level, nonviolent offenders. Five years later, an evaluation by the National Institute of Law Enforcement and Criminal Justice found that the 1973 laws had failed to achieve the desired outcome. Heroin was still readily available and usage was on par with neighboring states and other major cities. The report also found that more types of drugs were in circulation after the law was passed, including cocaine, which was on its way to eclipsing heroin. Property crimes had increased from 1973 to 1975 and just as many were being committed by narcotics users. Although the predicted prison overcrowding had not occurred, the report cautioned that a backlog of cases remained to be adjudicated.[44]

The implications of the Rockefeller drug laws for incarceration were substantial. At one point, according to the nonprofit advocacy group Drug Policy Alliance, the number of individuals occupying prison cells in New York as a result of these laws reached twenty-three thousand. By 2009, it reported, over 66 percent had never been in prison before and 80 percent had never been convicted of a felony prior to their arrest. Contrary to the hopes of the "Black silent majority" that had called for more aggressive action to protect their communities, the new laws had a profoundly negative impact. Blacks and Latinos accounted for roughly 33 percent of New York's population, but 90 percent of those imprisoned for drug-related felonies. On the legislation's thirty-fifth anniversary in 2008, 20 percent of New York's eleven thousand prisoners were incarcerated under the Rockefeller drug laws at an annual cost of roughly $45,000 per prisoner.[45]

While the New York State Legislature was debating the legislation, seventeen states were considering reducing penalties on marijuana and some already had. Over the next decade, however, these efforts were abandoned as the idea of mandatory minimum sentencing was adopted by other states and the federal government. The results were staggering. In 1973, the US prison population was 330,000. Four decades later, while the population had risen by about 50 percent, the prison population shot up 600 percent, to some 2.3 million inmates, with 20 percent of these convicted of drug-related offenses. This led to a boom in prison construction and the dramatic increase in costs to states and the federal government of building, maintaining, and staffing the United States' criminal justice and corrections infrastructure. The increase in limited state funds often came at the expense of spending on education and other social services, further exacerbating the impact of addiction and crime in many communities. Meanwhile, the drug trade continued unabated and the reliance on a law enforcement approach ensured that it was more lucrative. The Rockefeller drug laws were also exported internationally as the United States sought to eliminate supply by targeting overseas traffickers.[46]

Washington's attempts to impose its narcotics control policies on the international community dated to the early postwar period. Led by the now infamous anti-drug crusader Harry Anslinger, commissioner of the Federal Bureau of Narcotics (forerunner of the BNDD), these efforts encountered resistance, including from Moscow and Beijing. The 1961 Single Convention on Narcotic Drugs built on treaties over the previous five decades. Anslinger, who represented the United States at the negotiations, was opposed to its ratification because he saw its restrictions on opium production as insufficient. Washington discouraged other countries from joining the Single Convention and did not become a party to it until 1967.[47]

Four years later, the Nixon administration pursued two international treaties that were aligned with the War on Drugs. The first was an amendment to the 1961 Single Convention that enhanced restrictions on narcotics, with an emphasis on enforcement. It was accompanied by the 1971 Convention on Psychotropic Substances. One of the issues with the 1961 Single Convention was that it defined addiction based on opiates. As a result, amphetamines and barbiturates were not classified as addictive—a determination that was in line with the preferences of major American and European pharmaceutical companies. Although this changed with the 1971 Convention on Psychotropic Substances, the regulatory controls provided by that convention were weak. Still, these combined conventions marked a new direction: the United States was beginning to export its enforcement model through international agreements.[48]

Three months after Governor Rockefeller presented his aggressive new plan to the New York State Legislature, and as the final US troops left Vietnam, President Nixon proposed to Congress a major reorganization of federal resources focused on drug enforcement. Combining four existing agencies—the BNDD, the Custom Bureau's narcotics investigation division, the Office of Drug Abuse Law Enforcement within the Department of Justice, and the Office of National Narcotics Intelligence—into one division of the Department of Justice, he argued, would reduce bureaucratic inefficiencies and improve coordination with other agencies like the FBI. Indeed, Nixon claimed that the proposed Drug Enforcement

Administration (DEA) was essential to his administration's "all-out global war on the drug menace." Even in the intensely political climate of the Watergate scandal, Nixon's reorganization was endorsed by a leading Democrat from the party's progressive wing, Senator Abraham Ribicoff of Connecticut. A former Secretary of Health, Education, and Welfare in the Kennedy administration, Ribicoff chaired the Senate's Committee on Government Operations and its subcommittee focused on drug enforcement. The DEA's initial budget was almost $75 million and it boasted nearly 1,500 special agents. Two years later, its budget had ballooned to over $140 million, allowing it to employ some 2,100 agents.[49]

As the main coordinating agency for drug enforcement with state and local bodies, the DEA institutionalized the War on Drugs over the next decade. It was also the lead agency for interfacing with law enforcement in other countries. As will be seen, it was particularly active in the Western Hemisphere.

EXPORTING LAW AND ORDER

Nixon's attempt to export his law-and-order campaign came even before the creation of the DEA. Turkey and Mexico were his main targets. The domestic and international efforts were linked, and the origins were in Nixon's campaign rhetoric and domestic politics. At a September 16, 1968, event in Anaheim, California, Nixon had promised that, as president, he would target the "source of drugs."[50]

A year later, Daniel Patrick Moynihan, then assistant to the president, argued for a more aggressive approach toward Turkey. In a September 18, 1969, memorandum to Attorney General Mitchell, Moynihan argued that, if the United States acted with "energy and determination," it "could cripple the heroin traffic in the course of twelve to twenty-four months." Moynihan had recently met with NATO's newly established Committee on the Challenges of Modern Society and, after leaving Brussels, traveled to Turkey and France to discuss the heroin trade with agents of the US BNDD. He came away convinced that the United States should work more aggressively to shut down cultivation in Turkey and processing in France. Much could be accomplished through a serious effort combining diplomacy, economic incentives, and sanctions, he wrote in a memorandum to Mitchell. "*The foreign policy establishment of the United States has never regarded the heroin traffic as serious,"* Moynihan asserted, "But it is serious. It has become a threat to the social stability of the United States." Although Moynihan's suggestions found a receptive audience in the Nixon White House, they encountered resistance from the State Department. Meanwhile, narcotics became a focus of the Committee on the Challenges of Modern Society.[51]

NATO's Committee on the Challenges of Modern Society represented a departure for the military alliance. As proposed by President Nixon, the committee's initial focus was on environmental issues. It was soon expanded to examine a range of problems, including narcotics. There were tensions, however, between the Nixon White House, as represented by Moynihan, and the State Department and National Security Council. Moynihan attempted to pressure Ankara to eliminate Turkish opium, which Washington claimed was responsible for 80 to 85 percent of the heroin in the United States. Meanwhile, Foggy Bottom and the National Security Council were reluctant to aggravate a NATO ally.[52]

The attention on Turkish heroin was politically motivated. Moynihan and others in the Nixon White House believed that Ankara was susceptible to pressure due to its reliance on American aid. The administration also exaggerated the danger of Turkish opium by claiming it represented over 80 percent of the heroin imported into the United States, yet that figure, sourced to administration officials, was frequently cited in the media.[53]

Although the combination of public and private pressure on Ankara was eventually successful, it contributed to significant domestic upheaval in Turkey. By April 1970, Prime Minister Süleyman Demirel's government had agreed to reduce opium cultivation and eventually to curtail it altogether. In addition to purchasing that year's crop from farmers, Ankara ratified the 1961 Single Convention on Narcotic Drugs regulating opium production. Over considerable domestic opposition, Demirel's government cut by nearly half the number of provinces authorized to cultivate opium. The decision, however, coincided with rising popular discontent over political and economic issues, especially among college students. The Turkish military deposed Demirel's government in March 1971. Negotiations between Washington and Ankara continued over the next several years and progress was interrupted by Turkey's 1974 invasion of Cyprus and Nixon's resignation. Turkish politics entered a period of instability that culminated in the 1980 coup, by which point Turkey was no longer a major heroin producer.[54]

Although Turkey represented the most successful aspect of Nixon's War on Drugs, it did not reduce the drug problem in the United States. The so-called "French Connection" from Turkey to France was challenged by higher-quality heroin from Southeast Asia. Meanwhile, heroin originating in Mexico made up an increasing share of the US market. Although it was of lesser quality than Southeast Asian heroin, and was also targeted by the Nixon administration and its successors, it had ready access to a stable market in the United States.[55]

As Moynihan focused his ire on Turkey and the French Connection, Attorney General Mitchell and the Special Presidential Task Force Relating to Narcotics, Marijuana and Dangerous Drugs argued for action against Mexico. Mexico accounted for roughly 70 percent of the marijuana entering the United States. The Task Force advocated a "concerted frontal attack" on marijuana's importation and sale.[56]

In September 1969, the Nixon administration launched a short-term operation designed to crack down on smugglers trying to cross the US-Mexican border at the height of the marijuana harvest season. As with Turkey, the approach had been to use promises of foreign aid and increased trade to persuade President Díaz Ordaz's government to find ways to reduce cultivation of cannabis in Mexico. Operation Intercept took a harder line, deploying a legion of Border, Customs, and Immigration agents across the two-thousand-mile border with orders to inspect every vehicle entering the United States. The effort virtually halted tourism and commerce, but scant quantities of marijuana were seized. While administration officials claimed this demonstrated the effectiveness of the operation, internal discussions offered a different explanation.[57]

The US embassy in Mexico warned that traffickers had likely modified their activities due to media coverage of the impending operation. An assessment by the Bureau of the Budget warned that the initiative was based on flawed analysis and that the focus on marijuana was a distraction from "hard drugs" like heroin. Citing its 1967 report on the issue, the Bureau of the Budget stated that enforcement efforts targeting hard drugs were "about 100 times as effective as equal resources used against marijuana." It also predicted that a policy focused on marijuana could lead to the rise of hard drugs as a substitute. It was a prescient assessment.[58]

Operation Intercept contributed to two subsequent initiatives. The first, Operation Cooperation, was to improve counternarcotics coordination between Mexico and the United States. This was followed by Operation Condor. Beginning with the Kennedy administration, Mexico was pressured to implement crop eradication. By 1975, it instituted aerial spraying. The CIA reported that the use of aerial herbicides was "politically unpopular" and for good reason.[59] A State Department assessment found that aerial defoliants had negative impacts on the cultivation of legal as well as illegal crops. Not only did they damage large amounts of agricultural land, they negatively affected the health of the local population and polluted the environment, exposing domestic livestock and wild animals in natural habitats to toxic water. Accompanying the use of defoliants was a deliberate campaign to target leading traffickers. The intention, however, was the assertion of governmental control over the narcotics trade rather than its elimination.[60]

In early February 1976, the CIA reported that Mexico had become the "main source of illicit narcotics, especially opiates," entering the United States. The report would have made for sober reading in the Ford White House, as similar assertions had been made about Turkey only six years earlier. The assessment rated the Mexican government's authority as "sporadic or nonexistent" in the key cultivation areas, which were described as "lawless." Absent from the assessment, however, was the Mexican government's role in facilitating or benefiting from the narcotics trade or the involvement of the state and police forces in trafficking. Indeed, Operation Condor served to subordinate trafficking under Mexican state authorities. By the 1980s, drug trafficking became more centralized and lucrative as Colombian cocaine transported through Mexico supplanted marijuana and heroin.[61]

There was a second, covert, phase of Operation Condor that was rooted in US foreign policy goals and interests. Six months after Nixon's second term began, President Juan Maria Bordaberry dissolved Uruguay's parliament. In coordination with the Uruguayan military, Bordaberry and key allies implemented civic-military rule that would last for the next decade. Prior to the coup, the US embassy in Montevideo reported on a meeting with members of the military. "I sense," wrote Frank Ortiz, deputy chief of the US mission, "that our future relations with Uruguay will of necessity be influenced by how we manage our relationship with various military leaders."[62] The challenge was not limited to Uruguay: by the end of the decade, dictatorships would dominate the Latin American states. Washington either encouraged the military coups before they were launched or eagerly welcomed the new juntas once in power.

Less than three months after the Uruguayan coup, the Chilean military deposed President Salvador Allende. Washington encouraged the coup and the brutal crackdown that followed. The US DEA also supported the targeting of Chile's leading cocaine distributors by General Augusto Pinochet's new regime. This intersection of Washington's foreign and domestic policies had intended and unintended consequences with regional and global implications.[63]

As military juntas came to power across South America's "Southern Cone" and targeted narcotics traffickers, traditional trading routes and networks were disrupted. Prior to the 1973 coup, Chile's leading cocaine traffickers expanded their distribution networks in Colombia. Like Mexico, Colombia was pressured to adopt crop eradication. The combination of Pinochet's crackdown on Chile's leading traffickers, Colombia's marijuana eradication, and the availability of coca paste from Peruvian and Bolivian farmers created an opportunity for ambitious smugglers. Colombia's geographic location was also ideal for establishing a new hub for cocaine production and distribution.[64]

The overt and covert parts of Operation Condor intersected and had long-term implications for the United States and the hemisphere. They were also rooted in the American experience and failure in Vietnam. While the covert activity was politically oriented and targeted leftists across the region, the overt effort ostensibly focused on counternarcotics in Mexico. The covert part was initiated in the fall of 1975 and accelerated after a March 1976 military coup toppled Argentinian President Isabelle Peron. Writing in early August 1976, Assistant Secretary of State for Latin America Harry Shlaudeman reported that Chile, Uruguay, and Argentina believed they were "embattled." The feeling in Southern Cone juntas, he wrote, was that they were caught between, on one side, "international Marxism and its terrorist exponents" and, on the other side, "the hostility of the uncomprehending industrial democracies misled by Marxist propaganda." With Operation Condor, the juntas were "joining forces to eradicate 'subversion,' a word which increasingly translates into non-violent dissent from the left and center left." Shlaudeman noted that the countries had a "siege mentality shading into paranoia," even though the juntas had presided over a "near decimation of the Marxist left." Not only did the regimes "insist that the threat remains and the war must go on," but some described the fight against radical terrorism as a "Third World War" in which the Southern Cone served as "the last bastion of Christian civilization."[65]

Shlaudeman attempted to rationalize the position of the Southern Cone dictatorships by sharing their views that they were engaged in "counterterrorism every bit as justified as Israeli actions against Palestinian terrorism" and that Western critics applied a "double standard." Shlaudeman recommended that Washington focus on and distinguish between the individual countries rather than treating them as a bloc, and that it challenge rhetorical exaggerations, particularly of a "Third World War."[66]

Instead of distancing Washington from Operation Condor, Secretary of State Kissinger encouraged it. As with the Phoenix Program in Vietnam, the United States provided training as well as technical and intelligence support. At least 171 opponents of the Southern Cone juntas were killed, including prominent critics of the Pinochet regime assassinated in car bombings in Washington and Buenos Aires.[67]

Notions of a Third World War were shared by the Southern Cone regimes and American conservatives. Driven by the belief that the insurgencies across Latin America and the broader Third World were united and orchestrated by Moscow, the conservative counterrevolutions sought a similar level of coordination and shared purpose. Thus, Operation Condor was just one part of the larger, dirty wars in the Western Hemisphere and more broadly across the Third World. In southern Africa, Washington also embraced unsavory regimes that insisted they were locked in a civilizational struggle.[68]

A NIHILISTIC NIGHTMARE

While Nixon's law-and-order campaign at home centered on racial discord, the southwestern region of Africa offered the administration an opportunity to demonstrate its support for racial equality. Nixon, however, did not rise to the occasion. This was a consistent pattern for Nixon on issues of race, dating to the 1960 election. Before his first run for the presidency, Nixon had been considered the most progressive member of the

Eisenhower administration in the realm of race relations. But Nixon chose a different political path in 1960. Even though he lost that election, White anger would revive his chances eight years later. As Nixon entered office, the White-minority regimes in southern Africa faced international opprobrium and increasing isolation. Yet key figures in the American foreign policy establishment and the Nixon administration sought to align the United States with the regimes rather than sever ties.[69]

In November 1965, Rhodesia unilaterally declared its independence from the United Kingdom. Although the Rhodesian government of Prime Minister Ian Smith framed independence as necessary for "the preservation of justice, civilization and Christianity," the declaration was not welcomed internationally. Subsequent negotiations with London quickly reached a stalemate and Whitehall imposed trade sanctions. The UN supported UK Prime Minister Harold Wilson's efforts to isolate the Rhodesian government. In December 1966, the UN Security Council applied selective, mandatory economic sanctions against Rhodesia. Eighteen months later, in May 1968, the UN imposed comprehensive sanctions against the White-minority regime.[70]

The colony of Southern Rhodesia was founded in 1923. Named after the British mining mogul Cecil Rhodes, its White population was roughly 35,000. Although not incorporated into the Union (later Republic) of South Africa, Rhodesia emulated that country's apartheid policies toward the overwhelming Black majority. Apartheid, the Afrikaans word for separateness, was a multilayered series of racist and discriminatory laws, policies, and practices instituted over time in South Africa and adopted by neighboring White-minority regimes. When it declared unilateral independence in 1965, Rhodesia had a population of seven million Blacks and nearly 224,000 Whites. Faced with international opposition, Smith wanted Rhodesia to function as a bulwark against the forces of decolonization and communism. He found support in Washington.[71]

In an early April 1969 memorandum to Nixon, Kissinger judged the situation as "not an immediate crisis." He doubted that recent raids by "Black terrorist" groups into Rhodesia and reprisals by White militias would escalate into "the first rounds of the long-predicted race war." Kissinger predicted that the White minority regimes could easily contain potential military threats, while cautioning Nixon that the looming confrontation would carry political ramifications.[72]

The administration's policy review was influenced by former Secretary of State Dean Acheson, one of the storied group of Cold War foreign policy advisors known as the "Wise Men." Acheson had been largely responsible for the Truman administration's support for the reimposition of French colonial rule in Southeast Asia and decision to ignore Vietnamese independence in the early postwar period. He continued supporting a hardline approach in Vietnam until the 1968 Tet Offensive. Acheson took a different lesson from the Vietnam experience, however, and applied it to southern Africa. In a memorandum to Kissinger, Acheson advocated that the Nixon administration break with Johnson's policy toward the region. He argued that the policy was contrary to Washington's interests and the goals could not be achieved.[73]

In December 1969, a National Security Council paper initiated by Kissinger was circulated to brief members on US interests and policy options with regard to southern Africa. It recognized that, while the United States had no vital security interests in that region, it did have important political and material interests, beginning with the "racial repression by White minority regimes" and its "international political ramifications." Non-White people around the world, the paper warned, "deeply resent the continuation of discrimination, identify with the repressed majorities in southern Africa and tend in varying degrees to see relationships of outside powers with the white regimes as at least tacit acceptance of racism." It was a resentment, moreover, that communist states had already shown eagerness to exploit. Intensifying this pressure on America not to cooperate with the White regimes was the fact that "other countries tend to see our relationships with southern Africa as reflections of domestic attitudes on race." And it hardly helped that South Africa's laws would apply to any Black Americans visiting the country. Refusing American travelers' visas or subjecting them to segregation would surely complicate relations between Washington and Pretoria.[74]

In mid-December 1969, Nixon assembled his National Security Council for a "frank discussion" about US relations with White-minority governments in southern Africa—a matter that, although it was peripheral to national security considerations, was "an important question, as there are moral and domestic political issues involved." Reacting to a colleague's comment that there was little the US could do to exert influence over nations like Rhodesia and South Africa, Secretary of State Rogers spoke up:

"There is the moral argument. If we could do anything then we would have a moral responsibility. But since we can't do anything, there is no responsibility." Nixon pointed to the intractability of the problem: "The whites can't go home. It is a practical problem we have come up against. They are there to stay."[75]

Nixon asked Acting Secretary of Commerce Rocco Siciliano about trade between the US and African countries. Siciliano explained that American business investment amounted to about $1 billion in South Africa alone, and "investment in black Africa is about equal" to that number. Disengagement would mean commercial losses—the United States was running a favorable trade balance with South Africa of $200 million—and remove access to certain natural resources. Corning Glass, for example, used a mineral in its manufacturing process called petalite, of which Rhodesia was the only source at the time. Closing the US consulate in Rhodesia might lead to Corning shuttering a plant in West Virginia.[76]

"I think we have to be realistic on this question and straddle it," Nixon argued. "It is obvious that we have to avoid the colonialist label but we must analyze where our national interest lies and not worry too much about other peoples' domestic policies." The policy option Nixon would go on to select was one dubbed the "tar baby option" by those at the State Department who opposed it, because they worried that adopting it would entail a commitment that was hard to back away from: Washington would be stuck with it, and that might create vulnerability. Its appeal to Nixon, however, was that, by partially relaxing the measures the United States had taken against the White regimes and at the same time providing aid and pursuing diplomatic efforts to benefit the Black population, this option would allow Washington to have it both ways. America would enjoy greater trade and investment while publicly claiming to abhor racist systems of government.[77]

Nixon and a coalition of American conservative groups perceived African liberation movements through the dual lens of domestic politics and the global containment of communism. Already disdainful of the civil rights movement, the conservative groups observed the rise of the New Left on American university campuses and increased Black militancy with alarm. One of the most prominent was the Friends of Rhodesian Independence, which was founded in 1966 and had 180 chapters. It also shared members with other right-wing groups. These organizations found ideological bedfellows in the White-minority regimes of southern Africa, which they believed had a shared settler colonial identity and heritage. Meanwhile, the regimes actively courted support from, and at times sought to mimic, the American white supremacists, including the Ku Klux Klan. Yet they also attempted to differentiate their regimes from the segregationist American south. South Africa argued that segregation in the United States was racial discrimination, but it claimed that apartheid's goal was the eventual sovereignty of Blacks in independent homelands.[78]

The liberation groups in southern Africa found increased popularity at home and legitimacy abroad. Insurgents from South Africa's African National Congress and the Zimbabwe African People's Union conducted operations inside Rhodesia. For the first seven years after Rhodesia's secession, the military operations did not constitute a major threat to either Salisbury or Pretoria. In Washington, however, they evoked fears of a broader race war. The State Department was also concerned that they offered openings for Soviet influence. Even a slight increase in assistance from Moscow, the State Department's Bureau of Intelligence and Research reported in August 1970, "may give the various movements a boost."[79]

The Nixon Doctrine, as applied in Southern Africa, meant providing funds and supplies but relying on local allies to fight real or perceived Soviet influence. Just as Israel and Iran had welcomed that arrangement, South Africa, with the strongest economy and military in the region, if not the continent, was eager to do so. As with the Arab-Israeli conflict, however, America's reliance on a perceived stabilizing force in a precarious regional order provided only a temporary respite. Less than a year after the Paris Peace Accords were signed, and within months of the October 1973 Arab-Israeli War, a coup in Lisbon expedited the end of the Portuguese empire in Southern Africa. Angola and Mozambique became independent, but not conflict-free. Meanwhile, South Africa and Rhodesia retrenched. Rhodesia's military was heavily reliant on South Africa. Less than two years after Salisbury's secession, South African forces were deployed inside Rhodesia.[80]

Nixon's policy toward the White-minority regimes needed support in the US Congress. Common ground was found on the issue of chrome ore, a mineral essential to US production of steel and arms. Since the Soviet Union sold 60 percent of the chrome to the United States, the Nixon administration sought to circumvent UN sanctions on Rhodesia. It was eventually aided by Senator Harry Byrd Jr. of Virginia, whose 1971 amendment had exempted chrome ore from sanctions. The Byrd amendment had been part of a larger military procurement bill, and debate had been guided by Cold War priorities as well as the necessities of the Vietnam War. A *New York Times* editorial criticized the Nixon administration for not exerting pressure to block the amendment, a failure it attributed to various factors, including the Rhodesian lobby's ability to marshal support from a coalition of racists in Congress and general anti-Soviet and anti-UN sentiments. The amendment was also endorsed by business groups in sectors affected by the high price of Soviet chrome. In response, Senator Byrd stressed the importance of imported chrome to American national security and the economy. The Byrd Amendment was hailed by White supremacists in the United States and in southern Africa, as Washington joined Lisbon and Pretoria in bucking UN sanctions. Although it provided Rhodesia with needed funds over the next six years, until it was repealed by President Jimmy Carter, the Byrd Amendment was ultimately unable to save the regime in Salisbury.[81]

As the struggle against White rule in Rhodesia intensified by the mid-1970s, it would be the Cuban intervention in Angola that would instigate a change in Washington's policies. The challenge to Portugal's rule in Angola had led to the emergence of three different liberation groups with opposing international sponsors. Moscow and Havana backed the People's Movement for the Liberation of Angola (MPLA), while Beijing armed the National Union for the Total Independence of Angola (UNITA). A third group, the National Front for the Liberation of Angola (FNLA), received support from neighboring Zaire (now the Democratic Republic of the Congo) and from the CIA. The Ford administration authorized a covert operation to counter Soviet and Cuban support of the MPLA. It also joined China and Zaire in funding UNITA and the FNLA. Kissinger later dismissed the Angolan operation as poorly implemented and managed. The concerns he shared with subordinates about the dangers of moderation based on the Vietnam experience were not, however, heeded by the CIA. Complicating the situation further, South Africa intervened in Angola and also armed and coordinated with UNITA.[82]

The CIA's involvement was eventually halted by Congress in late 1975. Democrats, already eager to rein in the executive branch after the Watergate scandal, also feared that the United States would become involved in an open-ended conflict. An amendment to the CIA Appropriations Act, sponsored by Democratic Senator John Tunney of California with the support of Republican Jacob Javits of New York, ended covert operations in Angola. While Tunney and his allies celebrated, President Ford said the vote was "a deep tragedy for all countries whose security depends on the United States." Soon, Democratic Senator Dick Clark of Iowa also sponsored an amendment to the US Arms Export Control Act of 1976 to impose permanent prohibitions on military and paramilitary support to any anti-government groups in Angola. "We are living in a nihilistic nightmare," Kissinger told Ford. "It proves that Vietnam is not an aberration but our normal attitude."[83]

Kissinger described the international ramifications and again displayed his penchant for melodrama and apocalyptic predictions. "No one will ever believe us again if we can't do this," he complained in a meeting with President Ford. "How can they believe we will back them?" Ford should "take on the Congress in the national interest," Kissinger argued, given how congressional intervention had hindered negotiations with Moscow. "We would have had Angola settled by January if these bastards had not been in town." Although Ford considered vetoing the bill, he decided not to take Kissinger's advice.[84]

As the Angola crisis developed, Kissinger's fears were heightened. He was nervous that Havana planned to extend its involvement from Angola to Rhodesia. These concerns were stoked by a CIA report that warned Cuban forces would be involved in Rhodesia by the end of 1976. Kissinger later wrote that he had feared the region would be destabilized by the presence of armed liberation groups in it, "much as the PLO was doing to the legitimate government of Lebanon."[85] Before leaving on a six-country African tour in April to announce the change in US policy, Kissinger began meeting with prominent American civil rights and anti-apartheid activists, including the Reverend Jesse Jackson and Dr. Leon Sullivan. The participants were generally supportive and praised Kissinger for the outreach and policy change.[86]

In Zambia, formerly the British colony of Northern Rhodesia, Kissinger publicly expressed American support for "African unity." He privately reassured Zambian President Kenneth Kaunda that the United States was "totally behind majority rule." Kaunda reassured Kissinger that none of the African leaders wanted to see Soviet or Cuban intervention in the region. He emphasized that a negotiated settlement was preferred, and that

Washington should play a key role both in facilitating an agreement in Rhodesia and in ending apartheid in South Africa and Namibia. Kissinger offered a staged diplomatic process, similar to his approach to the Arab-Israeli conflict, which began with Rhodesia and ended with South Africa. Kissinger's announcement of American support for majority rule in Rhodesia contrasted, however, with his personal view shared with President Ford and National Security Advisor Brent Scowcroft before the trip. "Basically I am with the whites in Southern Africa," he explained. "I think it is no better for the majority to oppress the minority than vice versa."[87]

Rhodesia became an unlikely campaign issue in the 1976 presidential election. Kissinger's trip came in the midst of the Republican primaries where Ford faced a difficult challenge from former California Governor Ronald Reagan. The announced policy change angered conservatives, and leading Republicans demanded Kissinger's resignation. Reagan won four primaries after Kissinger's speech in Zambia, as he declared on the campaign trail that he would send US troops to Rhodesia. Although Reagan's bid was unsuccessful, he became the conservative standard-bearer after Ford lost to Carter in November. White-minority rule in Rhodesia ended in 1979, but apartheid in South Africa remained. Meanwhile, the Nixon Doctrine was implemented in the Persian Gulf.[88]

"COVERT ACTION SHOULD NOT BE CONFUSED WITH MISSIONARY WORK"

For nearly two decades, Mohammad Reza Shah Pahlavi was hailed by Washington as a key Cold War ally in the broader Middle East. Since being reinstalled in a coup jointly orchestrated by the CIA and MI-6 in August 1953, the shah had cultivated relations with American politicians, including Nixon while he was Eisenhower's vice president. The UK's decision to withdraw from the Persian Gulf in 1968 created an opportunity for the Pahlavi monarchy.

In April 1969, the shah traveled to Washington to secure the Nixon administration's support for his regional ambitions. Vietnam hung over the conversations with key officials. Meeting with National Security Advisor Kissinger, the shah encouraged Washington to seek an "honorable solution" in Vietnam and hinted that Moscow was eager to cooperate. Minutes of a separate conversation with Secretary of State Rogers record his sharing opinions that the United States "had shown too many scruples in Vietnam." The shah believed that Washington had erred in ousting Diem, "who was a strong leader and was making some progress in combatting corruption," and "that it was unlikely that the US would want to get involved in many more Vietnams." In a subsequent meeting with Secretary of Defense Laird, the shah discussed his military needs to deter a "foolish aggressor." Although the State and Defense Departments opposed the shah's appetite for advanced military hardware, they were overruled by the Nixon White House. Over the next two years, the Nixon Doctrine was implemented as the shah relied on rising oil prices to underwrite skyrocketing defense spending.[89]

In neighboring Iraq, the July 1968 coup and emergence of the Ba'th party contributed to hostility between Baghdad and Tehran. Although Washington was not opposed to the coup, Iraq appeared to tilt toward Moscow afterward. Negotiated by Iraqi Vice President Saddam Hussein al-Takriti, the April 1972 Iraqi-Soviet Treaty of Friendship and Cooperation provided an opportunity for Tehran to demonstrate its usefulness to Washington. After the treaty was announced, the shah met with his old friend Kermit "Kim" Roosevelt in late April. Roosevelt was a key figure in the August 1953 coup and was also involved in CIA intrigues across the region throughout the 1950s. The shah told Roosevelt that the Iraq treaty was "most disturbing" and "a fulfillment of his worst dreams." A month later, the shah raised his concerns directly with Nixon. He was worried that Moscow and Baghdad would turn the Kurdish minority in Iraq and Iran from a "thorn in the side" into "an asset."[90]

The Kurds are one of the largest stateless populations in the world and their struggle for statehood dates to World War I. The failure to address Kurdish aspirations at the end of the war, however, left them in the minority in Turkey, Iraq, Iran, Syria, and the Soviet republics of Armenia and Azerbaijan. There were parallels between the Palestinian and Kurdish national movements, but while the Palestinians benefited from broader Arab nationalism and the transformational potential of a liberated Palestine, the Kurdish movement was perceived as a threat to the existing order by Arab and non-Arab states. By the 1960s, both the Kurds and the Palestinians had embraced armed struggle and sought regional and international support. In 1961, the Kurdistan Democratic Party (KDP), led by Mulla Mustafa Barzani, launched an insurgency inside Iraq with support from Iran and the United States. The insurgency persisted for nearly a decade and through two coups, by which point the Ba'th Party was in power. In March 1970, an autonomy agreement was reached among Iraq, the KDP, and Jalal Talabani's Patriotic Union of Kurdistan. But Baghdad steadily eroded the agreement. A census was delayed while the Iraqi government actively sought to change the demographic composition of the population. The Friendship Treaty with Moscow spurred regional and international support for a renewed insurgency.[91]

During a May 1972 meeting with the shah in Tehran, Nixon endorsed the Kurdish insurgency. Kissinger later wrote that covert action was necessary "to induce Baghdad to conduct a policy more respectful of the security concerns of Iraq's neighbors and the autonomy of the Kurdish minority." A study by State Department intelligence, however, suggested a different rationale. It argued that a sustained guerrilla war could replicate the success of the earlier Kurdish insurgency and bring the Ba'th party down. For the next three years, the Kurdish insurgency benefited from military and financial assistance from America's regional partners: Iran, Israel, and Jordan. While they were successful in using mountainous terrain to defend against attacks by Iraqi forces, Barzani and the KDP were unable to extend their advantage.[92]

In March 1975, Iran surprised Washington and sought a negotiated settlement with Iraq. The eventual agreement, signed two months later in Algeria, resolved a dispute between Tehran and Baghdad over the Shatt al-Arab waterway. While tensions between the two neighbors were reduced, this also left the Kurdish insurgency exposed. Tehran ended its military and financial assistance to the KDP, and the United States and Israel also abandoned the insurgency. The Iraqi military took full advantage of the agreement and, in a rout, inflicted heavy casualties on the Kurdish forces.[93]

The collapse of the Kurdish insurgency had domestic political implications. After Nixon's resignation due to the Watergate scandal, Democrats swept the 1974 midterm elections. Revelations about CIA monitoring of the antiwar movement published in the *New York Times* spurred congressional investigations. Although Vice President Ford was not implicated in the Watergate break-in or the conspiracy to conceal Nixon's involvement, his decision to pardon Nixon hindered attempts to reconcile the nation and move past the scandal. Meanwhile, Democrats were eager to limit executive power and score political points at the expense of a wounded

White House and Republican Party. Investigations were conducted by Senate and House committees throughout 1975 and resulted in two landmark reports on the abuses of the intelligence community.[94]

Led by New York Democrat Otis Pike, the House Permanent Select Committee on Intelligence was deeply critical of the CIA. The Pike report was leaked to the press and caused a stir. The report's discussion of the Kurdish insurgency blamed Washington and Tehran for failing to provide sufficient support for victory. It labeled the operation a "cynical enterprise." Although Kissinger acknowledged that the goal was "military stalemate and the gradual exhaustion of our adversary," he dismissed claims that Washington had betrayed the Kurds. But his blunt response at the time appeared to validate concerns that, in the grander scheme of things, Washington regarded the Kurds as disposable. "Covert action should not be confused with missionary work," Kissinger said. Kissinger's intrigues continued over the next year as the 1976 presidential election approached, but the wisdom of his attempts to limit congressional interference while solidifying his foreign policy goals would soon be tested, in Lebanon.[95]

MAKING WAR FROM PEACE

The congressional intervention on Angola was part of the post-Vietnam, post-Watergate shift away from the deference normally shown by the legislative branch to the White House on foreign affairs. Between this general shift, the specific pressure of the 1975 Church Committee investigation and report, and the subsequent reforms of the intelligence community, Kissinger and the CIA sought a way to circumvent oversight. Kissinger's efforts were aided by the developing relationship with Egyptian President Anwar Sadat. After the October 1973 Arab-Israeli War, Kissinger oversaw two sets of bilateral negotiations for disengagement agreements, one between Egypt and Israel in the Sinai Peninsula, and the other between Damascus and Tel Aviv for the Golan Heights. The disengagement agreements between Egypt and Israel were successful in reducing tensions and improved the relationship between Washington and Cairo. Meanwhile, the "special relationship" between the United States and Israel was enhanced.

This was not, however, without difficulties. During the negotiations over the second disengagement agreement, known as "Sinai II," Kissinger was unable to convince Israeli Prime Minister Yitzhak Rabin of the overall benefits and broader implications of improving relations with Egypt. But Rabin wanted a separate peace, which Sadat was not prepared to sign at the time. President Ford's attempt to publicly pressure Israel by announcing a reassessment of relations backfired. He faced congressional criticism and an unprecedented Israeli public relations campaign. Ford authorized Kissinger to resume negotiations and the Sinai II agreement was signed in September 1975. The agreement contained secret commitments from Washington to Israel that constrained future administrations, including toward the PLO.[96]

By 1974, the PLO was recognized by the Arab League and the UN as the "sole, legitimate representative of the Palestinian people." In Washington, there was not unanimity in the State Department and CIA on relations with the PLO. While the US embassy in Lebanon and CIA station chief Robert Ames were advocates of relations with the organization, the embassy in Jordan and CIA station chief Jack O'Connell were opposed, as was Kissinger. This disagreement was not limited to the conference rooms in Foggy Bottom and Langley or to angry telegrams exchanged between capitals. It played out in the streets of Amman and Beirut with escalating death tolls and had long-term implications for the United States and the broader region.[97]

As Washington debated policy, the PLO established bases of operations. While the PLO attempted to replicate the actions of the Algerian and Vietnamese revolutions, Washington sought to dismantle its para-states in Jordan and Lebanon, working with and through regional proxies. The PLO's para-states drew on the Palestinian refugee populations concentrated in both countries but also scattered regionally and internationally. Although the Nixon administration was successful in targeting the PLO in Jordan, the organization was able to shift its headquarters to Lebanon. This was, however, a contested process.

In 1969, the Lebanese Army attempted to prevent the emergence of an active Palestinian guerrilla force. Although the Lebanese military received some support from Washington, it was insufficient to overcome pressure from Egypt and Syria. Brokered by Egypt's president, Gamal Abdel Nasser, the November 1969 Cairo Agreement granted the PLO freedom of movement in southern Lebanon and in the country's Palestinian refugee camps. Signed by PLO Chairman Yasir Arafat, and General Emile Bustani, commander of the Lebanese army, the terms of the agreement were not initially revealed to the Lebanese public and were ratified in a closed session of the Lebanese Parliament. Under the agreement, the PLO agreed to establish security and intelligence coordination with the Lebanese Army. Inside the refugee camps, the organization had full autonomy, including security, administration, and social and health provisions. The Cairo Agreement provided the nucleus for the creation of a Palestinian para-state in Lebanon that expanded over the next decade.[98]

The Palestinian para-state in Lebanon had several major centers. Its backbone was the Palestinian refugee camps. In southern Lebanon, this included the Ein el-Hilweh, el Buss, and al-Rashidiya camps established after the 1948 Palestine War. By the mid-1970s, the PLO's factions established bases of operations in and around these camps and extended their area of control to the Mount Hermon area and Lebanon's border with Syria. The US State Department and CIA often referred to this area as "Fatah Land," because it was dominated by the largest PLO faction, Arafat's Fatah.[99]

In Beirut's southern suburb, the Shatila and Bourj el-Barajneh camps were home to large concentrations of Palestinian refugees as well as the organization's military and social operations. West Beirut's Fakhani District was the base for the PLO's major offices and de facto ministries. Later dubbed the "Fakhani Republic" by Palestinians in Lebanon, the district was also the site of businesses owned directly or indirectly by the organization. Following the October 1973 War and the surge in oil prices that accompanied the oil boycott, the PLO's budget swelled with remittances from Palestinians working in the Persian Gulf.[100]

The PLO also faced accusations of involvement in narcotics trafficking. But these allegations were often exaggerated and politically motivated. In some cases, narcotics trafficking funded Palestinian groups antagonistic to the PLO. Even when individuals associated with different Palestinian factions were arrested or indicted on trafficking charges, it is unclear if the PLO's leadership was aware of their involvement or directed their activities. Washington's focus on the PLO also obscured the role of traffickers associated with Lebanese Christian Maronite politicians and militias. As observed with the CIA and the KMT, this remained a consistent pattern into the 1980s and beyond.[101]

Replicating the situation in Jordan, the PLO's para-state in Lebanon became a site for local, regional, and international intrigues. In April 1975,

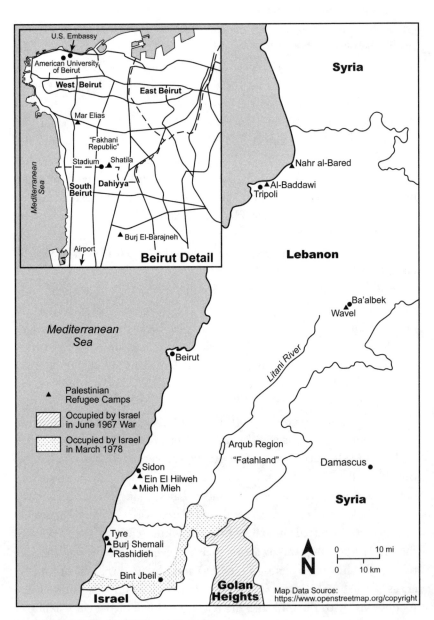

MAP 4. PLO PARA-STATE IN LEBANON

almost five years after the deadly civil war in Amman, the first stage of
the Lebanese civil war erupted. Although tensions had been building for
months, the spark came with an attack on a bus carrying Palestinian refugees returning to the Tel al-Zaatar refugee camp located in East Beirut. In
the ensuing conflict, the PLO formed a coalition with the leftist Lebanese
National Movement (LNM). It was challenged by old and new foes. Israel
and the United States sought to support the Lebanese Christian militias
against the PLO and LNM, and they were joined by King Hussein of Jordan. Drawing on his own experience battling the PLO, Hussein advocated for a harsh crackdown against the organization with the support of
CIA station chief O'Connell. They found a familiar ally in retired ambassador Dean Brown and an unlikely partner in Syria's Hafiz al-Asad.[102]

Kissinger asked Brown to mediate between the Lebanese factions.
Brown's tenure as ambassador to Jordan during the civil war should have
alerted the PLO and the LNM. Indeed, Brown warned the LNM that
failure to accept Asad's plan to end the fighting would trigger a Syrian invasion. The PLO was more supportive of Brown's efforts, which led to a
promising secret message from Kissinger to Arafat. Publicly, Brown served
as a mediator; privately, he helped to facilitate the arming of the Lebanese
Christian militias and strengthened their position in Lebanon.[103]

Over four decades later, Asad's rationale for intervening in Lebanon remains unclear. His publicly and privately stated goals were not consistent
with previous or subsequent policies. The most likely explanation is that
Asad feared a victory by the PLO-LNM forces would lead to an Israeli invasion of Lebanon and he would be forced to engage in a war he could not
win. If Asad stood by as Israel invaded Lebanon, he risked being overthrown by elements of the Syrian military and ruling Ba'th party that
supported the PLO.

Kissinger had his own calculations, factoring in the influence of domestic politics on foreign policy goals. He was concerned that, as the fighting in Lebanon escalated, the disengagement agreements between Israel
and Egypt would collapse. Kissinger also emphasized the difficulty posed
by US politics in a presidential election year. In June 1976, he confided to
regional ambassadors that his ability to conduct comprehensive negotiations or to develop relations with the PLO would be limited for a time:
"The Israelis will be impossible until the election." Attempting to deal
with the Arab-Israeli conflict before November would also be reckless in

terms of US voter sensitivities. "Anything including the PLO would run us into trouble with the Jews in the maximum condition for irresponsibility," Kissinger said, and would only benefit the Democrats.[104]

Meanwhile, Egyptian President Anwar Sadat accused Washington of attempting to destroy the PLO and threatening his own position at home. While the US ambassador to Egypt, Hermann Eilts, attempted to convince Kissinger that engaging with the PLO would resolve the conflict in Lebanon and could break the impasse in the Arab-Israeli conflict, Kissinger was unyielding. "We cannot deliver the minimum demands of the PLO," noted Kissinger, "so why talk to them?" Kissinger conceded, however, that he planned to talk to the PLO after the 1976 elections and only after other bilateral agreements were concluded. Otherwise, he feared that the PLO would "disrupt negotiations" with unacceptable demands.[105]

Syria's intervention was not as quick or decisive as Kissinger or Asad hoped. Indeed, Asad appeared to barely avoid a coup. In typical fashion, Kissinger presented a near apocalyptic outcome if Asad was overthrown. He predicted a "radical crescent" of states would emerge from Iraq to Libya that would pressure governments friendly to Washington. Kissinger claimed that this would hinder the developing relationship between Cairo and Washington and threaten the negotiations between Egypt and Israel. Kissinger's nightmare was avoided as Syria settled into a protracted occupation of Lebanon and an accommodation with the PLO. Although the PLO was weakened, its para-state in Lebanon remained.[106]

EXPORTING CHAOS

While the Syrian intervention in Lebanon was struggling to achieve its goals, the intelligence agencies of six countries signed a secret agreement to counter Soviet influence. Initiated by France and informally known as the Safari Club, it included the United States, France, Egypt, Saudi Arabia, Iran, and Morocco. The pact they signed on September 1, 1976, explicitly stated the development that concerned them all: "Recent events in Angola and other parts of Africa have demonstrated the continent's role as a theatre for revolutionary wars prompted and conducted by the Soviet Union, which utilizes individuals or organizations sympathetic to, or controlled by, Marxist ideology." After an initial meeting in Saudi Arabia establishing that the club would have administrative, planning, and operations divisions and a rotating chair, Cairo became the center for its ongoing activities. Its budget, in the millions of dollars annually, was funded in large part, and perhaps wholly, by Riyadh. Although the pact resembled Operation Condor in the Western Hemisphere, it was initiated by France. Taking the lead was Alexandre de Marenches, head of the French counterintelligence agency, the Service du Documentation et de Contre-Espionage, who coordinated closely with his friend, CIA Deputy Director Vernon Walters.[107]

The Safari Club's major test of countering Soviet influence was in the dispute between Somalia and Ethiopia. Somalia was a recipient of Soviet military assistance and provided the Soviet navy with facilities on the Red Sea. Over the previous two years, the Ethiopian revolution and overthrow of Emperor Haile Selassie had threatened relations between Washington and Addis Ababa. By the end of his administration, Ford's senior advisors were in disagreement over the policy stance the United States should take toward Ethiopia and its neighbors.

Moscow began supplying the Ethiopian military while maintaining its existing relationship with neighboring Somalia. The Kremlin believed it would be able to maintain ties with both, but also viewed an alliance with Ethiopia as more advantageous ideologically and politically. But Mogadishu was already following Cairo's lead and drifting away from Moscow. Irredentist sentiment in Somalia over the disputed Ogaden territory finalized the break. Somali President Mohammad Siad Barre established a proxy group, the Western Somali Liberation Front, which began attacking Ethiopian forces. As the Carter administration settled into office, the Ogaden dispute provided the Safari Club with an opportunity to demonstrate its utility.[108]

With assistance from Egyptian President Anwar Sadat and the Safari Club, Somalia's military intervened directly into the Ogaden. Emboldened by success in Angola and determined to secure the Ethiopian government of Haile Mariam Mengistu, Moscow began a massive airlift of supplies and advisors in September 1977. They were joined by Cuban advisors and elements of South Yemen's army. Coupled with Soviet and Cuban actions in Angola, the large-scale involvement did not go unnoticed in Washington and had implications for superpower relations.[109]

In his first few months as president, Carter was not focused on the escalating situation in eastern Africa. A policy paper prepared in the

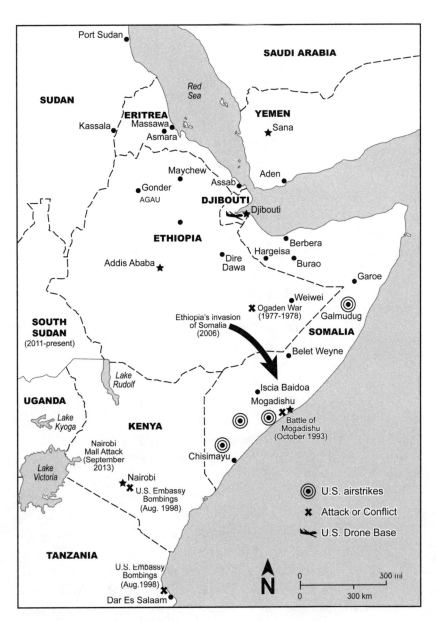

MAP 5. THE HORN OF AFRICA

administration's early months had declared that "Militarily the Horn [of Africa] is not of great strategic importance to the US." Carter emphasized a comprehensive settlement to the Arab-Israeli conflict, which was deemed a greater priority to US national interests. Domestic politics in the United States and Israel intervened, however. An influential group of Democrats had come to be called "neoconservatives" because they held hawkish positions on foreign policy. Led by Senator Henry Jackson of Washington, they strenuously objected to the inclusion of the Soviet Union in a proposed international conference. Carter's desire to include the PLO was also a source of friction. The victory of Israel's right-wing Likud party in its May 1977 elections contributed to a shift in Carter's approach. Instead of a comprehensive resolution to the conflict, Carter focused on Egypt and Israel, hoping that an agreement between them would lead to a broader settlement. The eventual breakthrough was assisted by the Safari Club, when Morocco's King Hassan II helped broker secret discussions between Egypt and Israel.[110]

Following the 1979 Egypt-Israel Peace Treaty and the Iranian Revolution that same year, Egypt supplanted Iran as one of Washington's most important partners in the region. One unintended consequence of the collapse of the Pahlavi monarchy was that it brought to light key documents on the creation of the Safari Club.[111] But the revelations did not hinder future coordination, as the Reagan administration would soon embrace Nixon's overt and covert Cold War by proxy.

CONCLUSION

In 1994, John Ehrlichman, Nixon's advisor for domestic affairs, told journalist Dan Baum that "the Nixon campaign in 1968, and the Nixon White House after that, had two enemies: the antiwar left and black people." The question was how to undermine their power. "We knew we couldn't make it illegal to be either against the war or Black, but by getting the public to associate the hippies with marijuana and Blacks with heroin, and then criminalizing both heavily, we could disrupt those communities," he explained. "We could arrest their leaders, raid their homes, break up their meetings, and vilify them night after night on the evening news. Did we know we were lying about the drugs? Of course we did."[112] At the time, even Baum ignored Ehrlichman's comment, leaving it out of his 1996 book about the War on Drugs. But his inclusion of it in a 2016 article created a stir, as many in the media (and on social media) saw it as evidence of an original sin behind Washington's policies. While skeptics dismissed Ehrlichman's statement as bitter hyperbole, it was an instructive glimpse into the making of Nixon's domestic policies and how they connected to efforts to stave off America's perceived decline due to Vietnam.

Richard Nixon inherited the war in Vietnam and domestic surveillance of the antiwar movement and radical political groups. He expanded both. Nixon also continued the attempts to contain the Vietnam War's impact based on the perception that America's global standing was diminished by it. The Nixon Doctrine was evidenced in overt and covert efforts, from the promotion of Iran as a regional hegemon to Operation Condor's targeting of leftist activists across the Western Hemisphere. After Nixon resigned in disgrace, the same doctrine was adopted by President Ford and Secretary of State Kissinger and applied in other regions of the globe.

There were domestic and international implications of Nixon's policies in the short and long term. Built on Johnson's War on Crime and intersecting with efforts to squelch dissent at home, the War on Drugs also countered national liberation movements abroad. Nixon's focus on law and order influenced how other Republican politicians campaigned, and draconian legislation was adopted across the nation and exported internationally. Similarly, the targeting of supply and introduction of eradication efforts in Mexico influenced future administrations. None of these efforts had an impact on the steady flow of illegal drugs into the United States. They did, however, directly contribute to the militarization of counternarcotics efforts and law enforcement over the next five decades. As will be discussed in future chapters, endemic police corruption coupled with harsh drug laws and enervated social services created a perception of urban badlands that was exacerbated when heroin and marijuana were supplanted by cocaine. Moreover, the COINTELPRO program which began under Johnson and targeted antiwar and Black activists continued under Nixon. It was expanded after the Munich Olympics to focus on Palestinian and Arab organizations and individual activists.

Kissinger's attempts to circumvent congressional oversight and involvement in foreign affairs entrenched conflicts across the globe. The overriding concern was America's interests, which Kissinger viewed narrowly and conflated with his own. His melodramatic warnings overstated the decline in the United States' international position, and exaggerated the implications of various events. The result was the adoption of policies that had negative short- and long-term implications and heavy civilian casualties. In Rhodesia and South Africa, the Nixon administration unnecessarily shifted policy. Even after Kissinger reversed course, it was only temporary. While Washington tolerated or embraced some para-states, others were targeted for destruction. The embrace of covert assassination and insurgency programs through allies, partners, and proxies extended the Vietnam counterinsurgency initiatives globally. These efforts expanded over the next decade.

CHAPTER THREE

Civilization's Thin Line and the Fear of Decline

> I want to talk to you right now about a fundamental threat to American democracy. I do not mean our political and civil liberties. They will endure. And I do not refer to the outward strength of America, a nation that is at peace tonight everywhere in the world, with unmatched economic power and military might. The threat is nearly invisible in ordinary ways. It is a crisis of confidence.
>
> —PRESIDENT JIMMY CARTER, 1979

"VERY SLOWLY, A STEP at a time, the hope for world peace erodes," the narrator ominously warned. As images of anguished children filled the screen, he continued: "Slowly we once slid into Korea, slowly into Vietnam, and now the Persian Gulf beckons." Ronald Reagan's "Peace Through Strength" television advertisement attacked incumbent President Jimmy Carter's "weak and indecisive leadership," which "vacillated before events in Ethiopia, Angola, and Afghanistan." It claimed that "Jimmy Carter still doesn't know that it takes *strong* leadership to keep the peace. Weak leadership will lose it."[1] Yet foreign policy rarely registers as a leading issue in American presidential elections, particularly in the midst of the kind of domestic economic turmoil seen in the 1980 campaign season. Nor were references to African and South Asian countries likely to sway many voters. Nevertheless, the Reagan campaign devoted two commercials to criticizing

Carter's foreign policies. Both advertisements rejected Carter's assertion that Americans suffered from a "crisis of confidence." The lack of confidence, Reagan argued, was in Carter's presidency. And by an overwhelming margin, voters agreed.[2]

This chapter argues that during Reagan's two terms in office, the themes of American renewal and decline were intimately linked and were tested at home and abroad, as aggressive policies in the Third World and renewed tensions with Moscow were matched in the domestic sphere. While Reagan expanded on Carter's policies abroad, he emulated the Nixon administration's approach to crime and drugs.

CONSTRUCTING AFGHANISTAN

Jimmy Carter's final State of the Union address was a somber affair. The previous twelve months had tested Carter and the nation. International tensions were high following the collapse of Iran's Pahlavi monarchy in January 1979, the hostage crisis that began eleven months later, and the Soviet invasion of Afghanistan at the end of the year. Meanwhile, the United States was mired in an economic recession with high inflation and spiking oil prices. To add to the White House's woes, Senator Ted Kennedy of Massachusetts announced he was challenging Carter for the Democratic Party's nomination. Yet Carter's approval rating was high, as the public endorsed his tough stance toward Moscow. Carter acknowledged the difficult situation the country faced: "It has never been more clear that the state of our Union depends on the state of the world."[3]

Carter attempted to secure domestic political support with a geographic imaginary that exaggerated the threat: "The region which is now threatened by Soviet troops in Afghanistan is of great strategic importance: It contains more than two-thirds of the world's exportable oil. The Soviet effort to dominate Afghanistan has brought Soviet military forces to within three hundred miles of the Indian Ocean and close to the Straits of Hormuz, a waterway through which most of the world's oil must flow. The Soviet Union is now attempting to consolidate a strategic position, therefore, that poses a grave threat to the free movement of Middle East oil." But Carter and his advisors knew that the aging Soviet leadership was preoccupied with the deteriorating situation in Afghanistan and the risk it posed to their southern border, not with threatening the flow of oil from the Persian Gulf. Indeed, the invasion of Afghanistan had already encountered significant resistance.[4]

Carter issued a stark warning to Moscow, vowing that the United States would defend its vital interests in the Persian Gulf region "by any means necessary, including military force." The following day, the *New York Times* underscored this explicit abandonment of Nixon's foreign policy, heralding a new "Carter Doctrine" and comparing the president's speech to Truman's over three decades earlier. Indeed, National Security Advisor Zbigniew Brzezinski had encouraged Carter to consider the similarity between this situation and the one Truman had faced in March 1947. Carter's speech went even further. In addition to the overt warning, he announced a range of public measures against the Kremlin, including increased defense spending. These were accompanied by secret programs, including funding for an anti-Soviet insurgency in Afghanistan.[5]

Carter's Afghanistan policy predated the Soviet invasion. Following the bloody coup in late April 1978 that overthrew the government of President Mohammad Daoud, a Special Coordination Committee Working Group was established to closely monitor the situation in Kabul. Although the new government of Nur Mohammad Taraki and the People's Democratic Party of Afghanistan was closely aligned with Moscow, its tenure was short. In September, the NSC informed Brzezinski that the "Soviets are likely to assert their position in Afghanistan forcefully if they see a counter-coup coming; they would be too fearful that a reactionary takeover would be anti-Soviet and put a regime friendly to the US right on their borders."[6] In response to the "Saur revolution," an insurgency emerged in Afghanistan's Nuristan province on the border with Pakistan and quickly spread. By early 1979, an Army garrison in the eastern city of Herat deserted and Saudi intelligence approached Washington about supporting the Afghan insurgency. The Carter administration debated the issue into the summer. On July 3, Carter authorized support for psychological operations by the insurgents and directed $695,000 in cash funds and nonmilitary supplies.[7]

Two months later, a second coup led by Foreign Minister Hafizullah Amin triggered reactions from Moscow and Washington. In an October 27 meeting with Acting Deputy Chief of Mission Archer Blood, Amin expressed his personal commitment to improving relations with Washington.

Meanwhile, the Soviet Union steadily built up its military presence in Afghanistan and on its borders. The Carter administration was aware of tensions between Amin and Moscow. Among the concerns that Soviet General Secretary Leonid Brezhnev faced was yet another country on its southern border openly aligned with the United States. Brezhnev and other Soviet leaders were also concerned about the Iranian revolution and its potential for destabilizing Muslim-majority Soviet republics. Coupled with the diminishing returns from détente and increasing pressure from Washington on human rights, Brezhnev and his key advisors believed the intervention would be quick and decisive. It was a fateful decision.[8]

After the April 1978 coup, the CIA cautioned that the press and public would connect the crisis in Afghanistan with Soviet involvement in the Horn of Africa. Instead, Brzezinski did so eight months later in a speech to the Foreign Policy Association. He warned that there was an "arc of crisis" encompassing "the shores of the Indian Ocean with fragile social and political structures in a region of vital importance to us threatened with fragmentation." "The resulting political chaos could well be filled by elements hostile to our values and sympathetic to our adversaries," Brzezinski asserted.[9] Although there were detractors inside and outside the US government, two weeks later an ominous *Time* magazine cover featured a bear looming over a "crescent of crisis" from East Africa to South Asia.[10]

Internal discussions were even starker. NSC staffer Fritz Ermarth warned that the invasion "sharply increases the prospect of eventual Soviet military domination of the greater Middle East and US exclusion from the region, except perhaps from Israel." He foresaw the "fearsome probability" that within a few years most of the Middle Eastern and South Asian states were either Soviet clients or allied with Moscow in a security pact. Although he conceded it was "not a certainty," Ermarth proposed a policy of "deeply echeloned containment" that would make it "as costly and painful as possible" for Moscow. "This will require extensive support to Soviet opponents wherever we find them," Ermath asserted, "not on the basis of their worthiness or chances of winning, but on the basis of their ability to tax Soviet power."[11]

Brzezinski's depiction was even bleaker. He emphasized in a memo to Carter that Afghanistan was the seventh state since 1975 in which communist parties had come to power with assistance from Moscow. He added that four had occurred since Carter became president, with the domestic political implications in an election year unstated. "I strongly urge you to make this a turning point at which you begin a sustained and comprehensive strategy for preventing the expansion of Soviet power projection," Brzezinski wrote. Although the Soviet military's actual performance exposed the disparity between Washington's perceptions and reality, Pakistan and Saudi Arabia emphasized the threat posed by Moscow. Ultimately Carter's response set in motion the policies that were adopted and promoted by Reagan.[12]

Several resistance groups benefited from the support of Islamabad, Washington, and Riyadh. Eventually dubbed the "Peshawar Seven" by US intelligence officials, the groups formed the Islamic Alliance for the Liberation of Afghanistan. By the end of the Afghan war, the alliance was known as the Islamic Unity of Afghan Mujahideen (or "holy warriors"). One of the most prominent was the Islamic Party (*Hizb-i-Islam*) led by Gulbuddin Hekmatyar with sixty thousand members. Even before the April 1978 Saur revolution, Hekmatyar benefited from his relationship with Pakistan's Inter-Service Intelligence (ISI) and targeted Afghan government forces. Over the course of the war against the Soviet Union, Hekmatyar was criticized for hoarding weapons but leaving the fighting to other groups. A competing group, Society of Islam *(Jamaat-e-Islami)*, was led by Burhanuddin Rabbani, a former professor at Kabul University. Rabbani was joined by Ahmed Shah Massoud, a graduate of Kabul University, who became one of the most respected military commanders of the conflict. While the other major groups were largely made up of the Pashtun ethnic group, Jamaat-i-Islami had support from Afghanistan's Tajiks and Uzebks. It claimed an initial following of twenty-one thousand.[13]

Two religious scholars led groups that took divergent paths. Sayed Ahmed Gailani's National Islamic Front of Afghanistan (*Mahaz-e Milli-ye Islami-ye Afghanistan*) was largely based in the country's eastern provinces. The group claimed a large membership, but it was likely less than ten thousand at the start of the war. Another religious scholar, Jalaluddin Haqqani, drew on recruits from majority Muslim and Arab countries. These recruits formed the so-called "Afghan Arabs." A remarkable 20 percent of aid from Islamabad and Washington—and likely a similar amount from Saudi Arabia and other Gulf Arab states—was funneled to Haqqani. Yet he and the members of his network eventually turned from

CIA assets to targets for indefinite detention or assassination after September 11, 2001.[14]

Before Carter left office, large quantities of weapons and funds were delivered to the *mujahideen* groups. Reagan expanded this practice dramatically. At least one observer calculated that the United States provided $3 billion in support to the anti-Soviet insurgency in Afghanistan, a figure that was matched by several other coalition members.[15]

The initial success of the anti-Soviet insurgency motivated even greater support. William Casey, Reagan's Director of Central Intelligence, quickly endorsed the CIA's program in Afghanistan. "This is the kind of thing we should be doing—only more. I want to see one place on the globe, one spot where we can checkmate them and roll them back," Casey declared.[16] Reagan and Casey were not willing to wait for only one spot, however. Casey proposed a broader program of support for groups across the "Third World." Echoing Che's call to create "many Vietnams," Casey wanted to create "half a dozen Afghanistans." This was eventually incorporated into the Reagan administration's policy toward the Soviet Union embodied in NSDD 75, which authorized containing and reversing Soviet expansionism through sustained competition "in all international arenas." The directive asserted that Washington needed to "support effectively those Third World states that are willing to resist Soviet pressures or oppose Soviet initiatives hostile to the United States, or are special targets of Soviet policy."[17]

In Afghanistan, Reagan continued relying on a broad coalition of states. Saudi Arabia, Pakistan, and Egypt were joined by China and Israel to fund, arm, and man the anti-Soviet insurgency. After Anwar Sadat's assassination in October 1981 by members of the Egyptian Islamic Jihad, Egyptian authorities led a crackdown on the group and a broad sweep of suspected Islamists. Over the next few years, Egyptian authorities released imprisoned activists and encouraged them to join the Afghan insurgency. This effort was replicated in other Muslim-majority countries from Algeria to Indonesia. Osama bin Laden, the son of Saudi construction titan Muhammad bin Laden, traveled to Afghanistan and Pakistan in the early 1980s and drew on his family wealth to fund charitable projects and support the *mujahideen*. As Part II explores, there were immediate and long-term consequences of this effort that were ignored at the time. By 1985, the United States provided the insurgency with advanced anti-tank and anti-aircraft missiles. The latter were shoulder-fired Stinger missiles that proved particularly effective against Soviet aircraft.[18]

More than six years after US support began, NSDD 166 outlined Washington's goals in Afghanistan, and the objectives remained consistent with those established by Carter. The directive advocated a combination of covert action and public diplomacy to achieve the removal of Soviet forces from Afghanistan. Support for the Afghan insurgency demonstrated America's "commitment to resisting Soviet aggression," with global implications, just as ending assistance would signal to Moscow and to anti-Soviet insurgencies that "our purpose in standing up to Soviet imperialism was not firm." NSDD 166 stressed that US propaganda was designed to isolate Moscow in the Third World and was aimed at Muslim-majority states. It also authorized attempts to improve coordination among the different insurgent groups and enhance their diplomatic and political effectiveness, while acknowledging that this would be difficult. Although unity proved elusive, Afghanistan remained a model for other conflicts across the globe.[19]

CONSTRUCTING CENTRAL AMERICA

In July 1981, Reagan signed NSDD 5, which established a new policy on conventional arms sales. NSDD 5 stated that the United States "cannot defend the free world's interests alone" and "prudently pursued, arms transfers can strengthen us." Among the goals of the new policy was for the US military and its allies to "project power in response to threats posed by mutual adversaries." Conventional weapons were described as "an essential element" of the United States' "global defense posture and an indispensable component of its foreign policy." Rather than contributing to escalating conflicts, the directive claimed that conventional arms would "foster regional and internal stability, thus encouraging peaceful resolution of disputes and evolutionary change" while enhancing the United States' domestic defense industry. The directive superseded the policies of the Carter administration and concluded with a thinly veiled swipe at the former president. "Both in addressing decisions as to specific transfers and opportunities for restraint among producers, we will be guided by principle as well as practical necessity. We will deal with the world as it is, rather than as we would like it to be." NSDD 5 was one part of Reagan's broader policy, whose ramifications extended beyond the Cold War.[20]

Shortly after taking office, the Reagan administration began supporting the creation of a Nicaraguan counterrevolutionary force based in neighboring Honduras. A series of high-level discussions over eleven months resulted in NSDD 17, which focused on Cuba and Central America. Approved on January 4, 1982, the directive sharply increased the pressure on Havana and Managua, while also committing the United States to defeating the insurgency in El Salvador. The directive authorized $50 million in military assistance and training for El Salvador and Honduras. The administration also sought improved regional intelligence-gathering and coordination and a robust public diplomacy effort. NSDD 17 approved a more aggressive policy toward Cuba, too, including heightened sanctions and military preparations, whether to counter the introduction of Cuban forces in the region or to take actions against Havana.[21]

Well before NSDD 17 was approved, the *Miami Herald* reported that forces opposed to the Sandinista regime had established bases of operation in Honduras. By the end of 1982, Washington had provided at least $1.5 million to the counterrevolutionary forces—the Contras—and had roughly 125 CIA employees based in Honduras to assist their efforts. The US embassy in Tegucigalpa was the center of covert activities and Argentinian and Honduran military officers served as liaisons with the Contras.[22]

The Contras unified under a broad coalition named the Nicaraguan Democratic Force. Its core leadership and armed forces of roughly three thousand men were derived from the National Guard of former strongman Anastasio Somoza Debayle. Somoza was overthrown by the Sandinistas in 1979 and assassinated a year later in Paraguay. The Nicaraguan Democratic Force's anti-Sandinista campaign was bolstered by former Sandinista commanders who had split from the revolutionary movement. They included Eden Pastora, known as Comandante Cero (Commander Zero), Fernando Chamorro, and Edmundo Chamorro. Pastora and the Chamorro brothers had originally been based in Costa Rica. The Chamorros had been expelled, however, and moved to Miami, where they had established a political party to rival the Nicaraguan Democratic Force. In a 1982 interview, Pastora dismissed the exile community in Miami as "crawling with *somocistas.*" The derogatory term referred to Somoza sympathizers and members of Nicaragua's Liberal Party, aligned with the deposed regime. During the Nicaraguan revolution, Pastora led the 1978 raid on Somoza's National Palace. Now opposed to the Sandinistas, he did not rule out raising money in Washington. "I would accept money from anyone who wants to give it to me," he freely admitted, "from the United States or from Fidel Castro." He would eventually find a steady source of funds in the narcotics trade.[23]

As the Nicaraguan opposition attempted to unify against the Sandinistas, the Reagan administration heightened the focus on the Western Hemisphere. In addition to supporting the Contras and counterinsurgency campaigns in El Salvador and Guatemala, Washington dramatically increased the sales of arms to the region. From 1975 to 1979, Washington sold $725 million in weapons to Latin American countries. The Reagan administration quickly eclipsed this figure and sold over $1 billion in arms in its first two years in office.[24]

The Contras embraced guerilla warfare and terrorism. From seventeen bases located either inside Nicaragua or across the border in Honduras, the Contras engaged in hit-and-run attacks against infrastructure and military patrols, targeted government offices, and carried out assassinations. Washington did not criticize these tactics, which were clearly laid out and rationalized in the Contras' manual, *Psychological Operations in Guerrilla Warfare*. "The force of arms is a need provoked by the oppressive system, and will cease to exist when the 'forces of justice' of our movement assume control," it declared. The manual was essentially a rewritten version of Che Guevara's *Guerrilla Warfare* and Mao Zedong's *On Guerrilla Warfare*. These texts were studied by the US military during and after the Vietnam War to develop counterinsurgency and propaganda strategies. Although the Contras presented their movement as one focused on the popular will, in contrast to Zedong and Guevara they were a "Christian and democratic crusade being conducted in Nicaragua by the Freedom Commandos!" In addition, the translated and declassified version of the manual sought to present violence as undesirable, but necessary.[25]

Washington's covert operation in Nicaragua did not remain a secret. During the 1982 midterm elections, press coverage about the Contras spurred congressional action. Led by Democratic Representative Edward Boland of Massachusetts, an amendment to the 1982 military appropriations bill prohibited funding to the Contras if it was used to oust the recognized government or instigated a conflict between Nicaragua and Honduras. Boland was chairman of the powerful House Permanent Select Committee on Intelligence, and his amendment was less restrictive than others proposed by his congressional colleagues. The amendment was also added

to the Intelligence Authorization Act of 1983, and Boland took the unprecedented step of reading the language on the House floor to reassure critics
of the administration's policies in Nicaragua. In response to the amendment, the Reagan White House stated, "We are complying with the law
now and will continue to do so." Boland told reporters he doubted that
the Reagan administration would defy Congress and continue funding
the Contras. "If there was any effort to use the funds" to topple the Sandinista government, he reasoned, "the administration would have to justify
it and I don't know how they would." This turned out to be overly optimistic, however, and as the Reagan administration sought to continue its
war against the Sandinistas, Boland's amendment had unintended as well
as intended consequences.[26]

American officials remained coy about the covert operation. At the center of the effort was the US ambassador to Honduras, John Negroponte.
Born in London on the eve of World War II, Negroponte was an alumnus
of Phillips Exeter Academy and Yale. After gaining his bachelor's degree in
1960, he entered the Foreign Service and within four years was a political
officer in Saigon at the height of the Vietnam War. Negroponte briefly
worked on the Paris Peace Talks with Philip Habib and Richard Holbrooke. However, Negroponte did not believe the US should withdraw
from Vietnam, which earned a rebuke from then National Security Advisor Kissinger.[27]

A December 1982 *Miami Herald* editorial noted that "Negroponte all
but smirked as he refused to discuss the allegations" that he was personally directing a covert war against Managua. Years later, however, Negroponte recounted how he was approached for the position of ambassador to
Honduras by Tom Enders, the Assistant Secretary of State for Latin America, with whom he shared a background of work in Vietnam and postings
in East Asia. Negroponte recalled that, shortly after Reagan's inauguration,
the administration had decided to use Honduras "as a rear for our interests both in El Salvador and Nicaragua," and that Enders believed "maybe
somebody with my kind of background would be suited for that kind of
work." It was made clear to him at the time that it "wasn't going to be just
any old sleepy Central American embassy." During his confirmation hearing, Negroponte informed the Senate Foreign Relations Committee that
the United States "must do our best not to allow the tragic outcome of
Indochina to be repeated in Central America."[28]

In Honduras, Negroponte oversaw the growth of the Contras. He was assisted by CIA station chief Vincent Shields. Shields was another veteran of the Vietnam counterinsurgency programs with experience in Laos. Negroponte described him as "a real expert in insurgency." Although Negroponte deemed the Contras a "special project," they never developed into an effective fighting force with popular support. However, they were implicated in human rights abuses, as were elements of the Honduran military and secret police. Evidence later emerged that during his tenure as ambassador there was limited reporting on human rights atrocities. Even as 150,000 refugees from neighboring countries sought shelter in Honduras from civil wars and insurgency campaigns across Central America, Negroponte actively undermined peace initiatives by Costa Rican President Oscar Arias. But his efforts were not enough to save the Contras. After Congress cut their funding, the Contras were forced to rely on former American military officials to secure weapons. The exiled Nicaraguan business community and American conservatives also provided financial support with assistance from Saudi Arabia, Israel, Taiwan, and South Korea. Another source of income was cocaine.[29]

REAGAN'S WAR AT HOME

Reagan's aggressive foreign policy stance was matched domestically. In April 1981, Attorney General William French Smith established a Task Force on Violent Crime. Among its members was Harvard's James Q. Wilson, a leading criminal justice expert whose research informed the efforts of the Johnson and Nixon administrations. The Task Force offered recommendations for laws that could be passed and initiatives that could be funded, but also considered what actions the Department of Justice could take without additional funds or legislation. Its final report, published four months later, noted that testimony from officials and scholars had stressed "the connection between drugs and violent crime." The task force recommended "a clear, coherent, national enforcement policy" for drugs that reflected "an unequivocal commitment to combatting international and domestic drug traffic."[30]

The proposed policies built on and amplified Nixon's War on Drugs. The report advocated a foreign policy to "accomplish the interdiction and eradication of illicit drugs wherever cultivated, processed, or transported;

including the responsible use of herbicides domestically and internationally." It recommended a more effective border policy that would "detect and intercept" narcotics even using, if necessary, the US military. Noting that 90 percent of illegal narcotics were imported, the task force wrote that "the international nature of drug trafficking most uniquely requires the powers and resources of the federal government," and that "state and local authorities are neither equipped nor empowered to conduct foreign relations or control access to this country by land, sea, and air." To achieve this, the Task Force recommended amending the Posse Comitatus Act of 1878, which prohibited the US military from serving as law enforcement within US borders.[31]

The Task Force also recommended criminal justice reforms. It advocated for more robust prosecution of drug cases, including limitations to habeas corpus petitions for state prisoners. This issue increased in prominence over the next decade and was implemented by President Bill Clinton working with congressional Republicans.[32] Although they garnered remarkably little media attention at the time, the Task Force's proposals had repercussions over the next four decades.

The recommendations were incorporated into the 1982 Defense Authorization Act. Passed in December 1981, the authorization included the Military Cooperation with Civilian Law Enforcement Agencies Act. As proposed by the Task Force, it marked a significant expansion in the powers of local law enforcement and its coordination with the US military. Although the law did not specify narcotics trafficking, that was the intended goal. The Act, and the Task Force recommendations it was based on, built on anti-drug legislation passed in the 1970s. In addition to amending the Posse Comitatus Act of 1878, the new law permitted sharing of relevant information obtained by the US military during operations with domestic law enforcement agencies. It also allowed the military to provide law enforcement with equipment and hardware, access to bases and other facilities, training, and advice. Rather than discuss the implications of the new law on civil liberties, media coverage emphasized the size of the appropriation ($199.7 billion).[33]

Before the Act was passed, President Reagan sought to build on the Task Force's recommendations. In late September, he spoke before the Annual Meeting of the International Association of Chiefs of Police in New Orleans. Reagan thanked the chiefs "for manning the thin blue line that holds back a jungle which threatens to reclaim this clearing we call civilization." He announced "an effective attack on drug trafficking" with key elements drawn from the Task Force report. *New York Times* columnist Tom Wicker noted the DOJ's intention to implement the task force recommendations and in some cases go beyond them. But Wicker, not overly concerned with the implications for Posse Comitatus, commented that "there seems no good reason why military intelligence collected in, say, West Germany, a center of heroin trafficking, should not be shared with customs and narcotics agencies." More important was the creation of federal, state, and local law enforcement coordinating committees that might help "make the streets safer for a lot of Americans."[34]

Reagan's other major anti-drug effort, aimed at marijuana, marked a departure from the Carter administration and also saw the president taking a more aggressive stance than Nixon. In July 1981, Reagan appointed Carlton Turner to the post of senior policy advisor for drug policy. Referred to as the "drug czar," Turner held a doctorate in organic chemistry and was the head of the University of Mississippi's Marijuana Research Project. Publicly, Turner and the administration promoted a balanced approach of enforcement and education. "The goal of this strategy," Turner said in October 1982, "is to create a condition in which the flow of drugs into the country is reduced, the number of Americans using illegal drugs will be reduced, and the effects on our society will be reduced."[35]

Behind the scenes, however, Turner announced a crusade. "We have to create a generation of drug-free Americans to purge society," he told staffers. But like other Reaganites, he targeted the federal bureaucracy first. Turner ended the emphasis on treatment and the provision of methadone, removed psychiatrists from federal agencies, and rid the National Institute of Drug Abuse of many advocates and officials. Turner was quickly promoted to Director of the Drug Abuse Policy Office, and the administration, in a high-profile launch in Reagan's home state of California, declared its war on marijuana.[36]

In April 1983, local authorities in California's Humboldt County reported that the previous year's marijuana crop in six Northern California counties was worth an estimated $400 million. The shocking figure was based on seizures, which they also believed accounted for only 10 percent of the total amount grown. A few months later, the Campaign Against Marijuana Production (CAMP) was launched. CAMP brought together federal, state, and local agencies with coordination through the California state attorney general's office. More than half of the budget was provided by the federal government. CAMP witnessed an unprecedented display of military force inside America's borders. Typically assigned to monitoring Soviet missile bases, U-2 spy planes were deployed over California to identify growing zones. Heavily armed National Guard and local law enforcement personnel descended from combat helicopters to manually eradicate the marijuana crops. CAMP boasted that over sixty thousand plants were seized in fourteen counties and nearly 130 people were arrested. The reported cost of the operation was between $1 million and $1.5 million, representing only a fraction of the amount reportedly grown.[37]

Perceived success bred repetition. The 1983 raids barely made a dent in marijuana cultivation and it remained one of the United States' major cash crops, rivaling corn and soybeans. Nevertheless, CAMP expanded in 1984 and nearly 400 raids were conducted at a cost of roughly $2.3 million. Over 200 individuals were arrested and 160,000 marijuana plants were seized that year. Media coverage was also more pronounced in 1984, often accompanying the helicopter overflights and raids. CAMP employed six spotter planes and seven helicopters; media reports referenced Francis Ford Coppola's *Apocalypse Now* to describe the operations. Meanwhile, some law enforcement officers sought to recreate one of the film's iconic scenes by broadcasting Richard Wagner's "Ride of the Valkyries" from the helicopters. Even the terminology used drew on the Vietnam experience. Officers were engaged in "search and destroy" missions, which included roadblocks to inspect cars and intrusive raids on suspected growers' homes. Despite these tactics, the 1984 campaign also encountered more difficulties as major growers adapted to the new enforcement strategy. Large plots were rare and growers scattered five to ten plants across rough terrain to make detection more difficult.[38]

The added media coverage also generated skepticism. At $500,000 per flight, U-2 spy planes were costly and did not produce any significant results. California State Senator Barry Keane, whose district included areas targeted by CAMP, also criticized the effort: "It operates on a Vietnam-type theory that if you inflict enough casualties on the enemy they will withdraw." But the raids were only "marginally successful" and the low-flying helicopters scared young children and were a nuisance for residents. In October 1984, as the CAMP raids were concluding for the year, a court order halted helicopter surveillance, barred their use below five hundred feet, and prohibited warrantless searches of properties.[39]

Reagan returned to the Wars on Crime and Drugs in his second term. In early February, DEA agent Enrique "Kiki" Camarena was abducted outside the US Consulate in Guadalajara, Mexico. He was tortured and killed by the Sinaloa Cartel. Camarena's body was found a month later by authorities. Thirteen months after Reagan met with Camarena's widow in the White House, he signed NSDD 221 on "Narcotics and National Security." NSDD 221 offered a rationale for a renewed drug war. "The international drug trade threatens the national security of the United States by potentially destabilizing democratic allies," the directive stated. In typical fashion for the Reagan administration, it noted that countries antagonistic to the United States—namely, Cuba, Nicaragua, and Bulgaria—facilitated the narcotics trade for "financial or political reasons." Mexico and Colombia were notably absent, even though their respective roles were far more pronounced, as were the Contras. Drawing on a still classified National Intelligence Estimate, NSDD 21 stated that narcotics trafficking threatened US interests by undermining "the integrity of democratic governments by corrupting political and judicial institutions." To be sure, there were suspicions about the involvement of corrupt Mexican officials in Camarena's murder—but the case also intersected with Washington's support for the Nicaraguan Contras.[40]

The events around Camarena's death would be depicted thirty years later in the Netflix series *Narcos*. In 2020, thirty-five years after he was killed, US prosecutors reopened the Camarena investigation, hoping to determine whether he was betrayed by colleagues. Despite the lingering questions, the War on Drugs was increasingly militarized on both sides of the US-Mexico border.[41]

Even before Camarena's murder, the discussion of narcotics and anti-narcotics efforts had pervaded American popular culture. It was embodied in the stylish hit television series *Miami Vice*. Created by Michael Mann, the series debuted on NBC in September 1984. The War on Drugs was fought on the streets of Miami with impossibly handsome undercover police played by actors Don Johnson and Philip Michael Thomas. Setting fashion trends and showcasing luxury cars and boats to a prominent soundtrack of the latest pop and rock music, *Miami Vice* exemplified the hollow reality of Reagan's War on Drugs. Meanwhile, drugs occupied the collective consciousness of Americans on the covers of major newspapers and magazines. Michael Sherry describes how media accounts adopted and applied the administration's rhetoric of a "war on drugs" and likened it to other conflicts from the Civil War to Vietnam. The increasing attention to illegal narcotics, especially cocaine, reached a crescendo in June 1986 with the high-profile deaths of college basketball star Len Bias and professional football player Don Rogers. By the end of the summer, and with midterm elections fast approaching, Congress moved quickly to pass high-profile anti-narcotics legislation.[42]

Anti-narcotics legislation had bipartisan appeal in an election year. In the Democrat-controlled House of Representatives, Speaker Thomas P. "Tip" O'Neill Jr. took particular interest in the issue. After convening the chairs of the House committees, O'Neill assigned the task of leading the legislative effort to Jim Wright of Texas, the House Majority Leader who would succeed him as Speaker of the House a year later. O'Neill and Wright wanted to take advantage of media interest in the issue. In an interview with the *New York Times*, Wright bemoaned the public's short attention span: "We walk along fat, dumb and happy until a crisis grabs us by the throat. Once it is off the front burner of nightly television coverage we go back to sleep."[43]

Republicans feared that Democrats would seize the law-and-order issue before the midterm elections. The high-profile effort also provided vulnerable incumbents an opportunity to benefit from media attention. At least two Republican senators, Alfonse D'Amato of New York and Paula Hawkins of Florida, made countering narcotics key pillars of their reelection campaigns. In a *New York Times* op-ed, D'Amato declared that the proposed law would "severely cripple the illicit drug industry." Meanwhile, President Reagan publicly praised Senator Hawkins's support of the legislation. Although D'Amato won reelection, Hawkins was defeated.[44]

A week before the 1986 midterm elections, Reagan signed the Anti-Drug Abuse Act into law. The $1.7 billion act emphasized harsher laws, the interdiction and eradication of narcotics, and education. Publicly, Reagan emphasized law and order. "The American people want their government to get tough and go on the offensive," Reagan declared, "and that's exactly what we intend, with more ferocity than ever before." Yet only two months

earlier, Reagan conceded that enforcement alone would not solve the problem. Instead, he asserted that a "national crusade" was needed to educate
about the dangers of drug use.[45]

However, the legislation only provided $200 million toward education.
The most visible, and easily derided, aspect of Reagan's anti-drug education efforts was First Lady Nancy Reagan's "Just Say No" Campaign.
Launched a month before the Anti-Drug Abuse Act was passed, the campaign also served to undercut a proposed education program by congressional Democrats. Nancy Reagan's campaign became easy fodder for co-
medians and critics of the administration, and it also diverted attention
from the Act's more aggressive aspects.

The more publicized aspects of the legislation focused on criminal penalties for federal offenses—in particular, life sentences for those convicted
of involvement in a "drug enterprise." Fines and penalties for drug possession offenses were also heightened. Other key features of the legislation
included over $300 million for new equipment and interdiction measures
along the US-Mexico border and in the Caribbean. Setting a precedent
for the future, $96.5 million was allocated for new Federal prisons. Some
of the more severe measures proposed in the House of Representatives,
including the death penalty and greater involvement of the US military,
did not make the final bill. They were not, however, forgotten.[46]

A key provision of the 1986 Anti-Drug Abuse Act that had long-term
implications but that did not receive coverage in the press served to extend America's borders and the reach of law enforcement. It prohibited
the production and distribution of illegal narcotics in other countries if
they were to be exported to the United States. This provision became an
essential tool for prosecuting foreign nationals in US federal court.[47]

The DEA's growth paralleled the expanding legal regimes. In the four-
year period leading up to the passage of the Anti-Drug Abuse Act, the
DEA reported that its convictions doubled and sentences for cocaine possession at the federal level increased by 35 percent. By 1990, the agency's
budget was three times as large as it had been a decade earlier. In addition,
it boasted nearly 2,200 agents in over forty countries.[48]

The DEA benefited from and influenced the increased media coverage
on narcotics. The DEA's New York office developed relations with key
media outlets, including CBS News and the *New York Times*. Both CBS

and NBC News had highly rated evening programs that focused on co-caine. Weekly news magazines were even more aggressive, with *Newsweek*, *Time*, and *US News and World Report* devoting cover stories to the subject. There were exceptions to the breathless media coverage. *The New Republic* criticized the rushed legislation and media attention. The magazine's roots were in the early twentieth-century progressive movement, but by the mid-1980s its politics were more centrist. The magazine also reflected a neoconservative agenda that generally supported Reagan's foreign policies. On illegal narcotics, however, the magazine firmly opposed the "drug mania" that swept Washington just before midterm elections.[49]

At least one congressman spoke against the hasty action. New York Democrat Charles Schumer lamented that the legislation was developed "too quickly and that the policies are aimed at looking good rather than solving the problem." Yet, two years later, Congress rushed through even more punitive anti-narcotics and anti-crime legislation with provisions omitted from its predecessor.[50]

DECONSTRUCTING LEBANON

While narcotics occupied media attention and popular culture in the United States, Washington was increasingly focused on the Middle East. In November 1981, Israel and the United States signed a strategic cooperation memorandum of understanding (MOU) that aimed to "deter all threats from the Soviet Union to the region." This was to be accomplished through greater military and intelligence coordination and collaboration. A month later, however, Israel annexed Syria's Golan Heights in December, which were captured and occupied in the June 1967 Arab-Israeli War. In response, Washington suspended the MOU. But the mini-crisis in US-Israeli relations was short-lived as ongoing regional tensions took precedence.[51]

Meanwhile, the Lebanese civil war settled into a bloody stalemate. The PLO's influence continued to expand in Lebanon and regionally. Syria maintained its occupation of Lebanon and abandoned its partnership with the Lebanese Christian militias. In March 1978, Israel invaded southern Lebanon and established a six-kilometer "security zone." The security zone was intended to halt cross-border raids into Israel and eliminate the PLO's "Fatah Land" in southern Lebanon, but neither goal was achieved.

Although relations between Damascus and the PLO improved, the Phalange militia led by Bashir Gemayel maintained its ties to Israel and began openly challenging Syrian forces.

Shortly after Reagan took office, rising tensions threatened a broader regional war. In the spring, the PLO and Israel exchanged fire across the Lebanon-Israel border and it quickly escalated. Israel launched punishing air raids, including against neighborhoods in West Beirut. Washington tasked Philip Habib, former under secretary of state, with resolving the crisis. Thirteen years earlier, Habib helped convince Secretary of Defense Clark Clifford that the Vietnam War could not be won militarily. President Reagan named Habib his personal representative to the Middle East. Habib negotiated understandings between Syria and Israel and between Israel and the PLO. Neither, however, would last for long.[52]

The 1979 Egypt-Israel Peace Agreement negotiated by President Carter could have contributed to regional negotiations and a comprehensive solution to the Arab-Israeli conflict. Although an autonomy provision for Palestinians under occupation in the West Bank and Gaza was part of the larger peace agreement, the terms were never finalized. Israeli negotiators were successful in stymying the autonomy discussions while Carter was still in office. Instead, Israel's emphasis was on preventing autonomy for the Palestinians under occupation or broader negotiations involving the PLO. The Reagan administration supported Israel's position and it informed the terms of the 1981 MOU.[53]

An assassination attempt on Israel's ambassador to the UK, Shlomo Argov, in early June 1982 initiated a new crisis. Although the PLO was not responsible, Israeli Prime Minister Menachem Begin and Defense Minister Ariel Sharon quickly blamed the organization and initiated planning for a large-scale invasion of Lebanon. Begin and Sharon had an ambitious plan to redraw the geopolitical map of the region. In addition to destroying the PLO's para-state, they hoped to annex the occupied West Bank, create a Christian Maronite state in Lebanon that would make peace with Israel, and chasten Syria. Neoconservatives in the Reagan administration endorsed Israel's plans.[54]

Launched on June 6, Israel's invasion of Lebanon resulted in heavy civilian casualties. Nearly fifty thousand civilians were killed and injured over eighty-two days. Following a nearly two-month-long siege of West Beirut, Ambassador Habib brokered the PLO's withdrawal from Beirut and

Washington agreed to safeguard the remaining Palestinian civilians. A multinational force that included US Marines as well as French and Italian contingents was deployed in Lebanon to monitor the PLO's evacuation. Over the next month, the PLO's offices and remaining members were targeted by Israeli forces, the Phalange militia, and Lebanese Army intelligence.[55]

In late August, Bashir Gemayel was elected president of Lebanon by the Lebanese parliament. On September 10, the US Marines withdrew from Lebanon. Four days later, Gemayel was assassinated. Although suspicions focused on Syria, the Phalange party was quick to blame the Palestinians. Two days later, Israeli forces encircling the Shatila refugee camp allowed the Phalange militia to enter. An estimated 800 to 2,000 Palestinian and Lebanese civilians were killed in the camp and the surrounding Sabra neighborhood. The massacre brought international condemnation and a new Multinational Force was formed with US, French, and Italian contingents.[56]

Announcing the new Multinational Force, President Reagan referenced his new peace plan for the Arab-Israeli conflict. Introduced on September 1, the Reagan Plan drew on the Egyptian-Israeli Peace Agreement and proposed autonomy for Palestinians in the Israeli-occupied West Bank and Gaza Strip. Israel rejected the Reagan Plan, but Arafat signaled his support. Hoping to establish relations with Washington, Arafat launched his own diplomatic initiative. Over the next year, Arafat improved relations with Jordan's King Hussein and Egypt's new president, Hosni Mubarak. However, Syrian President Hafiz al-Asad undermined Arafat's efforts. Asad wanted to diminish the PLO's presence in Lebanon and regionally. The PLO still maintained forces in northern Lebanon and in the Bekaa Valley. Arafat's attempts to augment the remaining PLO forces in Lebanon angered Damascus and contributed to a split within the PLO.[57]

Following the PLO's withdrawal from Beirut, several of Arafat's prominent deputies openly criticized his leadership of the organization and Fatah. Other Palestinian factions with ties to Damascus echoed the calls for internal reforms of the PLO. Libyan President Muammar el-Qaddafi joined Asad in encouraging the growing rift within the PLO. Qaddafi offered financial support and weapons to the dissident factions. By June 1983, fighting erupted between the dissidents and Fatah loyalists. Over the next six months, the dissident factions dislodged the loyalists from Lebanon.[58]

The destruction of the PLO's para-state in Lebanon had unintended consequences. In addition to the carnage visited on Lebanese and Palestinian civilians, Lebanon became less secure for American and European citizens and diplomats. Although the Multinational Force was supposed to have a defined role in Lebanon, the United States openly sided with Israel and the Lebanese Christian militias. The US Marines eventually became another party in the civil war and the repercussions were severe. In April 1983, the US embassy was leveled by a car bomb, killing sixty-three people, including CIA station chief Robert Ames. Six months later, a suicide truck bomb destroyed the Marine barracks, killing 241 personnel. In January 1984, a gunman murdered Malcolm Kerr, president of the American University of Beirut, in his campus office. William Buckley, the new CIA station chief, was also abducted and later killed.[59]

Responsibility for the attacks eventually settled on a new organization, Hizbullah, Lebanon's Party of God. Formally declared in February 1985, Hizbullah emerged out of Lebanon's Shiʻa community. Historically marginalized within Lebanon, Shiʻa political parties and militias were growing in power and size. Several key figures in Hizbullah had ties to the PLO as well as Iran's Revolutionary Guard. In June 1985, its members hijacked Trans World Airlines (TWA) Flight 847. Bound for Rome from Athens, the airliner was diverted to Beirut International Airport. Once on the ground, the hijackers demanded the release of 766 Palestinian prisoners held by Israel. An American sailor was murdered by the hijackers and seventeen women and children were released. The remaining passengers were forced off the plan and held in locations around Beirut's southern suburb, the Dahiyya. Ultimately, the Reagan administration negotiated a settlement to the crisis by working with Syria, Israel, and Iran. However, hostage-taking in Lebanon continued and contributed to a scandal that engulfed the Reagan administration.[60]

Meanwhile, Hizbullah's influence grew inside the country. Like the PLO, Hizbullah developed several major areas of operation. Indeed, these mirrored those of the PLO at its height. Hizbullah drew on the largely Shiʻa population in southern Lebanon, which included areas of the PLO's "Fatah Land." There were tensions between the PLO factions and the surrounding Lebanese villages, especially after Israeli raids and airstrikes. Those animosities shifted as Israel settled into an extended occupation of southern Lebanon. Hizbullah also established bases in the Bekaa Valley, where training was reportedly conducted with elements of Iran's Revolutionary Guard. Due to the Bekaa's role in opium cultivation, Hizbullah faced accusations of involvement in narcotics trafficking. As observed with the PLO, these allegations were often exaggerated and politically motivated. Hizbullah's increasing stature, continued hostage taking, and coordination with Iran led to a covert response from Washington.[61]

PREEMPTION

"In the past 15 years, terrorism has become a frightening challenge to the tranquility and political stability of our friends and allies," President Reagan declared in an April 26, 1984, message to Congress. He explained that over 3,500 people had been killed and 7,600 wounded in 6,500 terrorist incidents over the previous decade. Although Reagan did not define terrorism, he mentioned attacks from Lebanon to South Korea and argued Washington needed to increase cooperation with other governments to address "this growing threat to our way of life."[62]

NSDD 138 accompanied Reagan's public statements. Aimed at "preventing, combatting, and countering terrorism," the directive stated that the United States considered "the practice of terrorism by any person or group in any cause a threat to our national security and will resist the use of terrorism by all legal means available." NSDD 138 provided for linking acts of terrorism by groups with their state sponsors, and authorized "a full range of military options" against "anti-American terrorist groups," allowing for acts of preemption as well as retaliation. After September 11, preemption was applied to state and nonstate actors.[63]

The directive explained that a particular concern was direct or indirect Soviet support and guidance provided to terrorist groups. Yet over the previous decade the United States and terrorism experts had exaggerated Soviet intentions and involvement in terrorist attacks, allowing American policymakers to minimize or dismiss the root causes of conflicts. This was observed in the attempts by Israeli officials and neoconservatives in the Reagan administration to link the PLO to broader Soviet aims in the Middle East. However, Moscow sought to influence the PLO's moderates and recommended acceptance of the two-state solution. This advice was not in line with the maximalist positions of the PLO's leftist factions, who held the strongest ideological ties to the Soviet Union.[64]

Assassination was also selectively defined. President Ford's Executive Order 11905 prohibiting assassination did not delineate the term. Passed after the 1975 Church Commission investigations and report, the Executive Order was meant to reassure the American public about rogue policies and actions. But assassination was not defined in subsequent Excecutive Orders by Carter and Reagan.[65] Even though Reagan's Executive Order 12333 banned the direct or indirect involvement of US government personnel to "conspire or engage in assassination," the CIA determined that this applied only to heads of state. As the Reagan administration debated a response to attacks on Americans in Lebanon, targeting nonstate actors was deemed preemptive action.[66]

Paramilitary forces made up of CIA, FBI, and military special forces were established under NSDD 138. The directive authorized a range of actions against targets and their supporters, including military raids, sabotage, and the neutralization of individuals and groups. In targeting nonstate actors, the administration avoided killing the recognized heads of state of sovereign nations. NSDD 138 also approved efforts against states supporting insurgent movements, including Nicaragua, Cuba, Libya, Syria, Iran, and the Soviet Union. Thus, it deliberately blurred the line between actions against state and nonstate actors, and set a precedent for the future. Even though Executive Order 12333 remained in force until January 2002, there was flexibility in its application.[67]

At least one operation demonstrated the danger of this approach. Journalist Bob Woodward writes that, in March 1985, the CIA and Saudi Intelligence coordinated to assassinate Hizbullah's spiritual leader, Sayyid Muhammad Hussein Fadlallah, in retaliation for the attacks against the US Embassy and Marines compound. A car bomb placed near Fadlallah's home in Beirut's Dahiyya suburb killed at least 80 and wounded hundreds. Fadlallah was not harmed, however. Although the Saudi ambassador to the US, Bandar bin Sultan al-Saud, told Woodward a $2 million bribe was delivered to Fadlallah to prevent future attacks, TWA Flight 847 was hijacked three months later.[68]

The new policy led to a split within the Reagan administration. Secretary of State George Shultz favored an ongoing effort against terror networks. However, Secretary of Defense Casper Weinberger sought more limited operations. What became known as the "Weinberger Doctrine" drew on the experiences in Vietnam and Lebanon and appeared to constrain future military action based on several criteria. These included determining that the intervention was a vital US interest, the deployment of sufficient forces to ensure victory, clearly defined political and military objectives, the support of the American public, and the commitment of American combat forces only as the last resort.[69]

As with the prohibition on assassination, the Reagan administration implemented a covert effort that aligned with Shultz's approach. Drawing on NSDD 138 and NSDD 30, the administration established the Terrorism Incident Working Group. Publicly the working group was directed by Vice President George H. W. Bush and was presented as studying terrorism around the globe. This yielded a 1988 report with an introduction by Secretary of Defense Frank Carlucci, who wrote that, to effectively combat terrorism, "it is necessary to know the enemy." Carlucci acknowledged that terrorism was a tactic employed by groups from across the ideological spectrum with disparate and at time antagonistic goals. His description of the problem ignored root causes, however, in favor of an ideological rationale. The United States was "a prime target," Carlucci claimed, "because of our commitment to political reform and constructive change." Terrorists were opposed to reform, he added, because "it represents continuation of a system they abhor and coopts the revolution they hope to lead."[70]

Speaking to the press, members of the Reagan administration offered assurance that it would "endorse only the most cautious use of force in retaliation against terrorist acts." Vice President Bush argued a few days later that, while the administration rejected "wanton destruction of human life in order to show some muscle," military retaliation would be justified "where it could be surgically done." Bush and the working group oversaw covert military operations in a number of countries, including in Latin America and the Middle East. They received target lists developed by the CIA in conjunction with other agencies that included drug traffickers, terrorist networks, and Soviet allies. Although the Weinberger Doctrine limited military engagement between states, Shultz's approach was consistent with American actions over the next three decades.[71]

"FIGHTING EVIL ARABS"

Founded by Sabri al-Banna, the Abu Nidal Organization (ANO) had an outsized influence during the 1980s. Al-Banna was born in Jaffa, Palestine, and his family fled during the 1948 Palestine War. Originally a member of

Arafat's Fatah, he adopted the *nom de guerre* Abu Nidal or "father of the struggle." As one of Arafat's trusted lieutenants, Abu Nidal served as the representative of Fatah and the PLO in Iraq. In his dual role, he developed relations with Iraqi intelligence, which may have encouraged a split with the PLO's leadership. By 1974, as Arafat and the PLO gained international legitimacy and sought relations with Washington and eventual negotiations with Israel, al-Banna left the organization. He organized assassination plots of major Fatah leaders that were foiled. Although the PLO imposed a death sentence in absentia, that only seemed to inspire al-Banna to launch more attacks against his former compatriots. From 1978 to 1981, the ANO was responsible for a string of attacks that killed or wounded PLO officials and representatives across Europe and the Middle East. It also targeted the foreign ministers and government officials of Syria and Egypt. The ANO's attempted assassination of the Israeli ambassador to the UK was used as a pretext for Israel's invasion of Lebanon described earlier. Considering its close ties to Iraqi intelligence, there was speculation that the ANO's assassination attempt was a reprisal for Israel's June 1981 attack on Iraq's Osirak nuclear reactor.[72]

As the Reagan administration was developing its counterterrorism strategy, the ANO launched a high-profile attack that appeared to further justify the need for a policy. In late December 1985, two teams of ANO members fired on the ticket counters of Israel's El Al airlines at the Rome and Vienna airports. Eighteen were killed in the simultaneous attacks, including five Americans, and over one hundred were wounded. The CIA developed a response that drew on key veterans of previous covert operations. Duane Clarridge, the CIA's chief of European operations, promoted a Counterterrorist Center to pull together experts from across the agency, including operations, intelligence, and the CIA's Special Operations Group paramilitary service. Before serving in Europe, Clarridge had led the covert effort to fund and train the Nicaraguan Contras. Although he was assigned as head of the new terrorism center, his tenure was clouded by the Iran-Contra scandal.[73]

In addition to Iraq, the ANO had relations with Libya's Muammar al-Qaddafi. Qaddafi came to power in a September 1969 military coup that overthrew King Idris. Styling himself after Egypt's Nasser, Qaddafi embraced a similar combination of Arab nationalism, Pan-Arabism, and Pan-Africanism. After nationalizing Libya's oil industry in 1973, Qaddafi took full advantage of the spike in oil prices through the 1970s to support revolutionary movements across the developing world and purchase large quantities of Soviet weapons. By 1981, Qaddafi's relations with neighboring states had deteriorated. He openly criticized Egypt's peace treaty with Israel and scolded the North African states for their insufficient support of the Palestinian national movement. As evidenced by his later ties to the ANO, however, Qaddafi also had inconsistent relations with Arafat and the PLO.

Shortly before Reagan took office, Libya had intervened in the ongoing civil war in Chad. Qaddafi had also developed relations with the Sandinista government in Nicaragua. Reagan's Director of Central Intelligence, William Casey, and Secretary of State Alexander Haig identified Qaddafi as a target for covert operations. According to a former State Department intelligence analyst for North Africa, Lillian Harris, "Qaddafi presented this marvelous target because you could fight the Soviets, you could fight terrorism, and you could fight evil Arabs." Almost four years later, Libya's state-run media praised the ANO's attack on the Rome and Vienna airports. The Reagan administration quickly obtained evidence that linked Tripoli to the operation, largely due to the NSA's success in breaking Libya's diplomatic and intelligence codes—but also facilitated by Qaddafi's careless use of unencrypted phone lines. It was Libya's declaration extending its territorial waters into the Gulf of Sidra that offered a pretext for an American military challenge. Qaddafi's so-called "line of death" in the Gulf provided the necessary provocation for Washington to escalate tensions and embarrass Tripoli.[74]

On August 19, 1981, fighter jets from the aircraft carrier USS *Nimitz* flew air patrols over the Gulf of Sidra. When two Libyan jets attempted to intercept the F-14s they were shot down. After the incident, the Reagan administration claimed that Qaddafi dispatched assassination teams to kill President Reagan and target other senior officials. Although Qaddafi denied these claims on American television, the Reagan White House insisted that the story was true. It later quietly acknowledged that the intelligence reports were incorrect. The story of Libyan assassination squads roaming around the United States, however, became enshrined in American popular culture four years later with the blockbuster summer film *Back to the Future*. In addition, the Gulf of Sidra dogfight was transplanted to the Indian Ocean, where Soviet-made fighter jets from an unnamed country engaged with two American F-14A jets in *Top Gun*.[75]

The Reagan administration expanded its efforts to contain Libya and undermine Qaddafi. By December 1981, the administration placed embargoes on the import of Libyan oil and the export of American products to the country. The prohibitions were expanded over the next year and the Reagan administration also sought the withdrawal of American workers from Libya.[76] Following the Rome and Vienna attacks, the administration increased the pressure on Tripoli. In NSDD 205, Reagan declared that Libya's support for terrorist organizations constituted "an unusual and extraordinary threat to the national security and foreign policy of the United States." In addition to demonstrating American "resolve" to "mounting terrorist activity," the Reagan administration instituted a total ban on trade with Libya and worked to isolate it diplomatically and economically. Washington also prohibited any new loans to Libya or to government officials and entities, and barred Libyan-flagged vessels from US ports. In an appendix (later partially declassified), Reagan authorized a show of military force in the Mediterranean. This included dispatching a second carrier battle group and conducting naval exercises in international waters, including the Gulf of Sidra.[77]

The new policy had the desired effect and the "line of death" again proved to be an albatross for the Libyan military. In March, the US Navy engaged in a lopsided battle with Libyan patrol boats and anti-aircraft batteries. Although the Libyan military was embarrassed, Qaddafi responded through indirect means. In early April, the Reagan administration linked two separate attacks in Europe to Libyan sponsorship. The first was the bombing of a TWA flight traveling from Athens to Rome on April 2 that killed four Americans. Three days later, a disco in West Berlin was bombed and two Americans were killed. Washington debated how to respond to the attacks, including regime change and assassination. The ban on assassinations should have precluded an attack on a head of state. Reagan's chief concern, however, was whether Qaddafi would be present when the airstrike was conducted, as he was known to frequently change locations. On April 14, the United States launched airstrikes against targets in Libya, including the presidential palace. Qaddafi's adopted daughter was among those reported killed. Less than two years later, a bomb downed Pan Am flight 103 in December 1988. The New York–bound flight exploded over Lockerbie, Scotland, killing 268 on board and nearly a dozen on the ground. Speculation over the perpetrators finally settled on Libya, and UN sanctions were imposed on Tripoli in 1992, lasting until it cooperated with the investigation.[78]

While it sought to undermine Qaddafi, the Reagan administration also targeted the ANO. Washington drew on regional allies and partners to disrupt the organization. Exiled in Tunisia, the PLO's leadership found common cause with US goals and coordinated with the CIA. This was not the first time that Arafat and the PLO attempted to improve relations with Washington and coordinated with US intelligence. Unlike the previous episodes, however, this also directly benefited the PLO beyond public relations. The ANO had conducted a decade-long assassination spree of PLO officials and implicated the organization in its deadly attacks. To be sure, the PLO had problems with the discipline of its own factions, as demonstrated by the October 1985 attack on the *Achille Lauro* passenger ship. These attacks on civilian targets caused the PLO, the ANO, and the broader Palestinian national movement to be broadly associated with terrorism, and that association would prove difficult to shake even after the PLO developed formal relations with Washington. Nevertheless, operations against the ANO were conducted across the Middle East, and surveillance was conducted within the United States.[79]

The CIA was successful in finding a combination of incentives and threats with the ANO's state sponsors to reduce or eliminate their support. This contributed to, and was compounded by, internal fighting within the organization. By the end of Reagan's second term the ANO was severely diminished and the effort was considered a major success for the CIA's Counterterrorism Center. But Abu Nidal did not go quietly. In 1991, Arafat's longtime deputy and head of the PLO's intelligence bureau, Salah Khalaf (Abu Iyad), was killed along with two other officials in Tunisia. Prior to his assassination, Khalaf had publicly admitted that the PLO had helped to dismantle the ANO and that he had served as the main intermediary with the CIA. The assassin later confessed that he had acted on orders from Abu Nidal.[80]

"WHEN YOU ARE IN POWER YOU ARE RIGHT!"

As in Lebanon, Reagan inherited an active civil war in Angola. And it was exacerbated over the next eight years. By 1979, the Carter administration was taking steps toward recognizing the government of Agostinho Neto

and the Popular Movement for the Liberation of Angola (MPLA). Carter
received reassurances from Angolan representatives that Cuba's influence
was on the wane. Neto had also publicly criticized Moscow, which indicated a degree of independence that Washington could exploit. Meanwhile, Pretoria supported the separatist forces of Dr. Jonas Savimbi's National Union for the Total Independence of Angola (UNITA). The Soviet
invasion of Afghanistan, however, changed the Carter administration's
perspective. This was compounded by Neto's untimely death due to cancer
and Savimbi's persistent revolt. Five days before Carter's State of the
Union address and announcement of the Carter Doctrine, the NSC recommended that the regional and international conditions warranted arming
Savimbi rather than unconditional recognition of Angola.[81]

Washington's policies toward Angola were further complicated by South
Africa and Namibia. A former German colony, Namibia was placed under a League of Nations Mandate administered by South Africa. In May
1967, the UN Security Council terminated South Africa's mandate. Four
years later, the International Court of Justice ruled that the territory was
illegally occupied. Pretoria ignored the ruling and the UN Security Council approved Resolution 385 in January 1976. Resolution 385 demanded the
withdrawal of South African troops and UN-administered elections, with
the goal of self-rule. This was affirmed by the UN Security Council two
years later with Resolution 435. Pretoria engaged in negotiations while its
forces continued occupying Namibia. Areas controlled by South Africa
served as a base for UNITA to launch raids into Angola targeting MPLA
forces. Meanwhile, in Namibia, the South West Africa People's Organization (SWAPO) and its military wing, the People's Liberation Army of Namibia (PLAN), received support from the MPLA, Cuba, and the Soviet
Union. Beginning in May 1978, the South African military launched a
major operation against PLAN bases inside Angola. South Africa's successful intervention, coupled with the international community's failure
to levy additional sanctions against Pretoria, had regional implications. In
place of large, fortified bases, SWAPO and the PLAN adapted to a guer-
rilla-style insurgency. The operation also began a transition from low-level
counterinsurgency to large, conventional battles fueled by American and
Soviet weapons over the next decade.[82]

Less than a year after Reagan took office, Savimbi visited Washington.
Prior to his arrival, efforts to repeal the Clark Amendment prohibiting the

MAP 6. SOUTHERN AFRICA, 1969–1989

United States from providing support to UNITA failed. Nevertheless, Savimbi met with Secretary of State Al Haig. Savimbi held a doctorate in Political Science from the University of Lausanne, was fluent in English, and was a former Marxist. These credentials made him a darling of American conservative groups and think tanks. While he was in Washington, Savimbi was hosted by Freedom House, the Heritage Foundation, and the American Enterprise Institute, all think tanks allied with the Reagan administration. Through Reagan's first term, Savimbi and UNITA continued to receive support from South Africa. This limited UNITA's appeal within Angola and across the continent.

In a lengthy profile published in the *Washington Post*'s Style section, Savimbi dismissed complaints about UNITA's relations with Pretoria by pointing out that other states in the region also traded with the apartheid regime. "They are in power!" Savimbi exclaimed. "When you are in power you are right!" He expected a different dynamic in the future: "When we come in power no one will speak of our relations with South Africa." Four years later, the atmosphere in Washington was more favorable.[83]

The Reagan administration began implementing new policies toward southern Africa shortly after reelection. In July 1985, Congress repealed the Clark Amendment as part of a $12.6 billion foreign aid bill that provided military and economic assistance to anti-communist forces in Cambodia, Afghanistan, and Angola. The bill reaffirmed Washington's refusal to negotiate with the PLO until it recognized Israel and sent emergency financial assistance to Tel Aviv. Republican Henry J. Hyde of Illinois said that eliminating the Clark Amendment showed "we're no longer paralyzed by Vietnam-guilt legislation." Vin Weber, a Republican from Minnesota, explained, "We're really enunciating a Reagan doctrine in the Congress— that we will support resistance movements around the world."[84]

Eight months later, Reagan approved NSDD 212. Although specifically drafted for Angola, the directive demonstrated how interwoven the conflicts in southern Africa had become. The administration committed to continuing negotiations with Angola over the withdrawal of Cuban troops as part of a broader agreement on Namibian independence and a power-sharing agreement between the MPLA and other parties, including UNITA. In addition, the Reagan administration sought to "encourage change away from apartheid and reform in southern Africa." At the same time, NSDD

212 authorized applying greater pressure on the MPLA while increasing support for and promoting UNITA internationally.[85]

As it did in Angola, the Reagan administration initiated a new policy toward South Africa during the second term. South Africa was at the heart of regional issues. With the largest economy and most advanced military, Pretoria was directly or indirectly involved in the neighboring conflicts. Approved on September 7, 1985, NSDD 187 acknowledged the United States' political, commercial, and strategic interests in South Africa. But it also confirmed that domestic criticism of US policy toward Pretoria was growing in Congress and among the general public. The goal of NSDD 187 was to prevent revolutionary change and limit Soviet involvement while influencing a peaceful transition from apartheid to majority rule. To achieve change in South Africa, the directive authorized a combination of "quiet" and public diplomacy. This included urging and pressuring Pretoria to institute reforms and conduct negotiations with Black leaders. Washington also sought expanded relations with Black organizations in South Africa and tried to encourage nonviolent resistance. Meanwhile, the Reagan administration wanted to limit the imposition of new sanctions by Congress on Pretoria.[86]

Congressional support for Reagan's policies in southern Africa was a boon to UNITA and reinforced Pretoria's military and political position. By the time the new directives were implemented, UNITA was dependent on South Africa for its continued survival. Large areas of operation were carved out in northern and southern Angola and formed a UNITA parastate. Meanwhile, South Africa's defense relationship with Israel inspired a more aggressive strategy. Pretoria hoped to copy the perceived success of Israel's 1982 invasion of Lebanon and the October 1983 US invasion of Grenada. It encountered stiff resistance, however, from Angolan forces, which were buttressed by Cuban troops and Soviet advisors. In addition, UNITA was unable to operate effectively without support from the South African air force.[87]

South Africa's plans for regional diplomatic and military dominance were stymied by a sustained uprising in the country's Black townships. Although the apartheid regime hoped to present a different face to the Reagan administration and the rest of the world, the attempts to suppress the uprising brought even more opprobrium. Under President P. W. Botha,

Pretoria retrenched and rejected calls for universal suffrage. Thus, Reagan's policies offered South Africa a lifeline to delay majority rule while resuming support for UNITA.[88]

The influx of funds and weapons to UNITA did not lead to a decisive victory on the battlefield. Although a settlement in Angola was possible before the CIA resumed operations, Savimbi was opposed. Secretary of State George Schultz reportedly believed that US involvement would force the MPLA leadership to make concessions. Washington provided UNITA with roughly $15 million, plus advanced anti-aircraft and anti-tank missiles, but the results, in contrast to the Afghanistan experience, were inconclusive. In December 1988, a settlement was reached that led to the withdrawal of Cuban and South African forces from Angola and also to independence for Namibia. UNITA was not a party to the agreement; a separate cease-fire was negotiated six months later between it and the MPLA government. But the cease-fire did not last long. By the time the settlement was fully implemented in 1991, a hundred thousand Angolans had been killed. Within a year, Savimbi had rejected the UN-monitored election results in Angola and reignited the civil war. Fighting would continue to the end of the century.[89]

In contrast to Savimbi, Nelson Mandela of the ANC spent 27 years in South African prisons for sabotage. The CIA shared information with South African intelligence that assisted in Mandela's 1962 arrest. Released in February 1990, Mandela negotiated the end of White-minority rule in South Africa and was later elected president in the country's first post-apartheid election. Even though he was hailed internationally as a statesman and received the Nobel Peace Prize, Mandela remained on the United States' Terrorism Watch List until 2008.

THE SCANDAL

Unlike in Angola, Reagan's landslide victory in the 1984 presidential election did not change congressional opposition to the Contras. Five months before the election, Congress eliminated funding to the Contras. Yet Reagan continued to publicly promote the anti-Sandinista forces and skirted the edge of legality. Meanwhile, a coalition of conservative groups in the United States and its allies provided them with assistance. Even without Washington's direct aid and supervision, the Contras persisted. One source of funding was cocaine.[90]

In 1982, the Reagan administration launched Operation Bahamas, Turks, and Caicos (OpBat). Vice President Bush oversaw the OpBat Task Force, which was notable for the extensive deployment of DEA and Customs officials, US military helicopters, and the US Coast Guard in coordination with Bahamian anti-narcotics strike teams. Radar balloons provided the Task Force with the ability to track flights into the area. Although OpBat's first year of seizures made headlines, they declined precipitously afterward as trafficking routes shifted.[91]

Transportation and humanitarian aid organizations based in Honduras and Costa Rica were involved in supporting the Contras and they also shipped narcotics back to the United States through Mexico. The planes were operated by Southern Air Transport, a CIA front company based in Miami. Much like the Kuomintang forces in Southeast Asia's "Golden Triangle," discussed in Chapter 2, illegal narcotics provided a consistent and lucrative source of funding when Washington's support was uncertain or threatened.[92]

In South Central Los Angeles, an enterprising narcotics dealer named Ricky Ross relied on the Mexican route to build a crack cocaine empire. Known as "Freeway Rick," he was introduced to the smokable form of cocaine in 1979. Crack was typically sold in rock-like form for small dollar amounts. Often mixed with baking soda and other additives, crack produced a short, intense high. By 1986, Freeway Rick claimed he was selling half a million crack vials a day and had accumulated $2.8 million in cash.[93]

That same year, on March 3, President Reagan hosted a meeting with leading members of the Contras at the White House. In his comments to the press, Reagan emphasized the danger to Americans. He argued that failure to provide funding ensured their defeat with dire consequences. "It'd be a major defeat in the quest for democracy in our hemisphere, and it would mean consolidation of a privileged sanctuary for terrorists and subversives just two days' driving time from Harlingen, Texas," Reagan declared.[94]

He returned to this assertion in a televised address two weeks later. Reagan portrayed Nicaragua as the center of global turmoil and a threat to the United States. "Gathered in Nicaragua already are thousands of Cuban military advisers, contingents of Soviet and East Germans and all the elements of international terror—from the PLO to Italy's Red Brigades," he warned. Reagan quoted Libya's Qaddafi that supporting Nicaragua meant "fighting America near its borders. Fighting America at its door-step." He asserted that the Nicaraguan government had supplied weapons and support to "radical" groups throughout the hemisphere and planned to destabilize Mexico as part of its efforts with Moscow and Havana to eventually undermine the United States. This was compounded by Mana-gua's involvement in the drug trade, where Reagan said the highest-level officials were complicit in the transportation of narcotics to the United States. "There seems to be no crime to which the Sandinistas will not stoop—this is an outlaw regime," Reagan declared. Congress, however, remained unconvinced. And the Contras' involvement in the drug trade was not discussed by administration officials.[95]

As Reagan warned the American public and Congress of the conse-quences, his administration was already subverting the prohibition on funding the Contras. Reagan's NSC coordinated the effort. This included working with retired US Army General John Singlaub, who helped arm and train the Contras. It also included selling arms to Iran and directing the funds from those sales to the anti-Sandinista forces. Although Reagan and his advisors certainly knew that such sales violated US sanctions against Tehran dating back to the hostage crisis, they hoped they would facilitate the release of American hostages held in Lebanon by Hizbullah. Iran, locked in a bloody war with Iraq, needed weapons and spare parts. The secret transfers created a cycle, however, whereby new hostages were seized in Lebanon after others were released. Iraq's 1980 invasion of Iran was en-couraged by the Carter administration and Saudi Arabia. During the Reagan administration, Washington publicly sold large quantities of weap-ons to Baghdad, including precursor materials for chemical and biological weapons. The weapons sales to both countries ensured that neither Bagh-dad nor Tehran emerged victorious.[96]

Considering the numerous actors across multiple countries, it is re-markable that the Reagan administration believed its actions would remain a secret. Only seven months after hosting the Contras at the White House, they were exposed. In early October 1986, the Nicaraguan military shot down a C-123 cargo plan. The Southern Air Transport plane took off from Ilo-pango Air Base in El Salvador carrying ammunition and weapons for the Contras. The only surviving crew member was Eugene Hasenfus, a veteran of CIA operations in Laos who had ignored standing orders to commit suicide rather than be captured. Hasenfus was detained and then transported to Managua, where he was brought before the international press.[97]

The intersection of conflicts in the Middle East and Central America quickly began to unravel. In early November, *al-Shiraa*, a small Arabic-language newspaper based in Beirut, claimed that the United States was trading arms to Iran in exchange for the release of American hostages held in Lebanon. After the *New York Times* carried a similar report, the Reagan White House was besieged by reporters and members of Congress. Although Reagan initially sought to downplay the size of arms transfers, his administration was unable to squelch the controversy. Further revelations that the funds from the arms sales were transferred to the Nicaraguan Contras spurred a congressional investigation with the potential for a Constitutional crisis.

The Iran-Contra hearings and investigation clearly established that President Reagan and senior members of his administration sought to flout US law and congressional oversight. In addition, several administration officials, including National Security Advisor Admiral John Poindexter, destroyed important documents. Both Poindexter and Lt. Colonel Oliver North, a National Security Council staff member, negotiated immunity before testifying at the congressional hearings, but were later indicted and convicted. North's conviction added to his celebrity status, especially in conservative circles, where he was viewed as a sympathetic patriot unfairly maligned by Democrats and the press.

The congressional report detailed the simultaneous and contradictory policies that were enacted in public and secret. It found that the participants deliberately sought to obscure the operations from Congress, Cabinet members, and the press. The majority report blamed President Reagan for the policy failures and the atmosphere of lawlessness that pervaded the NSC. Although the key participants were ensnared in lengthy legal battles, they were ultimately pardoned by President George H. W. Bush as he prepared to leave office in December 1992. Bush also managed to obscure his prominent role in the operations and scandal.[98]

Although it was generally ignored when it was released, the minority report arguably had greater impact over time. Along with the Iran-Contra hearings it offered insights into Richard (Dick) Cheney's views of executive power and privileges. Cheney represented Wyoming in the House of Representatives and he believed that Congress was attempting to exert authority over the president in the same way it had during Watergate. The minority report was authored by a Cheney appointee to the minority staff, Michael Malbin, a former resident fellow at the American Enterprise Institute. It dismissed the "hysterical conclusions" of the Committee Report and insisted there was "no Constitutional crisis, no systematic disrespect for the 'rule of law,' no grand conspiracy, and no Administration-wide dishonesty or coverup." By the time of the Iran-Contra hearings, Malbin's think tank was undergoing a political shift. For over a decade it had represented the mainstream conservatism of the Republican Party. By the mid-1980s, however, its political stance had aligned with the neoconservative movement. This became even more pronounced a decade later, when Cheney joined its board of directors in 1996.[99]

In asserting the president's constitutional powers over foreign policy, the minority report provided an insight into the post–9/11 future. The Malbin authored, and Cheney approved, minority report offered an expansive view of executive power in the realm of foreign policy. It chastised congressional attempts to limit that power. Not all of the committee's Republican members agreed, however, with the assertions in the dissent and it was dismissed by Republican Senator Warren Rudman of New Hampshire, who served as a vice chairman of the Senate investigating committee.[100]

In May 1987, Senator John Kerry of Massachusetts initiated hearings related to the Iran-Contra affair. Kerry was a member of the influential Senate Foreign Relations Committee, and his subcommittee on Terrorism, Narcotics, and International Operations had probed how the United States' support for the Contras had led to its facilitating narcotics trafficking. In his opening statement, Kerry noted the frustration of American law enforcement officials and the general public with the government's inability to halt the flow of narcotics into the country. He added that federal policy was "essentially a war that is being waged against the citizens of this country." Congress had addressed the issue the previous year with the Anti-Drug Abuse Act, he acknowledged, but had failed to make a dent.[101]

The hearings initially focused on corruption in the Bahamas that facilitated narcotics trafficking into the United States. Senator Mitch McConnell of Kentucky, the ranking Republican on the Committee, observed that "we have dedicated millions of dollars, tons of equipment, and hundreds of personnel, yet the problem gets worse." Despite the diminishing returns, the interdiction effort persisted for decades after the hearings.[102]

During the Iran-Contra hearings, Alan Fiers Jr., chief of the CIA's Central American Task Force, testified that "a lot of people" in the "Southern Front," based in Costa Rica, were involved in narcotics trafficking: "We knew that everybody around [Comandante Cero Edén Pastora] was involved in cocaine." In addition to direct trafficking of narcotics, Lieutenant Colonel Oliver North proposed redirecting seized funds in a DEA sting operation to the Contras. The DEA, however, rejected the proposal. The Kerry report noted that North's failed attempt highlighted "the potential appeal of drug profits for persons engaged in covert activity."[103]

Eight years later, Gary Webb of the *San Jose Mercury News* published a multipart report on his investigation into the CIA's involvement in cocaine trafficking with the Contras during the 1980s. Webb built on the Kerry Committee report and focused on the crack epidemic, especially in California. Webb focused on Freeway Rick and his connection to a leading Nicaraguan trafficker with ties to the CIA-Contra network. With the series creating a great deal of consternation in the CIA, some national media outlets quickly worked to discredit Webb's reporting. Under sustained pressure and criticism, the *Mercury News* retracted the series. Webb published his investigation as a book, however, with additional reporting and a forward by Democratic Congresswoman Maxine Waters of California. Even though the book was not subjected to the same criticism by his peers, Webb's career never recovered. He died of an apparent suicide in 2004. A feature film released a decade later, *Kill the Messenger*, starring Jeremy Renner as Webb, portrayed the journalist as a hero. Its depiction of his media critics and the CIA was far less flattering.[104]

As the Kerry Committee examined official malfeasance, the Reagan administration exported its anti-narcotics policies. This was accomplished through the United Nations Convention against Illicit Traffic in Narcotic Drugs and Psychotropic Substances of 1988. The new convention was the result of a four-year negotiation. It expanded on the previous conventions with an emphasis on enforcement. In a hearing of the Senate Foreign Relations Committee in August 1989, Attorney General Richard Thornburgh testified that "it is a law enforcement convention, providing new tools for police, prosecutors and judges from the signatory nations to more effectively carry out their responsibilities across international borders, while preserving each nation's sovereignty." Asset seizure was one of the US practices exported as part of the new convention. It also emphasized interdiction,

placing increased onus on commercial carriers to ensure that illegal narcotics were not transported on their vessels, and promoted crop eradication. The 1988 convention also amended existing extradition treaties to
include offenses for drug trafficking and money laundering. Washington's
European allies were not, however, willing to accept more robust extradition provisions that applied to their citizens.[105]

Thornburgh dramatically overstated the agreement's benefits and its potential impact. If the agreement were fully implemented, he claimed that
the world would be "cleansed of drug abuse." He asserted that drug trafficking organizations would be dismantled, their leadership imprisoned,
and their "seized illicit profits plowed back into more effective law enforcement." While the 1988 convention was a reflection of American power
and influence, it coincided with a debate about American decline.[106]

PREDICTING DECLINE

In April 1988, the *New York Times* featured a lengthy discussion of the question of American decline. "It is not morning in America," the article's lead
sentence declared, an unambiguous reference to Reagan's presidential campaign commercial four years earlier. The article was published in the midst
of the 1988 election campaign. With a large number of Republican and
Democratic candidates jockeying to succeed Reagan, the debate over America's present and future was ubiquitous. Entering into the debate was Paul
Kennedy's *The Rise and Fall of the Great Powers*. A Yale History professor,
Kennedy book tapped into America's anxieties at the end of the Reagan
era. *The Rise and Fall of the Great Powers* was a bestseller and was widely
discussed and debated in the media. Kennedy offered a broad examination
of the relationship between military and economic power from the mid-
sixteenth century to the 1980s. He warned that America's military spending
and global commitments resembled the imperial overstretch of previous
powers and the United States was in danger of decline. The most immediate threat was not from the Soviet Union, but from America's postwar
allies, Germany and Japan.[107]

Kennedy asserted that Germany and Japan could translate their remarkable postwar economic growth into military power that would increase
tensions between the allies. In contrast, the US's defense spending as a
percentage of Gross National Product was no longer sustainable. He was

skeptical that Soviet Premier Mikhail Gorbachev's reforms would succeed and believed that the Soviet Union would remain a status quo power. Kennedy cautioned that Washington's continued predominant position ensured that its relative decline would be greater than that of the Soviet Union, even if Moscow was in a weaker position. However, he did not predict the end of the Cold War, its peaceful conclusion, or the collapse of the Soviet Union. Instead, Kennedy cautioned that imperial withdrawal and collapse were unpredictable and often costly.[108]

Kennedy was joined by other scholars in warning about American decline. The *New York Times* profiled a "School of Decline" that included commentator Walter Russell Mead and David Calleo of Johns Hopkins University's School of Advanced International Studies. In the midst of the presidential campaign, Kennedy, Mead, and Calleo were frequently interviewed by media outlets. Politicians, including presidential candidates, also sought their counsel. Yet their message was often simplified by the media and detractors.[109]

Prominent neoconservatives dismissed the claims of American decline. Jeane Kirkpatrick, Reagan's former ambassador to the UN, argued against retrenchment. She wrote that "it is more often a symptom of decline rather than a cure." Norman Podhoretz of *Commentary* dismissed Kennedy's central arguments about defense spending and imperial overstretch. Rather, he wrote, "our 'problem' is loss of national will."[110]

Members of both parties also weighed in on the debate. New York Democratic Senator Daniel Patrick Moynihan blamed Reagan's fiscal policies. "A foolish domestic political strategy failed and now has foreign-policy consequences," Moynihan argued. James Schlesinger, President Ford's Secretary of Defense, asserted that the discussion of decline was exaggerated. "We sometimes forget as we watch for those indicators of marginal decline how powerful this nation is and how remarkable that power is in relation to virtually all of human history," Schlesinger wrote.[111]

Kennedy offered a vigorous defense in a *New York Times* op-ed. He rejected the accusations of "liberal defeatism" and explained that the causes of American decline were not irreversible or inevitable. Instead, Kennedy reminded readers and critics that a range of policy options were available if the United States sought to avoid the fate of other great powers. Yet as the Cold War concluded, Kennedy's warnings were largely ignored.[112]

CONCLUSION

In early December 1987, Soviet Premier Mikhail Gorbachev flew to Washington for a summit meeting with President Reagan. The two leaders were scheduled to sign the intermediate nuclear force (INF) treaty to eliminate medium-range ballistic missiles. Press coverage evinced a guarded optimism about the future of superpower relations. In the *New York Times Magazine*, Hedrick Smith reported that Gorbachev was pursuing a grander strategy, and using this pact as just "a springboard to an array of arms agreements that he is now dangling before the West and that are vital to his drive to transform the stagnant Soviet economy into the modern apparatus of a 21st century superpower."[113]

The CIA portrayed Gorbachev's intentions as even more ominous. In a pre-summit memorandum for President Reagan, CIA Deputy Director Robert Gates argued that optimism over Gorbachev's reforms and personal style were merely the latest iteration of Western hopes and disappointments for a change in Russian and Soviet behavior. "Gorbachev intends improved Soviet economic performance, greater political vitality at home, and more dynamic diplomacy to make the USSR a more competitive and stronger adversary in the years ahead," he wrote. Amidst the pageantry of the summit, Gates warned that "a sober—even somber—reminder of the enduring features of the regime and the still long competition and struggle ahead will be needed."[114]

Within a year, Gorbachev was frustrated with Washington's apparent reluctance to embrace his vision for a less antagonistic relationship between the superpowers and a different future. Instead, as embodied in the Gates memorandum, the United States remained wary of Gorbachev's intentions. Nor was this limited to the military rivalry between Washington and Moscow or maintaining the Warsaw Pact. Gates later acknowledged that he did not believe that Gorbachev would move so quickly on foreign policy and the removal of Soviet forces from Eastern Europe. Moreover, Gorbachev was eager to abandon existing commitments in the Third World. But the end of the Cold War did not usher in an era of peace or end American suspicions of rivals and threats. Although American triumphalism overshadowed the arguments of pending decline, Part II demonstrates this was illusory. Notions of decline persisted as the United States expanded its military dominance and the number of interventions around the world increased in response to real and perceived dangers.[115]

The combination of Reagan's Cold War by proxy and militarized drug war had intended and unintended consequences. Across the Third World they served to entrench conflicts. In Lebanon, the destruction of the PLO's para-state and Israel's continued occupation contributed to the rise of Hizbullah. In addition, South Africa sought to replicate Israel's example in Namibia and Angola. Pretoria's military offensives were inconclusive and within a few years the apartheid regime was dismantled. Vietnam's legacy continued to haunt America's proxy wars in Afghanistan and Nicaragua. Once again, counterinsurgency veterans were deployed to apply their Vietnam experience but with mixed results. While the Soviet Union became bogged down and eventually suffered a humiliating defeat in Afghanistan, the Contras and UNITA were stymied in Nicaragua and Angola.

Reagan expanded the Wars on Crime and Drugs at home and abroad. These intersected with foreign policy, as observed in the Iran-Contra scandal and funding of the Contras. Although the Kerry committee's revelations continued to reverberate into the next decade, the War on Drugs intensified. The Mexican route only grew in importance after the Nicaraguan civil war and the Cold War were over. Indeed, traffickers benefited from and built on the relationships and networks established during the Reagan administration. The Cold War was an opportunity to reassess US domestic and foreign policies, but instead both were increasingly militarized.

The Reagan administration established the early parameters for the Global War on Terror. From assassinations and hunter-killer teams to the doctrine of preemption, Reagan's policies served as a bridge between Vietnam-era counterinsurgency and post–9/11 counterterrorism operations. As will be seen in Part II, the ghosts of Vietnam reemerged in the Badlands.

PART II

BADLANDS

IT WAS AN UNREMARKABLE Friday night in North Philadelphia. Two narcotics officers and a reporter sat in an unmarked Plymouth. They watched cars on Interstate 95 taking the exit ramp into the city's Kensington district in the early spring evening. A striking number of the cars followed a similar pattern: they slowly approached various street corners where they were met by young males and then, after quick exchanges of cash for crack cocaine, they returned to the highway.

A few days later, the front-page headline in the *Philadelphia Inquirer* appeared: "In the Badlands of the City, Drugs Still Riding High." The article noted that the neighborhood where this activity was observed was "a place narcs call the Badlands."[1] That moniker would soon become ubiquitous in the local media and, over the next five years, the Badlands boundaries shifted. Meanwhile, residents and community activists struggled to challenge the notion that their neighborhood was populated by irredeemable drug dealers. They even attempted to rename the area "the Good Lands," to no avail.[2] Many of the individuals were not even from the neighborhood, they tried to point out, but drove *into* North Philadelphia to ply

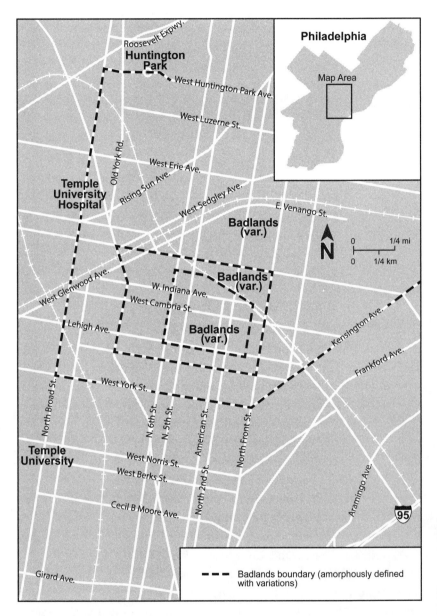

MAP 7. PHILADELPHIA'S BADLANDS

their trade, sometimes in cars registered in other states, and then left. The police and the news reports rarely emphasized the demand side of the drug trade; it was all about the suppliers.

Only a few weeks earlier, the United States had marked the end of the First Persian Gulf War. With Desert Storm fading from the headlines, media attention returned to the ongoing war against drugs and the "crack crisis." As crack became increasingly prevalent, it was sensationalized in national media. High-profile stories warned about "crack babies" and speculated about a generation of youth lost to addiction even before birth.[3]

Crack also pervaded popular culture in the lyrics of rap and rock songs and the scripts of films like the 1991 action movie *New Jack City*. Directed by Mario Van Peebles and starring Wesley Snipes, Chris Rock, and rapper Ice T, *New Jack City* applied elements of Frank Lucas's heroin trade in 1970s New York to crack twenty years later. It also drew on and frequently referenced Brian De Palma's 1983 classic, *Scarface*, itself an update of a 1932 gangster film inspired by Al Capone. De Palma's version had cast Al Pacino in the lead role and made him a Cuban exile in 1980s Miami.[4]

During the Prohibition era, the ring of neighborhoods between Chicago's central loop and its wealthier outlying residential areas had become known as the "ganglands" or "badlands." In the mid-1920s, sociologist Frederic Thrasher conducted the first scientific and comprehensive study of the city's gangs. Thrasher mapped this "Empire of Gangland," across which he identified 1,313 gangs, into three areas: the North Side Jungles, the West Side Wilderness, and the South Side Badlands. "In some respects these regions of conflict are like a frontier; in others, like a 'no man's land,' lawless, godless, wild," Thrasher explained.[5] As a vivid metaphor and a conveniently short headline word, the references to badlands would persist into the twenty-first century.[6]

Prohibition had brought the rise of the South Side's most notorious resident, Al Capone. Six decades later, as a different vice grabbed headlines, politicians again passed harsh laws and endorsed aggressive law enforcement tactics. By the late 1990s, the "crack crisis" appeared to have subsided. But this was not due to a resounding victory in the War on Drugs. Nor was it the result of addressing systemic racism and entrenched inequality following the 1992 Los Angeles riots. Revelations of abusive tactics and corruption in the anti-gang units of major police departments, including in New York City and Los Angeles, did not lead to a fundamental reevaluation of the US criminal justice system and associated legal regimes. Instead, the issues of crime, drugs, gangs, and police brutality and corruption were overwhelmed by the War on Terror.[7]

After September 11, 2001, the geography of the badlands shifted from American cities to the border area of Pakistan and Afghanistan. As US forces targeted the Taliban and al-Qa'ida, media coverage emphasized that the region was a lawless "badlands." The US invasion and occupation, the reports suggested, would impose order where chaos and brutality were endemic. Similar language was adopted after Mexico launched its War on Drugs to describe the southwest border area with the United States. As the War on Terror expanded, the term was applied to conflicts and crises in other regions as well.[8]

At the intersection of the Wars on Drugs and Terror, badlands did not just describe an arid landscape.[9] It represented the difficult terrain with a hostile population that engaged in, or gave tacit support to, illicit and violent activities. Drawing on the myth and mythology of the American West, the penalties were severe and easily justified. After all, these were badlands.

Part II examines how in the post–Cold War era, American policymakers confronted real and perceived enemies at home and abroad. Emboldened by notions of American exceptionalism, Cold War triumphalism, and liberal hegemony, the policies they enacted globalized and reified the badlands.

CHAPTER FOUR

The Limits of Primacy

The final lesson of Vietnam is that no great nation can long afford to be sundered by a memory.

—PRESIDENT GEORGE H. W. BUSH, 1989

A BEAMING PRESIDENT George Herbert Walker Bush walked through the cheering crowd of twenty thousand as "Hail to the Chief" blared from the loudspeakers. Bush had traveled to Shaw Air Force Base in Sumter, South Carolina, to greet American troops returning from the Persian Gulf. "You all not only helped liberate Kuwait, you helped this country liberate itself from old ghosts and doubts," Bush declared. "No one in the world doubts us anymore. What you did, you helped us revive the America of our old hopes and dreams." Bush's remarks were part of a larger narrative that presented the Persian Gulf War as the overwhelming victory that erased the shame of Vietnam. Yet lingering doubts accompanied the euphoria, especially as the United States sank into an economic recession that helped scuttle Bush's reelection bid.[1]

The end of the Cold War and victory in the Persian Gulf War did not translate into either a peace dividend at home or fealty abroad. Instead, this chapter argues that the United States faced stubborn domestic and foreign policy challenges and the new world order looked remarkably similar to the old. In the years before September 11, America's place in the

world was still depicted as insecure and the legacy of Vietnam was difficult to bury.

THE NEW WAR ON DRUGS

Even though Bush emphasized his experience and national security credentials in the 1988 presidential campaign, he trailed Massachusetts Governor Michael Dukakis in the polls prior to the Republican National Convention in August. Prominent polls revealed that Bush was vulnerable on
the issue of illegal drugs and that a majority of Americans disapproved of
the Reagan administration's handling of the issue. As vice president, Bush
led the task force targeting drug trafficking into Florida through the Caribbean. Although the task force claimed early successes, by 1988 policymakers acknowledged that seizures were reduced to a trickle and trafficking routes had shifted. Bush reversed the deficit in the polls with the
help of his campaign manager, Lee Atwater, and a political action committee called the National Security PAC.[2]

The now notorious "Willie Horton ad" the PAC ran labeled Dukakis
as weak on crime. Horton was a Black man serving a life sentence in Massachusetts for first-degree murder. He escaped from a furlough program
and raped a White woman and stabbed her fiancée. Although the program had been the state's policy for over a decade, Dukakis took owner-
ship of it when he overrode the Massachusetts legislature's attempt to
make murderers ineligible for furloughs. Bush's campaign capitalized on
the shocking story with a September ad that has forever since been seen as
the epitome of racist dog-whistling, with its stark presentation of Horton's
mugshot as the face of "rape and murder."[3]

The following month, the Dukakis campaign returned fire. It released
an ad featuring Angel Medrano, a heroin dealer who had also been on
furlough—in his case from a halfway house for drug offenders, where he
was serving a *federal* sentence—when he raped and murdered a young,
pregnant mother of two and then fled to Mexico. Dukakis was damaged
by the Horton ad and the *Los Angeles Times* reported that the campaign
"was frantically trying to find a case like Medrano's to use in counter-
punching Bush." The "Medrano ad" criticized the Reagan-Bush administration for allowing "thousands of drugs dealers" to be furloughed from
federal prisons. Meanwhile, Congress was preparing to pass harsher drug

laws suited for election year campaigning. The 1988 Anti-Drug Abuse Law expanded on the 1986 legislation with civil penalties for possession and introduced the death penalty for drug-related homicides.[4]

The influence of the contrasting ads was obvious when, a few weeks before the election, CNN moderator Bernard Shaw opened the second presidential debate by asking Dukakis if he would favor the death penalty for the killer if his own wife, Kitty, were "raped and murdered." Dukakis responded by dispassionately restating his opposition to capital punishment, saying he had never seen "any evidence that it's a deterrent." He quickly pivoted to a more energetic vow to fight "a real war" on drugs as opposed to "the phony war" that the vice president had been waging. "We have much to do to step up that war," Dukakis said, "to double the number of drug enforcement agents, to fight both here and abroad." Bush's response underscored the sharp "difference of opinion" on the death penalty. He also defended what had been accomplished in the drug war and endorsed the 1988 Anti-Drug Abuse Law. Post-debate analysis critiqued Dukakis's unemotional response about Kitty, and concurred on a verdict that he lost the debate. Bush won the election in a landslide.[5]

Six months into his administration, Bush expanded the War on Drugs with National Security Directive (NSD) 13. NSD 13 declared that preventing the flow of cocaine into the United States was a major foreign policy objective with an emphasis on interdiction. The directive authorized the expansion of the runway at the Santa Lucia base in Peru to accommodate C-123 aircraft. Designed by Vietnam War veterans, Santa Lucia was intended to be the United States' largest anti-narcotics base in the hemisphere. Construction began in 1987, but it was not completed by the time NSD 13 was signed. The base was located in Peru's Upper Huallaga Valley, which at the time was the source of nearly 60 percent of coca grown in the world. It housed a task force of DEA agents, helicopters, and Peruvian drug police. NSD 13's recommendations built on the existing US-Peruvian counternarcotics program in the valley.[6]

Almost three months later, on September 5, 1989, President Bush addressed the nation from the Oval Office. Bush prefaced his remarks by underscoring the seriousness of the topic: "This is the first time since taking the oath of office that I felt an issue was so important, so threatening, that it warranted talking directly with you, the American people." He had no doubt his audience would feel the same. "All of us agree that the gravest domestic threat facing our nation today is drugs. . . . Drugs have strained our faith in our system of justice. Our courts, our prisons, our legal system, are stretched to the breaking point." In fact, Bush declared, "Drugs are sapping our strength as a nation." He held up a plastic bag of crack cocaine that, he said, agents had just purchased in the park across from the White House. It was later revealed that Keith Jackson, the nineteen-year-old Black high-school student who sold the cocaine to DEA agents, had not even known where the White House was located before he was lured to Lafayette Square by DEA agents to provide the president with a compelling anecdote and prop for the televised speech.[7]

While the juries in two trials failed to reach a verdict on the charge that Jackson had been the dealer in Lafayette Square, the second jury did find him guilty of three other counts of selling cocaine—and because one transaction was within a thousand feet of a school, he was sentenced to the mandatory minimum of ten years in prison without parole. Judge Stanley Sporkin regretted that, due to provisions in the 1988 Anti-Drug Abuse Act, he was forced to apply the harsh sentence. Sporkin, a former CIA general counsel appointed to the DC District Court bench by President Reagan, sympathized with the young man, saying that the president "used you, in the sense of making a big drug speech," but advised that Jackson's best hope for a shorter sentence was to ask for a commutation from Bush himself.[8]

Although the collapse of the Berlin Wall was still two months away, and few predicted its peaceful fall, Bush suggested a new era of conflict was already at hand. He declared that Washington would provide $250 million in military and law enforcement assistance to Colombia, Bolivia, and Peru in "the first part of a five-year, $2 billion program to counter the producers, the traffickers, and the smugglers." This program formed the core of Bush's "Andean Initiative" and counternarcotics provided a new rationale for intervention in place of anti-communist counterinsurgency. The program was augmented by $1.5 billion in interdiction efforts that relied on "greater interagency cooperation, combined with sophisticated intelligence-gathering and Defense Department technology." In short, America's Cold War arsenal would now prevent narcotics from crossing into the United States.[9]

America's arsenal was also pointed inward. As part of the National Defense Authorization Act for 1990 and 1991, the "1033 Program" was established. The program allowed for the transfer of military equipment to local police for counternarcotics. Six years later, in the aftermath of the Oklahoma City bombing, the program was expanded to include counter-terrorism operations. And the type of equipment provided to local law enforcement was more fitting for a battlefield than urban, suburban, or rural environments. This included machine guns, body armor, grenade launchers, armored personnel carriers, and modified tanks. Once the equipment was delivered, however, usage was not restricted to counternarcotics or counterterrorism. Over the next two decades, the 1033 program helped drive the militarization of local law enforcement across the United States.[10]

The Andean Initiative did not have an auspicious start. In Peru, the Bush administration encountered resistance from the Peruvian military over the Santa Lucia base. Although Washington wanted to expand the runway and add additional helipads, raising the cost of the base to roughly $3 million, the Peruvian military believed the priorities were misplaced. Of greater concern was a leftist insurgency led by the Sendero Luminoso (or Shining Path). Peruvian officials also endorsed a policy of crop substitution instead of the eradication efforts implemented by Washington. American officials agreed to suspend eradication in response to criticism from Lima, but tensions remained, especially as the US State Department accused a Peruvian general who opposed the Andean Initiative of benefiting from the drug trade.[11]

The militarized emphasis on supply was accompanied by an enlarged and more punitive criminal justice system. "We need more prisons, more jails, more courts, more prosecutors," Bush asserted in his Oval Office address. He requested that Congress increase drug-related spending by $1.5 billion.[12] Bush's proposal built on the 1986 and 1988 Anti-Drug Abuse laws, which continued the trend of increasing penalties on recreational drug use. It introduced the death penalty for murders committed by individuals involved in drug trafficking or, if the victim was a law enforcement official, involved in any narcotics-related crime. Although the law expanded funding for treatment and education, including federal support to build new centers, it also increased the role of the military.[13]

Despite six years' effort, the US military had yet to demonstrate results that justified their continued role. The Government Accountability Office (GAO) reported that funding for drug abuse control was almost $4 billion in fiscal year 1987, which was more than triple the $1.2 billion allotted in 1981. Of this amount, $1.4 billion was designated for interdiction efforts. Yet the GAO "found no direct correlation between resources spent to interdict and the long-term availability of imported drugs in the domestic market." It added that law enforcement lacked the ability to determine the amount of illegal narcotics entering the United States to evaluate the effectiveness of interdiction. Success was gauged by the number of seizures and arrests, but it was not possible to correctly evaluate their impact.[14]

Military support for law enforcement efforts was even more uncertain. The GAO found that the use of advanced Air Force surveillance aircraft was expensive and ineffective. The Air Force deployed its Airborne Warning and Control System (AWACS) to assist with interdiction. But AWACS aircraft are intended to identify fighter jets flying at high speed and altitude rather than the smaller and slower twin-engine planes favored by smugglers. In 1987, the AWACS flew 591 hours at a cost of $2.6 million. The flights resulted in six seizures and ten arrests. Although the Navy and Coast Guard had better results, it was a larger and more expensive deployment. Naval operations in 1987 involved 2,500 ship days for a combined cost of $40 million in 1987. That year, 20 ships were seized, 110 arrests were made, and over 225,000 pounds of marijuana and 550 pounds of cocaine were confiscated. The GAO reported that in the first few months of 1988, interdictions had already resulted in fewer seizures and arrests. Yet the Bush administration ignored the report and its conclusions.[15]

Like heroin in the 1970s and cocaine in the early 1980s, crack cocaine dominated headlines and popular culture by the early 1990s. The parallels were not superficial. As observed with the Rockefeller Drug Laws, influential Black Congressmen, including California Democrat Ronald Dellums, supported the 1986 Anti-Drug Abuse Act. The Act's provision for far greater penalties for crack cocaine as opposed to the powder form in the federal courts proved to disproportionately impact minorities. In California, this was accompanied by new legislation and heightened law enforcement operations that targeted gangs. Further demonstrating the relationship between the Wars on Crime, Drugs, and Terror—and the penchant of lawmakers for hyperbole—the "Street Terrorism Enforcement and Prevention Act" became California state law in 1988. The law enhanced charges against gang members with as much as five additional years in prison per charge. Subsequent amendments over the next twelve years increased the penalties.[16]

Meanwhile, militarized policing and aggressive new laws added to the challenges faced by Black and Latino communities in Los Angeles. Mass incarceration was the preferred solution and further contributed to California's problems. From 1977 to 2000, the California Department of Corrections prison population skyrocketed from 19,623 to 162,000. In 1988, Blacks comprised over 37 percent of the state's prison population, but only 7 percent of its residents. In comparison, Latinos were 25 percent of the state's population and almost 28 percent of prisoners. Two years later, when Bush expanded the War on Drugs, roughly 34 percent of new admissions to California prisons were on drug-related charges.[17]

If there was one face most associated with the 1990s War on Drugs, it was Pablo Escobar's. The story of Escobar's rise and fall as the head of Colombia's Medellin drug cartel has been well chronicled. Four months before Bush's Oval Office address, the CIA's Counternarcotics Center warned that "Colombia's billionaire drug lords are intensifying their grip on the country by investing in legitimate business enterprises and by financing paramilitary groups." Although the Colombian government had instituted measures to counter the influence of the country's drug-trafficking organizations, the CIA asserted that it was "unlikely to prevent the situation from deteriorating further." The report detailed that Escobar owned at least 335 residential properties, including sixteen in an exclusive Medellin neighborhood. It noted that, over the previous decade, an estimated $5.5 billion in drug profits had been used to purchase real estate in Colombia. Since 1983, narcotraffickers had bought one million hectares of land, concentrated in Colombia's north-central region.[18]

Escobar's activities went beyond buying land. He also used his wealth to build a base of support for his political ambitions, mainly by funding housing projects and underwriting a welfare system in his hometown of Envigado. This largesse contrasted sharply, however, with the ruthlessness he displayed in the war between the Medellin Cartel and the Colombian government. Escobar's brazen acts of political violence, terrorism, and assassination blurred the line between narco-trafficking and insurgency— and similarly, Washington and Bogota erased the differentiation between the responses that criminal and political acts of violence should elicit.[19]

One underreported aspect of the Bush administration's efforts was empowering the DEA to engage in massive bulk collection of telephone records through a DEA program dubbed "USTO." It began in the final year of the Bush administration and continued for the next two decades. The DEA subpoenaed the phone records from providers for "all calls" made from the United States to 116 countries that were determined to be part of the "nexus of drugs." Although the content of the calls was not obtained, the DEA was able to secure the telephone metadata, which included the origination, the date and time, and the duration of a call. It was not unusual for DEA agents to perform three hundred searches of the call database in a day. A study conducted by an inspector general at the Department of Justice (DOJ) after the USTO program was halted found that the criteria for collection changed over time. The agency consistently focused, however, on countries linked to the narcotics production, narcotics trading, and money laundering. The DEA and DOJ tried to justify the lengthy program by saying it targeted the "command and control" layer of the leading narcotraffickers, whose international organizations were responsible for a "significant percentage" of the drug trade in the United States.[20]

DEA officials involved in the inception of the USTO program claimed it was created because the agency had not been able to infiltrate the Medellin Cartel or obtain a firm understanding of its infrastructure through human intelligence. With the assistance of the Pentagon, the DEA established the program to target the cartel's leadership.[21] The program's timing, however, may not have been coincidental. President Bush had declared a War on Drugs, but it was proving to be a losing struggle and election season was approaching. Drug-related crime rates were higher and, as demonstrated in North Philadelphia's "Badlands," there was no discernible impact on the daily trade.

The DEA and DOJ insisted that the collection program was successful and contributed to major investigations. The DEA has not, however, disclosed which kingpins were arrested. After the program was canceled in 2013, government agencies claimed that the lack of a similar data collection effort hindered investigations. In spite of this secret, two-decade-long program there has been no discernible impact on the narcotics trade. While the major Colombian cartels of the 1990s were dismantled, they were replaced. The major site of trafficking has moved closer to the United States. Recently, the National Security Agency (NSA) reportedly met with DEA officials to discuss the similarly extensive surveillance and collection program it had implemented after the September 11 attacks. In the USTO's final year, the DEA expanded the program to focus on "narco-terrorism" and sought information on the funding of terrorist activities through drug trafficking.[22]

JUST CAUSE

Reduced Cold War tensions and the Bush administration's emboldened efforts against narcotics trafficking contributed to an effort by the CIA to revisit prohibitions against the assassination of foreign leaders. In mid-October 1989, the *New York Times* reported that CIA Director William Webster sought "greater latitude" in coordinating with and supporting coup attempts. Webster asserted that the 1976 Executive Order signed by President Gerald Ford and reaffirmed by Presidents Carter and Reagan was interpreted as barring assistance to coups that would result in the death of a foreign leader. Two weeks earlier, a failed coup in Panama contributed to the CIA's desire to challenge the EO's perceived limitations. Although the White House publicly supported Webster's request, key members of Congress were not persuaded that a change was needed. Indeed, they argued that this was an attempt by the Bush administration to deflect criticism of their policies in Panama.[23]

By the end of the year, as the world embraced the end of the Cold War and dismantling of the Berlin Wall, the United States launched an invasion of Panama. Dubbed Operation Just Cause, the intervention ostensibly targeted the involvement of Panama's General Manuel Noriega in drug trafficking and money laundering. The case against Noriega had begun in spectacular fashion nearly four years earlier, when a pilot abandoned his twin-engine Cessna aircraft on Interstate 75 in south Florida. Authorities found nearly two thousand pounds of cocaine stashed in the plane. Although the DEA uncovered evidence that linked Noriega to the flight and other shipments, there was reluctance to indict him due to his cooperation with other investigations. By 1988, revelations about Noriega's involvement in the drug trade during the hearings held by Massachusetts Senator John Kerry and the Senate Foreign Relations Subcommittee made the Panamanian a political liability.[24]

Noriega was indicted by a Florida grand jury in February 1988. Although he did not hold the title of president, Noriega was Panama's de facto leader. As the head of G-2, Panama's intelligence service, Noriega personally

selected individuals for key political positions. A month after the indictment, the first of two unsuccessful coups was launched to remove Noriega
from power. The failure to unseat Noriega as head of the Panamanian Defense Forces and the subsequent removal of Panama's President Eric Arturo Delvalle led Washington to impose economic sanctions. By September, however, the US intelligence community reported that the sanctions
were unlikely to force Noriega to step down, instigate a coup, or provoke
civil unrest. As an additional embarrassment to the Reagan administration,
the CIA reported that Noriega was "managing the situation skillfully."
While Noriega carefully controlled expenses, Panama was receiving financial assistance from Washington's staunch opponents: Libya, Cuba, and
Nicaragua.[25]

The stalemate with Washington continued into the first year of the Bush
administration. On September 1, 1989, President Bush approved NSD 21
to establish a policy toward Panama. NSD 21 asserted that, since Noriega
was unwilling to accept the legitimacy of elections held four months earlier, Washington would recognize only a government based on a democratic process. It also encouraged other governments to adopt the same
policy and maintain sanctions. NSD 21 did not, however, specifically
authorize Noriega's removal from power. A month later, a second failed
coup attempt embarrassed the Bush administration. After this coup was
squelched, a smiling Noriega greeted journalists, apparently undaunted
by the temporary crisis. That did not last, however.[26]

In mid-December, the United States invaded Panama to depose and
capture Noriega. Although there was a sharp disparity in power, the intervention did not go as planned. Noriega was able to elude American forces
and sought amnesty in the home of the Vatican's representative before
finally surrendering to US forces. The civilian death toll and long-term
damage from the attack was disproportionate to the threat. Considering
Noriega's reputation at home and abroad, it also appeared to exceed his
limited base of popular support. US special forces deployed in the invasion also suffered heavier casualties than expected. Noriega was ultimately
tried and sentenced to forty years in prison, but the drug trade continued
unabated.[27]

Secretary of Defense Dick Cheney claimed that the Panama invasion had
been a "trial run" for an overt use of force. Although Noriega's extradition
and imprisonment were applied to leading drug traffickers, Washington

increasingly relied on counterinsurgency tactics instead of an overt invasion. Counternarcotics initiatives were also subject to less criticism than the Cold War era anti-communism policies and interventions in the Western hemisphere. Within a year, events in the Persian Gulf allowed the Bush administration to directly apply the lessons from Panama.[28]

THE PERSIAN GULF WAR AND ASSERTING AMERICAN PRIMACY

Ten months before Iraq invaded Kuwait, President Bush had authorized NSD 26 to establish a policy toward the Persian Gulf region. One recommendation had been to establish "normal relations" with Iraq that would "serve our longer-term interests" and promote regional stability. With the Iran-Iraq War over, the directive had recommended creating economic and political incentives "for Iraq to moderate its behavior and to increase our influence" and finding ways for American companies to assist with reconstruction efforts. These goals, however, were superseded by events.[29]

Iraq's August 1990 invasion of Kuwait had its roots in regional and domestic politics. Iraq claimed victory in its brutal eight-year war with neighboring Iran. But Baghdad was more than $80 billion in debt, mostly to other Arab Gulf states. The collapse of oil prices in the mid-1980s made it difficult for Baghdad to repay the loans. By the spring of 1990, Iraq complained that Kuwait was exceeding its production quotas and accused it of stealing oil from the Rumaila oil field through slant drilling. Heated rhetoric between Kuwait and Iraq quickly escalated and one hundred thousand Iraqi troops were massed on the Kuwaiti border by late July. The invasion and occupation were quick. Baghdad was expected to install a puppet regime and withdraw its forces. The Iraqi military stayed in Kuwait, however, and appeared to threaten Saudi Arabia. Under questioning by FBI and CIA interrogators over a decade later, Hussein conceded that the invasion had been a mistake.[30]

Although President Bush's initial reaction to the invasion was muted, he soon adopted a more bellicose stance. A rapid military buildup in the Persian Gulf and the deployment of forces inside Saudi Arabia quickly followed.[31] The diplomatic effort was equally robust, as Secretary of State James Baker coordinated with allies at the UN Security Council while also working with the Soviet Union and China to ensure that they did not hinder efforts to compel an Iraqi withdrawal. By early January 1991, as

President George H. W. Bush requested that Congress vote on an authorization of military force, the US-led coalition consisted of over thirty countries, including contingents from Egypt, Syria, and Saudi Arabia. The specter of the Vietnam War hung over the congressional debate. Senator William Cohen of Maine (later Secretary of Defense) warned that "we are walking in the shadows of Munich and Vietnam, and the path is dark and dangerous." The authorization passed narrowly in the Senate but there was a more comfortable margin of support in the House of Representatives.[32]

Iraqi forces were overwhelmed by a punishing air campaign and swift ground offensive. After Iraq was expelled from Kuwait, Saddam Hussein faced twin uprisings in the north and south, which were defeated, but with long-term repercussions. In response, the United States advocated for and enforced two UN-sanctioned "no-fly zones" over Iraq. The northern no-fly zone contributed to the establishment of a Kurdish para-state. In the south, however, Iraq's Shi'a majority was heavily suppressed. As will be discussed in Chapter 5, Shi'a political parties and militias emerged as a dominant force in the fractured country after the 2003 US invasion.[33]

Following the Persian Gulf War, as the Bush administration sought to ensure American primacy in perpetuity, the Pentagon's Office for Defense Policy developed its 1992 Defense Planning Guidance. In an effort overseen by Under Secretary of Defense Paul Wolfowitz, the document was initially drafted by Zalmay Khalilzad, head of policy planning at the Defense Department. The goal, Cheney later wrote, was to create a Guidance document that described "the challenges America faced and the strategic position we should adopt to meet them throughout the 1990s and beyond."[34]

The initial draft delivered to Cheney presented a vision of American military predominance. He described it as "brilliant." With the Soviet Union a memory, the document asserted that it was "improbable" a global rival would emerge from the "Eurasian heartland for many years to come." "Our strategy must now refocus on precluding the emergence of any potential future global competitor," it declared. Among the draft's recommendations were maintenance of existing bases, the prepositioning of equipment, and military exercises. Preserving the United States' collective defense system, the draft argued, allowed Washington to coordinate with allies and partners to ensure security interests while also minimizing defense spending.[35]

Cheney later wrote that the draft reflected a strategic shift from planning for the global threat posed by the Soviet Union to preparing for regional challenges. This presented the United States with the "opportunity to meet threats at lower levels and lower costs—as long as we are prepared to reconstitute additional forces should the need to counter a global threat reemerge." The draft also identified regions of critical importance, in particular the Middle East. It asserted that "our overall objective is to remain the predominant outside power in [the Middle East] and preserve US and Western access to the region's oil." In the wake of the 1991 Persian Gulf War, the draft claimed it was "fundamentally important to prevent a hegemon or alignment of powers from dominating the region."[36]

As further evidence of a Pax Americana alignment of domestic and foreign policy goals, the draft Defense Planning Guidance also addressed the drug trade. "Countering drug trafficking," it declared, "remains a national security priority of the Department of Defense." In addition to "attacking" the trade at the source and along transit routes, the Pentagon was involved in counterinsurgency efforts linked to narcotics trafficking and coordinating with American enforcement agencies. Yet, in the post–Cold War era, the illegal narcotics trade was not the only arena where American primacy was contested.[37]

MAD MAX WORLD

Two months before the 1992 presidential election, President Bush ordered a deployment of over 2,400 Marines and Air Force commandos to Somalia. Following the Persian Gulf War, Somalia was an unexpected destination for American forces. It was, however, experiencing a famine brought on by drought and exacerbated by civil war. The Somali civil war was one of several post–Cold War conflicts that garnered international attention. As discussed in Chapter 2, the conflict with Ethiopia and Somalia's failure to retake the Ogaden territory had weakened the government of President Mohammad Siad Barre. By 1988, Barre had faced internal divisions, amplified by a harsh crackdown on the opposition. Within three years, Somalia had descended into civil war and Barre had fled Mogadishu. But he had retained the loyalty of one of several heavily armed groups. As these groups, tied to major clans, competed for power and territory, they routinely took possession of UN relief supplies and prevented their distribution to rival areas. Media coverage featured haunting scenes of emaciated children, and reported death tolls of several thousand Somalis per day. American forces were tasked with providing support to a UN-led mission made up of five hundred Pakistani troops guarding aid distribution.[38]

The Somalia intervention was driven by media coverage and frustration at the UN. National Security Advisor Brent Scowcroft would later recount a May 1992 meeting between President Bush and UN Secretary-General Boutros Boutros-Ghali, in which the latter reported a growing belief in developing countries that the UN Security Council "was turning into an instrument of the Europeans and Americans." Scowcroft added that "Third World countries, Black countries, southern hemisphere countries, were just not on the agenda," and this was exemplified by Somalia. Yet Scowcroft insisted that the decision to intervene was "90, 95 percent humanitarian."[39]

On December 3, veteran journalist and *NBC Evening News* commentator John Chancellor called Somalia "Mad Max country in real life." The reference was to the popular *Mad Max* trilogy of films, directed by George Miller and starring Mel Gibson, which depicted a society ruined by nuclear war and overrun by leather-clad motorcycle and hot-rod gangs. "The Mad Max world is scary and so is Somalia," Chancellor elaborated, describing the African nation as a "lawless landscape where heavily armed gangs ride around in armored trucks, killing each other and stealing from honest people." Unlike Iraq and Panama, sites of other recent interventions, Somalia did not have a functioning government. "The problem in Somalia," he underscored, "is both political and humanitarian."[40]

The following day, President Bush addressed the nation. He expanded the original support mission and ordered a combined force of Marines and Army units to provide security for the UN's relief efforts. Over a quarter of a million Somalis had already died, Bush reported, and unless action were taken quickly, an additional 1.5 million could also perish from a combination of famine and a UN effort prevented from delivering and distributing relief supplies. Bush echoed Chancellor's commentary: "There is no government in Somalia. Law and order have broken down. Anarchy prevails." The United States was the only country with the capability to intervene quickly in Somalia, he emphasized, while allowing that the mission would have to focus on targeted objectives and that American forces could not stay indefinitely.[41]

The Bush administration relayed the decision to President-elect Bill Clinton's incoming national security team. Scowcroft informed Samuel "Sandy" Berger, who served as a deputy national security advisor in Clinton's first term, that the mission was merely to open supply lines and that US troops would be withdrawn by inauguration day. Clinton's first national security advisor, Anthony Lake, later recalled that there had been no firm mission or exit strategy. A veteran of the Johnson, Nixon, and Carter administrations, Lake disputed the notion that the mission had changed under Clinton: "It wasn't mission creep, it was mission creation." He added that the Clinton administration had attempted to coordinate with the UN to determine how to maintain stability in Somalia after the United States withdrew its forces.[42]

Media coverage of Somalia also influenced the incoming Clinton administration. Once it became clear that US troops would remain in Somalia after the inauguration, Clinton was briefed on the mission. In February, Samuel Lewis, Director of Policy Planning at the State Department, developed a "strategic agenda" for the administration's foreign policy. In a memorandum to Secretary of State Warren Christopher, Lewis noted that the goal for Somalia was a successful transition to the second stage of the UN mission, UNOSOM II.[43]

Conditions in Somalia deteriorated by the summer. The Clinton administration was faced with a difficult choice as both the CIA and Admiral John Howe, UN Special Envoy to Somalia, advocated capturing Somali General Mohammad Farrah Aideed. Aideed was a local warlord and his Somali National Alliance (SNA) militia had an estimated two thousand fighters, of which roughly one quarter were in Mogadishu. In June 1993, Aideed's militia ambushed Pakistani peacekeepers returning from an inspection visit and killed twenty-seven. The SNA also targeted UN personnel, including six Somali employees of a UN-run newspaper.

A month later, the CIA delivered an assessment to President Clinton. It argued that Aideed intended to harass the UN mission rather than engage in a direct confrontation. His goal was to intimidate UN officials while also coercing greater support among Somali civilians and thwarting rival warlords. The CIA asserted that Aideed's rivals would question the "UN's competence and resolve" if he was not dealt with swiftly. It concluded that arresting Aideed offered the best opportunity to "restore credibility" to the peacekeeping mission. Admiral Howe was similarly hawkish and Colin

Powell, then chairman of the Joint Chiefs of Staff, also endorsed a special forces mission to capture Aideed as the SNA's guerilla campaign persisted.[44]

Almost nine years later, Lake recalled that the administration had made several fundamental mistakes. The first was personalizing the conflict with Aideed. An even more important mistake was ignoring Somalia's political context. This topic, he said, had been broached in a September meeting at the UN between Clinton and Boutros-Ghali, but the UN secretary-general had not been convinced that a political solution could be found. Lake conceded that that the Clinton administration "could have raised it a lot harder and a lot earlier." Indeed, he said, "I should have known better from experiences in Vietnam and other places." Despite arguments by Ambassador Robert Oakley, Clinton's envoy to Somalia, that the conflict should be resolved through political dialogue, the choice was made to proceed militarily. "This was the same mistake we used to make in Vietnam," he said, "and I should have known better, quicker." But Lake was not the only member of Clinton's national security team with Vietnam experience. Colin Powell had been a young officer in Vietnam and he also favored targeting Aideed. At the same time, Clinton was able to overcome criticism of his lack of military service in Vietnam to win the 1992 presidential election. It is unclear how that influenced his decisions on Somalia.[45]

Domestic politics intervened in the Clinton administration's policy deliberations. The continued targeting of American and UN forces in Somalia by the SNA contributed to congressional skepticism. Although the US forces accounted for only four thousand of the twenty-five thousand total UN forces in Somalia, issues with aligned command and control coupled with the population's increasing hostility to put the mission in jeopardy. Among the opponents was Senator Robert Byrd, a West Virginia Democrat. Byrd criticized the Somalia mission in an August 19 *New York Times* op-ed, predicting a repeat of the ill-fated Lebanon mission discussed in Chapter 3.[46]

When the debate moved from the newspapers to the Senate floor, Lebanon was evoked by members of both parties. Byrd continued his criticism and advocated a "hard-nosed reassessment." In a negotiated agreement with the Clinton White House, the Senate voted 90-7 in favor of a nonbinding resolution that an extension of the US deployment in Somalia past November 15 required congressional approval. In one of his final acts as chair of the Joint Chiefs of Staff, Colin Powell warned the Senate not to "cut and run because things have gotten tough." Privately, however, he told President Clinton that the situation was untenable and the United States and UN should withdraw. The Senate debate and Powell's warnings were, however, too late.[47]

The decision for a military confrontation had immediate and long-term consequences. On October 3, US forces launched a raid targeting Aideed's key associates. Although 24 men were captured, the US forces were ambushed by the SNA. In the ensuing battle, 18 Americans were killed and 84 wounded, while 312 Somalis were killed and over 800 wounded. Two US Black Hawk helicopters were downed and one pilot was held captive by Aideed's forces. The graphic footage of the body of an American soldier dragged through the streets of Mogadishu and a video of captured pilot Michael Durant under questioning were ubiquitous on American news channels. This served to heighten the criticism from Congress, which was described by *NBC Evening News* anchor Tom Brokaw as a "chorus of outrage."[48]

Looking back, Lake challenged the notion that Clinton had immediately decided to withdraw from Somalia due to high-profile casualties. The administration met with congressional leaders and they urged Clinton to pull out. Although Lake faulted how Clinton handled the discussions, the administration was able to come to a negotiated agreement on the withdrawal of US forces. Indeed, the United States increased the number of troops supporting the Somalia mission while it developed and implemented the full withdrawal plan by the end of March 1994. General Aideed announced a unilateral cease-fire a week after the battle, and the UN eventually abandoned the warrant for his arrest. Even though the SNA suffered heavy losses in the engagement with US forces, Aideed was perceived as the victor. This was coupled with a broader perception that the American public was unwilling to accept casualties and would limit support for future humanitarian relief and peacekeeping operations.[49]

Shortly after US forces withdrew from Somalia, civil strife in the Central African nation of Rwanda culminated in a genocide. The Clinton administration's failure to respond or intervene was heavily criticized. And the ghosts of Vietnam, Lebanon, and Somalia hung over the deliberations on Rwanda and Bosnia.

RECONSTRUCTING THE BALKANS

Yugoslavia's dissolution and the civil war in Bosnia was another international crisis that Clinton inherited from Bush. Yugoslavia was an ethnically and religiously diverse country that grew out of the remnants of the Ottoman and Austro-Hungarian Empires and the experience of two World Wars. For over three decades, the country was held together by Marshal Josip Broz Tito and ruled by the Communist Party. Of its six republics and two autonomous provinces, the most prosperous were Slovenia, Croatia, and Serbia. After Tito's death in 1980, power was increasingly consolidated in the republics. In October 1990, a National Intelligence Estimate (NIE) warned that Yugoslavia "will cease to function as a federal state within one year, and will probably dissolve within two." It determined that neither the Yugoslav Communist Party nor the national army (JNA) would be able to hold the country together. The NIE cautioned that Washington would be "drawn into the heated arena of interethnic conflict and will be expected to respond in some manner to the contrary claims of all parties." The NIE was ignored in the midst of the Persian Gulf crisis, with fateful consequences.[50]

Yugoslavia's collapse contributed to two related conflicts. The first crisis erupted after Croatia declared independence in June 1991. Over the next six months, heavy fighting broke out among Croatia's new military, the Serbian militias, and elements of the JNA. After a ceasefire was declared and the JNA withdrew in early January 1992, the UN established a protection force for key areas in Croatia. Bosnia-Herzegovina, however, with a population roughly 43 percent Muslim (Bosniak), 32 percent Serbian, and 18 percent Croatian, proved more difficult. Two months after the ceasefire in Croatia, a plebiscite on independence was held in Bosnia. With the Bosnian Serbs boycotting the referendum, the plebiscite passed and civil strife quickly followed. A humanitarian and political crisis emerged as major cities, including Sarajevo, were besieged by Serbian militias supported by the JNA.[51]

Unlike Somalia, the Bush administration did not believe that an intervention in Bosnia would be quick or easy. The administration's response was hindered both by internal disagreements and by Germany's aggressive diplomacy. This was compounded by the European Union's desire to take the lead in resolving the crisis. Scowcroft and Deputy Secretary of State

Lawrence Eagleburger had prior experience in Yugoslavia and Serbia. Eagleburger had served as ambassador to Yugoslavia and both men spoke Serbian. In Washington, Powell and the Joint Chiefs of Staff did not support an intervention, a sentiment shared by the Pentagon. Scowcroft later explained that he and Eagleburger had believed there was an opportunity for American influence. Neither President Bush nor Secretary of State James Baker felt US national interests were at stake in Bosnia, but they agreed that a spillover into the Kosovo province threatened to draw in Turkey and Greece and fracture NATO. Meanwhile, like Somalia, the images of atrocities in Bosnia made it difficult to ignore the conflict.[52]

Once in office, the Clinton administration found America's NATO allies unable or unwilling to develop a strategy to end the fighting. A UN arms embargo served to reinforce the disparity in military forces between the Bosnian Serb militias supported by the JNA and the Bosniaks. Complicating a resolution to the crisis, Boutros-Ghali was not in favor of a UN deployment in Bosnia. Clinton was successful, however, in obtaining his support for airdropping humanitarian supplies.

In his memoir, Clinton echoed the assessment by his envoy, Richard Holbrooke, of the failure to resolve the conflict. Another foreign service veteran of Vietnam, Holbrooke argued that the main error was the faulty assumption that "ethnic strife was too ancient and ingrained to be prevented by outsiders." The "triumph of nationalism," Holbrooke claimed, over democracy or a unitary state reinforced these flawed perceptions. Holbrooke also noted that Yugoslavia's diminished importance after the Cold War coupled with the Bush administration's reluctance to engage in another major military intervention after the Persian Gulf War compounded the problem. This was further complicated by Washington's decision to defer to its European allies, rather than NATO, and the "confused and passive European response" to the escalating violence. Clinton added that "some European leaders" were opposed to the emergence of a Muslim-majority state "fearing it might become a base for exporting extremism, a result that their neglect made more, not less, likely."[53]

Two years after taking office, Clinton split with his predecessor. The impetus was escalating violence in Bosnia, exemplified by a massacre of eight thousand Bosniak men and boys in Srebrenica and the mass rape of Bosniak women. Although the town was identified as a UN-protected "safe haven," Bosnian Serb militias intimidated the UN peacekeepers from the

Netherlands. As the massacre unfolded, a draft NSC memorandum argued that the United States had "important strategic and humanitarian interests in Bosnia." The proposed strategy advocated containing the conflict and promoting a peaceful resolution that maintained Bosnia's political independence and territorial integrity with "a reasonable division of territory among its ethnic groups." Following Srebrenica, the Clinton administration convinced NATO to adopt a more aggressive defense of the remaining UN safe areas. The combination of NATO airstrikes, Croatian and Bosnian counteroffensives against Serb forces, and a US-led diplomatic effort contributed to ending the conflict. Holbrooke and Secretary of State Christopher presided over grueling negotiations in Dayton, Ohio. The eventual agreement was a difficult pill for Bosnian President Alija Izetbegović to swallow, but he ultimately agreed under pressure from Clinton. Yet there were broader implications to the Bosnian conflict that emerged by the end of the decade.[54]

THE BASE

In late November 1989, Abdullah Yusuf Azzam was entering a mosque in Peshawar, Pakistan, when a remote-controlled car bomb killed him and his two sons. Although Azzam's death garnered very little media attention in the United States, it was an important moment in the emergence of al-Qa'ida. A Palestinian originally from the West Bank town of Jenin, Azzam had lived in Pakistan since the late 1970s. With a doctorate in Islamic law from Egypt's prestigious Al-Azhar University, Azzam first taught in Saudi Arabia and then moved to Islamabad. He was a member of Egypt's Muslim Brotherhood and played a role in the establishment of the Palestinian Islamic Resistance Movement (Hamas). After the Soviet invasion, he established an organization to assist Afghan refugees, the Office of Services (*Maktab al-Khidamat*). His activities were not, however, limited to humanitarian work. Azzam drew on his religious credentials and education to author influential works that inspired a generation of radical Islamists. He wanted to apply the example of the Afghan insurgency to the broader Muslim world, especially the secular governments of the Arab states that were home to many of the "Afghan Arabs" that Azzam helped recruit.[55]

In *Join the Caravan*, Azzam encouraged devout Muslims to liberate Afghanistan from the Soviet occupation. He emphasized that it was a religious duty to end the occupation of Muslim lands, especially Afghanistan and Palestine. Azzam's contribution to Islamist thought was in promoting the notion of a global jihad that drew on a trained and devout cadre of *mujahideen*.[56] After the Soviet withdrawal, rifts emerged over strategy between key figures and groups. Some advocated challenging secular Arab regimes first, especially Egypt's Hosni Mubarak, that they considered apostates. One of the leading proponents for this course of action was Dr. Ayman al-Zawahiri of the Egyptian Islamic Jihad (EIJ). This issue remained unresolved as the Afghan insurgency came to an end, but it reemerged a few years later.

Exactly who was responsible for Azzam's death remains unclear. By 1989, he had developed an impressive list of enemies inside and outside the Afghan insurgency. In addition to his rivals among the *mujahideen*, the intelligence services of Israel and the Soviet Union had motives for his assassination. Azzam is not the only high-profile member of the anti-Soviet coalition whose suspicious death remains unsolved. Fifteen months earlier, a plane crash killed Mohammed Zia ul-Huq, the president of Pakistan; General Abdur Akhtar Rahman, the head of Pakistan's Inter-Services Intelligence; and the US ambassador to Pakistan, Arnold Raphel. Zia and Akhtar had been central figures in the planning and implementation of the covert effort to arm and supply the Afghan insurgency. The post-crash investigation's finding of mechanical failure did not entirely dispel suspicions that the Soviet KGB had a hand in it.[57]

Azzam's death provided an opening for one of his former students, Osama bin Laden. With his ties to Saudi intelligence and the royal family and access to his family's wealth, bin Laden had been able to build training and medical facilities for the Afghan insurgency in the mid-1980s. Relations with Azzam became increasingly strained as bin Laden gravitated toward *takfiri* Islamists like Zawahiri. Rather than remaining in Afghanistan after the Soviet withdrawal, bin Laden returned to Saudi Arabia. His relationship with the Saudi royal family, however, was quickly tested by the Iraqi invasion of Kuwait.[58]

Bin Laden reportedly implored Saudi King Fahd not to rely on American forces to deter Saddam Hussein. Instead, he suggested replicating the insurgency against the Soviet Union and relying on the network of "Afghan Arab" fighters to counter an Iraqi invasion. After Fahd rejected his proposal, bin Laden's criticism of the royal family over hosting the

US-led coalition continued. Under surveillance by Saudi intelligence, bin Laden left for Sudan in 1991. Led by Omar al-Bashir, Sudan's military government seized power in a 1989 coup. After consolidating power, it became a source of support for Islamist parties and movements.[59]

Bin Laden's time in Sudan intersected with the US intervention in Somalia and the Bosnian civil war. After US forces withdrew from Somalia, reports emerged that fighters affiliated with bin Laden assisted General Aideed's forces during the Battle of Mogadishu. Meanwhile, as the violence in Bosnia escalated, the Clinton administration circumvented the UN arms embargo with an arrangement that relied on Washington's allies and foes. According to a Dutch investigation into the Srebrenica massacre, the Pentagon coordinated with Saudi Arabia, Turkey, and Iran to funnel weapons to the Bosniaks. The weapons were delivered via Iran Air flights and were funded by Riyadh.[60]

In a development reminiscent of the Afghan insurgency, Bosnia became a magnet for fighters from Muslim-majority countries. The CIA was apparently opposed to the operation, and it was conducted by the Pentagon in coordination with the Clinton White House. Estimates of the number of *mujahideen* ranged from two hundred to four thousand. Clinton later wrote that, in the summer of 1995, Bosnian Croats and Muslims in central and western Bosnia had been able to circumvent the UN arms embargo and obtain weapons. He also claimed that the United States had thwarted attempts by the *mujahideen* to "take over" postwar Bosnia. Clinton exaggerated, but there is evidence that the United States both pressured Bosnian President Izetbegović to disband the *mujahideen* militias and facilitated their departure from Bosnia. The Clinton administration was also successful in driving a wedge between Bosnia and its supporters in Iran, which had been a major source of weapons for its militias, and Hizbullah, which had assisted with their training. Reportedly, Tehran had also donated $500,000 to Izetbegović's reelection campaign. Following the Dayton Accords, such ties were limited.[61]

HIZBULLAH'S PARA-STATE

As discussed in Chapter 3, Israel's 1982 invasion of Lebanon led to the destruction of the PLO's para-state. Although Israel hoped that this would contribute to the emergence of a Maronite Christian rump state in Lebanon and extinguish the Palestinian national movement, instead it contributed to the emergence of Hizbullah. Prior to the invasion, PLO Chairman Yasir Arafat made alliances with a range of groups and individuals inside Lebanon. These relationships continued after the PLO's leadership was forced to leave Beirut. Among the key figures was Imad Mughniyeh. Mughniyeh was a member of Arafat's select bodyguard and intelligence unit, Force 17, and he was instrumental in establishing Hizbullah.[62]

The United States and Israel held Mughniyeh responsible for a number of attacks. He was implicated in the 1983 bombings of the US embassy in Beirut and the US Marine compound as well as the 1985 hijacking of Trans World Airlines Flight 847. Mughniyeh later emerged as the head of Hizbullah's military wing.[63]

Over the next decade, Hizbullah's influence inside Lebanon grew, as did its ties to the PLO. Prior to Israel's invasion, Arafat maintained a relationship with Sayyid Muhammad Hussein Fadlallah, a leading Shi'a cleric in Lebanon. By the mid-1980s, Fadlallah emerged as Hizbullah's spiritual leader. This was more than just cordial ties, as Hizbullah received arms and funding from Arafat's Fatah faction. Meanwhile, Hizbullah facilitated the reintroduction of Fatah fighters into Lebanon's Palestinian refugee camps. Hizbullah and the PLO allied against the Syria military and rival Palestinian factions and Shi'a militias. The most prominent was Amal (Arabic for hope), which sought to prevent the PLO from reestablishing a presence in Lebanon. With support from Damascus, Amal's militia besieged the major Palestinian refugee camps around Beirut and in southern Lebanon. Hizbullah helped the PLO counter Amal's forces and brought the "War of the Camps" to an end.[64]

Joint PLO-Hizbullah operations were also directed against the Israeli forces occupying southern Lebanon. Israel's six-kilometer "security zone" in southern Lebanon dated to 1978. It was reinforced after the 1982 invasion and maintained by Israel's proxy force, the South Lebanon Army (SLA). Israeli forces and the SLA patrolled the villages within the zone, which was frequently attacked by Hizbullah and Palestinian guerrillas. The sweeps served to harden attitudes and further bolstered Hizbullah's recruitment. Hizbullah drew on funding from Iran and a network of expatriate supporters to implement public works projects in southern Lebanon. This included rebuilding houses destroyed by Israeli raids, improving roads, providing scholarships to Shi'a students, and establishing social

welfare organizations for residents of an area that was historically neglected by the Lebanese state. Meanwhile, Hizbullah expanded its military infrastructure, including training centers, underground bases, and
tunnels. By the late 1980s, Hizbullah expanded its base of support, largely
at Amal's expense.[65]

Israel's security zone proved difficult to maintain. Israel was unwilling
to abandon the zone or the SLA, however, or to launch another full-scale
invasion. Instead, it maintained an occupation that generated additional
support for Hizbullah. Although Washington and Israel believed Amal
was more moderate than Hizbullah, neither was willing to negotiate with
Israel. Even though the PLO was eager to engage in talks, the United
States and Israel continued to reject it as a negotiating partner.[66]

By late 1987, however, Israel's occupation of the West Bank and Gaza
appeared to be increasingly untenable. The outbreak of the first Palestinian *intifada* (or "uprising") challenged Israel's claims that its occupation
was benign. Exiled in Tunisia, the PLO's leadership sought to exert control over the daily management of the *intifada* while also benefiting from
the international criticism of Israel. As the Reagan administration was
preparing to leave office, Arafat and the PLO finally acceded to American
and Israeli demands that it accept UNSC Resolution 242 and Israel's right
to exist. In return, the PLO and the United States established diplomatic
relations, but at a far lower level than Arafat hoped. The *intifada* persisted
for the next four years, but Arafat and the PLO were increasingly diminished by regional and international events from the end of the Cold War
to the Persian Gulf War. Yet the Bush administration and Israel were unable to completely marginalize the PLO from negotiations sponsored by
Washington after the Persian Gulf War. Although the PLO was not invited to participate in the Madrid conference or subsequent negotiations,
the Palestinian negotiators were members of the organization and did not
hide that they were unable to make any major decisions without Arafat's
approval.[67]

Israel's occupation of southern Lebanon and the West Bank and Gaza
intersected with long-term implications. In the midst of the Bush-Clinton
transition, Israel expelled over four hundred members of Hamas and
Palestinian Islamic Jihad into southern Lebanon. Over the previous five
years, Israel had tried in various ways to crush the Palestinian *intifada*.
Although the uprising was lagging in late 1992, the expulsion of such a

large number of Palestinians brought additional international opprobrium, along with criticism within Israel.[68]

Hamas began as the Palestinian branch of the Muslim Brotherhood and it emerged in Gaza in the mid-1980s. Israel was initially more tolerant of Hamas, hoping that it would be an alternative to the secular PLO. Although Hamas was less popular than the PLO, the first Palestinian *intifada* and the subsequent Oslo Accords served to increase the movement's support in the West Bank and Gaza. Among those expelled by Israel were Hamas leaders Abd al-Aziz al-Rantisi and Mahmud al-Zahar. They found assistance both from Hizbullah and from Hamas and Islamic Jihad members based in Lebanon. As part of a negotiated agreement, roughly half of the deportees, including Rantisi and Zahar, were allowed to return to the occupied Palestinian territories. As Chapter 5 will show, the coordination between Hamas and Hizbullah, and their joint support by Iran, were among the unintended consequences of the expulsion.[69]

Less than nine months after the expulsion, there was a breakthrough. With Norway's assistance, Israel and the PLO agreed to a limited autonomy agreement for parts of the Gaza Strip and the West Bank city of Jericho. After the initial declaration of principles was signed in a White House ceremony overseen by President Clinton, the Palestinian National Authority was established to implement the Oslo Accords. The interim agreement included confidence-building measures and was only to last for five years until final status negotiations were concluded. Hamas's influence grew as the negotiations stalled and the occupied Palestinian territories became enmeshed in the Global War on Terror.[70]

CONSTRUCTING CRIME

Throughout the 1992 presidential campaign, Arkansas Governor Bill Clinton claimed he was a "New Democrat." Clinton sought to distinguish his record from previous Democratic aspirants whose campaigns faltered on the issues of crime and national security. Clinton's campaign was initially hamstrung by revelations of chronic infidelities, his failure to serve in Vietnam, and an absurd admission by denial of prior marijuana party use. Yet the combination of a weak economy, a vibrant third-party candidate in business executive Ross Perot, and President Bush's clumsy reelection campaign was sufficient to secure an election victory. To demonstrate that he would be tough on crime, Clinton carried out the execution of two Arkansas death row prisoners during the campaign, one of whom was mentally challenged. Having opposed the death penalty early in his political career, Clinton abandoned that stance on the road to the White House.[71]

Clinton continued Bush's War on Drugs and it became integral to US domestic and foreign policies. In November 1993, Clinton approved Presidential Decision Directive (PDD) 14, which addressed narcotics trafficking in the Western Hemisphere. PDD 14 stated that Washington considered international criminal narcotics syndicates a "serious national security threat" that required "an extraordinary and coordinated response" by civilian and military agencies. It asserted that the United States would act unilaterally and with other nations to implement an international strategy to address narcotics trafficking. While maintaining the United States' existing interdiction policy, PDD 14 emphasized destroying narcotics organizations and assisting producing nations' efforts to establish and enhance institutions to combat trafficking. As the foundation of the Clinton administration's approach over the next seven years, PDD 14 was the basis on which subsequent directives addressed organized crime, heroin, human trafficking, and terrorism.[72]

Later that month, Democratic Senator Joe Biden of Delaware spoke in support of a bill he crafted. "We must take back the streets," Biden declared. The Violent Crime Control and Law Enforcement Act ("Crime Bill") was presented as a response to a dramatic increase in crime. This was accompanied by a deluge of media coverage over the previous two years on crime-related issues. According to the Vera Institute, media coverage of crime doubled from 1992 to 1993. Although the FBI's Uniform Crime Report (UCR) found that the violent crime rate in the United States reached a thirty-year high of 758.2 per 100,000 persons in 1991 (757.2 in 1992), questions about the accuracy of the FBI data persisted. In comparison to the UCR, the National Crime Victimization Survey (NCVS) revealed crime rates were significantly lower. Although both increased by the early 1990s, they revealed a consistent difference between total crimes and violent crimes. While total crimes increased sharply over two decades, violent crimes remained steady, with slight increases from 1985 to 1993. When President Clinton signed the Crime Bill in September 1994, crime was already declining and continued to decrease for almost a decade.[73]

While the Crime Bill had only marginal impact on reducing actual crime, its effects on minority communities were profound. On top of its more severe penalties for drug-related convictions, the new legislation set mandatory minimum sentences and increased the time served. The federal death penalty was expanded to include sixty new offenses, such as "terrorist homicides" and "large-scale drug trafficking." It also adopted the "three strikes" mandatory life sentences for federal offenders, applied to individuals convicted of three or more violent felonies or drug trafficking convictions. To accommodate the harsher sentences, the bill also incentivized the building of prisons at the state and local levels. The final bill slashed proposed funding for prevention programs.[74]

By 2014, two decades after the Crime Bill's passage, the federal prison population increased by 125 percent.[75] Less pronounced, but still significant, was the 45 percent increase in state prison populations during this period. A 2015 study found that, after controlling for variables, "increased incarceration had a minimal effect on reducing property crime in the 1990s and no effect on violent crime." Nevertheless, by 2018, over 1.3 million inmates were incarcerated in state prisons, with 718,000 held for violent offenses and 200,000 for drug-related felonies.[76]

On the morning of April 19, 1995, a massive blast destroyed the front of the Alfred P. Murrah Federal Building in Oklahoma City. The explosion originated from a 4,800-pound bomb in a rental truck parked near the building's entrance. One hundred sixty-eight people were killed and over five hundred were injured. Among the dead were nineteen children who were in a second-floor day care center, which was crushed by the blast. Initial suspicion and speculation focused on three "Middle Eastern looking" men that were observed leaving the scene. The assumed connection to the Middle East was reinforced by the news media, with some commentators stating that the scene looked like Beirut. Meanwhile, Secretary of Defense William Perry suggested the attack might have been orchestrated by Iran or an organization based in the Middle East. The claims were abandoned, however, as authorities quickly arrested and charged Timothy McVeigh, a US Army veteran who had served with distinction in the First Persian Gulf War.[77]

McVeigh and his accomplice, Terry Nichols, clearly espoused anti-government and white supremacist opinions. Yet the legislation that was passed in the wake of Oklahoma City focused on the initial rumors and speculation, rather than the actual perpetrators. The Antiterrorism and Effective Death Penalty Act (AEDPA) and the Illegal Immigration and Reform and Immigrant Responsibility Act, both passed in 1996, did not target right-wing hate groups. Rather, their emphasis was on international terrorism.

The impetus for the two acts was not in Oklahoma City or the 1993 World Trade Center bombing. Rather, it was in the contentious politics of the mid-1990s. Five months before the Oklahoma City attack, Republicans swept the 1994 midterm elections. In control of the House and Senate, the Republican Party was determined to undermine the Clinton presidency. Among the targets was the 1994 Crime Bill. In response, Ron Klain, then chief of staff to Attorney General Janet Reno, proposed that Clinton adopt a more aggressive response on crime. Klain had previously served as chief counsel of the Senate Judiciary Committee, when it was chaired by Biden, and had been Clinton's main advisor on criminal justice issues, including the Crime Bill. Aspects of Klain's proposal were incorporated into the AEDPA.[78]

Two months after the Oklahoma City bombing, Clinton approved a policy on counterterrorism. PDD 39 addressed domestic and international terrorism as a "potential threat to national security as well as a criminal act." Not limited to minimizing the impact of terrorism, the directive focused on deterring terrorist acts, including state-sponsored attacks. To this end, it emphasized the extradition of indicted terrorists to the United States, which was already practiced with narcotics traffickers.[79]

Clinton seized the opportunity to recapture the winning issues of crime and national security from the Republican Party. Nixon's law-and-order stance was adopted by a Democrat, and the public debate on crime was transformed into anti-terrorism legislation. Although Clinton faced opposition from his own party, he was able to muffle a key Republican political talking point in the 1996 election season. Initial proposals were to extend the FBI's surveillance powers and expand the range of criminal charges subject to the death penalty. Clinton asserted that the efforts were to "strengthen law enforcement and sharpen their ability to crack down on terrorists, wherever they're from, be it at home or abroad."[80] The eventual legislation had a greater impact on crime, however, than on domestic or international terrorism. In his signing statement accompanying the

AEDPA, Clinton lamented that Congress was unwilling to grant the FBI greater investigative authority.[81]

Clinton also criticized the AEDPA's changes to immigration law as "ill-advised" and "having nothing to do with fighting terrorism." Only a few months after the bill was signed, the law was used to target resident immigrants who had been previously convicted of a crime, including some misdemeanors and minor drug possessions. While the administration and allies in Congress attempted to mitigate the damage of the AEDPA to immigrants, it further demonstrated the use of antiterrorism legislation to achieve other political goals. This became more pronounced after September 11.[82]

Six months after the Oklahoma City bombing, Clinton continued the emphasis on crime and terrorism domestically and internationally. Building on previous directives, PDD 42 targeted international organized crime. The directive placed organized crime within the broader context of post–Cold War globalization, asserting that "the scale and extent of international organized criminal activities has become complex, global and threatening." Money transfers, human and narcotics trafficking, and weapons sales now happened on a much larger scale. Like previous directives, PDD 42 declared that this was a national security threat as well as a law enforcement problem. Despite the general language of the directive, its specific actions were focused on Colombia.[83]

FROM MEDELLIN TO PLAN COLOMBIA

Pablo Escobar's death in 1993 and the dismantling of the Medellin Cartel did not end cocaine trafficking. Indeed, it made efforts to disrupt drug trafficking *more* difficult. Yet the Clinton administration continued to expand its efforts. In October 1995, Clinton signed Executive Order 12978, which identified narcotics traffickers in Colombia as "an unusual and extraordinary threat to the national security, foreign policy, and economy of the United States." EO 12978 declared a national emergency and applied the International Emergency Economic Powers Act (IEEPA) to the leaders of the Cali Cartel. Even though the rivals to Escobar's organization were less brazen about their activities, they were not immune to the politics of the War on Drugs. Invoking the IEEPA allowed for the seizure of the property and assets of Gilberto Rodriguez Orejuela, Miguel Angel Rodriguez

Orejuela, José Santacruz Londono, and Helmer Herrera Buitragoto. A
month later, Clinton authorized PDD 42 for organized crime, and PDD
44 for heroin control. Like the directive on organized crime, PDD 42 had
an international focus, linking heroin production and trafficking from
East Asia to South America. It approved a cooperative effort to reduce
heroin production in Burma and Afghanistan while continuing support
for counternarcotics efforts in Colombia and Mexico.[84]

By the end of Clinton's presidency, the Cali Cartel's core leaders were
either imprisoned or dead. Predictably, even after the Medellin and Cali
Cartels were destroyed, coca cultivation increased throughout the 1990s.
In 1994, the year after Pablo Escobar was killed, coca cultivation accounted for 44,700 hectares. When Plan Colombia was launched in 2000,
it had increased to 163,300 hectares. The DEA's 1994 Intelligence Report
on the Cali Cartel offers one explanation for this failure. It describes the
group as "a loose association of five major, independent drug trafficking
organizations." As the Medellin and Cali organizations were successfully
targeted, their remnants (as well as other suppliers) shifted strategies. They
began selling cocaine wholesale to Mexican drug organizations that were
responsible for transporting it to the United States. Even though cocaine
trafficking persisted, Clinton later wrote that the effort against the Cali
Cartel yielded a benefit, as the IEEPA was used to target bin Laden and
al-Qaʻida.[85]

The DEA applied a label and logic to the Mexican drug trafficking organizations similar to those in Colombia. "Cartels were shorthand, a convenient fiction," writes Benjamin Smith. "They gave a name to what was a
fluid, amorphous, and (though they dared not say it) unbeatable market-
place ecosystem." The term *cartel* was deliberately reminiscent of another
public villain of the 1970s and 1980s: the Organization of the Petroleum
Exporting Countries. But the similarities ended there. Colombian cocaine
producers sold to large and small groups of Mexican smugglers and the
DEA attempted to organize them into larger organizations with a rigid hi-
erarchy. But the cartel label obscured more than it revealed—in particular,
the power of the Mexican state that allowed these organizations to exist.[86]

Another unintended consequence of targeting the Medellin Cartel was
the bolstering of right-wing paramilitary groups. The most prominent was
led by the Castaño brothers, which maintained ties to the Colombian

military and government. Although they previously had ties to the Me-
dellin Cartel, the Castaño brothers (Fidel, Carlos and Vicente) broke with
Escobar in 1989. Their militia, nicknamed "Los Pepes" (or *Perseguidos Por
Pablo Escobar*, People Persecuted by Pablo Escobar), embarked on a cam-
paign against the Medellin Cartel with active support from Bogota and
Washington.[87]

Three years after Escobar's death, the United Self Defense Forces of Colombia (AUC) emerged as the most feared right-wing paramilitary group.
Drawn from the combined forces of Escobar's former enforcers and the
Castaño family militia, the AUC's main source of revenue was drug trafficking. In coordination with elements of the Colombian military and security services, the AUC began targeting leftist rebel groups, including
the Revolutionary Armed Forces of Colombia (FARC) and the National
Liberation Army.[88]

By 1998, Clinton was wounded by a sex scandal and the threat of im-
peachment hearings. Congressional Republicans attempted to regain the
initiative on crime policy by criticizing the Clinton administration on
drugs. This was compounded by the Democratic Party's internal polling,
which found a perception that drug use was on the rise and Democrats
were to blame. Yet *Newsweek* later reported that the poll was commis-
sioned by military contractor Lockheed Martin, which produced the P-3
radar planes used to monitor narcotics trafficking, Lockheed Martin had
encountered opposition from congressional Democrats to future purchases. A majority of those polled also supported $2 billion in additional
funding for tracking planes in drug cultivation areas.[89]

Plan Colombia's origins were in Washington and Bogota. Although official US government reports found that drug use was static or decreasing,
the Clinton administration began developing Plan Colombia in 1998.
Washington had a willing partner in Colombia's new president, Andrés
Pastrana. R. Rand Beers, director of the State Department's Bureau of International Narcotics and Law Enforcement Affairs, told the press the goal
was to "eliminate Colombian cocaine and heroin from American streets
in several years"—quickly adding that, "by several, I mean three." When
the new strategy was announced, Colombia was responsible for almost 80
percent of the cocaine in the United States. To achieve its ambitious goal,
the administration requested a mere $21 million in aid.[90]

Both Democrats and Republicans criticized the new plan, but it only expanded in size and scope. General Barry McCaffery, director of the Office of National Drug Control Policy, and General Charles E. Wilhelm, commander in chief of the United States Southern Command, convinced the Pastrana administration of the need for a combined counterinsurgency and counternarcotics effort. Prior to serving as "Drug Czar," McCaffery had also led Southern Command, as Wilhelm's predecessor, and his military recommendations carried considerable weight in Washington and Bogota. In a shift from earlier in the decade, however, the cartels were no longer the focus. Instead, the primary target was the FARC.[91]

FARCLANDIA

By the end of the 1990s, the FARC was the oldest insurgent group in Latin America. Founded in 1964, it had started out as a Marxist-Leninist organization with ties to Havana and Moscow, then survived the post–Cold War reconciliations that swept the region. With twelve thousand to fifteen thousand fighters, it relied on narcotics trafficking, abductions, and extortion to fund its operations. In Putumayo, a department in southern Colombia bordering Ecuador and Peru and roughly the size of Switzerland, it also controlled a large swath of territory that the Colombian military derisively called "Farclandia." Sparsely populated, the region accounted for roughly half the land used for coca cultivaton in Colombia. As in other para-states, the FARC had set up its own de facto area of control, militia, systems of justice, trade and taxation, political organs, and diplomatic relations with other movements and states.[92]

The Clinton administration quickly escalated efforts in Colombia. Within two years, Washington increased its military aid to Bogota from less than $100 million per year to $1.3 billion. In addition to selling Black Hawk helicopters to Bogota, Plan Colombia emphasized military and intelligence coordination, training, and equipment. For its part, Bogota announced a $7.5 billion effort over six years to eliminate coca and encourage the cultivation of alternative crops. Of this amount, $3 billion was to be raised from the international community. Another $40 million was designated for Putumayo, plus $150 million for the "Routes for Peace" infrastructure project to link three southern cities. Plan Colombia, however, met with local skepticism, encountered resistance from the FARC, and generated concern around the region.[93]

MAP 8. COLOMBIA AND THE FARC

Skepticism about Plan Colombia was warranted. The new policy was rooted in the domestic politics of both nations. President Pastrana embarked on a renewed peace process with both the FARC and the smaller National Liberation Army. He encountered opposition, however, from US Republicans and Colombian right-wing paramilitaries, and suspicion from the FARC. During the 1980s, right-wing paramilitary groups actively targeted politicians aligned with the FARC and the Union Patriotica party from participating in Colombian politics. A decade later, Pastrana's renewed peace process was undermined by the FARC's abduction and murder of three Americans, among other attacks. Under pressure from Republicans, the US State Department abandoned support for Pastrana's negotiations. Instead, Washington favored a military solution over difficult negotiations. The emphasis on military aid was intended to force concessions from the FARC at the negotiating table. Washington was convinced that a larger and more effective Colombian military would either dictate terms to the FARC or impose a victory should the peace process fail.[94] Reminiscent of American hubris in Vietnam, this continued as a recurring theme across regions and conflicts in the post–Cold War era.

The Clinton administration's embrace of Plan Colombia was also driven by domestic politics in a presidential election year. *Washington Post* columnist Jim Hoagland warned that Plan Colombia would not defeat drug trafficking or use. Instead, it fostered "the illusion that Washington is coping with an intractable social and criminal problem at home that shows no sign of going away." *New York Times* columnist Anthony Lewis warned that the United States had "no convincing strategy with no end in sight." Unless demand was reduced, he argued, there would always be a ready supply and large profits to be made. Domestic politics, however, overwhelmed logic.[95]

Bernard Aronson, former assistant secretary of state for inter-American affairs, raised similar concerns. Writing in the *Washington Post*, Aronson claimed that the new Colombia policy was influenced by election year politics in the United States. He linked negotiations with the FARC to conflicts in the Middle East, Latin America, and Northern Ireland. Washington needed to "find a formula to talk with the Colombian guerrillas, and a cease-fire in our domestic political wars would make that possible," Aronson wrote. But the detractors were ignored and Plan Colombia was eventually transformed from counternarcotics to counterterrorism.[96]

STRIKING THE FAR ENEMY

Less than three years after the Dayton Accords ended the Bosnian conflict, a new crisis emerged in the Kosovo province. During the Bosnian conflict, tensions had arisen between Kosovo's ethnic Albanians and Serbs, which had continued after the agreement was implemented. Kosovo was excluded from the Dayton Accords and the Clinton administration was determined not to repeat the mistakes that contributed to the bloody conflict in Bosnia. Hoping for a diplomatic resolution, Washington engaged in direct negotiations with Serbian President Slobodan Milošević while also applying pressure through the UN Security Council. By March 1999, Washington was leading a NATO intervention, ostensibly to prevent a humanitarian crisis. As National Security Advisor Sandy Berger would later put it, Clinton was "not going to watch a million Kosovars being expelled from Kosovo by the Serbs so that the last act of the twentieth century would be an act of ethnic cleansing."[97]

In the ensuing conflict, the United States relied on airpower and the threat of a large ground assault. Behind the scenes, Clinton engaged in diplomacy with Russia. Although Clinton's approach had detractors, they were ultimately silenced when it succeeded. Presented as a humanitarian intervention, the Kosovo conflict established a precedent for the United States' later invasions in Iraq and Libya. Predator drones also made their first appearance, as they were first deployed in Kosovo with limited effectiveness—and then put to greater use over the next decade.[98]

In contrast to the very public war in Kosovo, a secret conflict was brewing in Afghanistan. Exiled in Afghanistan, bin Laden made two separate but related announcements threatening to kill Americans. Neither bin Laden nor al-Qaʿida, however, was a household name yet. Indeed, bin Laden's now infamous 1998 *fatwa* (religious decree) received minimal coverage in the mainstream press. The *Washington Post* reported that, even though this was the first religious decree sanctioning the killing of American civilians, US intelligence analysts questioned the religious credentials of the group issuing the *fatwa*. Not discussed in the media reports at the time was that the decree represented a new strategy adopted by bin Laden and the "World Islamic Front," which represented a union between al-Qaʿida and the EIJ. The strategy was to target the United States first (the "far enemy") to bring down the "near enemy" of Arab regimes supported by Washington.[99]

A few months after the *fatwa* was issued, *ABC News* reporter John Miller traveled to Afghanistan to interview bin Laden. In the interview, bin Laden repeated aspects of the decree threatening American citizens. He also warned that action would be taken against Americans in the Persian Gulf region in the next few weeks. Although the timing was accurate, the attack was not in the Gulf.[100]

On August 7, 1998, nearly simultaneous explosions occurred eight hundred kilometers apart in Kenya and Tanzania. The targets were the US embassies in Nairobi and Dar es Salaam. Over two hundred people were killed and thousands were injured as the areas around the buildings were heavily damaged. Discussing the attacks, Clinton described bin Laden as "eerily like the fictional villains in James Bond movies." He said bin Laden was "a transnational presence suspended above allegiance to any government, with enormous private wealth and a network of operatives in many countries, including our own."[101]

The twin embassy bombings led to an immediate response from the Clinton White House. On August 20, Clinton signed Executive Order 13099. EO 13099 drew on the experience with the Cali Cartel and applied the IEEPA to bin Laden, two of his lieutenants, and al-Qaʻida as an organization. It did not, however, specifically reference the embassy bombings. Instead, the EO focused on the Middle East peace process and built on a 1995 executive order that had targeted several Palestinian factions. These included the leftist Popular Front for the Liberation of Palestine, Hamas, and Palestinian Islamic Jihad. Two right-wing Israeli organizations were also named, as was Lebanon's Hizbullah. To go along with the new EO, Clinton authorized missile strikes against a pharmaceutical plant in Sudan and al-Qaʻida bases and camps in Afghanistan—which turned out to be empty when the missiles hit. When the owners of the pharmaceutical plant denied any connection to al-Qaʻida, the Clinton administration had difficulty explaining the attack to journalists.[102]

To add to the complicated situation, Clinton was mired in a sex scandal that consumed the latter part of his presidency. Skeptical journalists and commentators likened the missile attack to the 1997 political comedy *Wag the Dog*, directed by Barry Levinson. The film chronicles a manufactured international crisis to distract from a scandal engulfing the White House. Secretary of State Madeline Albright later recalled that "people thought that Clinton had made it all up, the wag-the-dog part. So rather than being critical of us for not doing enough, people thought we were using too much force. Somalia had a lot to do with that." Although there was some criticism from Congress over the missile strikes, National Security Advisor Berger kept the House and Senate leadership informed of the administration's deliberations and rationale. The CIA continued its attempts to capture or kill bin Laden over the next two years, but without success. Meanwhile, al-Qaʿida was on the offensive.[103]

Algeria's civil war in the mid-1990s contributed to al-Qaʿida's growth. In December 1991, the Islamic Salvation Front (ISF) won a near majority in the country's first freely contested National Assembly elections. A month later, the Algerian military canceled the runoff elections, arrested the ISF's acting president, Abdelkadir Hachani, and jailed journalists from a newspaper that had published ISF communiques. It also banned public assemblies near mosques. The military crackdown on the ISF (and opposition more broadly) had escalated into open fighting by the end of the year. The armed insurgency numbered some twenty-five thousand fighters, with one of the main groups being the Groupe Islamique Armé (GIA). Over the next four years, Algeria was the site of horrific violence committed by state security services and opposition groups. Although the Bush administration rebuked the Algerian military over canceling the elections, the criticism was muted as Washington and Paris offered Algiers support during the civil war. The GIA sought assistance from broader Islamist movements and networks and there were some indications that it developed ties to al-Qaʿida. In sharp contrast to Algeria's inspirational role to national liberation movements across the developing world in the 1960s, it became a cautionary tale of the post–Cold War era. In December 1999, the broader implications of Algeria's civil war were apparent when a planned attack on the Los Angeles International Airport by a former GIA member affiliated with al-Qaʿida was thwarted.[104]

Ten months later, a small, explosive-laden boat piloted by two al-Qaʿida suicide bombers struck the USS *Cole* in the harbor at Aden, Yemen, where it had stopped for refueling. The attack severely damaged the ship, killing seventeen sailors and wounding thirty more. The fact that the 2000 presidential election was less than a month away might explain why Clinton was reluctant to respond. There was also a disagreement between the intelligence community and the military, both about bin Laden's involvement in the *Cole* attack and regarding the appropriate response.[105]

As Clinton's presidency drew to a close, there were two related attempts to capture bin Laden. The first involved the CIA coordinating with forces led by Ahmed Shah Massoud. Massoud was a famed former commander of the anti-Soviet insurgency and served as Defense Minister of Afghanistan after the Soviet withdrawal and the unity government established by the 1992 Peshawar Accords. By 1998, however, Massoud was part of the Northern Alliance, whose rule of Afghanistan was limited to roughly twenty percent of the country. The CIA reportedly began coordinating with Massoud on a plan to capture bin Laden. It would, however, be abandoned by late 2000.

A separate initiative involved negotiations with the Taliban. The Taliban ("students") emerged in the early 1990s with support from Pakistan's Inter-Services Intelligence. The group consisted of soldiers drawn from the Afghan refugee population and several former commanders of the anti-Soviet insurgency. For Islamabad, the Taliban helped ensure some stability in its western neighbor after it was racked by civil war when the 1992 Peshawar Accords collapsed. The Taliban routed or coopted the competing warlords that had divided Afghanistan. By 2000, the Taliban government controlled roughly 80 percent of Afghanistan, holding the country's five largest cities and its vital east and west border crossings. The Taliban's Islamic Emirate of Afghanistan was also recognized by Saudi Arabia, the United Arab Emirates, and Pakistan. Islamabad and Riyadh attempted to broker relations between the Taliban and Washington. One area of potential collaboration was a proposed oil pipeline from Turkmenistan through Afghanistan to Pakistan. Although Unocal (later acquired by Chevron) had the rights to the pipeline, the contracts were signed with the warlords deposed by the Taliban. Washington was in favor of the pipeline, but bin Laden's presence in Afghanistan and the embassy attacks were the main impediments to a resolution.[106]

The Clinton administration attempted to a broker an agreement with the Taliban through allies and unlikely envoys. After discussions with Pakistan and Saudi Arabia failed to yield the desired results, the State Department turned to a former member of the *mujahideen* residing in Texas. Kabir Mohabbat had maintained contacts with the Taliban and the Northern Alliance after coming to America, and was able to initiate, before the September 2000 attack on the USS *Cole,* a negotiation with Taliban leaders about surrendering bin Laden. Mohabbat stressed in these negotiations, which included American officials, that the United States would depose the Taliban to capture bin Laden. According to Mohabbat's memoir, the Taliban agreed to turn over the Saudi exile and even suggested they could provide his exact location to assist an American cruise missile strike or special forces raid. The deal was not finalized, however, before Clinton left office in 2001. In the months leading up to September 11, the incoming George W. Bush administration did not prioritize its completion.[107]

CONCLUSION

"The West's victory in the Cold War has not produced triumph but exhaustion," Samuel Huntington wrote five years after the Soviet Union's collapse. Initially published in *Foreign Affairs* in 1993, Huntington's "Clash of Civilizations" article argued that the end of the Cold War would not translate into perpetual peace. In the book-length treatment of his thesis, Huntington warns of Western decline through a "clash" both external and internal to the United States. He predicts that the immigration of Muslims to Western Europe and Latinos to the United States will contribute to internal cleavages and strife. "In the clash of civilizations," Huntington writes, "Europe and America will hang together or hang separately." He extends this claim to the "greater clash, the global 'real clash,' between Civilization and barbarism." Huntington argues that the "world's great civilizations" will "also hang together or separately." Despite its flaws and detractors, Huntington's thesis found influential adherents in academia and the national security establishment. And after September 11, its arguments, not nuanced to begin with, were simplified even further. Proponents of the argument saw the book as a seminal guide to understanding the changing world order, clarifying that America was not just engaged in a Global War on Terror but in a War for Civilization itself. On the other side was barbarism and the badlands.[108]

Huntington was correct that the end of the Cold War did not lead to peace at home or abroad. Instead, President George H. W. Bush's administration attempted to amplify the policies of his predecessor with an even more aggressive War on Drugs that had implications for domestic law enforcement and the judicial system. In the wake of the Persian Gulf War, the Bush administration also sought to ensure American primacy into the next century. Yet neither policy was truly successful. Although the United States remained the world's strongest political, economic, and military power this did not translate into uncontested authority. Instead, conflicts in East Africa, the Middle East, and Southeastern Europe tested Washington's resolve, as did the inability to stem drug trafficking through interdiction

and eradication. At home, the acquittal of four Los Angeles police officers
in the highly publicized beating of motorist Rodney King and subsequent
riots exposed decades of police brutality, systemic neglect of American
cities, and increased racial tensions. These challenges and frustrations
were depicted as symptoms of American decline in the face of a shifting
world order.

Although Bill Clinton promised a new beginning, he maintained and
expanded the policies of the Reagan and Bush administrations. Clinton
embraced American hegemony and continued the War on Drugs throughout his presidency. He signed a draconian Crime Bill that had long-term
implications for the incarceration of minorities in the United States. But
the ghosts of Vietnam lingered in Somalia, Bosnia, Kosovo, and Rwanda.
Although Clinton was criticized after September 11 for the failure to kill
or capture bin Laden, the policies he authorized influenced future US
counterterrorism programs.

CHAPTER FIVE

Constructing Global Terrorism and the Long War for Civilization

We wage a war to save civilization itself. We did not seek it, but we will fight it, and we will prevail. This is a different war from any our Nation has ever faced, a war on many fronts, against terrorists who operate in more than 60 different countries. And this is a war that must be fought not only overseas but also here at home.

—PRESIDENT GEORGE W. BUSH, 2001

STANDING ON TOP OF a damaged fire engine, President George W. Bush addressed a crowd of rescue workers through a bullhorn. "I want you all to know that America today is on bended knee," he said, with one arm draped around retired firefighter Bob Beckwith, "in prayer for the people whose lives were lost here, for the workers who work here, for the families who mourn." It was only three days after the shocking September 11 attacks, and the smoldering fires in the remains of the World Trade Center still permeated the air with smoke. Towering cranes and the shattered skeletons of the buildings provided a sobering backdrop to Bush's impromptu speech. After a member of the crowd shouted that they couldn't hear him, Bush responded, "I can hear *you*! . . . The rest of the world hears you, and the people who knocked these buildings down will hear all of us soon."[1]

Bush's bravado in the "Bullhorn Speech," meant to bolster a shaken nation, became the administration's prevailing ethos. This chapter argues that the Bush administration promoted a militarized foreign policy that created and entrenched even more instability around the globe. Like the Wars on Crime and Drugs, the Global War on Terror was presented as a fight for civilization at home and abroad. Foreign and domestic policies were linked and these conflicts converged. By the end of the Bush presidency, the combination of the global financial collapse, an insurgency in Afghanistan, and simmering conflict in Iraq contributed to existential angst and perceptions of American decline.[2]

AUTHORIZING PERPETUAL FORCE

Two days after September 11, a *New York Times* front page article was headlined "No Middle Ground." It offered a preview of the Bush administration's new policy declaring there were "no neutral states and no clear geographical confines." The administration, it reported, planned a lengthy campaign that involved targeting governments as well as nonstate actors. The guiding principle was simple: "You must choose sides. Us or them. You are either with us or against us." A week later, President Bush used similar language in presenting the early version of his doctrine to the nation and the world.[3]

Meanwhile, both houses of Congress authorized the use of military force. The resolution's language was sweeping and in subsequent years the Bush administration and its successors interpreted it even more broadly. The Senate voted 98–0 in favor of the resolution and there was a lone dissenter in the House, California Democrat Barbara Lee. Lee warned that the resolution was a "blank check" for interventions on a global scale. Derided at the time, she was proven correct.[4]

Negotiations with the Taliban leadership continued through several channels. Although the Taliban publicly demanded evidence of bin Laden's involvement in the September 11 attacks, privately they were willing to surrender him without conditions. On October 7, the United States commenced military action. President Bush rejected the Taliban's offer to surrender bin Laden to a third country if the United States halted its air campaign. The US invasion displaced the Taliban from power, but Mullah Mohammad Omar and most of the Taliban's core leadership escaped, as did bin Laden and Ayman al-Zawahiri. Within a year, the Taliban launched an insurgency that challenged the American-led coalition and newly established Afghan security forces.[5]

In developing a strategy for Afghanistan, Secretary of Defense Donald Rumsfeld argued that the US effort must be fully integrated to achieve its goals. The draft strategy discussed with Douglas Feith, Under Secretary of Defense for Policy, was prepared as the invasion of Afghanistan was already underway in October 2001. The goals combined the immediate tasks for the US invasion and occupation with overt demonstrations of American power. They embodied Bush's reliance on unilateralism if necessary. Meeting with his national security team at Camp David after the September 11 attacks, Bush put it bluntly: "At some point we may be the only ones left. That's okay with me. We are American."[6]

As a result, the goals for Afghanistan were overly ambitious and proved difficult to achieve. This mistake was repeated in Iraq. Rumsfeld wrote that, in addition to eliminating al-Qaʿida's leadership and fighters, the United States must deal with the group "in a manner that clearly signals to the rest of the world that terrorists and terrorism will be punished [*handwritten addition*: and stopped]." Demonstrating to the world that "harboring terrorism will be punished severely" also meant terminating the Taliban's rule, since "making an example of the Taliban increases US leverage on other state supporters of terrorism." Yet Rumsfeld noted that "the US should not commit to any post-Taliban military involvement since the US will be heavily engaged in the anti-terrorism effort worldwide." In another handwritten note on the draft, he added the caveat that "the US needs to be involved in this effort to assure that our coalition partners are not disaffected."[7]

Feith's reply revealed the fundamental miscalculations that haunted the next two decades. Washington, he wrote, "should not allow concerns about stability to paralyze US efforts to oust the Taliban leadership. . . . Nation-building is *not* our strategic goal." Only six months later, Rumsfeld conceded that the approach was flawed: "We are never going to get the US military out of Afghanistan unless we take care to see that there is something going on that will provide the stability that will be necessary for us to leave."[8]

Bush signed an executive order to accompany the authorization of military force. The EO authorized lethal force against al-Qaʿida and was followed by National Security Presidential Directive (NSPD) 9. Approved on October 25, 2001, NSPD 9 stated that the United States sought to "eliminate terrorism as a threat to our way of life and to all nations that love freedom, including the elimination of all terrorist organizations, networks, finances, and their access to [weapons of mass destruction]." In addition to al-Qaʻida, NSPD 9 asserted that part of the United States' overall strategy was to "eliminate the threat from other terrorist groups that attack Americans or American interests." At the time of the September 11 attacks, al-Qaʻida had fewer than a thousand core members. The directive cast a wide net on targeted groups and identified those that affiliated with al-Qaʻida like the Egyptian Islamic Jihad as well as those that did not, like Lebanon's Hizbullah and Hamas in the occupied Palestinian territories. NSPD 9 authorized the adoption of a "comprehensive approach employing all instruments of national power and influence in a coordinated manner for a sustained national campaign against terrorism." It committed the United States to acting in concert or alone to achieve these objectives. But the expansive approach undermined the United States' efforts globally. It was compounded by the assertion that terrorism was an ideology, rather than a strategy. This allowed for a similarly sweeping association of nationalist and Islamist political groups whose only relationship with al-Qaʻida was shared tactics of political violence and terrorism.[9]

In support of these goals, Bush and his advisors insisted that the traditional law-enforcement approach to terrorism must be abandoned. Instead, an aggressive policy of preemption was needed. "We needed a new way forward," Vice President Dick Cheney later wrote in his memoir, "one based on the recognition that we are at war." The United States "needed to go after the terrorists where they lived, rooting them out before they could attack" and that included holding states responsible.[10]

Although the Bush administration emphasized the use of force, it was a more traditional measure that yielded greater success. Bush signed EO 13224 on September 23 to target the financial networks of terrorist organizations. It drew on Clinton's International Emergency Economic Powers Act discussed in Chapter 4 and listed twenty-nine individuals and organizations with direct ties to al-Qaʻida. Four months later, EO 13224 was accompanied by UN Security Council Resolution 1390. The resolution maintained the sanctions regime and travel ban against bin Laden and al-Qaʻida. Washington found widespread support and cooperation from allies and partners for targeting al-Qaʻida's funds and unraveling its financial network. But expanding the Global War on Terror proved contentious.[11]

Cheney promoted an even more aggressive stance. In late November 2001, he introduced what became known as the "1 percent doctrine" or the "Cheney Doctrine." Journalist Ron Suskind described the approach: "Even if there is just a one percent chance of the unimaginable coming due, act as if it's a certainty." The impetus was an intelligence briefing by CIA Director George Tenet that Pakistani scientists might be assisting an al-Qaʿida affiliate group with developing a nuclear weapon. "It's not about our analysis, or finding a preponderance of evidence," Cheney said. "It's about our response." Cheney's skepticism of the intelligence community dated to the 1970s. He later confided to the 9/11 Commission that the attacks revealed there were "problems in analysis, with data collection, and with integration" at the CIA and he was reluctant to give it new authority. At the same time, Cheney's response to the intelligence report followed anthrax attacks inside the United States that had not been solved. The failure to capture or kill bin Laden ensured that the campaign combining the Bush and Cheney Doctrines was applied beyond Afghanistan and at home.[12]

The domestic component to the Global War on Terror was embodied in the USA PATRIOT Act. Over 340 pages long, the Act represented a remarkable expansion of the national security state into the daily lives of Americans and others around the globe. Yet it was quickly passed and signed on October 26. Among the most glaring provisions were preventive detention, secret searches and electronic surveillance without probable cause, the permitted searching of residences without informing the individuals in advance or at the time of the search (known as "sneak and peak" warrants), and the expanded coordination between intelligence agencies and law enforcement.[13]

Michael Chertoff, then an assistant US attorney general in the Criminal Division and later secretary of Homeland Security, helped shape the legislation. Chertoff would later point to the perceived need to erase the division between "intelligence information and criminal information, which had been the prevailing rule of the Justice Department." Chertoff's perspective was also influenced by the Zacarias Moussaoui case. Moussaoui had been enrolled in a Minnesota-based flight school and had raised suspicions by telling his instructors he was not interested in learning how to land airplanes. He had been arrested before September 11 for an immigration violation. Because the charges had not been related to an intelligence or criminal complaint, there had been no sufficient probable cause to search his laptop computer. It was searched after September 11, however, and found to have information pertaining to the planned attacks. Chertoff dismissed the criticism of the Patriot Act and noted that its provisions related to wiretaps were already in use for narcotics cases: "Our general rule was, if it's legal to do something in a drug case, for marijuana, it should be legal to do it in a terrorism case."[14]

The Patriot Act was not the only legal tool used by the Bush administration. Indeed, a range of executive orders and existing laws justified the actions taken. Chertoff recalled that the post–September 11 investigations were not constrained legally—"You could usually find a legal tool that would allow you to do what you needed to do"—but acknowledged that "some of them were imperfectly adapted."[15]

This legal approach also benefited from Vice President Cheney's perspective on executive power. With support from White House lawyers and advisors, the administration argued that the president had unlimited powers in wartime. Under the "unitary executive theory," Cheney and other administration officials asserted that as commander-in-chief during a conflict, the president had authority that could not be limited by Congress or the Supreme Court. The proponents of this theory included Deputy Assistant Attorney General John Yoo and David Addington, chief counsel to Vice President Cheney. As discussed in Chapter 3, Cheney also made similar arguments in the minority report of the Iran-Contra investigation. The Bush administration extended the president's unlimited authority to international law and treaties. In effect, Cheney and his advisors claimed that there were no internal or external checks on the president. Jack Goldsmith, assistant attorney general, said the administration's "conception of executive power and its agenda for executive power informed everything it did."[16]

"YOU ARE NOT GOING TO LET ME LOSE FACE ON THIS, ARE YOU?"

Bush embraced assassination and torture. In the late 1990s, the CIA deployed the Predator drone over Afghanistan to provide real-time surveillance in the hunt for bin Laden. After September 11, it was armed with Hellfire missiles and became an assassination tool for the US military and the CIA. The assassination ban first authorized in the mid-1970s was intended for foreign leaders and not nonstate actors. Over the next two decades, however, the ban was tempered. In mid-November 2001, the US military deployed the armed Predator in Afghanistan to assassinate Mohammad Atef. Originally from Egypt, Atef was the third-ranking member of al-Qaʿida and its military head. He was considered responsible for the 1998 embassy bombings. A year later in Yemen, the CIA carried out a drone strike on the suspected organizer of the USS *Cole* attack, Qaed Salim Sinan al-Harethi, and six others. Among the dead was Kamel Derwish, an al-Qaʿida recruiter connected to one of the earliest domestic applications of the Patriot Act.[17]

In the spring of 2001, six Yemeni-American men from the town of Lackawanna in upstate New York traveled to Afghanistan and received training at an al-Qaʿida camp near Kandahar. A few months later, the FBI received a tip that the men might be involved with a terrorist organization. Later known as the "Lackawanna Six," the men were arrested with great fanfare. Yet the most prominent charge against them was for material support of al-Qaʿida.[18]

David Cole and James Dempsey note that material support has been a frequent tool in federal terrorism prosecutions even when the government has not demonstrated that the actions abetted a terrorist act. Ultimately, five of the defendants pled guilty to material support and the sixth to conducting illegal transactions with al-Qaʿida and all were sentenced from seven to ten years in prison. Lawyers for the six men rejected the government's claim, however, that they were an al-Qaʿida "sleeper cell" and said their guilty pleas were the result of threats to detain the men indefinitely, presumably in the newly established prison at the United States' Guantanamo Bay base in Cuba. Kamel Derwish facilitated their travel to, and training in, Afghanistan. Derwish's death in the November 2002 airstrike prevented determining the level of the Lackawanna Six's commitment to al-Qaʿida. After their release from prison, three of the men were given new identities by the federal government, raising questions about the threat they posed and their cooperation with authorities. Meanwhile, armed drones continued to be a tool for the US military and the CIA.[19]

Even more than the drone assassination campaign, the torture of detainees undermined America's standing in the world and served as a recruitment tool for al-Qaʿida and other groups. In January 2002, the DOJ determined that the Geneva Conventions did not apply to the conflict in

Afghanistan. It declared that members of the Taliban and al-Qaʿida were "illegal enemy combatants" and not entitled to prisoner of war status or protections from torture and abuse. A month later, President Bush modified this determination. He affirmed that the Geneva Conventions applied to the Afghanistan War but not to Taliban and al-Qaʿida fighters captured in the country.[20]

The United States established an archipelago of secret bases for the detention and torture of captured individuals. This was coupled with an expanded program of extraordinary rendition of suspects to US allies and other countries where torture was expected, if not encouraged. "If you want a serious interrogation, you send a prisoner to Jordan," former CIA officer Robert Baer told a journalist. "If you want them to be tortured, you send them to Syria. If you want someone to disappear—never to see them again—you send them to Egypt." Baer's chilling comments shed light on practices dating to the Reagan administration. Some seventy individuals were subjected to extraordinary rendition before September 11, 2001.[21]

The CIA's "enhanced interrogation" program was set in motion after the capture of Zayn al-Abidin Muhammad Husayn (known as Abu Zubaydah) in March 2002. Detained in Pakistan, Abu Zubaydah was falsely identified as a high-ranking al-Qaʿida member and his capture was promoted by President Bush and other administration officials as a major success. By August, the DOJ's Office of Legal Counsel drafted several memoranda that validated harsh interrogation methods. Although the CIA claimed that Abu Zubaydah was unwilling to cooperate, the main concern appeared to be shielding its interrogators from criminal prosecution.[22]

In an August 2002 memorandum to White House Counsel Alberto Gonzalez, the Office of Legal Counsel claimed that the interrogator must have specific intent to harm the detainee for the federal ban on torture to apply. Disingenuous excuses were offered for the use of drugs, threatening to kill the detainee, and the application of mental and physical pain. For example, the memorandum claimed that physical pain only qualified as torture if it was associated with the detainee's death or the failure of their vital organs. Even though evidence quickly emerged that Abu Zubaydah did not have a leadership role in al-Qaʿida and likely suffered from psychological disorders, this was ignored for political reasons.[23]

President Bush pressed the issue in a meeting with CIA Director George Tenet. Reminding him that he had publicly said Abu Zubaydah "was important," he asked Tenet: "You are not going to let me lose face on this, are you?" Tenet's reputation was damaged by the September 11 attacks and after reassuring Bush, he successfully pressured the White House Counsel's Office as well as the CIA general counsel for the necessary legal determinations. Abu Zubaydah was flown to a "black site" prison in Thailand and waterboarded eighty-three times. Four years later, the CIA determined that he was not an al-Qaʿida member. He remains, however, incarcerated in Guantanamo Bay.[24]

The architects of the torture program were two former US Air Force psychologists, Bruce Jessen and James Mitchell. In early 2002, Jessen and Mitchell were tasked by the CIA with developing a program for the "enhanced interrogation" of detainees. In designing the methods, Jessen and Mitchell later claimed that they were told by the CIA to "walk right up to the edge of the law" to produce "learned helplessness" among the prisoners. The program was ruthlessly implemented and it went well beyond the edge of legality. It was also lucrative for Jessen and Mitchell, as they established their own company in 2005 to administer the $81 million CIA contract.[25]

The CIA later admitted that thirty-nine detainees were subjected to enhanced interrogation. The methods included forced drowning (known as waterboarding), sleep deprivation, prolonged confinement in a small cell, and manhandling (or "walling") of detainees. Waterboarding was deployed eagerly, especially on "high-value detainees" like Abu Zubaydah and Khaled Sheikh Mohammad. Khaled Sheikh Mohammad (often referred to as KSM) was the organizer and financier of the September 11 attacks. His interrogation began almost a year after Abu Zubaydah, and he was waterboarded over 180 times. At least one prisoner, Gul Rahman, died in custody and a number of others were released without charge.[26]

Mitchell later defended his actions in *Enhanced Interrogation*. He and Jessen also claimed that they had reined in other interrogators' uses of even harsher methods and objected to the treatment of some prisoners, including Rahman. Both men, however, settled a lawsuit brought by the American Civil Liberties Union on behalf of Rahman's family and two detainees who had been tortured and released from Guantanamo Bay without being charged.[27]

The released prisoners continue to suffer from the torture. There were no consequences, however, for the CIA officials who authorized the program or any member of the Bush administration who justified its legality. Indeed, Dick Cheney insisted that "the program was safe, legal, and effective" and that the intelligence it yielded had "saved American lives." Cheney's claim was disputed by a declassified Senate Intelligence Committee Report on the torture program, discussed in Chapter 6.[28]

Accompanying the Patriot Act was a robust global surveillance program run by the National Security Agency. As discussed in previous chapters, the NSA conducted large-scale surveillance programs of domestic and foreign targets before, but these were dwarfed by the post–September 11 campaign. Approved on October 4, 2001, the NSA's "Terrorist Surveillance Program" was widespread and contrary to the title not only targeted at suspected terrorists. It allowed for warrantless wiretapping of an indiscriminate nature. Within a few months, the NSA established secret rooms within AT&T telecommunications facilities in major cities across the country. The rooms allowed the NSA to copy all of the internet data transmitting through AT&T's fiber optic cables. The information was not limited to AT&T customers, however, as the locations were part of the "common backbone" of data traffic. This allowed the NSA to access the internet data of other providers through the AT&T network. After September 11, the NSA benefited from a larger profile within the Bush and Obama administrations and the agency's director had a more prominent role in deliberations.[29]

Revelations about the surveillance program did not emerge until after Bush was reelected. The administration and the NSA deflected criticism and claimed that surveillance was only on a limited number of domestic targets with a far larger number overseas. It was far more pervasive and invasive, however, than the administration originally claimed. Nevertheless, Bush publicly defended the program and vowed it would continue. Cheney wrote that mass surveillance was one of the programs he was proudest of: "If I had it to do all over again, I would in a heartbeat."[30]

Although Bush campaigned on reducing the role of government in American lives, he oversaw a massive expansion after September 11. This included the creation of the Department of Homeland Security (DHS) led by a new cabinet-level secretary position. Merging twenty-two existing agencies, DHS's mandate included monitoring for domestic terrorism

CONSTRUCTING GLOBAL TERRORISM AND THE LONG WAR   195

threats. The bureaucratic goal was to combine the agencies outside the Defense Department responsible for borders, transportation, and infrastructure, and the agencies responsible for prevention and response, into a single entity. There was significant overlap in intelligence collection and analysis. DHS was tasked with using available data-mining tools to analyze and assess the streams of information gathered across different agencies for potential threats. President Bush also authorized the FBI to establish a Terrorist Screening Center to collect and analyze information about suspected individuals. A second body, the Terrorist Threat Integration Center, assessed information from foreign and domestic sources. This would be merged, after the Intelligence Reform Act of 2004 was passed, into the National Counter-Terrorism Center. Yet the fact that these entities were created without clearly defined powers on collecting data domestically created the potential for civil rights abuses—potential that was soon realized in criminal and immigration cases.[31]

While data collection was secret, DHS's most public efforts were the color-coded Homeland Security Advisory System and the "See Something, Say Something" advertising campaign. Both initiatives were widely derided, and subsequent studies found that they were ineffective, or had the negative impact of contributing to domestic racial and religious profiling.[32]

Mirroring its efforts overseas, the Bush administration boasted about its domestic successes in the Global War on Terror. Like the case of the Lackawanna Six, however, these cases raised troubling questions about the government's claims and the actual actions of the defendants. One of the highest-profile cases occurred in Tampa and did not involve al-Qaʿida. Dr. Sami al-Arian, a University of South Florida computer science professor, was indicted in February 2003 with seven others, including his brother-in-law. The indictments culminated a decade of monitoring by federal agents as well as accusations by a controversial journalist that al-Arian supported terrorism, in particular the Palestinian Islamic Jihad (PIJ). At a press conference, Attorney General John Ashcroft accused al-Arian of helping to fund the PIJ, which was responsible for terrorist attacks that killed Israelis and Americans.[33]

A year later, the al-Arian case became a point of contention in the 2004 Senate race between Democrat Betty Castor and Republican Mel Martinez. Both candidates sought to brand the other as soft on terrorism through television ads that featured al-Arian in what was essentially a proxy issue for the larger presidential campaign and the floundering war in Iraq. Castor was president of the University of South Florida and Martinez claimed that she allowed al-Arian to run a "terrorist cell" on campus. Castor countered that the Bush administration embraced al-Arian during and after the 2000 presidential campaign, even hosting a White House visit. Al-Arian campaigned for Bush and other Republican candidates in Florida's Arab-American and Muslim-American communities.[34]

Although prosecutors had hundreds of hours of wiretaps and secret evidence, it proved to be far less than they claimed. Over five months, prosecutors argued that al-Arian played a key role in financing and directing PIJ attacks. He was acquitted on eight of the seventeen charges and the jury was deadlocked on the remainder, with ten jurors favoring full acquittal. Rather than face a lengthy retrial, al-Arian pled guilty to a single count of conspiracy to provide support to a terrorist organization. The assistance he provided was related to assisting a family member with an immigration and visa issue. The plea deal allowed al-Arian to be deported with time served and the DOJ to claim victory, even though the case was an obvious failure. The presiding judge ignored the plea arrangement, however, and sentenced al-Arian to an additional eleven months. While in prison, federal prosecutors attempted to compel al-Arian's testimony in terrorism-related cases. He remained incarcerated for two more years. Al-Arian served an additional six years under electronically monitored house arrest before the DOJ finally relented and he was deported in 2015.[35]

It was not a coincidence that Mazen al-Najjar, al-Arian's brother-in-law, was held on immigration charges and secret evidence for three years before he was deported. Existing immigration laws were used to detain Muslim immigrants after September 11. Chertoff admitted that immigration violations allowed for indefinitely detaining individuals and this was readily used after the attacks. At least 1,200 individuals were arrested in the months after the attacks, of which 738 were detained for extended periods of time.[36] While some individuals had expired visas, others had cases under review or were challenging the determinations of their immigration status. Yet the individuals were treated not as committing minor civil offenses, but as terrorism suspects. Predawn raids were conducted to

CONSTRUCTING GLOBAL TERRORISM AND THE LONG WAR

arrest individuals and they were held in custody without the possibility of posting bond. Nor were they allowed to contact attorneys, families, or journalists as they were subject to a "communications blackout." In some instances, families were separated, especially those with young children born in the United States or with different visa status from their parents. The detainees were held in federal as well as state and local facilities, including maximum security institutions. For example, the Metropolitan Detention Center in Brooklyn, New York, held a significant number of detainees. Yet none were ever charged with terrorism related crimes. It is also unclear if the individuals that were deported faced interrogation and possible torture in their home countries.[37]

The 2003 DOJ Inspector General report criticized the FBI and the Immigration and Naturalization Service. In addition to the communications blackout and denial of bond, the Inspector General noted that detainees, their families, and their attorneys alleged that they were given false and incorrect information. The report also found that some detainees were subjected to harsh and abusive treatment. Although the policies toward immigration detainees were not as punitive as those applied to enemy combatants, they were part of a spectrum of abuse toward individuals suspected of involvement with terrorism. For the immigration detainees, that suspicion was based largely on their religious identification and country of origin. This became even more pronounced in Iraq.[38]

IRAQ

The Bush administration deliberately sought to conflate Iraq with the September 11 attacks to justify an invasion. At the September 15 Camp David meeting, Vice President Dick Cheney, Secretary of Defense Donald Rumsfeld, and Deputy Defense Secretary Wolfowitz argued for attacking state sponsors of terrorism. Wolfowitz and Rumsfeld promoted an invasion of Iraq in addition to or instead of Afghanistan. Rumsfeld noted that Iraq offered a richer number of targets and the opportunity for immediate success in the Global War on Terror. Secretary of State Colin Powell objected, however, to the focus on Iraq. Unlike Afghanistan, Powell argued that Washington could not maintain an allied coalition for an invasion of Iraq.[39]

Rumsfeld dismissed Powell's concerns. He asserted that the "argument that the coalition wouldn't tolerate [an invasion of] Iraq argues for a different coalition." Rumsfeld argued that the Global War on Terror would be "a sustained campaign" that should be treated "like a political campaign with daily talking points." He stressed that this would require broad domestic support and take "years, not months." Indeed, the emphasis on domestic politics and public relations was essential to building the case for war, its prosecution, and the occupation. Powell later recollected Bush's words at Camp David: "We'll do Afghanistan first." For Powell this implied that "he already had Iraq on his mind."[40]

To help maintain domestic support, Rumsfeld hired Victoria Clarke as director of public affairs. Clarke was a former executive with a public relations firm, Hill and Knowlton Strategies. At the Pentagon, Clarke recruited a bipartisan collection of consultants, public relations experts, and lobbyists. Known as the "Rumsfeld Group," one of its major achievements was to recommend, based on focus groups, that the Bush administration link terrorism to nations rather than just to a shadowy transnational network. This "messaging" advice served to validate Rumsfeld's arguments at the September 15 Camp David meeting, and helped to make Iraq the primary focus of the Global War on Terror.[41]

As the administration was preparing its public response to the September 11 attacks, President Bush initiated planning for Iraq. Bush spoke with Rumsfeld privately after an NSC meeting in mid-September. Rumsfeld later recorded in his calendar that the president told him, "I want you to develop a plan to invade Ir[aq]. Do it outside the normal channels. Do it creatively so we don't have to take so much cover." In his memoir, Rumsfeld would later offer his interpretation of Bush's cryptic request. He understood that the president did not want an invasion to be similar to the plans for the 1991 Gulf War, but that he had not made a final decision on attacking Iraq.[42]

After September 11, Vice President Cheney recommended that Bush have the war plans for invading Iraq updated. Cheney later claimed that this was based on his experience in preparing for the 1991 conflict. Cheney also urged Bush to have the planning completed in the headquarters of Central Command (CENTCOM) in Florida, where it was less likely to leak to the press.[43]

Meanwhile, Rumsfeld offered an expansive view of US goals in the War on Terror. In a September 30 "strategic thoughts" memorandum drafted for President Bush, Rumsfeld argued that a key aim was to "to persuade or compel States to stop supporting terrorism." "If the war does not significantly change the world's political map, the US will not achieve its aim," he added. "There is value in being clear on the order of magnitude of the necessary change." Rumsfeld declared that the United States' goal should be "new regimes in Afghanistan and another key State (or two) that supports terrorism (to strengthen political and military efforts to change policies elsewhere)."[44]

When the United States began the invasion of Afghanistan in October 2001, US Ambassador to the UN John Negroponte relayed a warning to his Iraqi counterpart, Ambassador Mohammed Aldouri. Iraq was told not to "take advantage of the situation." Negroponte later recalled that it was "the first indication *I* saw, of this very early fascination, if not obsession, with Iraq." By the end of 2001, CENTCOM completed initial planning, and General Tommy Franks briefed Bush, Cheney, and senior administration officials. Less than a month later, in his January 2002 State of the Union Address, Bush labeled Iraq as part of the "Axis of Evil" and set the invasion plans in motion.[45]

War planning and domestic politics intersected throughout 2002. As the Pentagon continued refining its invasion plan into the summer, Bush's chief political advisor, Karl Rove, drafted a strategy for the November midterm elections that aligned with the administration's aggressive foreign policy approach. This included selecting candidates for the election. In a secret June presentation to California Republicans, Rove emphasized that the Global War on Terror was the centerpiece of the administration's election strategy. He presented the themes of terrorism and the war as advantages for Republican candidates, and deployed this strategy particularly against Senate Democrats seeking reelection in conservative states.[46]

Meanwhile, the Bush administration began publicly building the case for invading Iraq. In June, Bush's commencement address at the US Military Academy outlined the Bush Doctrine and made the case for preemptive wars. "Containment is not possible," he declared, "when unbalanced dictators with weapons of mass destruction can deliver those weapons on missiles or secretly provide them to terrorist allies." Less than three months later, the 2002 National Security Strategy emphasized preemption and democracy promotion to counter the threat posed by rogue states and terrorist organizations. "In an age where the enemies of civilization openly and actively seek the world's most destructive technologies, the United States cannot remain idle while dangers gather," it warned.[47]

As Congress prepared to deliberate an authorization of military force, Bush indicated a willingness to seek a UN resolution that was "tough" but would not hinder his freedom of action. White House Spokesman Ari Fleischer insisted, however, that regime change remained US policy.[48]

A week later, President Bush spoke in Cincinnati, Ohio. The site of the speech in a midterm election year was not coincidental. Bush won Ohio in the 2000 election and the state was essential to his reelection hopes. Bush linked Saddam Hussein to al-Qaʻida through a "common enemy"— the United States. He asserted that confronting Iraq was "crucial to winning the war on terror." "America must not ignore the threat gathering against us," Bush warned. "Facing clear evidence of peril, we cannot wait for the final proof—the smoking gun—that could come in the form of a mushroom cloud." This ominous warning and others were repeated over the next several months by Vice President Cheney and National Security Advisor Condoleezza Rice.[49]

The warnings were coupled with manufactured connections to amplify the potential threat. Vice President Cheney promoted the unfounded claim that the leader of the September 11 hijackers, Mohammad Atta, had met with Iraqi intelligence in Prague on the highly rated NBC News program *Meet the Press*. He also misled congressional allies, including House Majority Leader Dick Armey, about Iraq's weapons programs. An unreliable defector code-named "Curveball" provided false information to leading journalists about Iraq's WMD programs and ties to al-Qaʻida. Prominent experts at leading think tanks with ties to both political parties endorsed the administration's claim that Saddam Hussein posed an imminent threat to the United States. Thus, the administration's claims and deliberate disinformation were recycled through Congress and the press to sustain a fear-provoking echo chamber. By October, a majority of Americans believed Iraq was linked to the September 11 attacks.[50]

The Bush administration's efforts were endorsed by British Prime Minister Tony Blair. Blair's government produced two dossiers within six months that purported to demonstrate Iraq had an active WMD program based on the latest available intelligence. While the September 2002 dossier exaggerated the evidence and potential threat, the February 2003 report was partially plagiarized from a graduate thesis. In its 2016 report, the Chilcott inquiry offered a damning assessment of the Blair government's deliberate attempts to deceive the public and the rush to war. While Blair sought to maintain the UK's influence with Washington, his advice on securing international support and postwar planning was ignored by the Bush White House.[51]

Accompanying the scare tactics and deception was democracy promotion and empire. Iraq was central to Bush's "Freedom Agenda" and vision for a new Middle East. Administration officials and allies in the media and think tanks argued that the overthrow of Saddam Hussein would begin the democratic transformation of the region. The combination of force and American imperial guidance, they asserted, would sweep away hostile authoritarian governments. This would also break the stalemate in negotiations between Israelis and Palestinians and eradicate support for Hamas and Hizbullah. The position of friendly authoritarian governments in this policy was uncertain and like NSPD 9, it conflated Hamas and Hizbullah with al-Qaʿida.[52]

Congressional debate on military intervention favored the Bush administration's position. Although Democrats hoped to emphasize the weakening economy and corporate scandals tied to the administration for the midterm elections, Iraq dominated the political discourse. Leading Democrats, including potential candidates to challenge Bush in the 2004 election, advocated removing Saddam Hussein from power. Hawks like Senator and former vice presidential candidate Joe Liberman supported the Bush White House. Joe Biden, then chairman of the Senate Foreign Relations Committee, worked with Republican colleagues on a compromise that emphasized disarming Iraq's WMD programs and coordinating with allies as part of a UN resolution. The authorization for military force passed overwhelmingly with bipartisan support in the House and the Senate less than a month before the midterm elections.[53]

Although Democrats facing reelection hoped to benefit from voting in favor of military intervention, the election vindicated Rove's strategy. Republicans gained control of the Senate and added to their majority in the House. More important, the Bush administration had two related but distinct authorizations of military force that justified wars for the next two decades.[54]

As the administration pressed its case in the media and in world capitals, the Pentagon deployed forces to the Persian Gulf. Indeed, the presence of US forces became another rationale for invasion. As *Washington Post* columnist Roger Cohen put it, "Great Powers must not bluff."[55]

In early February 2003, Secretary of State Powell addressed the United Nations Security Council. With CIA Director George Tenet and Ambassador Negroponte seated behind him, Powell presented the US case for war. In a signature moment, Powell held up a small vial containing an undisclosed white powder. He explained that roughly the same amount of anthrax sent in an envelope had shut down the US Senate, killed two postal workers, and caused several hundred people to need medical attention. Eight years earlier, he said, Iraq had declared 8,500 liters of anthrax to UN inspectors and that nation had the capacity to produce much more. While Powell did not state that Iraq was linked to the unsolved anthrax attacks, the implication was strong.[56]

Although Powell's speech was initially praised in the US press afterward, it did not convince key American allies in Paris or Berlin to support an invasion. Nor did it persuade other Security Council members that were already opposed. But the decision to invade had been made well in advance of Powell's speech, which was largely for domestic consumption. Powell had been selected by President Bush because he was far more popular than any other member of the administration. Meanwhile, the Bush White House dismissed the largest global antiwar protests since the Vietnam War. And the failure to find an active WMD program in Iraq after the invasion undermined Powell's credibility.[57]

Another aspect of Powell's speech that was generally overlooked was his reference to an obscure Jordanian terrorist, Abu Musab al-Zarqawi, then based in northern Iraq. Powell's claim that Zarqawi was the link between al-Qa'ida and Saddam Hussein must have been a revelation to both men. The Bush administration was later criticized for not having acted against Zarqawi when it had the opportunity, choosing instead to promote the notion that Iraq had been involved in the September 11 attacks.[58]

The United States' swift victory was accompanied by looting, sabotage, and revenge killings. While the Bush White House and Pentagon openly discussed its elaborate "shock and awe" air campaign, designed to eliminate the Iraqi military and decapitate Saddam Hussein's government, the lack of post-invasion planning was immediately apparent. Although the administration vociferously denied that Iraq's large oil reserves were a factor, the oil ministry was one of the buildings in Baghdad guarded by US forces. Infighting within the administration between Secretary of State Powell and Secretary of Defense Rumsfeld was compounded by the decision to deploy a minimal US force with limited occupation duties.

Six weeks after the invasion started, President Bush landed a Navy S3-B Viking jet on the USS *Abraham Lincoln* anchored off the California coast. The nuclear-powered aircraft carrier had only recently returned from the Persian Gulf, where its fighter squadrons had dropped nearly 1.9 million pounds of ordnance on Iraq. Bush shed his aviator flight suit for a more traditional business attire to announce the end of major combat operations in Iraq. Behind the podium, a "Mission Accomplished" banner was prominently displayed on the ship's island. Bush stressed that "the battle of Iraq is one victory" in the war on terror, and placed it within a broader civilizational struggle: "Any outlaw regime that has ties to terrorist groups and seeks or possesses weapons of mass destruction is a grave danger to the civilized world and will be confronted." The United States was "committed to freedom in Afghanistan, Iraq and in a peaceful Palestine," he said. "The war on terror is not over, yet it is not endless. We do not know the day of final victory, but we have seen the turning of the tide." He was mistaken.[59]

The Pentagon's Office of Reconstruction and Humanitarian Assistance of Iraq was initially tasked with overseeing the United States' postwar efforts, but quickly replaced by the Coalition Provisional Authority (CPA). Led by L. Paul Bremer, a former ambassador-at-large for counterterrorism, the CPA was established to oversee the occupation and transition to Iraqi self-government. Bremer implemented politically and ideologically oriented decisions that further exacerbated tensions inside Iraq. He disbanded the Iraqi army without pay and instituted an ill-conceived de-Ba'thification program. The CPA was increasingly insulated in the Baghdad "green zone," an area that included Saddam Hussein's former palace and was deemed safe for soldiers, diplomats, and contractors. This isolation was compounded by dysfunction and infighting as the CPA failed to provide even a modicum of competent governance. The rifts between the military commanders and the civilian leadership in Washington and Baghdad hindered the creation of Iraqi security forces and contributed to the instability. Meanwhile, Saddam Hussein and key members of the Ba'th party leadership remained at large.[60]

In late July 2003, US forces surrounded a house where an informant reported that Saddam Hussein's sons, Uday and Qusay, were hiding. Both men were killed and the Pentagon released photos of their bodies. Secretary of Defense Rumsfeld and President Bush defended the decision, claiming that it demonstrated to Iraqis that the regime would not return to power and would encourage others to provide information on officials evading capture. Between this, some high-profile incidents in which US troops killed Iraqi civilians at checkpoints and during raids, and the failure to resume basic services, Iraq was ripe for an insurgency.[61]

August 2003 witnessed three devastating suicide truck bombings that marked the beginning of a sustained insurgency and contributed to a sectarian civil war. The bombings were linked to Abu Musab al-Zarqawi's fledgling al-Qaʻida in Iraq (AQI). Zarqawi was born Ahmad Fadhil Nazzal al-Khalaylah and hailed from Zarqa, Jordan. Despite his impact on Iraq and the broader region, there are elements of Zarqawi's biography and his movement that remain unclear and contradictory. Zarqawi was a thug and petty thief who had reportedly joined the Afghan resistance after the Soviet withdrawal. Over the course of the next decade, Zarqawi did not distinguish himself on the battlefield, he lacked charisma, and his knowledge of Islamic theology was limited to basic memorization of the Qurʼan. He returned in the early 1990s to Jordan, where he was involved in poorly conceived and executed terror plots. After a stint in prison, Zarqawi was pardoned by Jordan's King Abdullah II as part of a larger amnesty of Islamist prisoners.[62]

In late 1999, Zarqawi traveled to Afghanistan for an audience with bin Laden. Zarqawi failed, however, to impress bin Laden, who suspected he had connections to Jordanian intelligence, among other issues. Yet other leading figures in al-Qaʻida believed that Zarqawi could be useful. Drawing on support from the *mujahideen* network presumably in Saudi Arabia, Zarqawi set up a training camp in western Afghanistan near the city of Herat. By the time of the US invasion he reportedly recruited two to three thousand fighters largely from Syria, Jordan, and Lebanon. After the US occupation of Afghanistan began, Zarqawi infiltrated the Kurdish autonomous area of northern Iraq in late 2002. He came to the attention of American intelligence officials and was thrust into the international spotlight by Powell's UN speech. As the violence in Iraq escalated through the fall, the Bush administration deliberately overemphasized Zarqawi's role to deflect blame for their decisions as well as to obscure the level of popular anger at the fledgling occupation.[63]

The insurgency was more than just Zarqawi and AQI. A marriage of convenience developed between AQI and elements of Saddam Hussein's regime, especially the intelligence services (*mukhabarat*) and Sunni tribes linked to Saddam through familial and patronage ties. In addition, nationalist rivals emerged and jockeyed for power. Even after Saddam Hussein was captured in December 2003, the insurgency remained and metastasized. Beginning with the August 29 suicide car bombing at the Imam Ali shrine in the city of Najaf that killed over a hundred Shi'a pilgrims as well as a leading cleric, Ayatollah Mohammad Baqir al-Hakim, Zarqawi embarked on a deliberate campaign targeting Iraq's Shi'a majority. Yet through 2003, most attacks on US and coalition forces were conducted by Iraqi insurgents, not foreign fighters.[64]

By June 2004, Bremer informed Secretary of Defense Rumsfeld that there had been four times as many attacks as in the previous year. The US embassy in Jordan also reported concerns that "disaffected youth" in Zarqa would become "prey to extremist messages and recruitment." Comparing it to Jersey City, New Jersey—Zarqa is Jordan's second-largest city and home to its heavy industry—the cable warned that Zarqawi's "brand of disaffection" was appealing to Jordanians and Jordanian-Palestinians, and the city would "remain a concern for the [Jordanian] regime for the foreseeable future." The US embassy argued that this was fueled by the lack of economic opportunity and political disaffection among the city's youth, and heavy pollution, as well as Zarqawi's rising fame. Yet the Pentagon also contributed to this dynamic through a well-funded propaganda campaign that sought to discredit the Iraqi insurgency by linking it to Zarqawi. As it had before the war started, the United States legitimized Zarqawi, with devastating consequences.[65]

Meanwhile, Shi'a militias supported and trained by neighboring Iran and Lebanon's Hizbullah emerged to challenge US and UK forces as well as AQI. Three major militias were active within the first year of the occupation: the Badr Brigade, the Mahdi Army, and the Da'wa Party. Internal CPA assessments referred to the militias as a "a ticking time bomb under the still fragile foundation we are laying for Iraq's democratic future" and

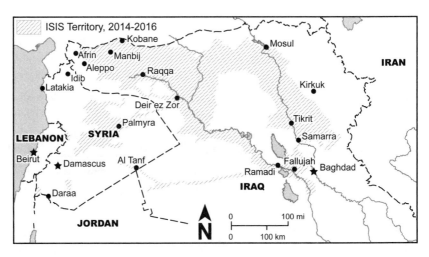

MAP 9. IRAQ, 2003–2020

advocated for their disarmament. Yet the negotiations were more difficult than the CPA or the Bush administration had hoped. This was compounded by the decision to disband the CPA in June 2004 and transfer its functions to a fledgling Iraqi government. The timetable for this decision was directly related to the US presidential election that year.[66]

"I'M A WAR PRESIDENT"

The 2004 presidential election was the rarity in American politics where foreign policy dominated the campaign. Terrorism and security were leading issues for the candidates as the United States was involved in two active conflicts while also conducting covert operations in multiple countries, and the September 11 attacks were still fresh. Yet the unresolved issues of a three-decade-old war also hung over the contest. Senator John Kerry of Massachusetts, the Democratic Party's candidate, contrasted his foreign policy credentials and distinguished military service with Bush's experience. Although Bush had been eligible for combat in Vietnam, he spent part of the war in the Texas Air National Guard before he was suspended in 1972 for failure to receive a medical exam. Even though Bush was honorably discharged, it appeared that he and others in the administration benefited from political connections to avoid serving in Vietnam.

In part, this was a reflection of the culture wars that emerged from the Vietnam era and continued to influence American political discourse. Conservatives viewed Kerry's war record as suspect and open for derision because he had publicly criticized the conflict as a member of Vietnam Veterans Against the War. In April 1971, Kerry had testified before the Senate Foreign Relations Committee and recounted the experiences of 150 Vietnam veterans who witnessed or committed atrocities. Although the prison abuse scandal at Abu Ghraib broke earlier in the year, Kerry generally avoided the controversy. Instead, he and Democratic Party surrogates argued that Kerry's experience in the Senate and on the battlefield made him a more qualified and competent commander-in-chief than President Bush. They also claimed a contrast with the Bush administration's aggressive foreign policy, dismissiveness toward US allies that opposed the invasion of Iraq, and open embrace of empire. Joining Kerry on the stage at the Democratic National Convention for his acceptance speech were several Vietnam veterans who had served with him on a patrol boat or "swift boat." Kerry opened his speech by stating, "I'm John Kerry and I'm reporting for duty," adding a military salute for emphasis.[67]

President Bush and his advisors chose to challenge Kerry's military record directly and indirectly. A political advocacy group named "Swift Boat Veterans for Truth" published a book and unleashed political advertisements that questioned Kerry's service in Vietnam, the medals he received, and his patriotism. The group suggested that Kerry's war record was inflated, if not completely manufactured. Although Bush denounced the political ads, Republican Party operatives eagerly adopted the line of attack. At the Republican National Convention, Kerry's purple heart medal—awarded to soldiers wounded in combat—was mocked by attendees that wore small bandages with purple heart shapes colored in by crayon or marker.[68]

While the unresolved politics of Vietnam were one source of tension in the campaign, September 11 and the Global War on Terror added more. The convening of the Republican National Convention at Madison Square Garden in New York City less than two weeks from the third anniversary of the September 11 attacks provided Bush with a poignant backdrop for his reelection campaign. "Ground Zero" was just a few miles from the convention site. The gaping hole in the ground where the twin towers once stood evoked terrible memories, but also served as a reminder of

Bush's "Bullhorn Speech." Kerry's criticism of Bush on Iraq, meanwhile, had been undermined by his support for the 2002 authorization of military force, and his clumsy attempts to explain that vote were eagerly exploited by the Bush campaign. Meanwhile, Bush embraced his record and rejected any notion that mistakes had been made. "I'm a war president," he said on NBC News *Meet the Press.* "I make decisions here in the Oval Office, in foreign policy matters, with war on my mind." Although polls showed a tight race through October, Bush maintained a consistent narrow advantage over Kerry.[69]

A few days before the election, bin Laden released a video message in which he referenced the September 11 attacks. Although both candidates were quick to condemn the video, Kerry attempted to demonstrate that he would be even more aggressive than Bush. "As Americans, we are absolutely united in our determination to hunt down and destroy Osama bin Laden and the terrorists," Kerry told reporters. "They are barbarians. And I will stop at absolutely nothing to hunt down, capture, or kill the terrorists wherever they are, whatever it takes. Period." Yet the bellicose posturing was insufficient. Bush was reelected, this time winning the popular vote as well as the electoral college.[70]

QUAGMIRE

Washington's desire to break the Iraqi insurgency contributed to a scandal that reinforced the intersection of America's Wars on Crime and Terror. The US military conducted numerous raids in Anbar province and arrested suspected insurgents. In Baghdad, the US military refurbished Abu Ghraib prison and used the facility to hold a range of detainees from petty thieves to leaders of the insurgency. Abu Ghraib was one of Saddam Hussein's notorious prisons, but during the American occupation it became infamous. Overseen by US Military Intelligence interrogators, the Military Police were ordered to make the detainees more amenable for questioning. This was achieved through physical, psychological, and sexual abuse. Prisoners were stripped naked and humiliated by the guards. Some were threatened with dogs and others were forced to commit sexual acts as the guards mocked them while photographing the abuse. Drawing on Orientalist notions that Arab men were susceptible to sexual humiliation, the photographs were intended to coerce the prisoners into becoming informants for the occupation. Although leaked photos of the abuse led to heightened criticism of the Bush administration less than seven months before the 2004 presidential election, the furor did not hinder Bush's reelection.[71]

In his investigation and subsequent report, General Antonio Taguba found that the treatment of prisoners at Camp X-Ray served as a deliberate model for Iraq. General Geoffrey Miller, the commander of the Guantanamo Bay base, recommended creating an environment in Iraqi prisons to serve the United States' broader intelligence needs. General Miller argued this could be accomplished in less than a month and his assessment influenced the decision to make Military Intelligence personnel responsible for the prisons. Taguba criticized these claims and the subsequent decisions as unsound practices and based on a flawed assessment of the types of prisoners held in Iraq. Even though the military determined that over 60 percent of civilian detainees at Abu Ghraib were not a threat, they were not released. In addition, Taguba identified similarities in the treatment of detainees held in Afghanistan and Guantanamo Bay.[72]

While Taguba admonished Military Intelligence personnel in his report, the military police faced the most severe punishments. The military police assigned to Abu Ghraib were originally tasked with traffic duties, but they were reassigned because some worked as correctional officers in the United States. Sergeant Ivan Frederick, a six-year veteran of the Virginia Department of Corrections, was placed in command of the night shift at Abu Ghraib. During his court martial trial, Frederick presented evidence confirming that military intelligence ordered the harsh treatment and torture of prisoners. This was based on a directive by the US Army Command for the detainees to be "broken." As part of a plea bargain, Frederick was sentenced to eight years in prison and agreed to testify against other soldiers. Although the courts martial emphasized the irregularity of the behavior at Abu Ghraib, what was unsaid was that physical and sexual abuse in American prisons is widespread. The Abu Ghraib scandal did not lead to a broader reassessment of the interrogation techniques or a discussion of the intersection between the prison cultures in the United States and at American military prisons overseas. Instead, Bush survived the scandal politically and the blame was placed on low-ranking military police. But the damage to US efforts and prestige remained, as did the insurgency.[73]

After the 2004 election, Bush insisted that he had a mandate from the American public to continue both the Global War on Terror and his domestic political program. Yet persistent violence in Iraq undermined the administration's claims that progress was being made. Ambassador Negroponte left the UN to serve as ambassador to Iraq after the CPA was disbanded. He contrasted the situation in Baghdad with his experience in Saigon four decades earlier: "Vietnam was a war for the control of the countryside, and the cities were basically pretty damn safe, except when they occasionally overran a province capital or something like that. In Iraq, it's a fight for the control of the cities so you're in danger the minute you walk out your door. And it was frightening." Another difference Negroponte observed was the size of the military deployment and reliance on reservists shuttling between Afghanistan and Iraq. This was compounded by a scandal in the care of wounded veterans that was reminiscent of underfunded and understaffed medical facilities during the Vietnam War.[74]

Ambassador Negroponte inherited two active insurgencies from the CPA. The Mahdi Army militia led by the young Shi'a cleric, Muqtada al-Sadr, challenged US forces, as well as more established Shi'a political parties and figures, with an uprising in the city of Najaf that spread to the southern city of Basra and Baghdad's Sadr city neighborhood. Meanwhile, in the city of Fallujah, four American military contractors that worked for the Blackwater corporation were ambushed and lynched in late March. Located in Iraq's Anbar province, dubbed the "Sunni Triangle" by the American military and policymakers, Fallujah was one of several cities where the insurgency was active. Although a reprisal operation was initiated, it was quickly abandoned after encountering stiff resistance and a public backlash in Iraq. By the summer, the US Marines reported that moderates and extremists were competing for control of Fallujah and it was a "denied area" for American forces. One implication was that $27 million in projects intended for the city were on hold. Similar initiatives were progressing in neighboring towns to convince the population that they would benefit from cooperating with the US occupation.[75]

While a negotiated settlement was brokered to end the Shi'a uprising before the November election, Fallujah remained unsettled. A week after Bush was reelected, US and Iraqi forces launched a major offensive in Fallujah. In addition to the heavy civilian casualties and critical coverage by the pan-Arab satellite television network Al Jazeera, the fighting in Falluja contributed to increased tensions and further stoked the insurgency.[76]

Bush indicated that he had no intention of changing or even altering course in his second term. Nor was there room for dissension. Secretary of State Powell was replaced by National Security Advisor Condoleezza Rice and Secretary of Defense Rumsfeld was retained. Although the administration was bolstered by the January 2005 parliamentary elections in Iraq, it was accompanied by an escalation in violence that included the assassination of leading political figures and candidates. Political parties representing the Sunni minority boycotted the January elections and were effectively sidelined by the results. By the summer, however, the US embassy in Baghdad reported that there was an initial but "surprising shift" by political leaders in Fallujah and Ramadi toward political engagement and participation in an October constitutional referendum. By the end of 2005, there was a sharp increase in political participation by Sunni political parties and leaders. This became even more pronounced over the next year and was part of a larger counterinsurgency effort that involved co-opting Sunni political leaders and undermining the insurgency as well as AQI. Washington's partners in the region, especially Jordan and Saudi Arabia, helped facilitate this political transformation.[77]

Increased sectarian violence accompanied the outreach to Sunni political leaders. The newly appointed ambassador to Iraq, Zalmay Khalilzad, warned in a March 13, 2006, cable to Washington that Shi'a militias, "acting both as extra-legal bodies and within government structures at multiple levels, will continue to pursue sectarian agendas that will undermine the government's ability to improve the security environment and will exacerbate sectarian tensions." The actions by the militias, he wrote, "may complicate outreach to insurgents who might otherwise start a dialogue with us." Khalilzad also informed Washington that Sunni insurgents were targeting Shi'a families in Baghdad neighborhoods. He noted that the insurgents outnumbered and outgunned the Iraqi security forces. In addition, American patrols were not frequent enough to offer sufficient protection. Shi'a militias were assisting families that were displaced by the violence, and Khalilzad cautioned that Lebanon's Hizbullah had offered similar services in the past. This was "especially effective," he noted, when the government was unable or unwilling to provide assistance. It is worth noting that many of Baghdad's neighborhoods and Iraqi families were not religiously homogenous. But one implication of the sectarian civil war

and creation of Iraqi refugees and internally displaced persons was to reduce religious diversity.[78]

The emergence of a sectarian civil war in Iraq and the resurgence of the
Taliban in Afghanistan belied the Bush administration's public assertions
that the dual occupations were successful. The ongoing challenges provided an opportunity to reassess the fundamental premise of the Global
War on Terror. One prominent reassessment drew on the Vietnam experience. Counterinsurgency specialist David Kilcullen argued that a new approach was needed to counter the "global *jihad*." He argued that, rather
than considering the different jihadist groups as monolithic and coordinated centrally, the United States needed to view the challenge as a globalized insurgency. Instead of "lumping together all terrorism, all rogue
or failed states and all strategic competitors," Kilcullen asserted that dis-
aggregating the movements was a more appropriate strategy. Disrupting
the links between the groups would enable Washington and its allies to
prevent the jihad from functioning as a cohesive global entity. Among his
recommendations was to revisit the Civil Operations and Rural Development Support (CORDS) program employed in Vietnam. Kilcullen claimed
that CORDS was "maligned (but extremely effective)." In promoting
CORDS as a model for a global counterinsurgency program in the
twenty-first century, Kilcullen deliberately downplayed its failure to achieve
any of its major goals. Nevertheless, his recommendations were incorporated into the US military's development of a counterinsurgency program
and deployed in Iraq.[79]

Vietnamization was another policy applied to Iraq and Afghanistan.
Negroponte later reflected that, in the US occupation of Iraq, he relied on
lessons learned in Vietnam regarding "how we organized to fight the war,
embassy, civilian-military relations, what you can and can't do about nation building, and probably most importantly, the question of 'Vietnamization.'" Negroponte had inherited a "Vietnamization" program in Iraq
that began slowly and without a defined plan. Indeed, there was only one
Iraqi Army battalion when he arrived in Baghdad. He presented a plan to
build a new Iraqi army and police force. It relied on the disbanded Iraqi
army and recruited former officers to help train the new force, "because
we didn't have anywhere else to turn." The Bush administration devoted
nearly $18 billion to develop the Iraqi security forces by fiscal year 2009.
But applying Vietnamization to Afghanistan lagged far behind Iraq and

was not initiated until after Robert Gates replaced Rumsfeld as Secretary of Defense. Like the original Vietnamization program, both efforts faltered within a few years.[80]

In contrast, police recruitment and retention in Iraq proved more difficult. Training occurred in neighboring Jordan and was further complicated by the reliance on cash payments that contributed to absenteeism among recruits and police officers. Even more problematic was the infiltration by insurgent groups and sectarian militias. This proved to be a consistent issue in Afghanistan as well.[81]

The Joint Special Operations Command (JSOC) has played a prominent role in the Global War on Terror. In Iraq and Afghanistan, JSOC was charged with tracking and detaining or assassinating key leaders of the insurgency. The effort expanded on operations discussed in previous chapters, from the Phoenix Program to the death of Pablo Escobar. But this was more than just a passing resemblance, as the initial commander in charge, General William Boykin, oversaw special forces operations in Somalia and Colombia. By the time of his appointment, Boykin was already a controversial figure due to derogatory statements he had made about Islam. Nevertheless, he oversaw the "hunter-killer" teams tasked with breaking the Iraqi insurgency. The insurgency persisted despite active special forces operations, proving the limits of purely military operations and assassinations. Still, hunter-killer teams were integrated into the United States' counterinsurgency strategy.[82]

By 2006, the US military began developing a counterinsurgency (COIN) strategy. Led by General David Petraeus, it drew on the example of successful operations in Iraq and previous conflicts as well as the expertise of military veterans in academia and think tanks. The COIN strategy sought to reduce the antagonism of the general population toward US occupation forces. It recommended abandoning previous behavior and actions that relied on brute strength. Intimidating the population through raids, mass detention, and harsh interrogation had only increased resentment and strengthened the insurgency. Proponents of the COIN strategy argued that improving relations between the population and the occupation forces as well as introducing more Iraqi security forces would improve the overall environment and provide a respite for a political solution. The proposed political solution relied on a power-sharing agreement that struck a balance between Iraq's sectarian political parties. While

Iraqis insisted that sectarian politics were imported with the US occupation, these politics had become reified with the civil war, the targeting of
mixed neighborhoods in Baghdad, and internal displacement and refugees. The January 2005 elections marked the ascendancy of Shiʿa political
parties and the resentment of the Sunni minority. A political solution also
required driving a wedge between Iraqi insurgents and AQI. The emergence
of the "Anbar Awakening" movement and Zarqawi's death in a June 2006
US airstrike provided that opening.[83]

COIN's implementation intersected with the 2006 US midterm elections. In a referendum on Bush's presidency, including his continued mis-
management of Iraq and ineffectual response to Hurricane Katrina, the
Democrats won majorities in the Senate and House. After the election,
Rumsfeld resigned as Secretary of Defense. The nomination of former
CIA director Robert Gates as his replacement signaled an end to the neoconservative dominance of the administration's foreign policy. Two months
later, Bush addressed the nation on a new strategy in Iraq involving increased US troop levels in Baghdad and Anbar province, and the deployment of Iraqi security forces. He did not mention any idea of co-opting
tribal leaders in Anbar province, but what would become known as the
"Anbar Awakening," or its "Sons of Iraq" militia, would prove to be far
more important than the infusion of new troops. It was also the most
fragile. By the end of the year, the "surge" was deemed a success by the
administration and the press as American and Iraqi casualties declined.
This narrative influenced the 2008 presidential campaign, as Democratic
Party candidates once critical of the Iraq War were pressed to endorse the
policy. This continued into the Obama administration and the same approach was adopted for Afghanistan.[84]

BIRTH PANGS

NSPD 9 applied the Global War on Terror rationale beyond al-Qaʿida.
After the failed July 2000 Camp David summit, the Israeli-Palestinian
peace process devolved. Less than two months later, Ariel Sharon, former
Israeli Defense Minister and leader of the opposition Likud party, led a
provocative visit to the al-Aqsa mosque in Jerusalem's Old City. Known as
the Haram al-Sharif (Noble Sanctuary) to Muslims, and as the Temple
Mount to Jews, it is a religiously sensitive site that remains a point of

heated contention in the negotiations between Israelis and Palestinians. Sharon's reputation as a hard-liner was well-earned and an image he embraced. His term as Minister of Defense during the 1982 Lebanon War evoked admiration among some Israelis and revulsion among others as well as the enmity of the Palestinians. Sharon's visit had the desired effect. It embarrassed an already politically weak Prime Minister Ehud Barak, angered Palestinian Authority President Yasir Arafat, sparked a wave of protests by Palestinians, and propelled Sharon and the Likud party to power. Israel's harsh response to the protests, intended to quell them with a strong show of force, had the opposite effect. Even though negotiations continued, they were stymied by Clinton's lame duck period and the pending Israeli elections between Barak and Sharon. Meanwhile, the second Palestinian *intifada* spiraled.[85]

A month after Bush's inauguration, Sharon was elected prime minister of Israel. With the second Palestinian *intifada* entering its fifth month and negotiations at an impasse, Sharon's election portended a more aggressive turn. He was welcomed by neoconservatives in the Bush administration. Even before Sharon was elected, President Bush indicated his determination not to follow Clinton's policies or approach. Instead, the Bush administration endorsed a show of force that only entrenched the violence. Meanwhile, Arafat's Fatah movement faced significant challenges from within and from its rivals, Hamas and PIJ. Secretary of State Powell planned to announce renewed peace talks with a Palestinian state as the end goal, but September 11 intervened.[86]

Israel had maintained bipartisan support in the post–Cold War era. Leading politicians from both parties viewed Israel as a reliable US ally in a vital region, as did the Pentagon. The American Israel Public Affairs Committee (AIPAC) was and remains an influential lobby, but it is not alone. Nor was identification with Israel limited to American Jews. Bush's 2000 election victory was due in part to the increased influence of Christian evangelical voters in the Republican Party. Although not a monolithic bloc, the majority of evangelical voters were consistently pro-Israel and inclined to view the Global War on Terror in civilizational and existential terms. They remained a significant base of support for Bush through his two terms in office. Even critics of Israel's ongoing occupation of the Palestinian territories focused on the negotiations brokered by Washington and the hope that it would conclude with a two-state solution. Although a

Palestinian state in the West Bank and Gaza had been controversial twenty-five years earlier, by the collapse of the 2000 Camp David summit and the end of the Clinton presidency it had mainstream political support. The outbreak of the second Palestinian *intifada* and September 11 altered the political landscape around the peace process.[87]

The US-Israel special relationship was enhanced into a strategic alliance with expanded counterterrorism cooperation and intelligence sharing. Meanwhile, diplomatic efforts focused on developing a roadmap for the resumption of talks with the Palestinians. As the *intifada* continued, however, military force remained the preferred solution. In late March 2002, Israel launched a large military operation inside major Palestinian cities and surrounded Arafat's headquarters in Ramallah. At a June National Security Council meeting, Bush offered a vision for resolving the conflict and its broader importance for his policies within the region: "Imagine how effective it would be if, right in the midst of all these undemocratic governments, a little flower begins to blossom. If we can take the Palestinians and make their lives better, we've roped the rest of the Arab world into the need to reform their own societies by putting a nice little laboratory in their midst."[88]

The Palestinian "laboratory" was integral to the Global War on Terror, the invasion of Iraq, and the Freedom Agenda. On June 24, Bush announced that the United States was breaking ties with Arafat. "When the Palestinian people have new leaders, new institutions, and new security arrangements with their neighbors, the United States of America will support the creation of a Palestinian state whose borders and certain aspects of its sovereignty will be provisional until resolved as part of a final settlement in the Middle East," he declared. Neoconservatives inside and outside the Bush administration argued that overthrowing Saddam Hussein was essential to a negotiated settlement between Israel and the Palestinians. Instead, as the invasion and occupation of Iraq faltered, the Bush administration did not prioritize brokering negotiations. In March 2004, Sharon announced a unilateral withdrawal from Gaza and approved the assassination of the founder and spiritual leader of Hamas, Sheikh Ahmed Yassin. Seven months later Arafat died under mysterious circumstances and Bush won reelection.[89]

The opportunity for renewed negotiations in Bush's second term and the realization of his vision of a Palestinian state never materialized. In early January 2005, Arafat's former deputy Mahmoud Abbas was elected president of the Palestinian Authority. With an active insurgency in Iraq and a resurgent Taliban in Afghanistan, Abbas's election appeared to offer the Freedom Agenda a political and public relations victory. But it was short-lived.

Abbas faced pressure from the United States and Israel to crack down on Hamas. Despite the Yassin assassination, Hamas had grown into a formidable political force by 2005. In contrast to the Palestinian Authority, Hamas established a reputation for a lack of corruption and efficient provision of social services. The 2006 legislative elections were yet another turning point for Hamas and the Palestinian national movement. Although the Bush administration and Abbas were certain that Fatah would win the elections, the decision by Hamas to participate under the banner of "reform and change" had unexpected consequences. Hamas's victory sent shockwaves across the region and in Washington.[90]

Hamas was unwilling to recognize Israel, renounce terrorism, or accept existing agreements as a condition for taking office. Washington coordinated with the European Union to impose sanctions on the Palestinian Authority and force Hamas to accept the Bush administration's demands. Over the next year, attempts to form a unity government between Hamas and Fatah to circumvent the sanctions were blocked by the United States and Israel.[91]

Condoleezza Rica later wrote that Hamas turned Gaza into "a terrorist wasteland that would explode repeatedly over the next three years." Yet the Bush administration helped light the fuse. Washington pursued a deliberate policy of isolating Hamas and punishing Palestinians in Gaza while rewarding Abbas and Fatah in the West Bank. Washington hoped the policy would force Fatah to challenge Hamas and attempted to expedite that process. Instead, in late June 2006, the al-Qassam Brigade, Hamas's military wing, dug a tunnel into Israel and attacked an army base. An Israeli private was captured and held in Gaza. Israel launched a major incursion into the territory that had broader regional consequences.[92]

Over the previous decade, Hamas and Lebanon's Hizbullah had developed a tacit alliance supported by Iran. While the PLO engaged in peace negotiations with Israel under the Oslo Accords in the 1990s, Hizbullah increasingly challenged Israel's security zone in southern Lebanon. Israel's mounting casualties on its northern border raised significant pressure on

political leaders to justify the continued occupation or launch a significant military response. When Israeli Prime Minister Shimon Peres chose
the latter in April 1996, it had implications for Israeli domestic politics as
well as relations with Hizbullah and the peace process with the Palestinians. The invasion was halted after Israel shelled a UN compound in the
village of Qana, killing over a hundred civilians and UN workers. A month
later, Peres lost the election to Benjamin Netanyahu of the Likud party.
Over the next two years, Netanyahu sought to derail the peace process with
the Palestinians. Meanwhile, Hizbullah continued its incursions against
Israeli positions in the security zone.

By May 2000, Netanyahu was no longer prime minister and Ehud Barak
was preparing to enter final-stage negotiations with the Palestinians. Barak
faced public pressure to withdraw from southern Lebanon and his cabinet
agreed that it would occur by the end of July. Israeli forces expedited the
evacuation, however, and by May 24 it was complete. Israel's proxy force,
the South Lebanese Army, also collapsed and its members sought shelter
in Israel. Two months later, the Camp David summit brokered by Clinton
failed weakening Arafat and Barak. Israel's unilateral withdrawal from
southern Lebanon, the failure of the Oslo peace process, and the second
Palestinian *intifada* further emboldened Hamas and Hizbullah.[93]

The September 11 attacks offered Washington an opportunity for a rapprochement with Hizbullah and Iran. Although Hizbullah was opposed
to al-Qa'ida and condemned the attacks, it was included in the secret
NSPD 9. Tehran shared intelligence with Washington about al-Qa'ida
members that were captured in Iran after fleeing the US invasion of Afghanistan. The cooperation ceased, however, after Bush's January 2002
speech placing Iran in the "Axis of Evil" with Iraq and North Korea. As
Washington was preparing for the invasion of Iraq, Deputy Secretary of
State Richard Armitage said that Hizbullah "may be the 'A-Team of Terrorists' and maybe al-Qaeda is actually the 'B' team. And they're on the
list and their time will come."[94]

In February 2005, a massive bomb blast shook downtown Beirut, killing Rafiq al-Hariri—a wealthy Lebanese businessman and Lebanon's former
prime minister—and twenty-one others. Hundreds more were wounded.
Hariri's company, Solidere, had been credited with redeveloping and revi-
talizing downtown Beirut after the civil war was over. He was also criticized
for the widespread fraud and corruption that accompanied reconstruction.

Suspicion focused on Syria, whose occupation of Lebanon was approaching its third decade. Although outrage at Hariri's death was shared across the country's political spectrum, divisions soon emerged between Syria's Lebanese allies and the opposition. A political accommodation was achieved between the March 8 coalition led by Hizbullah and the March 14 movement supported by Washington after Syria withdrew under international pressure. Tensions remained, however, over UN Security Resolution 1559, which called for the disarming of militias in Lebanon. Hizbullah considered implementation of the resolution a red line.[95]

Sixteen months later, as Israel invaded Gaza in July 2006, an army patrol in northern Israel was ambushed by Hizbullah guerillas. Washington claimed that the ensuing month-long conflict in Lebanon was part of the larger Global War on Terror. Secretary of State Rice asserted that the war was "the birth pangs of a new Middle East." Israel and the United States insisted that Hizbullah must be disarmed and dismantled to undermine Iran and Syria's regional influence, and to bolster American efforts in Iraq. Israel unleashed waves of aerial bombing attacks as part of what was termed the "Dahiya Doctrine," in reference to the Beirut neighborhood targeted by the sustained airstrikes. This policy, intended to make clear that any area lending latent or overt support to terrorist organizations would pay a heavy price, resulted in a thousand Lebanese civilians killed, hundreds of thousands displaced internally, and large-scale damage. Hizbullah responded with missile attacks inside Israel, heavily damaged an Israeli warship off the Lebanese coast, and repulsed Israeli armored incursions into southern Lebanon. Hizbullah emerged from the war with Israel victorious, but chastened.[96]

Meanwhile, Hamas was bruised by Israel's invasion, but it was not dislodged from Gaza. Instead of changing course, the Bush administration attempted to limit the impact to its broader regional goals. Over the next ten months, Washington pressured Abbas to confront Hamas. In May 2007, tensions between the rival militias erupted into open fighting. In yet another shock to Washington, Fatah's forces were routed.[97]

Over the next year, the Bush administration attempted to undermine Hizbullah in Lebanon and Hamas in Gaza. Neither policy was successful and both had repercussions. The Bush administration adopted a policy of rewarding Abbas in the West Bank with additional economic assistance and a renewed round of high-level peace negotiations beginning in November 2007. Washington coordinated with Israel and Egypt to tighten the siege on Gaza hoping to dislodge Hamas. But neither the siege, nor Hamas's attempts to circumvent it, achieved their goals.[98]

In Lebanon, Hizbullah focused on rebuilding the areas devastated during the 2006 war with Israel. Although the Bush administration promised large quantities of aid, it was never fully delivered or was siphoned off by Lebanese politicians with ties to Washington. As a result, Hizbullah's popularity in Lebanon increased in the ensuing two years as the movement developed a reputation for reliability. Washington sought to bolster anti-Hizbullah forces in the country and, working with Saudi Arabia, believed it had found a Sunni counterbalance in the Future movement led by Saad Hariri, the son and political heir of the assassinated former prime minister. Tensions escalated through the spring of 2008 following the assassination of Hizbullah's senior military commander, Imad Mughniyeh, in Damascus. Mughniyeh was wanted by both Israel and the United States for acts of terrorism dating to the 1983 bombing of the US embassy in Beirut.[99]

The political standoff turned violent after it was revealed that Hizbullah had secretly installed a fiber optic telecom network in parts of Lebanon. Hizbullah and allies from the Amal and the Syrian Social Nationalist Parties militias quickly routed the fledgling forces of Hariri's Future movement. Hizbullah was harshly criticized by the opposition March 14 coalition and across the region for redirecting its fighters from "resistance" against Israel to engaging in a domestic political dispute. Sectarian political conflicts expanded in Lebanon and regionally over the next decade.[100]

Washington's failure to counter Hizbullah and Hamas contributed to a new logic that influenced the second decade of the Global War on Terror. Writing in the *Washington Post*, David B. Rivkin Jr. and Lee A. Casey argued that Gaza was not occupied territory. Both served in the DOJ in the Reagan and George H. W. Bush administrations and were members of the UN Subcommission on the Promotion and Protection of Human Rights. For Rivkin and Casey, Gaza's status had broader implications than Israel's responsibilities and the rights of Palestinians in Gaza. The determination of Gaza's status, they wrote, "may well set a legal precedent for wars between sovereign states and nonstate entities, including terrorist groups such as al-Qaeda." They placed Gaza and Hamas in the broader category of "failed states or failed areas of states," where the government was unable or unwilling to establish control. "Such places—call them badlands—were once rare. Over the past 15 years, though, there has been an explosion in the number of such areas, notably parts of Afghanistan, Somalia and portions of Pakistan," Gaza, Rivkin and Casey declared, "is a classic example of a terrorist-controlled badland."[101]

At the end of his presidency, Bush's Freedom Agenda was in tatters. His visions of a new Middle East and a Palestinian state were unfulfilled. In early December 2008, Israel launched an invasion of Gaza that lasted twenty-two days and appeared to challenge the incoming administration of Barack Obama. The invasion reflected the view of Gaza as a badlands and Israel applied the Dahiyya Doctrine accordingly. Civilian areas were targets of indiscriminate airstrikes and shelling from land and sea.

Although there were hopes that Obama's election would herald a breakthrough in negotiations between Israel and the Palestinians that eluded previous presidents, these proved to be misplaced. Instead, the siege of Gaza imposed by Israel and Egypt was maintained. In place of one parastate under occupation, Palestinians had two. Israel launched repeated invasions of Gaza as well as frequent airstrikes and assassinations over the next decade. In justifying these operations Israeli military and political officials used metaphors like "mowing the grass" to emphasize the perpetual threat posed by Hamas and the need for enduring operations. Meanwhile, the United Nations warned of a pending humanitarian catastrophe in Gaza. As Chapter 6 argues, Gaza was not unique. Other badlands were reified through action and inaction—and also reproduced in popular culture.[102]

HOLLYWOOD'S WAR ON TERROR

Two months after September 11, the Peninsula Hotel in Beverly Hills hosted a remarkable meeting. A year earlier, the city was the site of lavish fundraisers for Bush's rival in the 2000 presidential election, vice president and Democratic Party nominee Al Gore. This meeting, however, featured Bush's chief political advisor, Karl Rove, and executives from movie studios, television networks, movie theater chains, and labor unions. It was cohosted by Jack Valenti, president of the Motion Picture Association and a veteran of the Johnson administration, and Jonathan Dolgen, chair of the Viacom Entertainment Group. In attendance were such titans of the entertainment industry as Sumner Redstone, the executive chair of Viacom; Sherry Lansing, chair of Paramount Pictures; and Disney's executive chair, Robert Iger. While the Bush White House sought support from a key American industry in the Global War on Terror, entertainment executives also wanted to move beyond the 1990s culture wars, when Hollywood was a frequent target of conservative critics.[103]

The nearly two-hour meeting focused on how the entertainment industry could cooperate with the administration in promoting American efforts abroad and supporting military personnel. After briefing the participants on the war effort, Rove promised he "did not come with a list of asks." He assured the group that it was "not our purpose to come here and say this effort should in any way, shape or form be directed by or coordinated by the government." Preempting any comparison to the Second World War alliance between Washington and Hollywood, Rove argued against any conception of direction by the federal government. Among his suggestions was that the industry could help emphasize that the war was against terrorism and not the religion of Islam. He added that it could also help the administration clarify its message to the international community that a global response was needed in the conflict against evil.[104]

Although participants denied that the meeting focused on content, there had been some indications before the gathering that the administration sought to recreate the kind of relationship that existed during the Second World War. Over the next seven years of the Bush administration, a range of television shows and films that drew on the Global War on Terror directly and indirectly were released.[105] While some glorified American efforts, others offered more complicated narratives about the history of US involvement in the Middle East and the implications. Yet only a few were commercially successful or critically acclaimed and none rivaled the cinematic classics of the New Hollywood era.

The Global War on Terror was best reproduced on television. September 11 and its aftermath coincided with the so-called "Second Golden Age of Television." Among the most popular shows was *24*, starring Kieffer Sutherland and cocreated by Joel Surnow. Purchased by Fox in 2000, its debut was only six weeks after September 11. Combining action and drama with political tension, *24* quickly became a pop-culture phenomenon. It won consistently high ratings as well as critical acclaim, including the 2006 Emmy Award for Best Drama Series. Its fans included conservative talk radio star Rush Limbaugh and members of the Bush administration. The show's title referred to the twenty-four hours that Sutherland's character,

Jack Bauer, and his Los Angeles–based counterterrorism unit had to re-solve a crisis. Each episode represented one hour in the day; a countdown clock was added for dramatic tension. Jack Bauer used any means neces-sary to resolve the problem—which invariably meant torture.[106]

Even after the Abu Ghraib scandal, President Bush publicly declared that "the United States does not torture." Yet he continued to defend the CIA's use of "harsh interrogation" as necessary to protect American lives. Meanwhile, on *24* and other television shows, Americans were treated to a regular diet of torture. Indeed, human rights groups documented the dramatically increased portrayal of torture on American television shows. Before September 11, torture was performed by the antagonists. After the attacks, protagonists engaged in the practice, presumably for noble means. The *New Yorker* reported that interrogators in Iraq watched epi-sodes of *24* on DVD and applied Jack Bauer's crude techniques on detained prisoners.[107]

Meanwhile, the Pentagon drew on *The Battle of Algiers* for training in combatting an urban insurgency. The classic film's harsh depiction of tor-ture was intended to shock viewers and discredit the French government and military. As with *24*, those lessons were lost. Nevertheless, the pro-ducers of *24* did not adopt a different approach until the Bush administra-tion was out of office. Its cultural moment passed, however, and the ninth and final season was in 2009.[108]

NBC's *The West Wing* offered another insight into the post–September 11 zeitgeist. Ostensibly representing the opposite sides of the political spectrum, both programs embraced an aggressive foreign policy approach. Created by Aaron Sorkin, *The West Wing* premiered in 1999 and featured an impressive cast led by Martin Sheen as President Josiah "Jed" Bartlet. The series was a critical and commercial success, earning twenty-six Emmy Awards, including Best Drama Series four times. It combined Sorkin's trademark rapid-fire banter among characters with contrived melodrama and sentimental American exceptionalism. Coinciding with Clinton's scandal-plagued final years, *The West Wing* offered Democrats an escapist fantasy of center-left politics. Sheen's Bartlet was a northeastern Catholic, Democratic president, equal parts devoted husband, father, politician, and intellectual. After September 11, however, the show fully endorsed lib-eral hegemony and promoted policies that went beyond those of the Bush administration.[109]

David Simon's *The Wire* was not directly related to the Global War on Terror. Debuting on HBO in June 2002, the series used the city of Baltimore for insight into the War on Drugs. Its gritty portrayal of police work and drug gangs, as well as the endemic corruption of city politics and the futility of the law enforcement approach to narcotics trafficking, earned critical accolades. *The Wire* critiqued the myriad failures of US policies targeting drugs and terrorism, suggesting that, while not achieving their stated political goals, they would drain vital resources and attention from America's struggling post-industrial cities. Meanwhile, that same lesson was on display in Colombia.

PLAN COLOMBIA

The Bush administration inherited Plan Colombia, but it was obscured by the September 11 attacks. With Washington's new focus on terrorism, combating drug trafficking was no longer a priority. Colombia, however, became another theater in the Global War on Terror. By early 2002, with over $1.3 billion spent, cocaine production was not reduced much less eliminated. Peace negotiations had collapsed between Bogota and the two largest leftist rebel groups, the Revolutionary Armed Forces of Colombia (FARC) and the National Liberation Army (ELN).[110]

In late May 2002, Álvaro Uribe Vélez was elected president of Colombia. A former mayor of Medellin and governor of the Antioquia province, Uribe adopted a tough stance toward leftist rebels. His father had been killed by the FARC in 1983 during a failed abduction, and Uribe himself had survived several assassination attempts. After his election, the Bush administration worked with the US Congress to remove limitations on aid to Bogota under Plan Colombia. Over the previous two years, US aid had been restricted only for counternarcotics efforts, not counterinsurgency against the rebel groups. Although this was flouted, the Global War on Terror and the increased violence that accompanied the collapse of negotiations helped overcome resistance from Capitol Hill.[111]

Less than two years later, a February 2004 cable from the US embassy in Bogota unironically declared "Mission Accomplished." The cable noted that, with American assistance, one of President Uribe's "top strategic objectives" had been realized. Colombian police had been deployed to all municipalities held by the FARC, including the two prominent areas of

Miraflores and Caruru. Miraflores had been captured by the FARC in August 1998 and served as a center for drug trafficking in the Guaviare department. The embassy reported that it could now serve as a base for aerial eradication programs.[112]

The relationship between Iraq and Colombia was not merely rhetorical. Indeed, Plan Colombia increasingly emphasized counterinsurgency and counterterrorism rather than counternarcotics. Critics of Uribe's hard-line campaign rhetoric were concerned that his policies only emboldened right-wing paramilitary groups. These concerns were realized. As in Iraq, paramilitary groups benefited from and exacerbated the violence. Uribe's government maintained ties to the United Self-Defense Forces of Colombia, a coalition of right-wing militias discussed in Chapter 4. The group had been designated by Washington as a terrorist organization before Uribe was elected, and the coalition was responsible for roughly 80 percent of civilian deaths in Colombia. According to leading Colombian human rights organizations, it had carried out at least a hundred massacres during the early years of Project Colombia. It did not commit these atrocities alone, however; it coordinated its actions with the Colombian military, from which it received logistical support.[113]

Following three years of negotiations with Bogota, the United Self-Defense Forces of Colombia was disbanded in 2006. Its 31,800 members were demobilized and 4,200 of them were charged under the 2005 Justice and Peace law. The law was intended to provide justice and reparations for victims, while also ending the fighting and ensuring the success of the peace process. Yet the protracted trials produced just fourteen verdicts and only thirty members of the group were extradited to the United States for drug trafficking.[114] The demobilization process had other flaws, too, including the failure to verify that the individuals involved in the demobilization were former members. It did not take long for the United Self-Defense Forces coalition to be replaced by successor groups, led by former mid-level commanders who had never demobilized. The new paramilitary groups continued committing atrocities and targeting human rights and union activists.[115]

The Uribe government also adopted a number of measures associated with the Global War on Terror, such as the use of large-scale surveillance to target its opponents and critics. Unlike the Bush administration, however, Uribe's government faced consequences for the abuses. In 2011, the Administrative Security Department (*Departamento Administrativo de*

Seguridad) was disbanded. Its director, Jorge Noguera Cotes, and several former Uribe aides, including Bernardo Moreno, Cotes's former chief of staff, were sentenced to lengthy prison terms for their involvement in wiretapping. Maria Pilar del Hurtado, the head of the Administrative Security Department, fled to Panama and was extradited to Colombia four years later. She was found guilty and sentenced to fourteen years in prison.[116]

On a parallel track, Colombia continued and expanded traditional anti-narcotics efforts. In addition to crop eradication, Bogota enhanced its asset seizure and forfeiture policies. In 2005, Colombia borrowed these policies from the United States and applied them to properties where coca plants were grown. The US embassy in Bogota hailed their potential to serve as a "powerful deterrent to illicit cultivation" that "should reduce high replant rates." The land was not, however, actually occupied by the Colombian government or military forces. The embassy reported that this was further complicated by an "onerous" bureaucratic process and the owners could appeal the decision. Moreover, the properties were located in difficult terrain and initial seizures led to a skirmish with the FARC.[117]

As Iraq descended into chaos, Colombia's security situation slowly improved. For four years from 2000 to 2004, Colombia had the highest murder rate in the world. It peaked in 2002 at 69.3 homicides per 100,000. Meanwhile, cocaine producers adjusted to the intervention and eradication policies. Although the number of hectares of coca crop cultivation decreased, the traffickers became more efficient with the land available and there was no discernible change in the wholesale price of cocaine. Contrary to the claims at the beginning of Plan Colombia, cocaine production and trafficking were not eliminated. Indeed, Colombia remains the largest producer of cocaine in the world. Yet proponents of Plan Colombia in Washington argued that it was a successful template for counterinsurgency and counternarcotics to be applied in Mexico and Afghanistan.[118]

THE FORGOTTEN WAR

A month into the US invasion of Afghanistan, President Bush hosted Pakistani President Pervez Musharraf at Camp David. Musharraf had seized power in a military coup two years earlier and relations between Washington and Islamabad were tense before September 11 due to Pakistan's nuclear weapons program. After the attacks, Musharraf quickly pledged

to support the campaign against al-Qaʿida. In return, the Bush administration promised a dramatic increase in military assistance with the goal
of transforming the Pakistani military toward counterterrorism operations. The reestablished relationship was quickly tested a few weeks later,
however, as US forces attempted to kill or capture bin Laden. Bush and
Cheney were briefed that the border between Afghanistan and Pakistan
was difficult to seal and the promised Pakistani troops were not deployed.
Bin Laden's escape raised questions about Islamabad's commitment to the
Global War on Terror. Indeed, Washington remained suspicious about
the relationship between Pakistan's Directorate for Inter-Services Intelligence (ISI) and the Taliban as well as al-Qaʿida.[119]

Over the next five years those questions were mitigated by Pakistan's
cooperation in arresting key al-Qaʿida members. These included Khalid
Sheikh Mohammad and Ramzi bin al-Shibh, both key figures in the
planning of September 11. Meanwhile, the Taliban was resurgent and bin
Laden and Ayman al-Zawahiri remained at large. In addition, Pakistan
faced internal unrest that proved difficult for the military to quell.[120]

The Bush administration insisted that Musharraf was a "western-
oriented modernizer." A 2006 cable from Islamabad advised that Musharraf espoused a "moderate and tolerant Islam for Pakistan as it finds its
way in a globalized world." Yet Washington's support was not focused on
improving Pakistan's economy or sustainable development to ensure that
Musharraf's moderation and modernization were successful. Instead,
roughly 75 percent of the over $12 billion the Bush administration pro-
vided Pakistan was devoted to military assistance. Only 10 percent of the
funds were intended for development.[121]

Islamabad's cooperation did not translate into stability or security in
Afghanistan or Pakistan. In 2006, an estimated 900 Pakistanis died and
over 1,500 were wounded due to 650 terror-related incidents. The majority
of these incidents and casualties were in three border provinces: Balochistan,
the North West Frontier Province, and the Federally Administered Tribal
Areas. At the end of that year, Musharraf began discussions with Washington about plans to end the unrest. He blamed Afghanistan's fledgling
government for its failure to support Pakistan's counterterrorism efforts
or help capture the leader of the Bolchistan uprising.[122]

After the Taliban was overthrown, the Bush administration endorsed
the interim government of Hamid Karzai in Afghanistan. Born and raised

MAP 10. AFGHANISTAN AND PAKISTAN

in Kandahar, Karzai was a member of the anti-Soviet *mujahideen*. After the Soviet withdrawal, he had briefly held the post of deputy foreign minister in President Burhanuddin Rabbani's government. When the Taliban came to power, Karzai had been offered the position of ambassador to the UN, but the Islamic Emirate of Afghanistan was never recognized as a member state. Karzai eventually abandoned the Taliban and sought exile in Pakistan. He returned in October 2001 with the assistance of US special forces. When President Bush was briefed on the progress of US military operations, Karzai was described as the "linchpin" of US efforts. The CIA believed that, as a member of the Pashtun ethnic group, Karzai could "unite" Afghanistan and provide the necessary political leadership

for the Northern Alliance, largely made up of members of the Tajik ethnic group. An additional factor was that the commander of the Northern
Alliance and former ally of the United States during the 1980s, Ahmed
Shah Massoud, had been assassinated by al-Qaʿida suicide bombers on
September 9, 2001. But, as Shah Mahmoud Hanifi later wrote, America's
emphasis on ethnic identities served to entrench them in Afghanistan.
This fetishization was most prominently recreated in the manufactured
"traditional" attire that adorned Karzai. Like the reification of sectarian
identities in Iraq, the ethnicization of Afghan society had immediate and
long-term implications for the US occupation.[123]

Karzai was a featured guest at President Bush's 2002 State of the Union
Address. Five months later he was elected president of Afghanistan for
two years in a stage-managed *Loya Jirga*, a grand assembly of local and
national leaders. While Karzai presented a respectable image to the world,
the main centers of power in his government were former warlords turned
ministers. One of the most powerful and infamous was General Abdul
Rashid Dostum. Although he was appointed deputy defense minister,
Dostum was implicated in war crimes against captured Taliban fighters.
Karzai won the 2004 national election, but there were allegations of widespread fraud. Afghanistan was no longer a priority, however, as the United
States had become mired in Iraq and Bush faced his own reelection challenge. Karzai remained dependent on the US military, including a Praeto-
rian guard of US special forces and private military contractors. In only
three years, Karzai's government was synonymous with corruption and
the Taliban had reemerged.[124]

In March 2006, Ronald Neumann, the US ambassador to Afghanistan, warned of the Taliban threat. His cable described a "grave" situation
in Uruzgan Province, the birthplace of the Taliban's Mullah Omar and
home to a population of roughly two hundred thousand people. Five years
into the US occupation, the provincial representatives of Karzai's government were considered weak and ineffectual, he wrote, and "abject poverty,
tribalism, illiteracy, tribal codes in lieu of modern law, isolation from Kabul, and radicalizing influences from Pakistan" created a "fertile recruiting ground" for the insurgency. "The Taliban and the poppy economy
have filled the vacuum left behind by the government's shrinking bubble
of authority," Neumann noted, and poppy production was expected to
be higher in the current year than the last. Government authority was

increasingly limited to the provincial capital, Tarin Kowt, and a significant minority of young men were Taliban supporters.[125]

A Vietnam veteran, Neumann had a distinguished career in the foreign service. He had served as the US ambassador to Algeria during the
Clinton administration and in the midst of the country's civil war. Neumann was assigned to the CPA in Baghdad before becoming ambassador
to Afghanistan. His father had also served as US ambassador to Afghanistan during the Johnson administration. He later reflected on how the
Vietnam experience influenced his perspectives on Afghanistan and Iraq:
"I learned that the US can't substitute for local political will, leadership,
and determination." The need for these was desperate in Uruzgan, a province he judged to be "at baseline zero by almost any measurable standard.
There is enormous work to be done concurrently in multiple sectors."
Neumann hoped this would be possible after the replacement of Jan Mo-
hammad, an incompetent and autocratic provincial governor with ties to
Karzai. Iraq continued to distract the Bush administration, however, and
Afghanistan remained the forgotten war. As Chapter 6 will show, the
Obama administration's renewed focus on Afghanistan did not improve
the situation.[126]

CONCLUSION

In December 2001, Rumsfeld dispatched two "snowflake" memos. The first,
on December 17, was to Wolfowitz and Feith: "We need to think through
what presence we want in Central Asia when the war on terrorism is over."
Ten days later, Rumsfeld forwarded a *New York Times* article to General
Tommy Franks and General Richard Myers about Saudi Arabia's failure
to closely monitor or detain citizens that had fought in Afghanistan,
Bosnia, Kosovo, or Chechnya over the previous decade. "It might give us
some thoughts as to how we want our footprint arranged in the Middle
East after things settle down," Rumsfeld wrote. "The time to get started
might be sooner rather than later."[127] By the time Rumsfeld resigned as
defense secretary in December 2006, the Global War on Terror was expanding rather than concluding. Al-Qa'ida cells were active from insular
Southeast Asia to East Africa.

The expanding map of conflict was the result of the Bush administration's insistence that a War on Terror was necessary if not essential, and

that it must be *global*. President Bush said the strategy was to "fight them over there so we do not have to face them in the United States of America."[128] The United States, however, conducted the war overseas *and* at home. Rather than learn the lessons of the failed War on Drugs, it allowed the two to become intertwined. As Afghanistan was deemphasized to focus on Iraq, the War on Drugs was a forgotten relic of the pre–September 11 era. In Colombia, the counternarcotics mission was replaced by counterinsurgency and was labeled a success. Anti-narcotics investigations and laws provided the template for the counterterrorism provisions of the Patriot Act. Chapter 6 discusses how these were merged into narco-terrorism.

The Bush administration's insistence that terrorism was an ideology, akin to fascism and communism, contributed to a sweeping policy devoid of historical and social contexts and geopolitical realities. Under the broad category of terror organizations with global reach, Washington included movements that did not share ideologies or goals. The administration eschewed diplomacy in favor of force either directly or through allies and partners in Lebanon and Gaza. This approach was affirmed in aspects of popular culture, as Americans were exposed to a steady regimen of terror-related and torture-filled television. When Washington's policies faltered, it again drew on the Vietnam experience. Flawed historical models were adopted and imperfectly implemented with predictable results.

The administration constructed a false narrative linking Iraq to the September 11 attacks to make an invasion more palatable to the American public. Bush and Rove deliberately framed the 2002 and 2004 elections as referendums on the Global War on Terror. By 2006, however, the administration's continued failure in Iraq had political consequences. This became even more pronounced with 2008's economic collapse. President Bush's average second term approval rating was 37 percent, 53 percent less than it was in the aftermath of September 11 and the "Bullhorn Speech." Bush's approval rating sank even lower after the US stock market crashed in September 2008 and leading banks announced staggering losses. The financial crisis had a devastating impact domestically and globally. Over $3.4 trillion in real estate value and $7.4 trillion in stock market gains were erased, 5.5 million Americans were unemployed, and US economic growth shrank.[129]

The wars in Iraq and Afghanistan coupled with the 2008–2010 financial crisis contributed to renewed existential distress about American decline. Although President Bush claimed the Global War on Terror was a fight for civilization, the policies employed undermined America's global standing and enervated the postwar international order. Contrary to the claims by neoconservatives inside and outside the administration, American power had limits. Chapter 6 explores the world Barack Obama inherited and his administration's attempts to manage and extend the Global War on Terror.

CHAPTER SIX

Dark Lands and the Geography of Empire

That's part of what makes us special as Americans. Unlike the old empires, we don't make these sacrifices for territory or for resources. We do it because it's right.

—PRESIDENT BARACK OBAMA, 2011

IT WAS A TYPICAL day in northwest Pakistan. American drones patrolled the skies while operators watched the live images on their screens thousands of miles away in the United States. A missile fired from one of the drones struck a small house, killing a husband and wife inside. Their ten-year-old daughter, Nadia, was at school at the time. Orphaned, Nadia then moved to a relative's home in a neighboring town. In 2010 she would tell investigators that, with her parents gone, she had "no source of income . . . my aunt looks after me now and I help her in the house . . . but I want admission to school. I want an education." Publicly, the Bush and Obama administrations claimed that the drone campaign was highly accurate and selective. They assured the American public that only members of the Taliban, al-Qaʿida, and affiliated groups were targeted. Nadia's parents did not belong to these organizations. They did, however, live in the badlands.[1]

In his 2020 presidential memoir, Barack Obama wrote that he "took no joy" in the drone campaign. "It didn't make me feel powerful," he added. "I'd entered politics to help kids get a better education, to help families get healthcare, to help poor countries grow more food—it was that kind of power that I measured myself against." Yet the civilian death toll from drone strikes was significantly higher than Washington claimed. Like Nadia's parents, these civilians experienced the deadly side of American power during the Obama presidency.[2] Pakistan was the key arena in Obama's drone campaign. The widespread use of drones to target suspected terrorists began under the Bush administration and it was embraced by Barack Obama in his first term.

The Obama administration expanded the Global War on Terror even after Osama bin Laden was killed in May 2011. Yet the United States began targeting far less influential actors operating locally rather than globally. This chapter argues that the Wars on Crime, Drugs, and Terror became deliberately intertwined. At home, these efforts were not only replicated in increased surveillance and the use of informants but in the targeting of immigrant and minority communities. The legal justifications for these efforts were enhanced, with intended and unintended consequences.

THE GOOD WAR

From the forgotten front in the Global War on Terror to the central battlefield under the Obama administration, Afghanistan exemplified the twin pillars of manufactured policy success and false equivalence to other conflicts. The surge policy introduced in Iraq was replicated in Afghanistan and exposed its failure in both arenas. The Afghanistan War also offered a remarkable parallel to, and eventually intersected with, Project Colombia.

In July 2000, Mullah Mohammad Omar, the leader of the Taliban, banned opium production. By the time of the US invasion in October 2001, opium cultivation had declined by an estimated 90 percent. The ensuing US occupation and Taliban insurgency, however, served to reinvigorate the opium trade. Opium grown in Afghanistan supplies over 80 percent of the world market for heroin and morphine. The United States, however, the world's largest consumer of illegal narcotics, receives heroin from Mexico and Colombia.[3]

In 2002, the United States identified counternarcotics as one of five priority areas for the reconstruction of Afghanistan. The UK led counternarcotics efforts, with an initial emphasis on crop destruction. Afghan farmers were paid $700 per acre of opium poppies. The World Bank

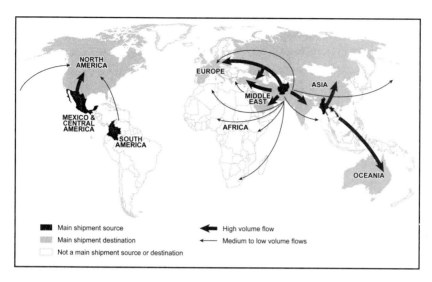

MAP 11. MAP OF INTERNATIONAL HEROIN TRAFFICKING

estimated that the gross domestic product per capita in Afghanistan at the time was $179. Instead of reducing the amount of opium cultivated, farmers rushed to expand their plots and take advantage of the poorly conceived program. It was not the last counternarcotics program to fail.[4]

Like Colombia, counternarcotics and counterinsurgency in Afghanistan became intermeshed. Over the next two years, opium cultivation spiked as the Taliban insurgency challenged Hamid Karzai's new government. The Taliban's previous prohibition on opium was unofficially scrapped. Meanwhile, key individuals in Karzai's government also benefited from the opium trade. By 2005, Washington attempted to apply its standard counternarcotics approach to Afghanistan: crop eradication. Two years later, William Wood, the US ambassador to Colombia, assumed the post in Afghanistan with the expectation that he would apply the perceived success of Plan Colombia to a new front. In Kabul, Wood earned the nickname "Chemical Bill" due to his support for aerial spraying. However, when the policy proved divisive, a manual eradication force was established. Over the next four years, crop eradication did not impact overall opium cultivation. Even when combined with USAID's economic development and crop replacement programs, America's more aggressive counternarcotics efforts were unsuccessful.[5]

In total, the United States spent $9 billion over eighteen years on counternarcotics efforts in Afghanistan. A 2018 report by the Special Inspector General for Afghanistan Reconstruction (SIGAR) offered an understated but devastating assessment. "No counterdrug program undertaken by the United States, its coalition partners, or the Afghan government resulted in lasting reductions in poppy cultivation or opium production," it concluded.[6]

Counterinsurgency efforts were also a failure. The US invasion displaced the Taliban from power, but the core leadership escaped, including Mullah Omar. Within a year, the Taliban launched an insurgency that began challenging the American-led coalition and newly established Afghan security forces. By 2006, the insurgency was successfully entrenched in more than half the country. The Taliban also established a "shadow government" that challenged Karzai's rule. Like other parastates, the Taliban's parallel government included judges, provincial governors, and military commanders. The Taliban's Islamic Emirate expanded as the United States implemented its counterinsurgency policy in Afghanistan.[7]

As it did in Iraq, the Bush administration began emphasizing counterinsurgency and security for Pakistan's Federally Administered Tribal Areas (FATA), bordering Afghanistan. The implementation was slow, however, and marred by continued violence as well as planned elections for early 2008. In discussions with Islamabad, Washington emphasized recent security deployments in Pakistan's Swat valley as a model for the FATA. Over the previous four years, the Pakistani Taliban challenged government rule in the area. Like their Afghan brethren, the Pakistani Taliban promised more effective and less corrupt rule than government authorities. They routed local government forces in a series of clashes. Although the Pakistani army was deployed into the area and directly challenged the Taliban, it was still unstable when the Bush administration began promoting the Swat valley as a model for the FATA. The assassination of presidential candidate Benazir Bhutto in late December 2007 exposed Pakistan's fragile state of security. As the Bush administration prepared to leave office it completed a review of Afghanistan that recommended emphasizing counterinsurgency. The Obama administration adopted this policy, but it was not successful.[8]

During the 2008 campaign, Democratic presidential candidate Obama blasted the Bush administration for diverting attention from Afghanistan to invade Iraq. After securing the party's nomination, Obama's criticisms were more muted as he conceded in media interviews that the "surge" in Iraq worked. Before taking office, Obama asked Vice President-elect Joe Biden to travel to Kabul and provide an assessment of the situation. Afterward, Biden advised that the administration's rationale for continued American involvement should be the presence of al-Qaʻida. In response, Obama prioritized Afghanistan and Pakistan and a combined "Af-Pak" strategy was conceived. Robert Gates remained as Secretary of Defense and was joined by Obama's new national security team, which included National Security Advisor General Jim Jones, CIA Director Leon Panetta, and Director of National Intelligence Admiral Dennis Blair. General Petraeus continued as the commander of CENTCOM, which oversaw the major combat zones of Iraq and Afghanistan. In May 2009, Obama replaced the military commander in Afghanistan, General David D. McKiernan. He also adopted elements of the "surge," including the infusion of thirty-two thousand troops into Afghanistan, as well as the broader adoption of the US military's counterinsurgency strategy. This was complemented with a more aggressive drone war campaign in the skies above Afghanistan and Pakistan.[9]

Four months before the 2008 election, Bush expanded strikes in Afghanistan and Pakistan. Of Washington's twenty-four top al-Qaʻida and other targets, fifteen were killed or captured. Yet the insurgency persisted and grew. Attacks by the Taliban steadily increased through 2009 and spiked in August as the country's presidential elections were held. The open corruption and electoral fraud that accompanied Karzai's victory did little to quell the insurgency. Nor did it restore confidence in Karzai's government inside Afghanistan or in Washington. Indeed, shortly after the election, the Obama administration began planning for a post-Karzai Afghanistan in which US troops were no longer present in the country. Obama and most of his advisors believed that this required a new strategy that combined counterinsurgency and the training of the Afghan National Army. That meant an additional commitment of forces, but Obama wanted to ensure that it would only be for a limited time and his decisions were driven in part by the domestic political calendar. Midterm elections were only a year away and his own reelection loomed.[10]

McKiernan's replacement, General Stanley McChrystal, was frustrated by the perceived lack of support from Washington. McChrystal's stark assessment of the situation in Afghanistan was deliberately leaked to *Washington Post* reporter Bob Woodward. McChrystal sought an additional ten thousand troops and warned that if the request was not fulfilled the mission would fail. Obama eventually agreed to a total of one hundred thousand American troops supplemented by fifty thousand NATO personnel. As demonstrated by the manufactured furor over the McChrystal report, Obama's Afghanistan policy was doomed from the start.[11]

The development and implementation of Obama's Afghanistan strategy was inhibited by infighting and poor policies. While McChrystal managed the war in Afghanistan, Ambassador Richard Holbrooke served as the special representative for Afghanistan and Pakistan policy. The third member of the team was Karl Eikenberry, the US ambassador to Afghanistan and a retired Army general. They were a team, however, in name only. The three men often clashed with each other and their superiors in Washington. Nor did they improve relations with Afghan President Karzai. Like the experience of the CPA in Iraq, this dysfunctionality reflected and reinforced the continuing policy failures in Afghanistan.[12]

Holbrooke's career began in South Vietnam and it shaped his view of counterinsurgency efforts. Interviews by the Special Inspector General revealed that Holbrooke "had political goals and spent most of his time promoting himself." In practice, this meant an emphasis on development efforts in rural Afghanistan. The "civilian uplift," or "civilian surge," had three main goals: build governing capacity "at all levels," improve the rule of law, and initiate sustainable economic growth. With the State Department serving as the lead agency, the number of American civilian employees in Afghanistan more than tripled from 2009 to 2011. At a cost of over $1.7 billion, the civilian surge was presented as the partner to military counterinsurgency efforts.[13]

Yet this proved to be one of the many issues that plagued the effort. US counterinsurgency strategy was summed up as "clear, hold, and build." After areas were "cleared" of Taliban insurgents and held for a period by coalition forces in conjunction with the Afghan National Army, civilian-led reconstruction and development efforts could be introduced. This had the unintended consequence of focusing funding and expertise on areas held by the Taliban, in particular the Helmand and Kandahar provinces.

Meanwhile, those provinces that already supported Karzai's government were often ignored.[14]

Neither the civilian nor the military surge achieved their respective goals. Barnett Rubin, an advisor to Holbrooke, admitted to the Special Inspector General that it "looked like [Holbrooke] believed in [stabilization] when he was doing it but would express doubts at night." Rubin added that Holbrooke had pushed stabilization mainly "as a way of establishing his bona fides" with the US military and the president, "but he knew stabilization wouldn't work because of Vietnam." Rubin recalled Holbrooke had "once told me that the only thing that's the same is that the policies still don't work." Further reflecting the Vietnam experience, Holbrooke wanted to pursue a negotiated settlement but there was "no political space for that." Lacking political support for negotiations or for an expanded war, the Obama administration settled on a strategy of prevention. As Rubin put it, Washington's policy was "not peace or stabilization." Instead, "it was preventing a safe haven" for al-Qaʻida. Despite his private reservations, Holbrooke argued that Afghanistan was different than Vietnam because the Vietnamese insurgency never posed an existential national security threat to the United States. Holbrooke and others insisted that al-Qaʻida did. The unwillingness to explore negotiations with the Taliban or to distinguish it from the Pakistani Taliban ensured that both insurgencies continued.[15]

Holbrooke's skepticism was matched by other senior team members. In December 2010, the *New York Times* published excerpts from leaked cables in which Ambassador Eikenberry criticized Afghan President Hamid Karzai. Eikenberry asserted that Karzai was not "an adequate strategic partner" and that he avoided responsibility for any of the burdens of governance, including security. The leaks damaged Eikenberry's relationship with Karzai beyond repair.[16]

Meanwhile, the faith in counterinsurgency proved to be misplaced. The surge in Iraq only proved to be a temporary success. In Afghanistan, the United States was unable to suppress the Taliban. A SIGAR assessment determined that US military efforts in Afghanistan suffered from a lack of strategy, changing mission parameters, and unrealistic goals. During the Bush administration, Afghanistan was neglected and there was also a missed opportunity to resolve the conflict through negotiations. Elements of the Taliban were willing to join Karzai's new government, but they were rebuffed by the Bush administration.[17]

Although the Obama administration prioritized Afghanistan, the military and political goals remained unrealistic. Like his predecessor, Obama was unwilling to refer to the conflict in Afghanistan as a "war" due to the implications under international law, especially for the treatment of prisoners. Reminiscent of the Vietnam War, the official goals for American and NATO involvement in Afghanistan were muddled. General McChrystal's 2009 assessment summarized them as follows: "Reduce the capability and will of the insurgency, support the growth in capacity and capability of the Afghan National Security Forces (ANSF), and facilitate improvements in governance and socioeconomic development, in order to provide a secure environment for sustainable stability that is observable to the population."[18]

Obama later wrote that he was skeptical of applying the counterinsurgency strategy from Iraq to Afghanistan. He claimed that with each review session "the expansive view of [counterinsurgency] that McChrystal imagined for Afghanistan not only went beyond what was needed to destroy al-Qaeda—it went beyond what was likely achievable within my term of office, if it was achievable at all." He also questioned the claims by the military leadership of the necessity to "send more troops in order to show 'resolve.'" Even though Secretary of Defense Robert Gates and the military leadership endorsed McChrystal's plan, they acknowledged that the United States could not stabilize Afghanistan if it had a corrupt and predatory government. Obama's announced deadline for the withdrawal of US forces undermined the infusion of US troops and civilian advisors. The June 2011 announcement surprised American military officials and diplomats. It had the unintended consequence of signaling to the Taliban and Pakistan that Washington's commitment to Afghanistan was limited. Islamabad was determined not to see a power vacuum in neighboring Afghanistan and sought to maintain its relations with the Taliban and the United States. Meanwhile, the Taliban adopted a flexible insurgency strategy designed to outlast the American military and political calendars.[19]

Washington's flawed approach was compounded by the dysfunctionality of the Afghan National Security Forces. Reminiscent of Vietnamization, the SIGAR review determined that the United States and its NATO allies had little to show for their nearly two decades of training. After spending $83 billion in security assistance during this period, Afghan forces were poorly trained, corrupt, ineffectual, and infiltrated by Taliban members. One NATO trainer from Norway estimated that 30 percent of the Afghan police recruits that deserted created criminal gangs that established fake checkpoints to extort travelers. An American Naval official and counter-insurgency advisor asserted that the Afghan police were the "most hated institution" in the country.[20]

Hanging over the continued problems in Afghanistan was the possibility of negotiations with the Taliban. In July 2008, former members of the Taliban offered to mediate between Karzai's government and the insurgency. By September, Karzai had announced that Saudi Arabia had agreed to broker talks. In response, Secretary of State Condoleezza Rice reinforced Washington's "redlines" on reconciliation. The Bush administration willfully misread the Taliban's interest in negotiations as a sign of rifts within the insurgency that could be exploited. Rice's guidance offered little room for concessions. Rice was adamant that, unlike the accommodation reached in Iraq, this one could not include the Taliban in a power-sharing agreement or other arrangement. In her words, this would "effectively reward insurgent violence and undermine the constitutional processes." Washington also rejected any attempts to create protected geographic areas or zones of control. Instead, any individuals or groups wishing to reconcile needed to surrender their weapons, recognize the constitution and the authority of Karzai's "democratically-elected government," refrain from criminal activity after returning to normal life, and have no association with al-Qaʻida.[21]

The administration's rigid stance was modified slightly over the next month as press reports emerged about the potential negotiations. Subsequently, Rice cabled that the United States would "consider whether to suspend military operations or activities" against individuals or groups engaged in negotiations. Riyadh's position on talks aligned with Washington. Thus we see in the Bush administration's attempts to dictate surrender terms to the Taliban another missed opportunity. There would be even more over the next eight years.[22]

Three years later, bin Laden was dead and the US efforts in Afghanistan were not demonstrating progress. In addition, Pakistan continued to struggle with a vigorous insurgency. Talks were initiated between Karzai and the Taliban with Qatar serving as an intermediary. Although expectations were low, the effort was endorsed by prominent diplomats. Even though public and secret talks continued, a breakthrough did not come before Obama left office.[23]

However, Obama did reduce the size of US forces in Afghanistan. By the time Donald Trump was inaugurated in January 2017, US troop levels were at their lowest level since 2002. Yet these figures do not account for military contractors deployed in Afghanistan to assist with security duties, training, and other functions. In addition, the Afghan National Army had yet to engage in sustained operations without US support. Meanwhile, the Taliban demonstrated the ability to maintain a sustained insurgency and effective shadow government that contrasted with the corruption and ineptitude in Kabul.[24]

THE WITCHES' BREW

Immediately after Pervez Musharraf's resignation in August 2008, in the midst of the US presidential campaign and an active insurgency in Pakistan, US Ambassador to Pakistan Anne Patterson sent a lengthy cable assessing possible ramifications. In it, she noted that Musharraf had been a "trusted ally who was closely identified with America; it was in US interests that he receive a dignified exit." His popularity had plummeted, however, and after leaving the army in November 2007 he had "lost influence over government and military policy." His commitment to the Global War on Terror had tied him closely to Washington, but he "never convinced his own people that this was their battle and not a war fought only for America and the West." Yet Patterson's assessment of Musharraf's performance centered on political failings and poor military strategy, not attempts to influence public opinion within Pakistan. From the "disastrous" two-year campaign in the tribal areas to flawed peace deals with insurgents, Musharraf had been unable to either impose governmental authority or reach an accommodation with the opposition. Nor had he managed to convince Pakistan's security services to abandon their proxies. Patterson reported that Islamabad was "losing ground to the militants every day" and had yet to "employ effective counter-insurgency strategy."[25]

Six months later, the Obama administration was preparing its "Af-Pak" strategy. For fiscal year 2011, it planned to double US assistance from $2 billion to $4 billion. Meanwhile, the situation in Pakistan had deteriorated. The Pakistani Taliban had seized the Swat valley, which only a year before the Bush administration had hailed as a successful example of counterinsurgency operations. Ambassador Patterson presented a case not for counterinsurgency or counterterrorism but for nation-building. She cabled in February 2009 that "defeating a growing witches' brew" of al-Qaʻida, the Pakistani Taliban, and assorted local extremists and criminal gangs would be "a long 10–15 year fight." It didn't help that "Pakistan hedges its bets on cooperation because it fears the US will again desert Islamabad after we get Osama bin Laden." The relationship between Islamabad and Washington, she wrote, was "one of co-dependency we grudgingly admit— Pakistan knows the US cannot afford to walk away; the US knows Pakistan cannot survive without our support."[26]

Pakistan's military operations reflected the lack of faith in Washington, the ambassador observed. While President Asif Ali Zardari (widower of Benazir Bhutto) and other political leaders had come around to seeing that the country's greatest threat was no longer war with India but the militancy spreading from its border with Afghanistan, the Army and intelligence community had "not turned that corner." This was complicated by the Pakistani government's habit of using "militant / tribal proxies as foreign policy tools." Islamabad encouraged Washington to engage in negotiations with former Taliban members, but that would not occur for two more years. Meanwhile, the Obama administration launched its drone campaign.[27]

UNDER A DRONE-FILLED SKY

Inside a nondescript trailer on a US military base, soldiers sit in cubicles facing fourteen video monitors. On the screens were images broadcast from drones flying over several countries. When a wanted target is identified and the order is given, the copilot presses a button that activates a laser for guiding the Hellfire missile. Holding a joystick, the pilot pulls the trigger and the drone releases its payload. A Hellfire missile travels at 950 miles per hour and the time to impact is swift. In less than twenty seconds, the judgment is often final.[28]

Washington's more aggressive strategy was adopted after Robert Gates replaced Donald Rumsfeld as defense secretary. Gates benefited from increased drone production and improved human intelligence. The new strategy was also informed by evidence of communications between Pakistan's ISI and the Afghan Taliban. "We're going to stop playing the game," Bush reportedly told his national security team. "These sons of bitches are killing Americans. I've had enough." Islamabad was informed of the strikes while they were underway or afterward. A combination of Predator and Reaper drones were unleashed on western Pakistan. During the Bush administration's last three years, at least 160 civilians were killed in Pakistan from drone attacks, including a hundred children. The administration focused on the deaths of al-Qaʿida's senior leadership and seven major figures were assassinated by the end of 2008. Despite the public criticism in Pakistan, newly elected President Zardari privately blessed the program.[29]

The drone war dramatically increased during Obama's first term in office. General Michael Hayden, former director of the National Security Agency and the CIA, later reflected that had been a "powerful continuity" from Bush to Obama. To justify the more aggressive drone campaign to President Bush, Hayden had pointed to the reemergence of training camps in Pakistan. The trainees, he said, were "people who wouldn't cause you to raise your eyebrow if they were next to you going through the passport line at Dulles in your latest flight from the United Kingdom." Over a year later, Hayden presented the same scenario to President-elect Obama.[30]

Obama abandoned detaining high-value targets. As Hayden observed ruefully, "We don't detain anybody anymore. Put interrogations aside. Interrogate someone? We don't *capture* anybody. I think that's a big deal, but other than that, amazing continuity." From 2009 to 2012, over 1,784 individuals were killed in Pakistan by drone attacks—of which at least 249 were identified as civilians, including 62 children—and another 875 were injured. The drones based at secret locations inside Pakistan accounted for 80 percent of the United States' attacks around the globe. Meanwhile, in Yemen, drone attacks had a similar pattern and consequences. During Obama's first term, at least 383 people were killed, including a hundred civilians and 26 children. Special forces targeting teams were on the ground to assist with identification of individuals. Although this should have helped limit civilian casualties, the Obama administration considered all military age males in the areas of operation to be combatants. Subsequent reporting by journalists and human rights organizations determined that civilian casualties far exceeded the administration's claims.[31]

Yemen was also the site of the drone assassinations of three American citizens. In late September 2011, Anwar al-Awlaki and Samir Khan were killed in a drone strike. The Obama administration asserted that they were actively involved in the leadership of al-Qaʿida in the Arabian Peninsula

(AQAP) and incited attacks against the United States. Two weeks later, al-Awlaki's sixteen-year-old son, Abdulrahman, was killed in a separate drone attack. Before he was on the kill list, Anwar al-Awlaki was an active religious leader in the Washington, DC area and widely quoted by leading media outlets. He served as the imam at George Washington University and led the first Muslim prayer service at the US Capitol. Born in Yemen, and holding dual US-Yemeni citizenship, al-Awlaki fought with the *mujahideen* in Afghanistan during the 1980s. Evidence later emerged that after fighting in Afghanistan, al-Awlaki served as a CIA informant. Although al-Awlaki may also have been associated with the September 11 hijackers, he never testified before the 9/11 Commission. Instead, al-Awlaki returned to Yemen and his online sermons were increasingly aligned with and praised al-Qaʿida. A Pakistani-American, Khan was the editor of *Inspire*, al-Qaʿida's English-language magazine.[32]

The extrajudicial assassinations of American citizens, including of a minor, raise questions about the violations of the right to due process and trial by jury. In 2012, the ACLU and the Center for Constitutional Rights filed a lawsuit challenging the constitutionality of the killings, but the case was dismissed two years later. Although Obama's memoir offers no insights or explanations into the legality of these assassinations, he reportedly confided in aides that it was "an easy choice."[33]

There were two separate but related drone programs. The CIA maintained one list of "high value targets" in Afghanistan, Pakistan, and Yemen. Operating out of CIA headquarters in McLean, Virginia, presidential approval was not required to eliminate targets on the agency's list. In contrast, the US military's targets were authorized by Presidents Bush and Obama. It took over a decade, however, for the drone program to reach this point. When Gates succeeded Rumsfeld, CENTCOM only had thirty-six drones in operation. The majority were deployed in Iraq, and Gates had difficulty obtaining drones for use in Afghanistan.[34]

The escalating drone campaign triggered a response. In April 2009, Ambassador Patterson reported that Baitullah Mehsud, leader of the Pakistani Taliban (*Tehrik-e-Taliban Pakistan*, TTP), had "declared war." The previous month, two separate drone strikes killed an estimated thirty TTP insurgents and the United States offered a $5 million reward for information leading to Mehsud's capture. In response, Mehsud promised to launch two attacks per week inside Pakistan. With an estimated forty to fifty

thousand fighters, the TTP controlled large swaths of the North West
Frontier Province and the FATA. Renewed attacks by the TTP extended
into the major cities of Lahore and Islamabad. The attacks claimed the
lives of at least seventy Pakistanis, including over forty military and security personnel.[35]

In February 2008, Mehsud and the TTP signed an agreement with the
Pakistani military to cease attacks inside Pakistan. The TTP planned to
focus only on American and NATO forces in Afghanistan. Ambassador
Patterson reported that the drone campaign and US bounty likely contributed to the group's decision to resume operations inside the country as
it sought to pressure Islamabad to end the drone attacks. The TTP was
further emboldened by its success in holding the Swat valley. Patterson
added that when the government "could no longer promise citizens law
and order the Taliban is ready to step in." Nor was Islamabad able to develop and implement a coherent strategy to challenge Mehsud and the
TTP. Over the next four months, the Pakistani military launched offensives against TTP positions. The US embassy in Islamabad warned that it
would be a "long haul" and the progress of the operations was limited by
internally displaced persons. But in early August, the drone campaign and
Pakistani military offensive claimed a major success, as Mehsud was killed
in Waziristan with his wife and two aides. The assassination was hailed
by several Pakistani newspapers and led to factional infighting within the
TTP.[36]

Although the United States had unchallenged air superiority over Afghanistan and Pakistan and the drone campaign continued for three
more years, it was inconclusive. The Obama administration continued to
declare major successes in the targeted assassinations of Taliban leaders
and fighters as well as al-Qaʿida members. It did not translate into quell-
ing the insurgency in Afghanistan, however, or to any marked improvement in stability or security. In addition, the continued assassinations and
revelations about civilian casualties that were far higher than the Pentagon's estimates raised questions about the efficacy of the effort. These
questions were even more pronounced after bin Laden was killed and the
drone assassinations of lower level al-Qaʿida and Taliban members continued. As the 2012 presidential campaign approached, the Obama administration began revising and streamlining the process for the assassination
campaign.

More than a decade after the Global War on Terror began, the lists of individuals to kill or detain were still updated and maintained. President Obama convened counterterrorism meetings every Tuesday where the list of targets was reviewed and updated. Referred to as the "disposition matrix," both the Pentagon and CIA contributed to the lists. As the 2012 election approached, the Obama administration conceded that the number of individuals on the list had been reduced. Roughly twenty-five individuals in Pakistan and Yemen remained to be killed or captured. Although they were not of the same stature as their predecessors, Washington believed that they were still a threat. Moreover, Obama's national security team indicated that there were plans to maintain the lists and the related assassination program for at least another decade. They asserted that they had developed an approach that was "bureaucratically, legally and morally sound," and would be a model for future administrations. Yet even former administration officials were critical of the reliance on assassination, which provided a short-term benefit without considering the long-term implications or precedents established that constrained future administrations. And the presumption of guilt in areas of operation was applied domestically as well.[37]

FUTURE CRIME, FUTURE TERROR

Only five months into his presidency, Obama was presented with a frightening intelligence report. At least twenty individuals holding American, Canadian, or Western European passports trained in Pakistan by al-Qaʿida were planning to return home and launch a wave of terror attacks. Subsequent FBI investigations based on additional intelligence yielded two arrests. But the threat was not over as new intelligence suggested at least a hundred individuals with a range of passports were trained in Pakistan. This provided part of the rationale for increased domestic surveillance.[38]

Monitoring potential threats adopted a familiar model. The War on Crime's emphasis on future infractions was applied to the Global War on Terror. In addition to the disposition matrix, and apparently informing it, are major databases that collect information on terrorism suspects. The Obama administration oversaw a tenfold increase in the number of suspects added to the "Terrorism Screening Database" (TSDB). Over 40 percent of the nearly 700,000 individuals in the database did not have an official affiliation with a designated terrorist organization. In contrast, roughly 33 percent belonged to one of several closely monitored groups: al-Qaʿida in Iraq, the Taliban, al-Qaʿida, Hamas, and Hizbullah. One reason for the dramatic growth of the watch list is that government officials only need "reasonable suspicion" to add an individual to the TSDB. In addition, the CIA adds information to the TSDB by relying on a program that secretly accesses and extracts information from the intelligence databases maintained by foreign governments.[39]

An assessment process determines if individuals should be added to the TSDB. This includes monitoring and evaluating constitutionally protected activities, like social media and travel habits. Biometric data is also collected on individuals and the database contains facial images, fingerprints, and iris scans. The assessment process also relies on a very broad definition of terrorism, that includes damaging government property or the computer systems of financial institutions. Once an individual is added, their family and friends can also be nominated for inclusion. The TSDB's data is shared with the US intelligence community, the military branches as well as law enforcement agencies, foreign governments, and military contractors. As observed with the FBI's Uniform Crime Report in the 1960s and 1970s, there is a presumption of guilt based on minimal evidence that an individual will commit an act of terrorism in the future. Individuals are not informed that they have been added to the TSDB and there is no legal recourse to be removed from the watchlist.[40]

Another database, the Terrorist Identities Datamart Environment (TIDE), is larger and requires even less evidence for inclusion. According to leaked documents, TIDE reached 1 million entries in late June 2013. This was an increase of 380,000 records in three years. Nearly seven years later, a press release from the Office of the Director of National Intelligence noted that the database was "a critical element" of "border and security screening," suggesting that the data entry has continued unabated.[41]

The growth of the databases aligns with the aggressive domestic policing and surveillance of Arab and Muslim-American communities since September 11. One of the most intrusive cases was in New York City. Although this new operation was initiated by the New York City Police Department's Intelligence Division after September 11, there were prior efforts dating to the 1970s. With support and training from the CIA, the Intelligence Division established a "Demographics Unit" that was tasked with inserting undercover officers into different neighborhoods as well as relying on informants. The program mapped the Muslim community across the greater New York City metropolitan area, including in New Jersey, Connecticut, and Pennsylvania.[42]

Targets ranged from individual religious and community leaders to businesses, community organizations, and educational and religious institutions. One former intelligence division officer told a reporter, "it's not a question of profiling. It's a question of going where the problem could arise." The "ancestries of interest" listed twenty-eight countries and territories as well as "American Black Muslims." But the lengthy investigation was not due to evidence of wrongdoing and the suspicions were purely speculative based on perceived religious beliefs. Information gathered by the investigation was shared with state and federal agencies, including for entry into the database watchlists.[43]

The 2013 lawsuit, *Razza v. City of New York*, was successful in its goal of exposing the program and its cessation. Even before the suit was filed, the head of the NYPD Intelligence Division conceded that for the six years he led the division the surveillance program did not produce any leads. Like COINTELPRO, the information collected was mundane and revealed more about the biases and misperceptions of the officers than a reality in the community. For example, to determine the level of radicalization the program sought reports on the number of times university students prayed per day on a Muslim Students Association rafting trip. Other indicators of radicalization included restaurants with televisions that broadcast Al Jazeera or that closed for daily prayers. In 2017, a settlement was reached in which the NYPD agreed to a number of reforms that limited surveillance programs. Restrictions were placed on the length of investigations as well as the use of undercover police and informants. In addition, the NYPD adopted an anti-discrimination policy and created a civilian representative position to ensure that the settlement was implemented.[44]

Another controversial aspect of the NYPD program was to encourage informants to instigate conversations related to terrorism. Called "create and capture," these attempts were deployed more successfully outside of New York City. Like the NYPD, the FBI relied on unscrupulous informants to identify potential domestic terrorists. The informants were often individuals with previous criminal records or charges and had financial and legal incentives to encourage, if not entrap, individuals in terrorism plots.[45]

One FBI informant, Shahed Hussain, translated his history of fraud and bankruptcy into a lucrative career for the federal government. He was involved in two major cases in New York State five years apart that were hailed by the FBI and the Department of Justice as major victories against terrorism. Neither the 2004 Albany case nor the 2009 "Newburgh Four" case, however, concerned al-Qaʿida. Instead, the FBI agents and Hussain instigated the plots and provided the money and weapons. In addition, James Cromitie, the lead defendant in the Newburgh case, had a history of addiction and mental illness. Although the presiding judge criticized the FBI's actions, she had no choice but to sentence the four men to the mandatory minimum of twenty-five years each. Meanwhile, Hussain was paid at least $96,000 for his efforts. In July 2023, US District Judge Colleen McMahon ordered the release of three members of the "Newburgh Four"—Onta Williams, David Williams, and Laguerre Payen—on compassionate grounds. Judge McMahon offered a scathing assessment: "the sentence was the product of a fictitious plot to do things that these men had never remotely contemplated, and that were never going to happen." Cromite, however, is not scheduled to be released until 2030.[46]

There were even more troubling cases of the FBI attempting to force individuals to become informants and reprisals when they refused. In one instance, three men—Muhammad Tanvir, Jameel Algibhah, and Naveed Shinwari—were placed on the no-fly list for five years because they refused to serve as informants. The men were not only prevented from reuniting with their families or visiting sick parents, they were subjected to harassment by FBI agents and suffered lost income. Their attempts to challenge the FBI in court were initially unsuccessful, but the US Supreme Court ruled in December 2020 that they could seek monetary damages.[47]

Building on its use of immigration laws to indefinitely detain thousands of people inside the United States, the FBI attempted to entice or threaten individuals to serve as informants based on their immigration status or that of a spouse or family members. In its internal policy guide, the FBI referred to this as the "immigration dangle" and it served to ensnare the majority of its fifteen thousand informants by 2017. Yet, since 2007, the "Attorney General's Guidelines Regarding the Use of FBI Confidential Sources," drafted by then US Attorney General Alberto Gonzalez, had prohibited making promises to potential informants related to immigration status. Nevertheless, the FBI agents continued the practice

even though they could not assist with resolving visa status issues for informants or their family members. Nor did it prevent them from making
outlandish promises that were beyond their capacity. In at least one case,
FBI agents promised to help with admission into a university in the
United States if an individual agreed to serve as an informant. The alternative was imprisonment and separation from a newborn child. These practices continued from the Bush to the Obama administration and into the
Trump presidency, as did the reliance on the Patriot Act.[48]

RENEWING THE PATRIOT ACT

Although the USA Patriot Act was originally passed and signed with little
debate after September 11, over the next five years it had become increasingly controversial. As the Act came up for renewal in the fall of 2005,
several prominent Republican Senators raised objections to making key
provisions permanent. While media attention focused on the compromise
to ensure passage, new provisions were incorporated that served to entrench the War on Terror and integrate it with the War on Drugs. In improving and reauthorizing the Patriot Act, Congress established "narco-
terrorism" as a new category of crime for enforcement.[49]

The new statue was a victory for the DEA. After September 11, the
DEA sought to link narcotics trafficking to terrorism. For the Bush ad-
ministration, it was an easy sell. In December 2001, Bush reauthorized the
"Drug-Free Communities Program" and made the connection explicit.
"Terrorists use drug profits to fund their cells to commit acts of murder,"
Bush said. "If you quit drugs, you join the fight against terror in America."
Less than two months later, the Office of National Drug Control Policy
produced a $4 million public service announcement that was broadcast
during Super Bowl XXXVI. The advertisement warned: "Drug Money
Supports Terror" and "If You Buy Drugs You Might Too." Like the construction of the cartels, narco-terrorism helped provide a new rationale for
the DEA. The combination of the new statute and the Obama administration's focus on Afghanistan was a lifeline.[50]

However, there was a complication. The statue was sponsored by Republican Henry Hyde of Illinois, who chaired the House International Relations Committee. It was largely crafted by the committee's counsel and
was deliberately written in a broad manner that allowed for the prosecution

of individuals for material support of a terrorist organization even if the drugs were not intended for the United States. Therefore, it aligned with the War on Terror's global battlefield. The DOJ attempted to clarify the new statue's language on terrorism, but it was rejected as unnecessary.[51]

Lawmakers sought to justify the statute's necessity. In October 2007, a House Subcommittee meeting was held on counternarcotics strategy and police training in Afghanistan. While Democrats used the hearing to criticize the Bush administration's policies in Afghanistan and Iraq, Republicans embraced the claims about the relationship between narcotics and terrorism. Representative Mike Pence, Republican of Indiana and future vice president, asserted that "it is clear from the growth of opium traffic and its close links to the insurgency that the war on drugs is a crucial piece of the war on terror."[52]

In his prepared statement, Ambassador Thomas Schweich, the Coordinator for Counternarcotics and Security Reform in Afghanistan, focused on the recently approved counternarcotics strategy. Notably absent were references to counterinsurgency or narco-terrorism, a point raised by California Republican Dana Rohrabacher. Rohrabacher pressed Schweich on the failure to apply the narco-terrorism statute in Afghanistan and claimed it was successfully implemented in Colombia. Schweich conceded that nineteen months since the Patriot Act was renewed, no individuals from Afghanistan were extradited under the narco-terrorism provision. This, however, was partially due to confusion over the legal status of the Taliban and applicability of the law. He acknowledged that several Taliban commanders were considered "high value targets" due to their involvement in opium production, and the United States was coordinating with the NATO-led International Security Assistance Force (ISAF) to have them arrested.[53]

A month later, the first individual to be convicted under the statue was flown to the United States. Arrested by the DEA thirteen months earlier, Khan Mohammad was affiliated with the Taliban but was not a high value target. Relying on an informant, the DEA arrested Mohammad for distributing 2 kilograms of heroin. The informant had previously recorded Mohammad discussing attacks on American forces. He was also enthusiastic about converting 11 kilograms of opium into heroin for sale in the United States. Several damning statements were presented to the jury during his trial. Mohammad told the informant that "jihad would be performed since they send [the heroin] to America . . . [m]ay God eliminate them right now, and we will eliminate them too. Whether it is by opium or by shooting, this is our common goal." In December 2008, Mohammad was sentenced to two life sentences.[54]

Speaking at the Washington Institute for Near East Policy in July 2008, Michael Braun painted a stark picture of the future. Braun had recently served as the DEA's Chief of Operations and he asserted bluntly that "the nexus between drug trafficking and terrorism is growing at quantum speed." He reported that the DEA linked nineteen of the forty-three organizations designated as terrorists by the United States to "some aspect of the global drug trade." "It is believed that up to sixty percent of terrorist organizations are connected with the illegal narcotics trade," he added. Braun argued that state sponsorship of terrorism was declining due to the War on Terror and US agencies had successfully targeted al-Qaʿidaʾs funding networks. This forced organizations to find alternate sources of funding and narcotics were more lucrative than other options. The Pentagon, Braun reported, expected the War on Terror to continue for "another thirty to fifty years." It lacked the expertise and infrastructure for narcoterrorism, however, and relied on the DEA "for advice on how to wage a war that has increasingly become a shared fight."[55]

Despite the DEA's claim that narco-terrorism was a rapidly growing threat, it failed to convict al-Qaʿida members for the new crime. This was resolved in December 2009, when three fledgling smugglers from Mali were indicted in New York City for narco-terrorism. Federal prosecutors argued that the case reflected "the worrisome alliance between Al Qaeda and transnational narcotics traffickers." The defendants did not have relationships with al-Qaʿida, however, and the FBI informants actively encouraged the extravagant scheme to transport drugs from Colombia to Europe via Mali. Nevertheless, the three defendants were found guilty and sentenced to five years in prison before they were extradited to Mali.[56]

As a sign that surveillance under the Patriot Act was normalized, five years later renewal only garnered minimal debate. Two measures from the legislation were extended for another four years. The first related to roving wiretaps that allowed government agencies to maintain surveillance of a suspect if they switched phones. The second provision allowed investigators to examine an individual's history of borrowing library books, purchases from bookstores, and business records even if the suspect was not involved in a terrorism related case.[57]

An analysis by the Electronic Frontier Foundation found a dramatic increase in the number of "sneak and peak" warrants from 2001 to 2013. Few
were related to terrorism, however, and the overwhelming majority were
for narcotics cases. From September 2001 to April 2003, only forty-seven
warrants were requested. Seven years later, the number of warrants skyrocketed to nearly four thousand. But only thirty-seven involved terrorism
and over three thousand were narcotics-related. The number of warrants
continued to dramatically increase during the Obama presidency. There
were 11,129 warrants in 2013—nearly three times as many as three years
before. Yet only 51 were related to terrorism and over 9,400 were for drug
cases. Considering the Patriot Act's origins were in applying standards from
narcotics investigations to those related to terrorism, it appears that federal agencies relied on the terrorism justification merely for more invasive
surveillance of suspects in a range of cases with limited, if any, oversight.[58]

MILITARIZING POLICE

The intersection of law enforcement and counterterrorism was not limited
to domestic spying and the use of informants. It was also directly evidenced
in the increased militarization of local police across the United States. This
became clear with the proliferation of Special Weapons and Tactics (SWAT)
teams. An analysis by the Congressional Research Service found that, by
the end of the 1990s, 80 percent of police departments serving areas with
populations of twenty-five thousand to fifty thousand people had SWAT
teams. The percentage was even higher, 89 percent, for departments serving
a population of more than fifty thousand. This has been matched by an
exponential increase in their use. From 1980 to 2000, there was a 1,400
percent increase in SWAT deployments. Yet this has only raised concerns
about SWAT training and the appropriateness of their deployments.[59]

Legislation passed nearly a decade before September 11 helped expand
the relationship between the Pentagon and local police departments. As
discussed in Chapter 4, the 1033 Program created by the National Defense
Authorization Act for 1990 and 1991 allowed for the transfer of military
equipment to local police for counternarcotics. It was further expanded
for counterterrorism. Over the next two decades, at least $7.4 billion in
equipment was delivered to more than eight thousand federal, state, and
local agencies across the country.[60]

Radley Balko demonstrates that narcotics task forces were increasingly prevalent in rural areas across the United States. Made up of local police officers, they featured SWAT equipment but not the same level of training and experience. In addition, their incentives were based on arrests and seizures of narcotics and money as well as property. This had dire consequences as aggressive raids occurred that were based on poor information or dubious informants. The raids and their implications were eerily similar to those conducted in Afghanistan and Iraq by heavily armed American soldiers, including some that served in law enforcement in the United States.[61]

Criticism of night raids in Afghanistan and Iraq date to the beginning of both occupations. A September 2011 report by the Open Society Foundation found that 1,700 night raids were conducted by the NATO-led ISAF from December 2010 to February 2011. The average of nineteen raids per night increased to forty per night in April 2011. Even when the raids did not result in civilian casualties, they angered the local population and the Afghan government. Resentment of the night raids persisted after the CIA transferred oversight of Afghan strike forces to Afghan intelligence in 2012. Human Rights Watch found that the Afghan strike forces were responsible for extrajudicial assassinations, arbitrary and extended detentions, and abusive tactics that qualified as war crimes.[62]

Similarities between the raids overseas and at home were deliberate as well. This was observed in Buffalo, New York when local police implemented "Operation Shock and Awe" in April 2006. The operation's name was borrowed from the US military's initial bombing campaign of Iraq three years earlier. It featured thirty-eight SWAT team counternarcotics raids around the Buffalo area that yielded less than two pounds of marijuana, some weapons, and a large number of arrests but few convictions. Like America's efforts in Iraq, the Buffalo police were not deterred by the obvious failure of the high-profile initiative as more operations were planned.[63]

After September 11, the Department of Homeland Security (DHS) implemented an anti-terrorism grant program for local law enforcement. Over the next decade $34 billion in grants were distributed that supported the purchase of military equipment and supplies. The impact was much greater than the 1033 programs. Police departments across the United States were awarded grants, including those that were unlikely to be targeted in a major terrorist attack. The program ensured that local law enforcement armed with the latest military equipment would find any excuse for deployment.[64]

This reality was demonstrated most vividly in August 2014 in Ferguson, Missouri. After local police killed Michael Brown, an unarmed, eighteen-year-old, Black teenager, protests gripped the small city outside St. Louis. In response, the police deployed a massive show of force, including armored personnel carriers. Wearing body armor and carrying high-powered rifles, the police did little to quell the anger of residents—and nor did their use of tear gas and "flash-bang" grenades. Democratic Representative Emanuel Cleaver of Missouri, an outspoken critic of police militarization, underscored the relationship between America's wars abroad and at home when he told reporters that "Ferguson resembles Fallujah."[65]

The national and international revulsion at the overwhelming show of force by local police led President Obama to reform the 1033 program. Signed five months after Brown was killed in January 2015, Executive Order 13688 prohibited the sale of certain types of equipment like armored personnel carriers and grenade launchers to law enforcement agencies. This EO was later rescinded by President Trump, who praised the 1033 program. An investigation by the US Congress's Government Accountability Office (GAO) found that there were insufficient controls and verifications in place. To conduct its study, the GAO established a fake law enforcement agency and was able to buy lethal surplus military equipment. Although further reforms were implemented after its report was issued, 1033 was just one of several unaccountable programs employed by the US national security establishment that had detrimental implications at home and abroad.[66]

"WE TORTURED SOME FOLKS"

During the 2008 presidential election campaign, both John McCain and Barack Obama promised to close the prison at the Guantanamo Bay base. Shortly after Obama's sweeping win, the Senate Armed Services Committee released a devastating report on the treatment of detainees held by the United States. The report listed the objections made by lawyers for the major military branches and rejected the claim that low-ranking military personnel were responsible for abuses. "The fact is," it stated, "that senior officials in the United States government solicited information on how to use aggressive techniques, redefined the law to create the appearance of their legality, and authorized their use against detainees." Quoting testimony from a Navy lawyer, it expressed the view that, more than anything else, "the symbols of Abu Ghraib and Guantanamo" were causing US troops to die in Iraq, because they were such potent recruiting tools for insurgent fighters.[67]

By the end of the Bush administration, the eighteen approved "enhanced interrogation" techniques were reduced to six. Shortly after entering office, President Obama signed Executive Order 13491 ending the indefinite detention program. EO 13491 also prohibited the use of coercive interrogation methods beyond those already approved in the Army Field Manual, which were in accordance with the Geneva Conventions for the treatment of prisoners.[68]

The Guantanamo Bay prison remained in operation at the end of Obama's presidency. Forty-one detainees were in limbo. Five of the men were cleared for release by the Bush administration but remained in custody. Another twenty-six were never charged or had a trial. A number of the detainees were seized as part of a bounty program to capture Taliban and al-Qa'ida members. Instead of apprehending high value targets, the program created a financial incentive to seize random individuals. By 2023, the Biden administration began releasing some of the detainees. The remaining prisoners are still waiting for trial in the military commission process established by the Bush administration, which Human Rights Watch called a "failed experiment in alternative justice." As of this writing, the US government has begun negotiations for plea agreements with five detainees linked to the September 11 attacks that were subjected to torture.[69]

A year before the Senate committee report was issued, the *New York Times* disclosed that the CIA had destroyed the detainee interrogation tapes. The rationale was that any leak or release of the tapes would place the easily identifiable interrogators and their families at risk. Deliberations within the CIA and with congressional oversight committees about how to proceed occurred over thirty-nine months. Ultimately, Jose Rodriguez Jr., the director of the National Clandestine Service, obtained legal approval from the CIA's Office of Legal Counsel over the objections of then Director of National Intelligence John Negroponte. Rodriguez incinerated the tapes in November 2005, but this did not become widely

known for two more years. Rodriguez defended his actions as "just get-
ting rid of some ugly visuals that could put the lives of my people at risk."
But in internal emails obtained by the American Civil Liberties Union,
Rodriguez was more blunt. He wrote that it would be "devastating" to the
CIA if "the tapes ever got into the public domain."[70]

Yet this history of the torture program was effectively erased in popular
culture. Considering the concerns raised in the Senate Armed Services
Committee report and the ongoing Senate Intelligence Committee investigation, a more cautious approach to the issue of torture and abuse of detainees was warranted. This was abandoned, however, with the Kathryn
Bigelow film *Zero Dark Thirty*. Released after Obama's reelection in 2012,
the film chronicled the search for Osama bin Laden through the main
character of a CIA analyst, Maya, played by Jessica Chastain. *Zero Dark
Thirty* was made with the assistance of, and final script approval by, the
CIA. The film portrays in extensive detail the torture of detainees, including waterboarding, sleep deprivation, and physical abuse and humiliation.
Like *24*, the film sought to demonstrate that these tactics were successful
and ultimately led to bin Laden. It also endorses the Bush administration's approach to counterterrorism after September 11.[71]

The narrative presented in *Zero Dark Thirty* was not merely for dramatic purposes. Indeed, it aligned with the CIA's media and operational
goals. Nearly seven years earlier, Phil Mudd, deputy director of the CIA's
Counterterrorism Center, had exhorted his colleagues in an internal email
to do more to create a positive impression of the group's work: "We either
get out and sell, or we get hammered, which has implications beyond the
media." Congress was influenced by negative press coverage, and he could
easily imagine a scenario in which "Congress reads it, cuts our authorities,
messes up our budget. . . . We either put our story out or we get eaten."
And, to be sure, the attempt to manage the agency's actions and policies
was not limited to the media or Hollywood.[72]

At an August 2014 press conference, Obama made a candid admission:
"We tortured some folks." Yet he also defended the CIA and its director,
John Brennan, after it was revealed that agency personnel had illegally ac-
cessed the computers of the Senate Select Committee on Intelligence
while it was investigating the detention and interrogation program. During the 2008 campaign, Brennan was a national security advisor to candidate Obama. Having served as director of the National Counterterrorism

Center after September 11, he was implicated in the interrogation and detention program and was not selected for a post that required Senate approval. He was named CIA director after Obama was reelected.[73]

Four months after Obama's press conference, in December 2014, the
executive summary of the Senate report offered a scathing assessment of
the CIA program. Just as the Senate Armed Services Committee had, its
findings contrasted sharply with the claims made by Cheney and Rodriguez in defense of torture and indefinite detention, as well as their portrayal in *Zero Dark Thirty*. California Democrat Diane Feinstein served as
chair of the committee and authored the foreword to its report. In it she
pointed to the fact that the CIA knew from its own experience with coercive interrogations that such techniques would "probably result in false
answers," and "had historically proven to be ineffective" Although the
agency's code of conduct forbidding their use had been abandoned after
September 11, the committee recommended that it be restored. The report
noted that seven of the thirty-nine detainees held and tortured by the CIA
"produced no intelligence" while in custody. It also found that the agency
exaggerated or falsified the benefits of coercive interrogation. The report
determined that there was "no relationship between the cited counterterrorism success and any information provided by detainees during or after"
the interrogation. It recounted how the CIA deliberately impeded efforts
at oversight by the White House, Congress, the State Department, the
FBI, and the CIA Inspector General. The agency also provided inaccurate
information to the DOJ.[74]

The committee report also faulted the agency on other grounds. It had
poorly implemented operations; six months after it was granted the authority to detain individuals, it was still unprepared for operations to commence.
The CIA had deployed untrained or inexperienced personnel for interrogations or oversight. It had subjected detainees to unauthorized interrogation techniques, and it had never evaluated the program to determine its
efficacy. Moreover, it appeared that internal criticisms had routinely been
rejected or ignored. Ultimately, between the negative media attention and
the complaints from America's allies it was generating, the detention program was deemed to be unsustainable. Despite two highly critical Senate
reports, no extensive reforms were made at the intelligence community or
limitations placed on its activities. Instead, the CIA was further emboldened with operations of questionable efficacy at home and abroad.[75]

THE OTHER DRUG WAR

Shortly after taking office in December 2006, Mexican President Felipe Calderón initiated a fateful policy. He authorized anti-narcotics operations in his home state of Michoacán, located in central Mexico's Pacific coast. A cable sent from the US embassy in Mexico City three months later summarized the orders given to the Mexican troops and federal police: "Their mission was to eradicate drug plantations, intercept drug cargos and wanted criminals, execute arrest warrants, and dismantle points of drug retailing." The results of the first week, however, were modest. Half of the nearly 6,800 troops deployed to Michoacán were engaged in eradicating marijuana crops and no major leaders of drug trafficking organizations were arrested. Calderón's administration boasted that drug-related killings were reduced by 72 percent. Yet this was only the beginning of Calderón's "War on Drugs."[76]

A month later, multiple operations were simultaneously launched targeting the major drug cartels. Almost four thousand troops were sent to Tijuana with the goal of challenging Felix Arellano's cartel. Over nine thousand troops and federal police were ordered to the "Golden Triangle" area, where the states of Chihuahua, Durango, and Sinaloa meet, to search for Joaquin "El Chapo" Guzman of the Sinaloa Cartel. A third operation in the state of Guerrero involved 7,600 soldiers and police, with a large contingent assigned to the city of Acapulco. By February, operations had been conducted in eight states. The language employed by Calderón's administration echoed that of the United States' War on Terror, as its "surge operations" were said to focus on "narco-transit zones" and major trafficking hubs. Attorney General Eduardo Medina Mora acknowledged that "the war would take 'years' to win."[77]

Critics in Mexico dismissed the operations as "political grandstanding" and argued they had not achieved concrete results. The US Embassy in Mexico City was, however, cautiously optimistic. The number of drug-related deaths had fallen sharply from the previous year in the eight states. A March 2007 cable claimed that Calderón was sending an important, if "partly symbolic," message. It advised that more sustained efforts were needed to challenge the cartels. Yet warning signs were also apparent. The cartels began attacking the police and military. Drug trafficking extended to new areas not targeted by the joint operations.[78]

Beginning in May, Washington initiated discussions with Mexico and Colombia. Led by DEA Administrator Karen Tandy, the meetings culminated in a counternarcotics coordination agreement. Colombian and Mexican police representatives were incorporated into the DEA's El Paso Intelligence Center. The three countries agreed to share law enforcement and intelligence information. Tandy emphasized to her Mexican and Colombian counterparts that "that long-term success in reducing the flow of drugs into the United States" was dependent on their collaboration. While the United States embraced Calderón and Uribe, American officials chided Afghanistan's Karzai for his unwillingness to tackle corruption and drug trafficking.[79]

Corruption still haunted Mexican and American efforts. As the coordination agreement was finalized, there were already significant concerns in Mexico about Calderón's key aides, Attorney General Mora and Secretary of Public Security Genera García Luna. Questions were raised about García Luna's finances and real estate holdings and Medina Mora's competence.[80]

By the end of 2007, the early benefits of Calderón's War on Drugs had evaporated. Indeed, Plan Mexico resembled Plan Colombia. The death toll for the year exceeded that of 2006. Human rights organizations warned of abuses by the security forces, particularly against indigenous communities in the southern state of Guerrero. Although US and Mexican officials pointed to major successes such as the arrest of the Sinaloa Cartel's Alfredo Beltran Leyva, and cited anecdotal evidence that the operations were disrupting the flow of cocaine to the United States, there were troubling signs. Over the previous year, violence was largely confined to the states where joint operations were conducted. Ambassador Garza warned in March 2008, however, that there were high-profile murders in Mexico City, including of operations staff at the Mexico City International Airport. Like the United States' Global War on Terror, Mexico's War on Drugs metastasized.[81]

Washington ignored the warning signs and endorsed Calderón's war with the Mérida Initiative. In March 2007, Bush and Calderón met in Mérida, Mexico and agreed that their two countries would expand counternarcotics cooperation. Approved in Bush's final year in office, the initiative sent over $350 million in anti-drug assistance to Mexico. Congress reduced Bush's original request over concerns about human rights abuses

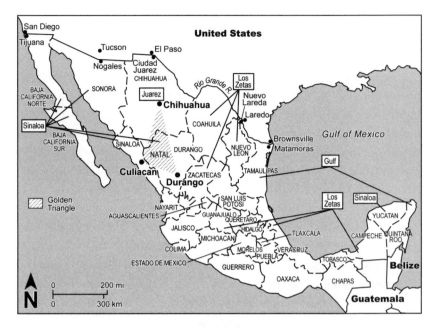

MAP 12. MEXICO AND LEADING DRUG TRAFFICKING ORGANIZATIONS, 2010–2017

by Mexican forces. This led to a rebuke from Mexican officials that the United States was not in a position to judge other countries based on its own actions. Nevertheless, the majority of US funding was devoted to providing military equipment as well as to support anti-corruption programs. An additional $100 million was intended for counter-narcotics efforts in neighboring countries. Yet greater funding and improved coordination did not have a discernible impact on narcotics trafficking.[82]

The Obama administration adopted the Mérida Initiative, even though it was not successful. Funding increased dramatically in the 2010 fiscal year to over $639 million. The majority of funding, $365 million was dedicated to narcotics control and law enforcement, and over $265 million for foreign military financing. Yet the violence continued to spiral. As in Afghanistan, a "surge" of American personnel from varying agencies were dispatched to Mexico. And there were few demonstrable improvements.[83]

Calderón and the Obama administration refocused the Mérida Initiative in 2011. A new emphasis was placed on institution building and economic development, especially for states on the US-Mexico border. Although funding for economic support programs increased over the next five fiscal years, it only accounted for 17.9 percent of the $964.7 million delivered. Funding for military equipment was shifted from the Mérida Initiative to bilateral military assistance.[84]

By any measure, Calderón's war was a failure. None of the militarized policies adopted on either side of the US-Mexico border prevented narcotics traffickers from meeting the demand for their products. Nor did the massive use of force by Mexican authorities dismantle a single drug trafficking organization. But it did result in a staggering death toll, leaving over 121,000 dead and at least 30,000 disappeared. Although violence decreased in Calderón's final year in office, it was far higher than under the previous administration. After five years, the death toll was over forty thousand and would only increase. Calderón appeared to acknowledge the limits of the military and law enforcement approach and suggested that the United States begin to evaluate "market solutions" to the narcotics problem. Nor did the candidates to replace Calderón embrace the war; instead, they focused on ending the violence.[85]

Although the Bush and Obama administrations supported Calderón's policies, there were consistent questions raised in Mexico by journalists and politicians about their effectiveness and the human and financial costs. There were also troubling indications that the crackdown appeared to be targeting the Sinaloa Cartel's rivals. In December 2019, Garcia Luna was arrested and the rumors about his ties to the Sinaloa Cartel were finally confirmed.[86]

Endemic corruption was only one part of the failure. Calderón consistently requested that the United States assist with efforts on its side of the border. Indeed, these remained the same for decades. The United States is the world's largest market for illegal narcotics and remained so despite the militarization on both sides of the border. The unwillingness or inability to address drug use and addiction in the United States drove narcotics trafficking. In addition, the flow of American weapons across the border into Mexico helps fuel the violence. The benefits to the US and Mexican financial systems of laundering the immense sums of money produced by narcotics trafficking have never been fundamentally addressed. Although this was one of the important successes of the War on Terror, the same cannot be said of counternarcotics initiatives. One area where there was success, was the extradition of major cartel leaders to the United States. But it has not been a significant enough disincentive to halt the endless

flow of drugs, weapons, money, or blood that accompanies the militarized
response to narcotics trafficking.[87]

CONSTRUCTING THE HORN

In late 2006, General John Abizaid, then commander of CENTCOM,
traveled to Ethiopia. Abizaid's trip concerned Ethiopia's neighbor, Somalia,
which was splintered between the UN-backed Transitional Federal Government (TFG) and an emerging force known as the Islamic Courts Union
(ICU). Over the previous year, the ICU and its al-Shabaab ("the youth")
military wing battled an alliance of Somali warlords known as the Alliance
for the Restoration of Peace and Counter-Terrorism (ARPCT). ARPCT
was the culmination of CIA efforts to establish local allies that would assist with capturing al-Qaʿida members in East Africa. The clandestine effort evolved into overt support from Washington for the ARPCT. This
did not translate, however, into success against the fledgling ICU. The
ICU's capture of the Somali capital of Mogadishu brought an end to over
a decade of clan and warlord rule. But it was another embarrassing failure
for the Bush administration, which was already faced with persistent insurgencies in Afghanistan and Iraq. The calm in Mogadishu did not last
long as Washington sought a new ally to challenge the ICU.[88]

The ICU was originally based in the port city of Merca, south of Mogadishu, and led by Hassan Dahir Aweys. Prior to establishing the ICU,
Aweys had led the Islamic Union (*al-Itihaad al-Islamiya*, AIAI), which
was affiliated with al-Qaʿida. AIAI had reportedly assisted with al-Qaʿida's
1998 attack on the US embassies in Kenya and Tanzania.[89]

In his meeting with General Abizaid, Ethiopian Prime Minister Meles
Zenawi declared that he could cripple the ICU "in one to two weeks."[90]
He was overconfident. Ethiopia quickly seized Mogadishu from the ICU,
and Washington embraced the operation as a model for the future. US
Special Forces coordinated with and supported the Ethiopian intervention. Utilizing a new base established in Djibouti, US Special Forces attacked al-Shabaab. Although the Djibouti base was intended to support
the capturing or killing of key al-Qaʿida figures, it had limited usage prior
to Ethiopia's invasion. Yet after al-Shabaab launched an insurgency, Ethiopia faulted Washington for its continued involvement in Somalia.[91]

By the end of the Bush administration, the Pentagon established Africa Command (AFRICOM) based in Germany. AFRICOM's zone of operations included fifty-three countries on the continent except for Egypt. Even though CIA Director Hayden claimed that al-Shabaab was "insignificant," Somalia became yet another entrenched battleground in the Global War on Terror and an arena for an expansion during the Obama presidency.[92]

Far from a model of a successful campaign, the Ethiopian intervention served to inspire al-Shabaab's recruiting. Drawing on ethnic Somalis and Somali refugees in neighboring Kenya, the group was able to identify young men that were willing to join its ranks. The US embassy in Nairobi actively monitored the city's Eastleigh suburbs where Somalis are the majority as well as Kenya's North East Province bordering Somalia for al-Shabaab activity. By June 2009, the embassy reported that the group's recruiting network had expanded and reached into the center of Kenya. At least sixty young men from Isiolo, Kenya, left for Somalia and two were reported to have conducted suicide operations in Mogadishu. The conflict also served to induce a small number of Somali Americans to join al-Shabaab.[93]

Al-Shabaab's recruitment in Kenya was evidence of the fractionalization of the conflict in Somalia. The US embassy in Nairobi reported that, due to the reemergence of clan-based militias, there was increased competition for fighters. In Kenya, "frustrated and aimless" ethnic Somali youth were a "prime target" for recruitment by al-Shabaab.[94] A network of mosques whose funding sources originated in Saudi Arabia helped recruit youth for al-Shabaab. But the militia remained relatively small, at roughly a thousand members.[95]

Before the Obama administration escalated in Somalia, another path was available. In a June 26, 2009 cable to Washington, Donald Yamamoto, the outgoing US ambassador to Ethiopia, warned that it was time for "Plan B" in Somalia. As the new administration was reviewing U.S policy in the country, Yamamoto argued that Somalia's five-year-old Transitional Federal Government (TFG) had failed to emerge as a national government. Nor was providing additional military assistance the answer as it was passed on to al-Shabaab or other groups. In addition, the policies of neighboring countries, especially Eritrea, exacerbated Somalia's instability. Yamamoto urged Washington to help the TFG build governing institutions, to demonstrate its benefit to the Somali people, rather than emphasize humanitarian relief. "By not assisting the TFG directly," he advised, "we are again applying medicine to the symptoms, rather than the root cause." Yamamoto also warned that no military solution was available, as the TFG could not defeat its opponents and al-Shabaab's capabilities had not been substantially degraded after two years of fighting. He proposed a combination of regional diplomacy, direct support for the TFG's capacity-building, and continued humanitarian assistance. Instead, Washington continued to focus on the symptoms rather than the root causes, in Somalia and at home.[96]

The conflict raised concerns about the potential for al-Shabaab to recruit Somali-Americans. With a population of roughly thirty thousand, the Minneapolis-St. Paul area is home to the largest Somali community in the United States. Like New York City, Minneapolis had also been engaged in a lengthy and extensive surveillance program of the city's Muslim community before the war in Somalia. Beginning in 2008 and over the next sixty months, roughly forty young men from the Minneapolis area traveled to Somalia and joined al-Shabaab. Although this was a tiny percentage of the overall community, it was sufficient cause for Minneapolis to be one of three pilot cities in the Obama administration's new Countering Violent Extremism (CVE) initiative.[97]

The CVE was announced in August 2011 only a few months after bin Laden was killed and as popular uprisings in the Middle East and North Africa challenged authoritarian regimes that traditionally benefited from Washington's support. The broader context and events should have challenged the basic assumptions underlying the CVE and its goals. Instead, the intent was to target individuals in the United States that could "acquire and hold radical or extremist beliefs that may eventually compel them to commit terrorism." CVE was presented as an open engagement with Muslim American communities as opposed to mass surveillance. That is not, however, how the program was implemented.[98]

Four months after CVE was announced, a strategic plan was developed. It sought to improve expertise on extremism in the government and law enforcement. The other goals were to counter extremist propaganda and strengthen the government's engagement with the communities around the country. Minneapolis was one of the three cities selected for the CVE pilot program. Noticeably absent from these goals was any attempt at conflict resolution in Somalia or addressing the root causes of instability in the region and sources of recruitment. Even before funding was delivered in 2014, the city's Somali-American community was already under FBI surveillance, and residents suffered from harassment. Although CVE was presented to the community as a humanitarian endeavor, it quickly became apparent that its intent was surveillance. Absent from the policy discussions about violent extremism or the focus on the Somali-American community was Washington's role in instigating Ethiopia's invasion and its repercussions. Nor did the CVE focus on attempts to address and resolve issues within the Somali-American community in Minneapolis. Instead, it fit neatly into, and served to justify the expansion of invasive spying programs.[99]

In Minneapolis, the CVE replaced an existing and successful community outreach program by the St. Paul Police Department. The outreach program was established in 2004 and included 250 community members in a Task Force that addressed the needs and concerns of East African immigrants in the city. It emphasized decreasing language barriers, improving cross-cultural understanding, and providing education on the US criminal justice system. This changed, however, with the CVE. Instead, local police departments shifted toward coordination with federal authorities, including maintaining lists of youth that were considered radicalized and providing the information to shared databases. Yet the indicators for radicalization were deeply problematic and included mosque attendance and opposition to US foreign policy.[100]

The change in emphasis of the community outreach programs did not go unnoticed. Indeed, by 2015 community organizations in Minneapolis-St. Paul objected to continuing the CVE program. Even though the CVE was reintroduced as "Building Community Resilience," the Somali-American coalition of organizations rejected the effort. They argued that it detracted from their own efforts at building resiliency while leaving their major concerns and issues unaddressed. In addition, it added to the stigmatization of Somali-American youth already facing disadvantages based on their socioeconomic status, language barriers, structural racism, and Islamophobia. Yet building on the pilot programs, the CVE awarded $10 million in grants to nineteen cities in 2016. An additional $10 million was awarded four years later.[101]

As the Obama administration was preparing to unveil the CVE, it launched drone strikes against al-Shabaab. Although it received less attention than the campaigns in Afghanistan and Pakistan, Washington's quieter conflict in Somalia had similar outcomes. Over the next six months, there were a series of airstrikes in which the TFG and the United States initially claimed to have killed leading al-Shabaab figures. The civilian casualties accompanying the strikes were, however, significant. In addition, al-Shabaab's leadership either were not harmed or were able to quickly replace those killed. According to the *Washington Post*, there were domestic limitations to the air campaign in Somalia. The Pentagon sought approval to strike at al-Shabaab camps where some Somali-Americans were believed to be training. But there were concerns that this would elevate the group from a regional to an international problem, with the potential for reprisal attacks on American soil. Nevertheless, the drone and special operations campaigns against al-Shabaab continued.[102]

Over the next two years, internal rifts emerged within al-Shabaab. A series of offensives by AMISOM against the group, coupled with support from US special forces and drone strikes, pushed al-Shabaab out of Mogadishu. In addition, Ahmad Abdi Godane, al-Shabaab's leader, increasingly antagonized other members of the group. The divisions were exacerbated by his decision to openly ally with al-Qaʿida and to spurn negotiations with the TFG. Godane was successful in ruthlessly consolidating his rule within the group and he expanded operations outside of Somalia. This included the September 2013 Westgate Mall attack in Nairobi, Kenya, that left over seventy dead and hundreds wounded. Thirteen months after the Nairobi attack, Godane was killed in a US airstrike. Although it was one of a number of high-profile assassinations of al-Shabaab and al-Qaʿida leaders in East Africa during the Obama presidency, both groups persisted. And as the final chapter discusses, US counterterrorism operations continued to expand.[103]

CREATING QUAGMIRES

As Washington escalated against al-Shabaab in East Africa, in the North African country of Tunisia a popular revolt had regional and international implications. The Obama administration's initial response to the popular uprisings against Arab authoritarian rulers was not inspirational. Washington coordinated with Paris to send riot control gear and tear gas to

Tunisia. It arrived too late, however, to save Zine el Abidine Ben Ali's dictatorship.[104]

In Egypt, the administration was similarly unwilling to abandon President Hosni Mubarak. During the December 2008 briefing by CIA Director Hayden, President-elect Obama was informed that the agency "owned" a number of foreign intelligence services in the Middle East. When Mubarak ignored the massive protests and rebuffed Obama's suggestion that it was time to step down, Washington relied on its ties with Egyptian military and intelligence services to pressure the longtime dictator. Mubarak was replaced by an interim military junta after Obama's initial choice, intelligence chief Omar Suleiman, was rejected by the protestors.[105]

As protests spread from Morocco to Iraq, the Obama administration appeared less interested in supporting democratic aspirations than in securing its regional allies. Washington only offered muted criticism of Saudi Arabia as it helped crush the uprising in Bahrain. Nor did the Obama administration object when Morocco, Algeria, Jordan, Oman, and Iraq quelled protests with increased subsidies and promises of reform as well as repressive security measures. The United States intervened directly and covertly in Libya and Syria, however, with devastating consequences.[106]

Obama finally enunciated his administration's response to the revolutions six months after they started. The speech was not delivered until after the United States and NATO had intervened in Libya and bin Laden had been killed in Pakistan. He stated that the United States would still be guided by its interests in the region: "We will continue to do these things, with the firm belief that America's interests are not hostile to people's hopes; they're essential to them." Obama pledged that the United States would promote reform and support democratic transitions. Yet this was abandoned within two years—if it was ever more than an empty promise.[107]

In the speech, Obama defended the Libyan intervention as necessary to prevent an "imminent massacre." After September 11 and the invasion of Iraq, Muammar el-Qaddafi attempted to improve relations with Washington and London. This included a public decision to abandon his nuclear and chemical weapons programs and admit responsibility for the December 1988 Pan Am 103 bombing. By 2009, Qaddafi's rehabilitation neared completion. Libya signed a $900 million agreement with British Petroleum for oil exploration and development. Members of the Libyan opposition exiled in the UK were renditioned to Libya, where they were jailed and tortured. In August 2009, Qaddafi and his son and national security advisor, Mutassim, met with Senators John McCain, Susan Collins, Lindsey Graham, and Joseph Lieberman in Tripoli. Qaddafi was "satisfied" that relations with Washington were improving. McCain assured his hosts that the United States "wanted to provide Libya with the equipment it needs for its security," and he pledged to assist with efforts to modernize the country's aging fleet of C-130 transport planes.[108]

Less than two years later, Qaddafi's regime faced its biggest test in four decades. Only a few days after Mubarak stepped down in Egypt, widespread protests gripped the country on February 17. Known as the "Day of Rage" protests, they were met with a harsh response from Libyan security forces. Yet even before February 17, exiled members of the Islamist opposition met in Switzerland to coordinate for a popular uprising. As in Tunisia and Egypt, the protestors called for an end to Qaddafi's four-decade rule. Unlike the neighboring countries, the Libyan protests quickly devolved into violence and open rebellion. In response, Qaddafi issued a threatening message on state television that was replayed incessantly by pan-Arab satellite television stations and was widely mocked on social media.[109]

Despite the threats and intimidation, the security forces were unable to quickly quell the rebellion. By the end of February, the National Transitional Council (NTC) was declared and featured prominent defectors and opposition leaders. Although the rebellion scored early victories and captured major cities and towns in eastern Libya, this was reversed by mid-March. As an armored division led by Qaddafi's youngest son, Khamis, approached the opposition capital of Benghazi, the UN Security Council weighed a response. Led by the United States and France, Resolution 1973 was passed establishing a "no fly zone" over the country. Approved on March 17, 2011, it also authorized the use of force to protect civilians from government and paramilitary forces. In addition, the resolution placed an asset freeze on Qaddafi's family and high-ranking government officials as well as an arms embargo. French Foreign Minister Alain Juppé argued that there were dire consequences to inaction if the UN "let the warmongers flout international legality." China and Russia did not block the resolution and it received the support of Saudi Arabia, the UAE, and Qatar. After it was passed, a token Arab League presence accompanied NATO in enforcing the resolution.[110]

The ensuing conflict carried on for six months. NATO provided air support to opposition forces on the ground. After months of stalemate and insincere negotiations, the opposition and NATO made significant advances in September. The NTC was recognized as the Libyan government and took the country's UN seat. On October 20, a combined air and drone strike by France and the United States on a convoy in the town of Sirte led to Qaddafi's capture. He was executed by opposition fighters that day. Mutassim Qaddafi was also captured and killed under similar circumstances. Khamis Qaddafi died in a NATO airstrike, and Seif al-Islam Qaddafi, the heir apparent, was captured attempting to flee Libya.[111]

Five years later, Obama conceded that the real goal of the intervention was regime change. Yet neither Washington nor its NATO and Arab allies had a plan for what replaced Qaddafi. Much like Iraq, this contributed to the chaos that followed. Obama described Libya's collapse as a "shit show," yet he had a leading role in creating the quagmire. Another central figure was French President Nicolas Sarkozy. While Sarkozy galvanized support for an invasion in March 2011, Seif al-Islam Qaddafi threatened to release details about secret bank transfers. At the time these accusations were dismissed by Sarkozy and the Libyan opposition. Indeed, as NATO warplanes decimated Libyan tanks and transports, opposition fighters praised Obama and Sarkozy. But an investigation was opened two years later by French prosecutors into apparent corruption in Sarkozy's 2007 election campaign. Sarkozy is accused of accepting as much as 50 million euros from Qaddafi, with some of the funds delivered in cash-filled luggage. In March 2021, Sarkozy was convicted on corruption charges in a separate case and the trial related to Libya is still pending.[112]

Libya's democratic transition was undermined by internal and external forces. The NTC proved unable to reestablish order or prevent a widespread campaign of revenge attacks by the same militias that helped overthrow Qaddafi. While the country's political and economic situation was tenuous for the first year, it became increasingly unstable. The September 11, 2012, attack on the United States' Benghazi consulate, in which Ambassador Christopher Stevens and three others were killed, exposed Libya's fragility to an American public whose attention had shifted after Qaddafi's fall. It also revealed the increasing prominence of Islamist political movements involved in the 2011 revolution and post-Qaddafi transition. This became more pronounced as the country slid into civil war. Turkey and Qatar played an important role in supporting Islamist parties and militias in Libya and Syria. Indeed, the two uprisings and civil wars became intertwined.[113]

The Libya intervention and the country's collapse influenced events in Syria. In his May 2011 speech, Obama also criticized Syrian President Bashar al-Asad. At the time, the Asad family's rule over Syria was in its fourth decade and the regime was maintained by a brutal security service (*mukhabarat*) that squelched dissent. Following the uprisings in Tunisia and Egypt, protests emerged in the southern city of Daraa and quickly spread. Although the protests were initially peaceful, the security services responded with typical force. Over the next few months, protestors were arrested and taken to the *mukhabarat*'s notorious prisons where there were routinely tortured. As a message to others about the price of dissent, the bodies of detained protestors bearing the marks of abuse were dumped in the street.[114]

The growing protests shattered the Asad regime's carefully constructed image of stability and repression. "President Asad now has a choice," Obama declared. "He can lead that transition, or get out of the way." A month later as Asad remained in power, the protests transformed into an armed revolution and civil war. The Free Syrian Army (FSA) was initially formed by defectors from the Syrian army and it boasted support from influential Syrian expatriates in the United States and the UK. It was not the only opposition group to emerge, however, and it was quickly challenged for primacy by the local al-Qa'ida affiliate, the Nusra Front (*Jabhat al-Nusra*).[115]

Washington coordinated with Saudi Arabia, Turkey, Qatar, the UAE, and Jordan to support the disparate Syrian opposition forces. The states, however, often worked at odds with each other, and supported competing groups. This served to exacerbate the lack of unity in the Syrian opposition. Like Libya, relations between Syria and the Arab Gulf states were strained before the Arab uprisings. Across the region, Saudi Arabia and the UAE sought to contain the wave of popular protests fearing that the movements would eventually challenge their holds on power. But they embraced regime change in Syria. Although Damascus had friendlier ties with Ankara and Amman, these were ruptured as the civil war escalated. Both Qatar and Turkey supported Islamist political movements, especially branches of the Muslim Brotherhood. In Syria, however, the Nusra Front co-opted or eliminated rival groups. While the FSA sought international legitimacy, especially support from Washington and London, it coordinated with the Nusra Front on the ground. Despite Washington's objections, this continued for the next four years. By 2013, the Nusra Front and other opposition groups were challenged by the even more extreme Islamic State in Iraq and al-Sham (ISIS). Yet the anti-Asad coalition still viewed the opposition as preferable to Asad's continuing rule.[116]

The US intervention in Syria was overt and covert. In April 2012, Secretary of State Hillary Clinton announced that the United States would begin paying the FSA's salaries and provide communications equipment, but not weapons. The goal was to encourage more defections from the Syrian army and signal to Asad that he was running out of options. By the summer, Clinton, CIA Director General Petraeus, and Secretary of Defense Leon Panetta proposed a secret plan to arm the opposition directly. President Obama rejected the suggestion, however. Instead, other members of the coalition continued funneling arms to the rebels. One major route for weapons transfers was from Libya through Turkey and paid for by Qatar. The transportation of men and arms linked the two conflicts. Ankara and Doha had little regard for the final destination of the weapons or their use. Instead, the prevailing ethos was that the defeat of Asad's regime was paramount.[117]

While the opposition was divided, the Syrian army was hapless. Syrian government forces relied on indiscriminate shelling and airstrikes to offset their poor performance. In late August 2013, reports emerged of a possible chemical weapons attack by government forces in East Ghouta, a Damascus suburb held by the opposition. Over the next month, it appeared that the United States would respond with limited airstrikes. Overt intervention was avoided, however, after Washington and Moscow reached an agreement to dispose of Syria's chemical weapons arsenal.[118]

Although Obama did not authorize airstrikes, he did approve the CIA's plan to arm the Syrian opposition. Known as Operation Timber Sycamore, the goal was to train and arm "moderate" rebels with money and weapons from the United States and Saudi Arabia as well as other partners in the coalition. The training occurred in Jordan and the goal was to improve coordination within the coalition as well as vetting of the opposition forces. It was also intended to ensure that advanced weapons were not transferred to al-Qaʿida affiliated groups. While the prior efforts were uncoordinated and irresponsible, Timber Sycamore proved to be a debacle. The CIA later admitted it spent over $1 billion on the operation, but it produced only a handful of viable candidates. Even more problematic was that trained fighters joined the more radical Nusra Front, which also obtained American weapons. A separate Department of Defense initiative to train fifteen thousand Syrian opposition soldiers also failed after spending $500 million. After three years, less than fifty men completed the training and the program was scrapped. In comparison, the Nusra Front boasted twenty thousand fighters.[119]

Like Iraq almost a decade earlier, Syria became a magnet for foreign fighters and weapons. One of the routes into Syria was through Lebanon. The eastern Bekaa Valley became a key staging ground for operations by the Nusra Front and other opposition groups into Syria. This brought them into direct conflict with Hizbullah and the Lebanese Army. The Bekaa is one of Hizbullah's main areas of operation in Lebanon and also serves as a land bridge for the delivery of weapons from Iran via Syria. While the Lebanese Army was unwilling to challenge Hizbullah directly, they engaged in escalating clashes with the Syrian opposition groups. Increasing sectarian rhetoric toward Shi'a Muslims in Syria and Lebanon, especially by the Nusra Front, coupled with the Syrian army's poor performance spurred Hizbullah to intervene. They were joined by Iran's Revolutionary Guard and helped to transform the Syrian army into a more effective fighting force, especially for urban combat. With the emergence of ISIS and a spate of suicide attacks in the Dahiyya suburb of Beirut, Hizbullah's Secretary General Hassan Nasrallah argued the party and its supporters faced an existential threat. Nasrallah adopted the language of the Bush administration in response. If Hizbullah had not fought ISIS in Syria, he claimed, they would have been forced to face them in Lebanon.[120]

By the end of 2013, there were over a million Syrian refugees in Turkey, Jordan, and Lebanon. An even greater number were internally displaced within Syria. Although UN brokered talks were conducted between Asad's government and the opposition, neither side was committed to a negotiated settlement nor were their allies and supporters. In short, the zero-sum approach to the civil war that ensured a quagmire also guaranteed that negotiations would fail. As will be discussed, the emergence of ISIS reshaped the Syria conflict and Washington's approach to the civil wars in Syria and Libya.

HOPE OR DECLINE?

The collapse of the US and global financial markets recast the 2008 presidential election. While Barack Obama's relative inexperience may have been an obstacle in previous contests against a seasoned politician and former prisoner of war like John McCain, it became an asset as fears of an economic depression grew. The irrational exuberance that surrounded Obama's election and embodied in the Shepard Fairey "Hope" campaign poster contrasted with, and was an antidote to, the dread that accompanied the unfolding economic catastrophe.

This tension was evidenced in the works of leading scholars that sought to reclaim American dominance. Princeton's G. John Ikenberry emphasized restoring the postwar international order constructed by Washington and enervated by the Bush administration. Harvard's Joseph Nye was also optimistic about Washington's potential to restore American primacy. He argued that no other country had the potential to match the United States' combination of hard and soft power in the near term. Josef Joffe, the publisher of *Die Zeit* and a distinguished visiting fellow at the Hoover Institution, disputed claims of American decline. Joffe argued that similar claims were made over the previous half century and ignored the United States' economic and political advantages.[121]

Other scholars, however, were more pessimistic about America's ability to navigate the challenges of the twenty-first century. Building on the thesis of the "rise of the rest," Fareed Zakaria saw a post-American world emerging. The financial crisis provided an additional rationale for Zakaria's argument. Others warned that China's meteoric rise would transform into a quest for dominance as the United States remained bogged down in the Middle East. Christopher Layne examined domestic and external factors to American decline and affirmed the claims of the 1980s decline school. He argued that American hegemony was undermined by a combination of debt, high defense spending, challenges to the US dollar as the global reserve currency, and rising great powers. Warning that "hegemonic decline always has consequences," Layne asserted that this would be the United States' main strategic preoccupation.[122]

Despite the predictions of decline, America's global standing and economy improved by the end of the Obama presidency. But the United States was still locked in the post–September 11 conflicts in the Middle East.

Meanwhile, domestic political, racial, and economic tensions contributed to persistent fears of American decline. Indeed, those fears were integral to Donald Trump's campaign and eventual victory.

CONCLUSION

Reflecting on his first term and policy debates over Afghanistan, Obama wrote that the threats the United States faced were "real but not existential, and so resolve without foresight was worse than useless. It led us to fight the wrong wars and careen down rabbit holes." "It made us administrators of inhospitable terrain and bred more enemies than we killed," he added. Yet these were not the policies he pursued. Indeed, the Obama presidency never achieved the lofty and unrealistic goals that its most ardent supporters hoped it would. Although he campaigned on a stark difference with the Bush presidency, there were a number of consistencies in domestic and foreign policies. Obama was hamstrung domestically by a hostile Republican majority in the House of Representatives after the 2010 midterm elections and four years later in the Senate. Nevertheless, as demonstrated by the response to the Arab uprisings, the Obama administration was more comfortable maintaining US foreign policy interests than challenging their underlying precepts. The quagmires in Syria and Libya and the maintenance of autocratic regimes across the region were evidence of this approach.[123]

At home, the Obama administration institutionalized the Global War on Terror and ensured its longevity. Domestic surveillance expanded and the terrorism watchlists and database entries increased after bin Laden was killed. The use of informants that helped manufacture terrorism cases and convictions represented a national security establishment whose goal was not to keep Americans safe but maintaining the rationale for their institutions and budgeting levels. By 2016, the Global War on Terror had replicated and intersected with the War on Drugs. This was most apparent in the use of the Patriot Act not for terrorism, but overwhelmingly for narcotics-related cases. The introduction of the narco-terrorism statue did not result in major convictions or even have a discernible impact on either narcotics trafficking or terrorist organizations. Instead, it provided the DEA with a rationale to support, and benefit, from the largesse of the Global War on Terror. Meanwhile, the increased funding was also shared with local law enforcement as the same military hardware deployed overseas patrolled American streets.

Obama inherited a drone assassination campaign that was expanded and institutionalized. As demonstrated in Vietnam a half century earlier, there were limits to what an air campaign and an assassination policy could achieve. One of the unintended consequences of the criticism of the United States' indefinite detention policy is that it was ultimately abandoned, but not for criminal justice proceedings or the flawed military tribunals created by the Bush administration. Capturing and interrogating high-value targets was no longer US policy. Instead, true to their name, the hunter-killer teams dispatched suspects, including American citizens. The implications of this more aggressive approach were not debated openly. While it served to eliminate key leadership figures, the assassinations were not accompanied by greater diplomatic efforts, increased development funding, or improved governance. Instead, they were followed by more assassinations as the disposition matrix was updated and new targets selected. This contributed to the fragmentation of some groups that reflected a conflict management approach rather than one designed to address and resolve root causes and issues. Even more troubling was that civilian casualties were far higher than the Pentagon or the Obama White House admitted. In short, even with the new technology, the assassination policy resembled previous efforts dating to the Vietnam War with similar results.

The Obama administration never fundamentally challenged the underlying assumptions of the Global War on Terror or the War on Drugs. This was demonstrated in Mexico and Colombia as well as Afghanistan. Although Obama inherited the counternarcotics efforts in these countries, his administration accepted the false narrative that Plan Colombia was not only successful, but a counternarcotics and counterinsurgency model that could be exported. Yet all available evidence demonstrated the opposite. The failure of counterinsurgency to maintain long-term stability without a political solution was fully exposed in Iraq. It provided fertile ground for the Trump campaign and presidency to portray America under siege from internal and external forces.

Epilogue

When was the last time you've seen our country win at anything?
We don't win anymore.

—DONALD J. TRUMP, 2015

"I KNOW FROM MY friends in the Border Patrol that there are countries—
radical Islamist countries, state-sponsored—that are cutting deals with
Mexican drug cartels for some of what they call the 'lanes of entry' into
our country." The speaker was retired Lt. General Michael Flynn, former
director of the Defense Intelligence Agency, and he made this claim in an
interview with *Breitbart News* in late August 2016. "And I have personally
seen the photos of the signage along those paths that are in Arabic," he
added. "They're like waypoints along that path as you come in. Primarily,
in this case, the one that I saw was in Texas and it's—literally, it's like signs
that say, in Arabic, 'this way, move to this point.' It's unbelievable."[1]

Flynn, whom President Obama had fired in 2014, went on in the interview to discuss the threats facing the United States at home and abroad.
He criticized the Obama administration's policies toward the Islamic State
and argued that listeners could expect the same of the Democratic Party's
presidential nominee, former First Lady and Secretary of State Hillary
Clinton. Flynn saw threats everywhere, from "radical Islamic" countries
and groups like Iran and Hizbullah, to the Islamic State and al-Qaʿida,
and to China, Russia, North Korea, and Cuba. There were internal threats,

too, Flynn asserted, as the United States was drifting toward socialism, hastened by changing demographics. To keep the country's belief system, Flynn argued, Americans must "fight for it overseas and fight for it here in the homeland."[2]

Flynn's remarks reflected a fear, prevalent in right-wing circles, that an unprecedented migration level represented an existential threat to America. In Europe, meanwhile, the civil war in Syria and resulting refugee crisis spurred even greater anxiety. As millions of Syrians fled the fighting, most headed for Lebanon or Turkey. Some of those sheltered in Turkey then attempted, by land or by sea, to reach destinations in Europe. The civil war in Libya exacerbated the situation, as traffickers relied on the Libyan coast for boats bound for southern Italy. A rift developed over the refugee crisis between the wealthier northern European states and those in the south. Italy and Greece demanded that the European Union member states live up to their responsibilities, but they were ignored. Similarly, the United States only accepted a fraction of the number of Syrian refugees that were sheltered by Eastern Mediterranean nations. Sympathy toward the refugees risking the dangerous journey was replaced by disdain after high-profile terrorist attacks were initially linked to the Islamic State in Iraq and al-Sham (ISIS). The importance of closing the US border to refugees, especially those from Syria, became a key talking point for Donald Trump's presidential campaign and was one of his earliest acts as president.[3]

Flynn advised the Trump campaign, and the online news site *Breitbart News* was an emerging hub in the right-wing media ecosphere. Founded by conservative firebrand Andrew Breitbart, the organization was transformed after his death. Under new executive manager Steve Bannon, and with funding from conservative billionaires Robert Mercer and his daughter, Rebekah, the site increasingly appealed to fringe opinions and reporting. This was particularly apparent after the 2008 financial crisis and Obama's election. *Breitbart's* coverage of immigration and refugees reflected Bannon's perspective on the issues. As evidenced by Flynn's claims in the August 2016 radio interview, the most outlandish assertions were accepted as fact. A former investment banker turned television and movie producer, Bannon shifted toward creating conservative political documentaries after the September 11 attacks. *Breitbart* embraced the Trump campaign and Bannon joined as its chief executive officer in August 2016,

less than three months before election day. After the election, he served as
Trump's chief political advisor and was instrumental in crafting early policies, especially related to immigration.[4]

Implicit in these sentiments and the resulting policies, and in Trump's
"Make America Great Again" campaign slogan, was the perception of
decline. Although there were obvious rhetorical differences between the
Obama and Trump presidencies, there were also remarkable consistencies.
In attempting to stave off decline, or the perception of it, the implemented
policies and their failings have served as a catalyst. This has continued
with Joe Biden's administration.

THE CALIPHATE

Standing in the historic Grand al-Nouri mosque in the Iraqi city of Mosul,
Abu Bakr al-Baghdadi declared the formation of a caliphate.[5] In his June
2014 sermon, Baghdadi deliberately sought to evoke memories of the historic Islamic empires and distinguish them from the externally drawn
borders of the region's nation-states. Over the previous eighteen months,
ISIS captured a broad swath of territory from eastern Syria to western
Iraq. The abrupt surrender of Iraqi security forces in Mosul, which significantly outnumbered the ISIS fighters, shocked Baghdad and Washington.
The Obama administration devoted extensive resources to the training
and development of the Iraqi military. Its rapid collapse in the face of a
lightly armed force was a major embarrassment for Washington. ISIS's
ability to capture and hold major cities in al-Anbar province revealed
the hollowness of the power-sharing agreement that had been brokered
by Washington and allowed for the withdrawal of US forces in December 2011. Shock turned to desperation as ISIS threatened to capture
Baghdad.[6]

Blame for the rise of ISIS has focused largely on the government of
Prime Minister Nouri al-Maliki. Not only did al-Maliki fail to implement
the power-sharing agreement, but he encouraged the targeting of Sunni
Muslim politicians and groups. Meanwhile, al-Maliki evidenced increasing authoritarian tendencies. Although the Bush and Obama administrations monitored this trend, Washington maintained its support. After
Maliki's State of Law Alliance lost the March 2010 parliamentary elections, the Iraqi Supreme Court ruled that it should be allowed to form a

coalition government. The ruling bore the hallmarks of political pressure and served to undermine confidence across Iraq's political spectrum. Maliki consolidated power over the next two years and added the defense ministry to his portfolio. Meanwhile, increasing sectarian tensions within Iraq were exacerbated by regional events.[7]

Washington, however, also deserves a share of the blame. The United States facilitated the emergence of Sunni militias such as the Sons of Iraq to counter al-Qaʿida in Iraq. As part of the power-sharing agreement, the militias were to be integrated into the Iraqi Security Forces or the government after the US withdrawal. Washington paid the salaries of the Sunni militias until December 2011 when Baghdad was expected to assume this responsibility. As with other aspects of the power-sharing agreement, this was not fully implemented. Members of the Sons of Iraq and the awakening movement were targeted by gunmen from the Shiʿa militias and the remnants of al-Qaʿida in Iraq that reemerged as the Islamic State of Iraq (ISI). Without a patron in Washington or protection from Baghdad, Sons of Iraq and Awakening members who were unable to flee or fight eventually joined ISI. In the summer of 2013, ISI launched its "Breaking the Walls" campaign, which freed prisoners held in Iraqi jails. The group expanded its ranks over the next year and pressed offensives across Anbar province culminating in the capture of Mosul.[8]

Although Maliki's government was able to weather the protests that swept the Middle East and North Africa in early 2011, the Syrian civil war created a new challenge. As Bashar al-Asad's government faced increasing resistance, al-Qaʿida in Iraq sought to extend its influence next door. This, however, was one in a series of decisions that had unintended consequences for the entire region. Initially led by Abu Mohammed al-Julani, the local al-Qaʿida contingent was rebranded as the Nusra Front and quickly became one of the leading opposition forces in the Syrian civil war. The failure of the Free Syrian Army to emerge as a viable military force and the Nusra Front's predominance undermined the Obama administration's Syria policy. But a rift also emerged between Julani and Baghdadi after the Islamic State was declared. Instead of uniting under the Islamic State banner, the two groups split and engaged in internecine fighting that ultimately benefited Syrian government forces.[9]

While the collapse of state institutions is one aspect of ISIS's story, state sponsorship is another. ISIS initially benefited from the support of several regional states, including Turkey, Saudi Arabia, the UAE, and Qatar. Although they later denied any association with ISIS, the coalition members facilitated transfers of weapons and money and the movement of fighters across international borders. ISIS also generated funds through extortion, the looting of artifacts, and the sale of Iraqi oil, usually to Turkey. But ISIS was transformed after capturing Mosul. The organization reportedly looted $500 million from Iraqi banks, dramatically filling its coffers. Able to expand its recruitment and propaganda, ISIS appeared to become even more brazen in its actions and behavior. This was demonstrated in Baghdadi's declaration and in its rampant abuses, including the atrocities committed against Iraq's Yazidi minority.[10]

Baghdadi's declaration of a caliphate was a departure from al-Qaʿida. Yet the emphasis on a state, or para-state, resembled other nonstate actors discussed throughout this book. The universal aspect of a caliphate, however, distinguished it from other groups. ISIS attempted to maintain aspects of a nation-state, including the collection of taxes and issuance of currency. It was not recognized by another country, however, even though it benefited from the support of regional powers.

The coalition against ISIS combined allies and foes and offered the prospect for future cooperation on regional issues. One flank was composed of the US and NATO forces coordinating with Kurdish militias. Also contributing were Saudi Arabia, Qatar, Turkey, and the UAE, who began to limit the flow of funds, weapons, and men into Syria and Iraq. The other flank included Russia, Syrian government forces, Iran's Quds Force, Hizbullah, and Syrian and Iraqi militias. Areas under ISIS control were slowly but steadily eroded over two years from both flanks. Tehran and Washington appeared to reach a common agreement, mediated by Moscow, to defeat ISIS. The completion of the Joint Comprehensive Plan of Action for Iran's nuclear program in July 2015, also portended an improvement in relations. Meanwhile, the Syrian civil war approached its bloody denouement. Russia's intervention in the Syrian civil war and coordination between Damascus, Tehran, and Moscow was decisive. In contrast, opposition forces and their state sponsors worked at cross purposes. The opposition was undermined by infighting as different intelligence agencies promoted rival groups and commanders. By late 2016, the United States began bombing Nusra Front and ISIS positions.[11]

President Trump continued the anti-ISIS campaign. By the time he left office, the organization's para-state was destroyed and it returned to a shadow insurgency inside Iraq. Trump also ordered the operations that killed Baghdadi and his successor, Abu Ibrahim al-Hashimi al-Qurayshi. In an attempt to mimic Obama's 2012 reelection messaging, Trump argued that Baghdadi's death was more important than killing bin Laden.[12]

The Islamic State's collapse displaced tens of thousands. Camps and prisons were established in Syria and Iraq to house suspected fighters and their families until their status could be determined. Although these were intended to be temporary, human rights organizations repeatedly warned that they were rife for a range of abuses under the control of Kurdish and Iraqi militias. Meanwhile, a secret arrangement allowed four thousand fighters and their families to escape from the Islamic State's declared capital of Raqaa when it was surrounded by coalition forces.[13]

Efforts to defeat ISIS were undermined by Turkey's October 2019 invasion of the Kurdish Autonomous Administration in northeastern Syria. The emerging Kurdish para-state was a product of the Syrian civil war. Ankara considered a second and distinct Kurdish para-state a direct threat. During the Turkish offensive, ISIS prisoners escaped camps controlled by the Syrian Democratic Forces, a Kurdish militia. Over the next year, Turkey sponsored the creation of new militias of fighters from Syrian opposition groups, including ISIS. These paramilitary groups were deployed in support of Ankara's regional goals in Libya, Syria's Idlib province, and Azerbaijan.[14]

Trump relied on the ISIS campaign to establish a US military presence in Syria. A small contingent of US forces continues to hold roughly a third of the country, including Syria's main oil wells, refineries, and agricultural lands. The Biden administration maintained this de facto occupation and it was a source of tension with local militias tied to Tehran and Damascus.[15]

The Syrian opposition's area of control has been reduced to Idlib province, bordering Turkey. Today, Idlib is home to roughly three million people, including foreign fighters, refugees, and internally displaced persons. It is also the main base of the Nusra Front, recently renamed the Organization for the Liberation of Syria (*Hay'at Tahrir al-Sham*), and remnants of the Free Syrian Army, as well as ISIS. Indeed, both Baghdadi and Qurayshi were killed in operations conducted by US special forces in Idlib. The

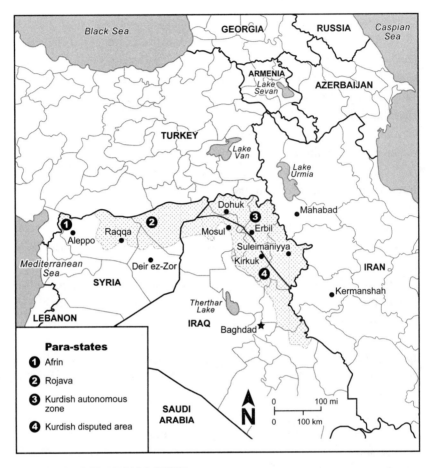

MAP 13. KURDISH PARA-STATES

United States has also conducted drone assassination strikes and other operations against suspected al-Qaʿida and ISIS targets in the province. By early 2021, HTS formally split from al-Qaʿida and Julani attempted to present a more moderate face.[16]

NATO's intervention in Libya directly contributed to the collapse of the state. The return of Islamist parties and militias from exile, facilitated by the UK's intelligence services to assist in Qaddafi's removal, served to undermine the authority of the transitional government. By June 2014, Libya descended into a renewed civil war. Like Syria, it became an arena for regional and international competition. The Syrian and Libyan conflicts

became intermeshed and mutually reinforcing. This was even more pronounced after ISIS emerged in Libya with direct ties to the organization's
leadership in Syria.[17]

Libya's internecine fighting featured its own dynamic. Local Islamist
groups in the "Dawn" coalition challenged ISIS and the secular forces of
the Libyan National Army led by General Khalifa Haftar. Haftar was a
former general in Qaddafi's army who joined the opposition in exile. He
returned to Libya in 2011 and was part of the coalition of forces that challenged Qaddafi. Although Haftar originally supported the transitional government, by 2014 he had his own ambitions. Haftar's army included former elements of Qaddafi's military and benefited from the support of the
UAE, Saudi Arabia, and Egypt. Meanwhile, Qatar and Turkey provided
funding and arms to the Dawn coalition, which included the Libyan Muslim Brotherhood. As in Syria and Iraq, ISIS has been diminished in Libya
but remains a source of instability. Although Haftar has the more established force, he was unable to defeat his rivals after seven years of fighting.
While Washington's regional partners competed on the ground through
proxy forces, the Trump administration's "active, but neutral" policy contributed to the stalemate. A fragile cease-fire was implemented in October
2020 and UN brokered talks five months later contributed to a controversial election in the Libyan House of Representatives. More than a decade
after Qaddafi was overthrown and killed, Libya remains fragmented with
two competing governments and rival forces jockeying for power.[18]

If the campaign against ISIS demonstrated the potential for improved
coordination, the civil war in Yemen reveals the limitations of proxy conflicts to achieve their goals. In March 2011, Yemen was gripped by protests
calling for the end of the two-decade rule of Ali Abdullah Saleh. Like his
counterparts in Syria and Libya, Saleh was unwilling to relinquish power.
Protracted negotiations and unfulfilled promises of reform culminated in
a June rocket attack on the presidential palace that severely wounded Saleh.
While he recuperated in neighboring Saudi Arabia, Vice President Abdu
Rabbu Mansour Hadi managed the affairs of state before assuming the
presidency in February 2012. Less than three years later, Hadi's tenuous rule
was challenged by coalition of Saleh and the Houthi militia (*Ansar Allah*).[19]

Both Saleh and Hadi cooperated with Washington in targeting al-Qaʿida
in the Arabian Peninsula (AQAP). The Obama administration was concerned about AQAP's ability to inspire or coordinate attacks on American

soil and the Pentagon coordinated with Houthi militias to counter the group. Drawn from Yemen's Zaydi Shi'a minority based in northern Yemen, the Houthi's had a contentious relationship with Saleh's government and with Saudi Arabia. The animosity between the Houthi movement and Saleh was temporarily placed on hold as Hadi's government was forced from power and Yemen descended into civil war. The marriage of convenience ended, however, when Houthi forces killed Saleh in December 2017.[20]

In March 2015, as the Obama administration was finalizing negotiations with Iran over its nuclear program, Saudi Arabia lobbied Washington to support an intervention in Yemen. Riyadh claimed it would be a six-week operation, but it persisted for over seven years. Presented as an opportunity to chasten Iran's regional ambitions and eliminate the Houthi militia as a military power, the Saudi-led intervention failed to achieve these objectives. Instead, the Houthis evolved into a battle-hardened militia with the ability to conduct sophisticated drone and missile attacks deep inside Saudi Arabia—attacks that negated the Saudi-led coalition's technological advantage. The Saudi intervention also emboldened AQAP and helped to promote the emergence of ISIS in Yemen. As Washington and London, the Anglo-American allies, actively engaged in the Yemen conflict, they provided the Saudi-led coalition with advanced weapons, logistical support, intelligence, and satellite imagery. The US Navy was responsible for the blockade of Yemen. Meanwhile, the United States continued its campaign against AQAP and ISIS in Yemen, including President Trump's first official military operation.[21]

By September 2023, a fragile cease-fire was in place, and it remained to be seen whether the cessation of fighting could be transformed into a long-term agreement to share power—or if Yemen would fragment into competing para-states with questionable viability. That this was entirely avoidable made the situation even more tragic.[22]

MAXIMUM PRESSURE

Shortly after landing at the Baghdad Airport on January 3, 2020, Iranian Major General Qasem Soleimani entered a sports utility vehicle. Soleimani and his entourage of Iranian officers were met by Abu Mahdi Al-Muhandis, the deputy chairman of Iraq's Popular Mobilization Units. These units, although part of the Iraqi government and military, were also Iran's local allies. As the head of Iran's Quds Force, Soleimani coordinated with Tehran's allies around the region, from Hizbullah in Lebanon and the Houthis in Yemen to the militias in Iraq and Syria. US military drones struck the SUVs, killing Soleimani, al-Muhandis, and their aides. That same January day, another drone struck far away, in Yemen, but missed. Its intended target had been another senior commander in the Iranian military.[23]

The Quds Force is a division of Iran's Islamic Revolutionary Guard Corps. It focuses on external operations and coordination with proxy groups and militias. A veteran of the Iran-Iraq War, Soleimani took the helm of the Quds Force in 1998. He emerged as a major regional player after the US invasion and occupation of Iraq. Soleimani served as the key intermediary between Tehran, Baghdad, and the Iraqi militias during the US occupation and the subsequent civil war. His role became even more pronounced with the rise of the Islamic State. As the Iraqi army collapsed in the face of ISIS, Iran responded by bolstering the training and arming of Shi'a militias to counter the threat. Soleimani led the coordination effort against ISIS.[24]

In May 2018, President Trump withdrew from the Joint Comprehensive Plan of Action agreement with Iran. Negotiated by the Obama administration three years earlier, the agreement placed limits on Iran's nuclear program. Although Washington's European allies had confirmed that Iran was generally in compliance with the agreement, President Trump insisted that the deal had to be scrapped. He wanted a new agreement that would also limit Iran's regional ambitions and missile program. Over the next year, tensions increased due to the Trump administration's "maximum pressure" campaign and renewed efforts for regime change. After Iran shot down an American drone in June 2019, it appeared that Washington would respond with airstrikes. Reports indicated, however, that President Trump settled for a cyberattack on Iranian missile batteries instead.[25]

Regional tensions continued to escalate through the final months of 2019. In September, the Houthi militia launched a combined drone and missile attack on the Saudi Aramco oil facility in Abqaiq. The successful use of drones showed that the cheap technology first deployed by the United States in Yemen and Afghanistan could be easily adapted and used by less powerful states and nonstate actors. Even though Houthi officials declared responsibility, Washington and Riyadh blamed Tehran. A December missile attack on a US military base in Iraq killed an American military contractor. The Trump administration claimed Iran and the PMU

were responsible, but Iraqi security forces later revealed that it was likely
an ISIS operation. Although the Pentagon was aware of the ISIS connection, Washington continued to blame Tehran. After protests at the US
embassy in Baghdad turned violent, the United States again argued that
Iran was the culprit. Washington used these events and accusations to
justify the assassinations of Soleimani, Muhandis and their companions.
Subsequent reports indicated, however, that the decision was made months
in advance. Following the assassinations, a wider conflict appeared imminent. Iran launched retaliatory missile strikes against a US military base
in Iraq. But the accidental downing of a civilian airliner departing Tehran's international airport that same evening demonstrated the implications of escalating tensions.[26]

These lessons were lost on advocates within the Trump administration
for maintaining the maximum pressure campaign. Only a few months
later, as Iran was hobbled by the COVID-19 pandemic, Secretary of State
Mike Pompeo lobbied for a military strike. Decisive military action, he
argued, would force a weakened and distracted Iranian leadership to accept a renegotiated nuclear deal on Trump's terms. But the Pentagon successfully resisted the efforts of Pompeo and others. Instead of chastening
Tehran, the maximum pressure campaign contributed to a major agreement between China and Iran. Meanwhile, attacks against US forces in
Iraq persisted over the next year demonstrating that neither the maximum
pressure campaign nor the assassinations were successful.[27]

After two years of negotiations, the Biden administration has yet to restore the Joint Comprehensive Plan of Action agreement with Iran. Meanwhile, Beijing has extended its influence in the Persian Gulf. China brokered the restoration of diplomatic ties between Saudi Arabia and Iran.
Although the long-term implications are uncertain, improved relations could
help reduce tensions and end proxy conflicts across the region.[28]

SANCTIONS REGIMES

As part of the effort to contain Iran's regional influence over the past decade, the United States has steadily increased pressure on Hizbullah in
Lebanon. In February 2016, the DEA announced that it uncovered a
money laundering scheme involving Hizbullah and Colombian cartels.
The DEA asserted that Hizbullah used the proceeds from narcotics

trafficking and money laundering to fund its global operations, including in Syria. Before Trump took office, far right think tanks advocated for the incoming administration to take more forceful action against Hizbullah to deter "illegal immigration." Indeed, three years before Flynn's August 2016 *Breitbart* interview, one analyst claimed that American intelligence officials were concerned Hizbullah was providing expertise on tunnel building to leading drug trafficking organizations. Demonstrating the geographic imaginary that has informed the Wars on Drugs and Terror, Matthew Levitt asserted that "the terrain along the southern US border, especially around San Diego, is similar to that on the Lebanese/Israeli border."[29]

In September 2017, Hizbullah's General Secretary Hassan Nasrallah claimed victory in Syria, but new challenges emerged. Three months later, *Politico* published an in-depth report on the DEA's investigation into Hizbullah's involvement in drug trafficking. The article claimed that the Obama administration hindered the operation to finalize the Joint Comprehensive Plan of Action agreement with Iran. The Trump White House and its congressional allies stressed the negative implications of the agreement and the benefit to Hizbullah. Meanwhile, Washington coordinated with Riyadh and Abu Dhabi to apply additional economic pressure on Lebanon and Syria. These measures dated to the final year of the Obama administration and expanded under Trump. Lebanon's ensuing economic and political crisis was exacerbated by the COVID-19 pandemic. By late 2020, the Trump administration expanded sanctions against Hizbullah and its coalition allies in the Lebanese government. Less than five months after taking office, the Biden administration extended sanctions further.[30]

As of this writing, the party and its militia remain the strongest force in Lebanon, even as the country remains on the brink of financial collapse. Indeed, Hizbullah's para-state has become intertwined with the Lebanese state. It has been a party in successive governments and its militia coordinates with the state security apparatus and with other state and nonstate actors across the region. Economic and political pressures have not reduced its popularity among its core base or forced it to make concessions. Yet Washington remains unwilling to accept Hizbullah as a legitimate political force in Lebanon or the broader region.

Syria has slowly emerged from regional and international opprobrium. Although it remains under sanctions by the United States and European Union, Syria has renewed relations with several Arab states and sought readmission to the Arab League. In September 2023, Damascus and Beijing announced a "strategic partnership" that includes reconstruction and a role in China's Belt and Road Initiative. But Syria has also been under increased scrutiny for its role in the trafficking of Captagon, an amphetamine. Media reports have suggested that the Captagon trade has helped al-Asad's government survive the existing sanctions regimes. As part of the broader rapprochement with Saudi Arabia and other states, Syria has offered to assist in curbing the production and trafficking of Captagon in return for investments and assistance with lifting sanctions.[31]

PERPETUATING FAILURE

Traveling in the stratosphere at altitudes of up to 65,000 feet, solar-powered balloons cover six American Midwestern states. Operated by US Southern Command, the balloons "provide a persistent surveillance system to locate and deter narcotics trafficking and homeland security threats." The balloons have the ability to monitor and track a range of vehicles in all weather conditions. As with previous efforts dating to the 1970s, the use of mass surveillance for counternarcotics efforts raises legitimate concerns about privacy and civil liberties protections.[32]

There is also the question of efficacy. Testifying before the Senate Armed Services Committee in February 2019, Admiral Craig Faller, head of US Southern Command, discussed the successful interdiction efforts over the previous year. The Joint Interagency Task Force South, he explained, was responsible for keeping "the equivalent of 600 minivans full of cocaine off US streets." He admitted, however, that only 6 percent of "known drug movements" were seized and that doing more would require far greater deployment of ships, aircraft, and American and international personnel. Thus, nearly three decades of Southern Command's involvement in counternarcotics and interdiction had not had a substantial impact on the flow of illegal narcotics into the United States. But the War on Drugs continues unabated.[33]

Fifteen years after Calderón's War on Drugs, the Mexican drug trafficking organizations have become more entrenched. Calderón's successors, Enrique Pena Nieto and Andrés Manuel López Obrador, have attempted to refocus counternarcotics efforts and reduce the violence. The folly of militarized anti-narcotics policies is evidenced in the emergence and fragmentation of Los Zetas. Its members were originally soldiers in Mexico's elite counternarcotics Airborne Special Forces Group (*Grupo Aeromóvil de Fuerzas Especiales*), and at least one of them received training from the US Army in the late 1990s. It was in 1997 that a contingent of the group's members abandoned the Mexican military and formed Los Zetas (Spanish for "the Zs," a reference to their commander's original radio code, Z1). For more than a decade, they served as the ruthless security force of the Gulf Cartel based in Tamaulipas. In June 2009, the US embassy in Guatemala reported that Los Zetas was purchasing heavy weapons and ammunition from elements of the Guatemalan military. Soldiers in the Kaibiles, the Guatemalan military's special forces unit, also joined their ranks. As they expanded their recruitment beyond the Mexican and Guatemalan militaries, Los Zetas developed a rigorous training program.[34]

By 2010, a rift formed between Los Zetas and the Gulf Cartel. Over the next seven years, Los Zetas embarked on a bloody campaign to eliminate their former patrons and other rival organizations. But their targets were not limited to the competition. Los Zetas were linked to the murders of Mexican security personnel, suspected informants, migrant workers, and innocent bystanders. The group became infamous for gruesome murders, beheadings, and mutilated corpses. Los Zetas diversified and expanded their operations beyond illegal narcotics to extortion, abductions, oil piracy, and the smuggling of weapons from the United States into Mexico. The group's operations crossed the border into Texas, where it was accused of involvement in several homicides and the death of a US Customs official in Mexico. As Los Zetas increasingly challenged the Gulf and Sinaloa Cartels, their rivals employed their own militarized responses, fueling a cycle of escalating violence.[35]

Emboldened by their success and expanding areas of operation, Los Zetas began taunting the Mexican government. The group claimed, with justification, that the Sinaloa and Gulf Cartels were able to thrive only due to official support. Both the United States and Mexico sought to counter Los Zetas, with Washington branding it an international threat. Meanwhile, government forces and rival militias captured or killed key Los Zetas leaders and gunmen. One indication of the group's declining status was that it increasingly relied on young, inexperienced fighters instead of former military personnel. By 2015, the threat of Los Zetas dominating the other organizations was eliminated. Its fragmentation spawned other mini-cartels, however, that mimicked its brutality and diversified operations.[36]

During the 2016 presidential campaign, Donald Trump evoked the threat of violence in Mexico crossing the border into the United States to justify his proposed immigration policies. Trump's campaign rhetoric was deliberately antagonistic and divisive. His policies as president matched his language. The two US agencies focused on the border adopted more aggressive postures, with Immigration and Customs Enforcement conducting mass sweeps, detentions, and deportations of undocumented individuals, and Customs and Border Protection subjecting migrants entering the United States with children to family separations. The administration also implemented a ban on travelers from seven countries and Syrian refugees, and prevented asylum seekers from entering the United States to present their claims. Thus a crisis at the United States' southern border, timed to the 2018 midterm elections, was manufactured by the administration, its congressional allies, and conservative media. Focusing on "migrant caravans," they intended to generate fear with images of an invading horde. Building on his campaign rhetoric, Trump focused attention on the MS-13 gang (*La Mara Salvatrucha*). Founded by Salvadoran migrants in California in the 1980s, the gang had grown in membership and impact over three decades. In early October 2018, Trump claimed that MS-13 members were "pouring into" the United States.[37]

After Democrats retook the House of Representatives, the Trump administration and its allies continued emphasizing the threat at the southern border. In July 2019, Senator Lindsey Graham appeared on Fox's *The Ingraham Angle*. He echoed the warnings of General Flynn three years earlier. "It's just a matter of time until a terrorist gets in this crowd and comes here and hurts us," Graham said. A year later, in the midst of the COVID-19 pandemic, the Department of Justice announced sweeping arrests and indictments of MS-13 members. This included the unprecedented indictment of the head of MS-13's Virginia branch for providing material support to terrorists.[38]

ENDING THE ENDLESS WARS?

As a presidential candidate, Donald Trump drew on the examples of Richard Nixon and Ronald Reagan. Trump adopted Nixon's "law and order" for domestic policy. In his September 2016 foreign policy address, Trump echoed Ronald Reagan and argued that "peace through strength" was his guiding philosophy. But Trump also suggested a different approach from either the George W. Bush or Obama administrations. "Our actions in the Middle East will be tempered by realism," he explained. "The current strategy of toppling regimes, with no plan for what to do the day after, only produces power vacuums that are filled by terrorists." In promoting the military and national security experts that endorsed his campaign, Trump asserted that they "know both how to win—and how to avoid the endless wars we are caught in now." Although he asserted that his administration would work with any party willing to fight against ISIS, he adopted a different approach once in office.[39]

While Trump continued the campaign against ISIS, he borrowed a page from Nixon and escalated in other conflict zones. The Pentagon implemented new rules of engagement and it result in higher civilian casualties. One study reported that in 2018 over five hundred civilians were killed in Afghanistan, the highest figure in nearly a decade. The following year, at least seven hundred civilians were killed due to airstrikes, the largest number since hostilities began in 2001.[40]

Similar trends were observed in Yemen and Somalia. In Yemen, there were two air campaigns. The first has been conducted by the United States against AQAP and ISIS targets. According to Airwars, a UK-based non-profit monitoring the situation, civilian casualties exceed the Pentagon's claims. The second campaign is conducted by the Saudi-led coalition with US support and has contributed to a humanitarian crisis and accusations of war crimes.[41]

Meanwhile, in Somalia, reporting and monitoring have been more difficult than in other areas. Airwars finds, however, that this is also a function of the internet-based database created by the US military for reporting civilian casualties from airstrikes. Only a small percentage of the population has internet access. Even fewer have access in areas controlled by al-Shabaab. Further limiting the reporting is that use of the website requires some fluency in English. Although the Trump administration withdrew US ground forces from Somalia, the air war continued. In May 2022, the Biden administration announced it was redeploying some number of US troops to support the Somali government's renewed campaign against al-Shabaab.[42]

The increase in airstrikes did not alter the situation on the ground in Afghanistan. Trump pursued negotiations with the Taliban with more fervor than prior administrations had. Led by Zalmay Khalilzad, the special representative for Afghanistan reconciliation, the resulting peace treaty acknowledged the reality in Afghanistan. It also effectively abandoned the government of President Ashraf Ghani, which did not participate in the talks. Instead, the Taliban agreed to some key US terms, including a split with al-Qaʿida. Four months after taking office, Biden announced that the United States would withdraw from Afghanistan by September 11, 2021. Vietnam's legacy hung over the announcement, and comparisons to the fall of Saigon were heightened as US forces withdrew. By August 2021, the Afghan National Army and government collapsed as the Taliban swiftly captured provincial capitals and Kabul. As in Vietnam, decades of policy failures and deceptive claims were exposed.[43]

Since the withdrawal, the relationship between the Taliban and Washington has remained tenuous. The Taliban remain subject to sanctions first applied in 1998. The US and its allies also withdrew recognition from Afghanistan's Central Bank and prevented it from accessing $9 billion in foreign reserves. Human Rights Watch reported that nongovernmental organizations operating in Afghanistan also encountered challenges accessing funds. Although the economic restrictions were intended to moderate the Taliban's policies, especially toward women and girls, they have not had the intended effect. By early 2022, the country was hit by economic and humanitarian crises. Yet the Taliban appear committed to the counterterrorism provisions of the peace agreement with the United States, especially against al-Qaʿida and the local Islamic State organization, ISIS-Khorasan. The Taliban's renewed prohibition on poppy cultivation has contributed to a dramatic decline in opium production, but it has also led to concern in Western Europe that more deadly drugs will be adopted instead.[44]

The US withdrawal from Afghanistan two decades after the September 11 attacks marked an end to America's longest war and the end of an era. Indeed, some observers and politicians made similar claims about the January 6, 2021, insurrection at the US Capitol. Two days after the riot, House Representative Elissa Slotkin, a Democrat from Michigan, declared on MSNBC that the "post–9/11 era is over." Before entering Congress, Slotkin had served as acting assistant secretary of defense for international security affairs in the Obama administration and as a Middle East analyst for the CIA. She drew on this experience to validate her claims: "It's the threat of domestic terrorism. It's that polarization that threatens our democracy."[45]

Having impeached President Trump, for the second time, for inciting the riot, Congress turned its attention to an expanded Patriot Act, with an emphasis on domestic threats. Yet, over the previous two years, the FBI's use of the Foreign Intelligence Surveillance Act, or FISA, for wiretaps and surveillance had dropped significantly. In 2018, over 1,800 FISA warrants had been issued, but the number fell to 451 in 2020. Surveillance of foreign targets experienced only a slight dip, from roughly 205,000 in 2019 to 202,700 in 2020. The reductions suggested that new legislation was not needed and would not have prevented the insurrection. Instead, initial investigations revealed that there had been sufficient warning and intelligence to prepare for January 6. However, the Capitol Police were hobbled by operational failures, bureaucratic delays, and poor decision-making.[46]

The legacy of the Global War on Terror will not end with the withdrawal from Afghanistan or the deaths of al-Qaʻida's senior leadership. It certainly will not end as the United States continues to engage in active conflicts in at least seven other countries. As the Vietnam War served as a catalyst for right-wing militias and movements that reached their apogee in the 1990s, the Global War on Terror is having a similarly galvanizing effect. Several new groups emerged in the wake of the 2008 financial crisis and Obama's election. The Oath Keepers, the Proud Boys, and the 3 Percenters embraced the Trump presidency and were present at the US Capitol riot. The Global War on Terror was also directly linked to the emergence of The Base, a neo-Nazi organization whose founder was a veteran of Iraq and Afghanistan and a former Department of Homeland Security employee. That the English translation of al-Qaʻida was adopted as the moniker of a white supremacist, militant group reflects one of the ironies of the policies pursued since September 11.[47]

But the logic and rhetoric of the War for Civilization remains resilient. In mid-August 2021, as the Taliban advanced on provincial capitals, former National Security Advisor General H. R. McMaster argued for a continued American military effort. Although McMaster authored a critical examination of the deceptions and poor decisions that contributed to the

Vietnam War, he was less nuanced on Afghanistan. The Taliban he explained were "the enemies of all civilization, of all humanity." "This is not an Afghanistan problem, this is a humanity problem on a modern-day frontier between barbarism and civilization," McMaster declared. Although McMaster's appeal was unsuccessful, only a few months later the civilizational rhetoric reemerged with Russia's invasion of Ukraine. Some commentators argued that liberal democracy, rather than race and religion, was the dividing line between civilization and barbarism.[48]

Russia's February 2022 invasion of Ukraine appeared to herald a shift from small wars toward renewed great power competition. Yet there are consistencies as Washington has not embraced a diplomatic solution. Instead, the United States has supplied Ukraine with vast quantities of weapons and funds with little oversight. This has increased the potential for an escalation and direct confrontation between Russia and the United States and its NATO allies. It has also heightened the likelihood of an extended proxy conflict and the creation of a badlands in Central Europe. Meanwhile, the United States continues to engage in extended counterterrorism operations while also preparing for larger conflicts.[49]

Thus, America's War for Civilization persists. Although some costs of the policies are known, others are hidden. According to one analysis, as of 2019, the United States had spent over $6 trillion dollars on the War on Terror. Unlike the Department of Defense, the authors of this study included spending by the Department of Homeland Security and costs incurred by Veterans Affairs and for debt service. The expenditures will only increase as military operations continue into a third decade.[50] Meanwhile, the War on Drugs has cost at least $1 trillion.[51] Quantifying spending on the War on Crime is even more difficult, and this is true even for the costs that are calculable. Going wholly unmeasured are the lives lost, those who have been wounded or incarcerated, and the soldiers and civilians whose physical and mental health have suffered. There has been no accounting for the detrimental effects on countries, societies, and communities and the diversions of funding from other essential priorities. All these costs are ongoing.

This book has shown that domestic and foreign policies are not distinct spheres. When the wars waged on crime, drugs, and terror over the past six decades are considered together, it becomes apparent that they are interlaced and mutually reinforcing. As elements of a larger War for

Civilization, these chronic issues have been consistently depicted as urgent threats to the American way of life. Civilization was synonymous with the United States and its allies, while barbarism was readily applied to real and perceived opponents. There have been several persistent features in this ongoing struggle.

Congress is not a monolithic bloc and it is a site for robust partisan politics. But on crime, drugs, and terror, majorities across the political spectrum have endorsed more punitive measures. As crime was racialized, punishment was emphasized. This was also observed with illegal drugs as Congress continued to pass draconian laws while decreasing funding for rehabilitation. Yet there is overwhelming evidence that drug rehabilitation is far more cost effective and punitive measures have not been successful in curbing supply or demand.[52]

During the Cold War, there was a bipartisan compact on containment and deterrence. Although a direct conflict with the Soviet Union was avoided, the overt, covert, and proxy wars from insular Southeast Asia to South America had a devastating toll that was often invisible to most Americans. Even though Congress attempted to limit covert actions at times, especially after Watergate, the foreign policy and national security establishments found legal, quasi-legal, and illegal avenues to bypass the legislative branch. In the post–Cold War era of American triumphalism and hyperpower, liberal hegemony has been endorsed by majorities from both parties.

US domestic policies were exported in overt and latent ways. Tactics like asset seizure were first implemented in Washington, DC and then adopted nationally before they were exported. The criminalization of dissent contributed to mass surveillance, which was conducted at home and abroad. Financial tracking and restrictions were applied in the United States for criminal investigations, including against organized crime syndicates, and applied to narcotics trafficking and terrorism. Yet underlying these policies was often flawed data accompanied by suspect analysis. From future crime to future terror, there has been and remains social scientists and media personalities eager to promote interventions abroad and harsh policies at home.

The wars on crime, drugs, and terror have all been parts of a larger War for Civilization. They have been influenced by race, racism, and notions of religious supremacy. From Indian Country to the Badlands, the territories and their populations have been depicted as hostile and lawless. A rogue's gallery has been compiled of bandits, criminals, gangsters, terrorists, and madmen. All the devils are in it: Geronimo, Capone, Che, Ho, Arafat, Saddam, Qaddafi, Escobar, bin Laden, Chapo, and Baghdadi. Dispatching the evildoers has been depicted as essential for victory and to maintain primacy. And the failure to do so has implied declining power and a lack of resolve.

The United States has employed a range of tactics to manage the hostile terrains. Assassination and torture as counterinsurgency tactics date to the early twentieth century, if not before. They are not uniquely American tactics, nor have they been features only of the Global War on Terror. They have, however, through political rhetoric and popular culture products, become acceptable—even when they involve assassinations of American citizens.

While political rhetoric has received significant attention, the relationship between Washington and Hollywood deserves greater scrutiny. Although Hollywood's products have often been flash points in the culture wars, the alignment of the Hollywood establishment with US foreign policy has been less discussed. Even during the Vietnam War and the emergence of the "New Hollywood" generation of filmmakers, mainstream movies like *Patton* were released alongside more critical fare like *M*A*S*H*. The late Cold War period witnessed a closer alignment with US foreign policy interests and promotion of the US military in blockbuster films like *Top Gun* and *Rambo II*. Even the less successful *Rambo III* praised the *mujahideen* in Afghanistan. After September 11, the Bush administration and leading entertainment conglomerates sought a more collaborative relationship. This continued into the Obama administration, as seen in *Zero Dark Thirty*, *Argo*, and *American Sniper*. Nor was this limited to movies, as the Second Golden Age of Television coincided with the Global War on Terror. This included series that are now considered classics like *The Sopranos*, *The Wire*, and *Breaking Bad*, and less well regarded programs directly related to politics, terrorism, drugs, and crime.

US intelligence agencies continue to conduct intrusive spying programs at home and abroad. Mass surveillance dates to at least the First World War and the initial Red Scare after the Bolshevik Revolution. The National Security Agency has acknowledged that there was never a distinct line drawn between domestic law enforcement and foreign surveillance.

The blurring of these activities preceded the Global War on Terror and has continued over the two decades since. Surveillance has also become normalized. Indeed, Americans and countless others around the globe freely offer their locations, personal and social network information, facial features, and biometric data to a range of applications and websites. In turn, surveillance technology has been used to target and suppress human rights activists and spy on journalists. Often unsaid in the discussion of mass surveillance, especially across borders, is that it is a violation of individual rights and state sovereignty.

The persistence of para-states during and after the Cold War has reified and challenged notions of sovereignty. Nonstate actors created para-states in part to replicate the functions of countries. This has typically happened when state services were lacking or nonexistent, or in response to discrimination by authorities based on nationality, ethnicity, race, or religion. The para-states featured de facto boundaries, legal systems, taxes, trade, diplomatic relations, and armed militias. The international community has not adopted a consistent approach to accommodate these movements or address their fundamental grievances. Indeed, there is a correlation between viewing the para-states and their related movements as challenges to state sovereignty and Washington's preference for conflict management over resolution. The United States maintains a predominant position on the world stage and has disproportionate influence. Thus, Washington's interests and preferences have often made it synonymous with those of the international community and impacted the aspirations for statehood of a range of movements. While some were achieved as in Kosovo and South Sudan, others like the Palestinians and the Kurds remain unfulfilled.

The United States has had a profound influence on international legal regimes related to narcotics and terrorism. Washington sought to impose its policy preferences on the international community from the 1961 Single Convention on Narcotic Drugs to the 1988 United Nations Convention Against Illicit Traffic in Narcotic Drugs and Psychotropic Substances. This was also reflected in the United States' designation of terrorist groups. The determination triggered a range of actions, from the application of sanctions, to tracking of financial transactions and asset seizures, to extradition or assassination. It also served to restrict potential interactions between Washington and the designated groups. At times, this has limited the potential for diplomatic resolutions.

A consistent refrain of American presidents from Lyndon Johnson to George W. Bush was their insistence that their policies were justified by an understanding of "the way the world is." But the United States was not a passive actor, especially in the developing world. American policymakers sought to dictate the world they *wanted* and it was reflection of the United States. During the Cold War this contributed to a range of policies that served to entrench conflicts. After the Cold War, the number of interventions increased as Washington sought to impose its vision of the world by force. Counternarcotics provided a rationale to apply America's military might internally. The Global War on Terror further reinforced this trend. It amplified the militarization of police, the monitoring of suspect minority communities, and the use of unscrupulous informants.

The inability to impose its terms on countries and conflicts in the developing world contributed to perceptions of decline. Beginning with the Vietnam War and through the occupations of Afghanistan and Iraq four decades later, American policymakers and national security experts were preoccupied with maintaining primacy and staving off decline. This was further influenced by the fear of rising crime and the constancy of drug trafficking. The combination of sensationalistic media coverage and unscrupulous politicians eager for campaign issues contributed to ineffective and ineffectual policies that were portrayed as a panacea. Instead, they served to institutionalize the War for Civilization with implications at home and abroad. The failure to rectify social ills reinforced notions of decline.

Yet there are indications of change. Several of the most populous US states with the largest economies have legalized marijuana. In October 2022, President Biden announced several marijuana reforms, including pardons for federal offenses for possession and a review of marijuana's Schedule 1 classification under the Controlled Substances Act. Drug courts have seen some success in reducing recidivism and substance abuse of defendants compared to incarceration. In addition, a number of US states and major cities have witnessed the benefits of harm reduction initiatives including naloxone, a drug that reverses opioid overdose, syringe service programs, supervised injection facilities as well as diversion programs for treatment instead of arrest. These are small but important steps. They also begin to challenge the emphasis on supply-side efforts through interdiction, eradication, and counterinsurgency. These policies, which are the lifeblood of the War on Drugs, are based on a flawed understanding of addiction to cocaine and opiates. Demand for "hard drugs" like cocaine and heroin is not elastic and increasing their price has not disincentivized abuse. Therefore the emphasis on supply will not have the desired results. Five decades of the War on Drugs have demonstrated this fallacy, as the United States remains the world's largest market of illegal narcotics. By contrast, Portugal's decriminalization policy offers an alternative to the alarmist rhetoric that has limited policy discussions on addressing addiction through a health-based approach instead of law enforcement and national security.[53]

The COVID-19 pandemic also served to challenge the central claims and assumptions underlying these policies. COVID-19's financial and societal impacts have been staggering and they have eclipsed the astonishing costs of the failed policies described in this book. Indeed, the widespread shortages of personal protective equipment, vital medical equipment and supplies, and frontline health care workers demonstrated the futility of military primacy, costly wars abroad, aggressive policing, draconian laws, and mass incarceration. Even more troubling is that that these issues were predicted, but the appropriate response plans were either ignored or not adopted.[54]

What kinds of lessons can be drawn from the post–Vietnam War era? The already robust literature on the Wars on Crime and Drugs is a humbling reminder of the limitations of scholarly analysis and its influence on institutionalized practices and policies. For the countless pages on the failures of America's domestic criminal justice, law enforcement, and anti-narcotics policies, they are even a great number of funds that have been devoted to their continuation. The powerful entrenched interests that ensure their persistence should not be discounted, but that is not an excuse for inaction. A decade ago, the Global Commission on Drug Policy declared that the War on Drugs had utterly failed. It recommended halting the criminalization of drug abuse and ostracism of addiction. The Commission's report also advocated creative approaches to legalization and an emphasis on health care approaches to addiction rather than punitive measures. Yet the Global Commission's recommendations have largely been ignored.[55]

This is not to suggest that drugs are not harmful or that they do not destroy lives, families, and communities. They obviously do. But aggressive law enforcement has not been successful in curbing demand or discouraging their sale. Instead, it has made the illegal market more lucrative and violent. The spending on military deployments, law enforcement, courts, and prisons has come at the expense of education, social services, and health care. As observed with the opioid epidemic, the emphasis on supply has been deeply flawed. The opioid epidemic was driven in part by avaricious business practices. Moreover, synthetic opioids like fentanyl are not subject to crop eradication and interdiction is challenging because of the regulated and unregulated precursor chemicals that are used in production. This is further demonstrated by the fact that since the 1980s, the US military's seizures have consistently accounted for less than 10 percent of the illicit narcotics entering the United States.[56]

Yet leading politicians returned to a familiar playbook in the 2022 midterm elections. California Republican Kevin McCarthy, who was later elected Speaker of the House, blamed China for the emerging fentanyl epidemic and suggested it was a deliberate attempt to weaken America. These assertions were part of the Republican party's broader narrative for the elections amplified by conservative media outlets that emphasized increased crime and immigration during the Biden presidency. Even though the strategy was not as successful as previous efforts. it has not prevented Republican candidates for president from advocating for applying the tactics used in the Global War on Terror against Mexican drug trafficking organizations. Although bellicose rhetoric may have immediate appeal on the campaign trail, grandstanding will not solve chronic social problems.[57]

Can similar lessons be applied to the Global War on Terror? The relationship between domestic and foreign policies evidenced over six decades demonstrates that the over reliance on force has been misguided. This is more than just blowback from overt and covert operations that have come back to haunt Washington. From Vietnam to Lebanon and Afghanistan to Iraq, there has been a consistent reliance on force over diplomacy. The attempts to obtain concessions through military action have not been realized. Nor has overstating the potential for military force to reshape countries and regions. From crime to drugs to terror, there have consistent attempts to claim that force will quickly resolve problematic situations. Instead, it has made resolutions more difficult and complex. This has been reinforced by Washington's preference in the post–Cold War era for conflict management rather than resolution.

Lost in the shock and horror of September 11 is the simple fact that the attack was carried out by 19 men armed with boxcutters. Several hijackers were known to and monitored by CIA Counterterrorism officials. The plan relied on knowledge of the United States' standard practice of dealing with airplane hijackings at the time. But the hijackers were not agents of a superpower or even a state. Al-Qaʿida was not the equivalent of the Soviet Union or Nazi Germany, nor would it have ever reached their size, power, and influence. In short, implementing a more dynamic and creative counterterrorism strategy would have been more effective. Only a fraction of the dollars spent on the Global War on Terror to date was needed to secure the homeland after the attacks. This includes improvements in intelligence gathering, analysis, cooperation and coordination, enhanced airline security, and investments in the United States' public health and physical infrastructure. Two decades later, only a small percentage of the total cargo that enters US ports is screened. At airports, Americans have settled for security theater in place of actual protection. As revealed by the COVID-19 pandemic, the United States' public health system is underfunded, underequipped, and not prioritized. Launching the Global War on Terror was a political decision with ideological overtones and disastrous consequences for the United States and the world.

This is not to suggest that diplomacy is a panacea. For proof that insincere diplomatic efforts will not result in a resolution we need only look to the unsuccessful negotiations between Israel and the Palestinians, the peace process in Colombia, or Ukraine. Even though Biden campaigned on restoring the Joint Comprehensive Plan of Action agreement with Iran, the negotiations have not been successful—yet this is evidence that more diplomatic effort is needed, not less.

Sometime in the fall of 2019 as tensions escalated in the Persian Gulf, the virus that became known as SARS-CoV-2 infected the first human. Over the next several months it spread rapidly around the globe. Rather than unify the nation and the world around a common threat, political and social schisms emerged in the United States over lockdowns, masks, and vaccinations. These reactions made responding and coping with the pandemic even more difficult. This was compounded by, and intersected with, the unprecedented mass protests against institutional racism and police violence after Minneapolis police officers murdered George Floyd. These societal and political rifts were exacerbated by the fallout from the

2020 presidential election and the subsequent insurrection. Three years later, leading polls reported deep dissatisfaction with governmental institutions and the state of the nation. It appears that the United States is unable to respond in a meaningful and consistent manner to major challenges, including climate change, systemic racism, an even deadlier pandemic, and decline. Addressing global issues will require a fundamental change in how Washington perceives and employs its power, and the development and implementation of domestic and foreign policies. Otherwise, the War for Civilization will endure and American policymakers will continue, at home and abroad, to see a world of enemies.[58]

ARCHIVAL SOURCES

NOTES

ACKNOWLEDGMENTS

INDEX

Archival Sources

ARCHIVAL COLLECTIONS

George H.W. Bush Presidential Library
   National Security Directives
George W. Bush Presidential Library
   National Security Presidential Directives
   Staff Member Office Files, Chris Henick and Karl Rove, Electronic and
      Textual Records
William J. Clinton Presidential Library
   Digital Library
Jimmy Carter Presidential Library
   Files of National Security Advisor Zbigniew Brzezinski
   Files of Chief of Staff Hamilton Jordan
Gerald R. Ford Presidential Library
   Files of National Security Advisor Brent Scowcroft
National Archives, College Park and Washington, DC
   Central Intelligence Agency (RG 263)
         CIA Records Search Tool (CREST) Records
         Freedom of Information Act Electronic Reading Room

State Department (RG 59)
>   Near Eastern, South Asian, and African Affairs Division
>   FOIA Virtual Reading Room

Drug Enforcement Agency (RG 170)
>   Drug Enforcement Administration

Richard M. Nixon Presidential Library

Files of National Security Advisor Henry A. Kissinger

Ronald Reagan Presidential Library

National Security Decision Directives
National Security Study Directives

ORAL HISTORIES

Madeline Albright, Miller Center, University of Virginia
Samuel R. Berger, Miller Center, University of Virginia
L. Paul Bremer, Miller Center, University of Virginia
Michael Chertoff, Miller Center, University of Virginia
Hermann Eilts, The Association for Diplomatic Studies and Training
Robert Gates, Miller Center, University of Virginia
Michael Hayden, Miller Center, University of Virginia
Richard Holbrooke, Dean Rusk Oral History Collection, University of
>   Georgia Russell Library
Robert Komer, John F. Kennedy Library
Anthony Lake, Miller Center, University of Virginia
John D. Negroponte, The Association for Diplomatic Studies and Training
>   Foreign Affairs Oral History Project
John Negroponte, Miller Center, University of Virginia
Colin Powell, Miller Center, University of Virginia
Harold Saunders, The Association for Diplomatic Studies and Training
Brent Scowcroft, Miller Center, University of Virginia

PUBLISHED ARCHIVES

Access Archival Database

Digital National Security Archive

Federation of American Scientists, National Security Collection

Federal Bureau of Investigations, The Vault

Counterintelligence Program (COINTELPRO) Files

Foreign Relations of the United States (Government Printing Office, Washington,
DC)

Eastern Europe, The Soviet Union, 1946, Volume VI
The Intelligence Community, 1950–1955
Vietnam, 1961, Volume I
National Security Policy, 1961–1963, Volume VIII
Cuba, January 1961–September 1962, Volume X
Near East, 1961–1962, Vol. XVII
Organization of Foreign Policy, Information Policy, United Nations, Scientific
    Matters, 1961–1963, Volume XXV
Iran, 1964–1968, Volume XXII
Arab-Israeli Dispute,1964–1967, Volume XVIII
Vietnam, 1966, Volume IV
Vietnam, 1967, Volume V
Vietnam, January–August 1968, Volume VI
Vietnam, September 1968-January 1969, Volume VII
Vietnam, January 1969–July 1970, Volume VI
Arab-Israeli Dispute, 1974–1976, Vol. XXVI
Southern Africa, 1969–1976, Volume XXVIII
Documents on Global Issues, 1969-1972, Volume E-1
Documents on Iran and Iraq, 1969–1972, Volume E–4
Documents on Africa, 1973–1976, Volume E-6
Documents on Mexico; Central America; and the Caribbean, 1973–1976,
    Volume E–11, Part 1
Afghanistan, 1977–1980, Volume XII
Horn of Africa, 1977-1980, Volume XVII
Soviet Union, January 1981–January 1983, Volume III
Soviet Union, March 1985–October 1986, Volume V
Soviet Union, October 1986–January 1989, Volume VI

Internet Archive

  Douglas Valentine Papers

National Security Archive

University of California, Santa Barbara American Presidency Project

Vanderbilt Television Archive

WikiLeaks

  Kissinger Cables
  State Department Cable Leaks
  Saudi Arabia Foreign Ministry Leaks

Notes

PROLOGUE

Epigraph: Viet Thanh Nguyen, *Nothing Ever Dies: Vietnam and the Memory of War* (Cambridge, MA: Harvard University Press, 2016), 2.

1. Mark Owen, *No Easy Day: The Autobiography of a Navy SEAL* (New York: Dutton, 2012), 87, 124; Barack Obama, *A Promised Land* (New York: Crown, 2020), 695. The "E" signified "Enemy," and "KIA" is an acronym for "Killed in Action." The SEAL Team's official name is the Naval Special Warfare Development Group.

2. Barack Obama, "Osama Bin Laden Dead," Obama White House Archives, May 2, 2011 https://obamawhitehouse.archives.gov/blog/2011/05/02/osama-bin-laden-dead.

3. Joseph R. Biden Jr., Vice Presidential Nomination Acceptance Speech, Democratic National Convention, Charlotte, NC, September 7, 2012.

4. Stephen W. Silliman, "The 'Old West' in the Middle East: U.S. Military Metaphors in Real and Imagined Indian Country," *American Anthropologist* 110, no. 2 (2008): 237–247; Alex Lubin, *Never-Ending War on Terror* (Oakland: University of California Press, 2021); Martin W. Lewis, and Karen Wigen, *The Myth of Continents: A Critique of Metageography* (Berkeley: University of California Press, 1997); Osamah F. Khalil, *America's Dream Palace: Middle East Expertise and the Rise of the National Security State* (Cambridge, MA: Harvard University Press, 2016).

5. Peter Dale Scott, *American War Machine: Deep Politics, the CIA Global Drug Connection, and the Road to Afghanistan* (Lanham, MD: Rowman and Littlefield, 2010); Jeremy Kuzmarov, *Modernizing Repression: Police Training and Nation-Building in the American Century* (Boston: University of Massachusetts Press, 2012); Stuart Schrader, *Badges without Borders: How Global Counterinsurgency Transformed American Policing* (Oakland, CA: University of California Press, 2019).

6. Nikhil Pal Singh, *Race and America's Long War* (Oakland, CA: University of California Press, 2017); Eric T. Love, *Race Over Empire: Racism and U.S. Imperialism, 1865–1900* (Chapel Hill, NC: University of North Carolina Press, 2004); Michael Hunt, *Ideology and U.S. Foreign Policy* (New Haven, CT: Yale University Press, 1987).

7. Robert A. Williams Jr., *Savage Anxieties: The Invention of Western Civilization* (New York: Palgrave Macmillan, 2012); Benjamin A. Coates, "American Presidents and the Ideology of Civilization," in *Ideology in U.S. Foreign Relations*, ed. Christopher McKnight Nichols and David Milne (New York: Columbia University Press, 2022), 53–73.

8. Dominique Kalifa, *Vice, Crime, and Poverty: How the Western Imagination Invented the Underworld* (New York: Columbia University Press, 2019); Deepa Kumar, *Islamophobia and the Politics of Empire* (New York: Haymarket Books, 2012); Louise Cainkar, "Racial Control under the Guise of Terror Threat: Policing of US Muslim, Arab, and SWANA Communities," *Critical Studies on Terrorism* 16, no. 1 (2023), 152–175; Sahar F. Aziz, "Race, Entrapment, and Manufacturing 'Homegrown Terrorism,'" *Georgetown Law Journal* 111, no. 3 (2023): 381–463; Robert L. Ivie, "Images of Savagery in American Justifications for War," *Communication Monographs* 47 (November 1980), 279–291; David Ebner and Vladimir Enrique Medenica, "Racial Bias Makes White Americans More Likely to Support Wars In Nonwhite Foreign Countries—New Study," *The Conversation*, June 16, 2021; Gabriel Kolko, *Confronting the Third World: United States Foreign Policy, 1945–1980* (New York: Pantheon Books, 1988); William Appleman Williams, *America Confronts a Revolutionary World, 1776–1976* (New York: Morrow, 1976); Perry Anderson, *American Foreign Policy and Its Thinkers* (New York: Verso, 2015); Paul Thomas Chamberlin, *The Cold War's Killing Fields* (New York: HarperCollins, 2018); Vincent Bevins, *The Jakarta Method: Washington's Anticommunist Crusade and the Mass Murder Program That Shaped Our World* (New York: Public Affairs, 2020); Max Boot, *The Savage Wars of Peace: Small Wars and the Rise of American Power* (New York: Basic Books, 2014).

9. There is a vast literature on the War on Drugs and its failures: Alfred McCoy, *The Politics of Heroin: CIA Complicity in the Global Drug Trade* (Brooklyn, NY: Lawrence Hill Books, 1991); Alfred W. McCoy and Alan A. Block, eds., *War on Drugs: Studies in the Failure of U.S. Narcotics Policy* (Boulder: Westview Press, 1992); Johann Hari, *Chasing the Scream: The Search for the Truth about Addiction*

(London: Bloomsbury, 2015); David Courtwright, *Forces of Habit: Drugs and the Making of the Modern World* (Cambridge, MA: Harvard University Press, 2001); Jonathan V. Marshall, *Lebanese Connection: Corruption, Civil War, and the International Drug Traffic* (Stanford, CA: Stanford University Press, 2012); Daniel Weimer, *Seeing Drugs: Modernization, Counterinsurgency, and U.S. Narcotics Control in the Third World, 1969–1976* (Kent, OH: Kent State University Press, 2011); Francisco E. Thoumi, *Political Economy and Illegal Drugs in Colombia* (Boulder, CO: Lynne Rienner, 1995); David Macdonald, *Drugs in Afghanistan: Opium, Outlaws and Scorpion Tales* (New York: Pluto Press, 2007); Ryan Gingeras, *Heroin, Organized Crime, and the Making of Modern Turkey* (Oxford, UK: Oxford University Press, 2014); Paul Gootenberg, *Andean Cocaine: The Making of a Global Drug* (Chapel Hill, NC: University of North Carolina Press, 2008); Kathleen J. Frydl, *Drug Wars in America, 1940–1973* (Cambridge, UK: Cambridge University Press, 2013); David Farber, *Crack: Rock Cocaine, Street Capitalism, and the Decade of Greed* (Cambridge, UK: Cambridge University Press, 2019); Jeremy Kuzmarov, *The Myth of the Addicted Army: Vietnam and the Modern War on Drugs* (Amherst, MA: University of Massachusetts Press, 2009). Paul Gootenberg and Isaac Campos, "Toward a New Drug History of Latin America: A Research Frontier at the Center of Debates," *Hispanic American Historical Review* 95, no. 1 (2015): 1–35.

10. Julian Zelizer, *Arsenal of Democracy: The Politics of National Security—From World War II to the War on Terrorism* (New York: Basic Books, 2009); Campbell Craig and Fredrik Logevall, *America's Cold War: The Politics of Insecurity* (Cambridge, MA: Harvard University Press, 2012); Daniel Bessner and Fredrik Logevall, "Recentering the United States in the Historiography of American Foreign Relations," *Texas National Security Review* 3, no. 2 (Spring 2020): 38–55; Daniel T. Rodgers, *Age of Fracture* (Cambridge, MA: Harvard University Press, 2012); Mary Dudziak, *Cold War Civil Rights: Race and the Image of American Democracy* (Princeton, NJ: Princeton University Press, 2000); Thomas Borstelmann, *The Cold War and the Color Line: American Race Relations in the Global Arena* (Cambridge, MA: Harvard University Press, 2001); Rick Perlstein, *Nixonland: The Rise of a President and the Fracturing of America* (New York: Scribner, 2008); Rick Perlstein, *The Invisible Bridge: The Fall of Nixon and the Rise of Reagan* (New York: Simon and Schuster, 2014); Sean Wilentz, *The Age of Reagan, 1974–2008* (New York: HarperCollins, 2008); Melvin Small, *Democracy and Diplomacy: The Impact of Domestic Politics on U.S. Foreign Policy, 1789–1994* (Baltimore: Johns Hopkins University Press, 1994).

11. Melani McAlister, *Epic Encounters: Culture, Media, and U.S. Interests in the Middle East, 1945–2000* (Berkeley: University of California Press, 2001); Lawrence Suid, *Guts & Glory: The Making of the American Military Image in Film* (Lexington, KY: University Press of Kentucky, 2002); Jonathan Kirshner, *Hollywood's Last Golden Age: Politics, Society, and the Seventies Film in America* (Ithaca, NY: Cornell

University Press, 2012); Stephen Prince, *Firestorm: American Film in the Age of Terrorism* (New York: Columbia University Press, 2009).

12. Natasha Zeretsky, *No Direction Home: The American Family and the Fear of National Decline, 1968–1980* (Chapel Hill: University of North Carolina Press, 2007); Stephen Wertheim, *Tomorrow, the World: The Birth of U.S. Global Supremacy* (Cambridge, MA, Harvard University Press, 2020); Josef Joffe, *The Myth of America's Decline: Politics, Economics, and a Half Century of False Prophecies* (New York: Liveright, 2014); Penny M. Von Eschen, *Paradoxes of Nostalgia: Cold War Triumphalism and Global Disorder since 1989* (Durham, NC: Duke University Press, 2022).

13. Elizabeth Hinton, *From the War on Poverty to the War on Crime: The Making of Mass Incarceration in America* (Cambridge, MA: Harvard University Press, 2016); Radley Balko, *Rise of the Warrior Cop: The Militarization of America's Police Forces* (New York: Public Affairs, 2013); Michelle Alexander, *The New Jim Crow: Mass Incarceration in the Age of Colorblindness* (New York: New Press, 2012); Michael Sherry, *The Punitive Turn in American Life: How the United States Learned to Fight Crime Like a War* (Chapel Hill, NC: University of North Carolina Press. 2020); Kuzmarov, *Modernizing Repression*; Schrader, *Badges without Borders*.

14. Andrew Bacevich, *The New American Militarism: How Americans Are Seduced by War* (New York: Oxford University Press, 2005); Mary Dudziak, *War Time: An Idea, Its History, Its Consequences* (New York: Oxford University Press, 2012); Rosa Brooks, *How Everything Became War and the Military Became Everything* (New York: Simon and Schuster, 2016).

PART I. THE FIREMEN

1. On the AFV, see Fredrik Logevall, *Embers of War: The Fall of an Empire and the Making of America's Vietnam* (New York: Random House, 2012), 755–758. On Donovan and the OSS, see Osamah F. Khalil, *America's Dream Palace: Middle East Expertise and the Rise of the National Security State* (Cambridge, MA: Harvard University Press, 2016), ch. 2.

2. John F. Kennedy, "America's Stake in Vietnam" speech, June 1, 1956, President's Office Files, Presidential Papers, JFKPOF-135-015-p0001, John F. Kennedy Presidential Library and Museum, Boston (hereafter JFK Library).

3. Arthur M. Schlesinger Jr., *Robert Kennedy and His Times* (New York: Houghton Mifflin, 1978), 712–718.

4. "National Security Directive on Covert Operations," NSC 5412, March 15, 1954, Doc. 171, Enclosure; and "National Security Council Directive," NSC 5412/2, undated, Covert Operations, Doc. 250, both in *Foreign Relations of the United States* (hereafter *FRUS*), *1950–1955: The Intelligence Community, 1950–1955*, ed. Douglas Keane and Michael Warner (Washington, DC: Government Printing Office, 2007);

"Memorandum for the Record," April 22, 1961, Doc. 169, *FRUS, 1961–1963: Volume X, Cuba, January 1961–September 1962*, ed. Louis J. Smith (Washington, DC: Government Printing Office, 1997); John Prados, *Safe for Democracy: The Secret Wars of the CIA* (Chicago: Ivan R. Dee, 2006), 148–151, 180–182.

5. Schlesinger, *Robert Kennedy and His Times*, 701–704.

6. Prados, *Safe for Democracy*, 298.

7. "Chargé in the Soviet Union (Kennan) to the Secretary of State," February 22, 1946, telegram 861.00/2-2246, *FRUS, 1946: Volume VI, Eastern Europe, The Soviet Union*, ed. Rogers P. Churchill and William Slany (Washington, DC: Government Printing Office, 1969).

8. John F. Kennedy, "Inaugural Address," January 20, 1961, JFK Library https://www.jfklibrary.org/archives/other-resources/john-f-kennedy-speeches /inaugural-address-19610120.

1. VIETNAM'S LONG SHADOW

Epigraph: Martin Luther King, Jr. "Beyond Vietnam—A Time to Break Silence," April 4, 1967.

1. Lyndon Johnson, "Peace without Conquest," speech, Johns Hopkins University, Baltimore, MD, April 7, 1965, American Presidency Project, University of California, Santa Barbara (hereafter American Presidency Project).

2. Lansdale memorandum to Gates, January 17, 1961, *Pentagon Papers*, vol. 5, V.B.4, Book I, 1–12 *The Kennedy Administration, Jan. 1961–Nov. 1963*, National Archives https://www.archives.gov/research/pentagon-papers.

3. Mark Atwood Lawrence, *The Vietnam War: A Concise International History* (New York: Oxford University Press, 2008), 64–65; Fredrik Logevall, *Embers of War: The Fall of an Empire and the Making of America's Vietnam* (New York: Random House, 2012), 788–789.

4. "Summary Record of a Meeting, The White House," January 28, 1961, Doc. 3; Rostow memorandum to Bundy, January 30, 1961, Doc. 4, both in *Foreign Relations of the United States* (hereafter *FRUS*), *1961–1963: Volume I, Vietnam, 1961*, ed. Ronald D. Landa and Charles S. Sampson (Washington, DC: Government Printing Office, 1988).

5. Jonathan Nashel, *Edward Lansdale's Cold War* (Amherst: University of Massachusetts Press, 2005), 25–31.

6. Alfred P. McCoy, *Policing America's Empire: The United States, the Philippines, and the Rise of the Surveillance State* (Madison: University of Wisconsin Press, 2009), 374–378.

7. Nashel, *Edward Lansdale's Cold War*, 30–42.

8. Nashel, *Edward Lansdale's Cold War*, 49–76; See also Logevall, *Embers of War*.

9. Larry Butler, "The First Wave of British Decolonization: Commonwealth Territories, the Indian Subcontinent, and the Gold Coast, 1945–1951," in *Crises of Empire: Decolonization and Europe's Imperial States,* ed. Martin Thomas, Bob Moore, and L. J. Butler, 2nd ed. (London: Bloomsbury, 2015), 56–58.

10. Martin Thomas, "Algeria's Violent Struggle for Independence," in *Crises of Empire: Decolonization and Europe's Imperial States,* ed. Martin Thomas, Bob Moore, and L. J. Butler, 2nd ed. (London: Bloomsbury, 2015), 193–199.

11. Thomas, "Algeria's Violent Struggle for Independence," 200–203; Logevall, *Embers of War,* 801.

12. Bosley Crowther, "Algiers: The Reality Recreated," *New York Times,* October 1, 1967; Mark Harris, "Cinema '67 Revisited: The Battle of Algiers," *Film Comment,* September 13, 2017.

13. Elaine Mokhtefi, *Algiers, Third World Capital; Freedom Fighters, Revolutionaries, Black Panthers* (New York: Verso, 2018); Pauline Kael, "Burn! Mythmaking," *New Yorker,* November 7, 1970; Tom Wolfe, "Radical Chic: That Party at Lenny's," *New York Magazine,* June 8, 1970; Michael Kaufman, "What Does the Pentagon See in 'Battle of Algiers,'" *New York Times,* September 7, 2003; Stuart Klawans, "Lessons of the Pentagon's Favorite Training Film," *New York Times,* January 4, 2004.

14. Lawrence, *The Vietnam War,* 78–79; Logevall, *Embers of War,* 812.

15. Robert W. Komer, interview by Dennis O'Brien, December 22, 1969, JFKOH-ROWK-05, John F. Kennedy Presidential Library; "National Security Action Memorandum 55," June 28, 1961, Doc. 32; "National Security Action Memorandum 124," January 18, 1962, Doc. 68, both in *FRUS, 1961–1963: Volume VIII, National Security Policy,* ed. David W. Mabon (Washington, DC: Government Printing Office, 1996).

16. "National Security Action Memorandum 162," June 19, 1962, Doc. 92, *FRUS, 1961–1963: Volume VIII.*

17. Lawrence, *The Vietnam War,* 76–80.

18. David Milne, *America's Rasputin: Walt Rostow and the Vietnam War* (New York: Hill and Wang, 2008), 195.

19. Michael Latham, *Modernization as Ideology: American Social Science and "Nation Building" in the Kennedy Era* (Chapel Hill: University of North Carolina Press, 2000), 151–207; Milne, *America's Rasputin,* 158–160.

20. Frank Leith Jones, *Blowtorch: Robert Komer, Vietnam, and American Cold War Strategy* (Annapolis, MD: Naval Institute Press, 2013), 102–127.

21. Komer memorandum to Johnson, July 1, 1966, Doc. 171, *FRUS, 1964–1968: Volume IV, Vietnam, 1966,* ed. David C. Humphrey (Washington, DC: Government Printing Office, 1998).

22. Komer memorandum to Johnson, June 14, 1966, Doc. 155, *FRUS, 1964–1968: Volume IV.*

23. Thomas Ahern, *Vietnam Declassified: The CIA and Counterinsurgency* (Lexington: University Press of Kentucky, 2010), 212–214.

24. Komer letter to Vance, April 7, 1967, Doc. 131; and "Notes of Meeting" (Johnson and McNamara), July 12, 1967, Doc. 238, both in *FRUS, 1964–1968, Volume V: Vietnam, 1967,* ed. Kent Sieg (Washington, DC: Government Printing Office, 1969).

25. *The Unexpurgated Pike Report: Report of the House Select Committee on Intelligence, 1976,* ed. Gregory Andrade Diamond (New York: McGraw-Hill, 1992), 72–75.

26. *Unexpurgated Pike Report,* 75–78.

27. Nick Turse, *Kill Anything That Moves: The Real American War in Vietnam* (New York: Metropolitan Books, 2013), 26–31, 48–51.

28. Alain C. Enthoven and K. Wayne Smith, *How Much Is Enough: Shaping the Defense Program, 1961–1969* (New York: Harper and Row, 1971), 295 (italics in text); Turse, *Kill Anything that Moves,* 41–48.

29. Douglas Valentine, *The Phoenix Program* (New York: William Morrow, 1990), 19; "Assessment of the Phoenix Program," December 16, 1968, CIA, "Phoenix Fact Sheet, August 10, 1968," National Security Archive https://nsarchive.files .wordpress.com/2010/11/phoenix.pdf; "U.S. Assistance Programs in Vietnam," October 17, 1972 (Washington, DC: Government Printing Office, 1972).

30. Lawrence, *The Vietnam War,* ch. 6.

31. Laird memorandum to Nixon, March 13, 1969, Doc. 38, *FRUS, 1969–1976: Volume VI, Vietnam, January 1969–July 1970,* ed. Edward C. Keefer and Carolyn Yee (Washington, DC: Government Printing Office, 2006).

32. McCoy, *Policing America's Empire,* 64; Turse, *Kill Anything That Moves,* 174.

33. Alfred W. McCoy, *A Question of Torture: CIA Interrogation, from the Cold War to the War on Terror* (New York: Metropolitan Books, 2007), 67–68; Seymour Hersh, "The Scene of the Crime," *New Yorker,* March 23, 2015.

34. John Boykin, *Cursed Is the Peacemaker* (Belmont, CA: Applegate Press, 2002), 14–16.

35. Boykin, *Cursed Is the Peacemaker,* 20–26.

36. Richard Holbrooke, interview by Richard Rusk, March 1985, RuskVV, Dean Rusk Oral History Collection, Russell Library, University of Georgia; Richard Holbrooke, "Foreword," in *Prelude to a Tragedy: Vietnam, 1960–1965,* ed. Harvey Neese and John O'Donnell (Annapolis, MD: Naval Institute Press, 2001), vii–ix.

37. Holbrooke, "Foreword," ix.

38. Holbrooke interview, March 1985; George Packer, *Our Man: Richard Holbrooke and the End of the American Century* (New York: Alfred A. Knopf, 2019), 131–132.

39. Holbrooke interview, March 1985; Jones, *Blowtorch,* 102–127.

40. Richard Holbrooke, "Presidents, Bureaucrats, and Something In-Between," in *The Vietnam Legacy: The War, American Society and the Future of American Foreign Policy*, ed. Anthony Lake (New York: New York University Press, 1976), 146–147, 164.

41. Lake quoted in Rennie A. Silva, "Idealism, Diplomacy and Power: Tony Lake's Story," Foreign Service Journal, December 2020, American Foreign Service Association https://www.afsa.org/idealism-diplomacy-and-power-tony-lakes-story.

42. Seymour M. Hersh, *The Price of Power: Kissinger in the Nixon White House* (New York: Summit Books, 1983), 176–178, 196; Anthony Lake interview, May 21, 2002, Presidential Oral Histories, Bill Clinton Presidency, Miller Center, University of Virginia; Silva, "Idealism, Diplomacy and Power"; Walter Pincus, "20-year-old Wiretap Suit against Kissinger Settled," *Washington Post*, November 13, 1992.

43. Anthony Lake, "Introduction," in *The Vietnam Legacy: The War, American Society and the Future of American Foreign Policy*, ed. Anthony Lake (New York: New York University Press, 1976), xvi–xvii.

44. Jon Lee Anderson, *Che Guevara: A Revolutionary Life*, rev. ed. (New York: Grove Press, 2010), 405–411, 581–584; Prados, *Safe for Democracy*, 332.

45. Anderson, *Che Guevara*, 586–589; Ernesto "Che" Guevara, "Address at the United Nations," December 11, 1964, in the *Che Guevara Reader: Writings on Guerrilla Strategy, Politics & Revolution*, ed. David Deutschmann (New York: Ocean Press, 1997), 297–298; Prados, *Safe for Democracy*, 273–279.

46. Timothy C. Field Jr., "Ideology as Strategy: Military-Led Modernization and the Origins of the Alliance for Progress in Bolivia," *Diplomatic History* 36, no. 1 (January 2012): 147–183.

47. Anderson, *Che Guevara*, 646–685.

48. Ernesto "Che" Guevara, "Create Two, Three, Many Vietnams (Message to the Tricontinental)," April 1967, in *Che Guevara Reader: Writings on Guerrilla Strategy, Politics & Revolution*, ed. David Deutschmann (New York: Ocean Press, 1997), 313–328.

49. Prados, *Safe for Democracy*, 334–335.

50. Walt Whitman Rostow, *The Diffusion of Power: An Essay in Recent History* (New York: Macmillan, 1972), 199.

51. Prados, *Safe for Democracy*, 332–336.

52. Odd Arne Westad, *The Global Cold War: Third World Interventions and the Making of Our Times* (Cambridge: Cambridge University Press, 2005), 185–186.

53. American Consulate Surabaya to American Embassy Jakarta, Telegram 187, National Security Archive https://nsarchive.gwu.edu/document/15717-document-21-telegram-187-american-consulate; December 10, 1965; and Jakarta Airgram A-408 to Washington, December 21, 1965, National Security Archive https://nsarchive.gwu.edu/document/15720-document-24-airgram-408-joint-weeka-no-48.

54. Komer and Lodge quoted in Westad, *The Global Cold War*, 188–189. On Sukarno, see "Minutes of National Security Council Meeting," January 25, Doc. 10, 1969, *FRUS, 1969–1976: Volume VI*.

55. Elizabeth Hinton, *From the War on Poverty to the War on Crime: The Making of Mass Incarceration in America* (Cambridge, MA: Harvard University Press, 2016), 87–88.

56. Hinton, *From the War on Poverty to the War on Crime,* 20–21.

57. James Q. Wilson, "Crime in the Streets," *The Public Interest* 5 (1966): 26–35. Emphasis in original.

58. Daniel S. Lucks, *From Selma to Saigon: The Civil Rights Movement and the Vietnam War* (Lexington: University of Kentucky Press, 2014), 111–114.

59. Tom Wells, *The War Within: America's Battle over Vietnam* (Berkeley: University of California Press, 1994), 129–131.

60. Kenneth Campbell, *The Beatles and the 1960s: Reception, Revolution, and Social Change* (London: Bloomsbury Academic, 2021), 138–141.

61. Steven M. Gillon, *Separate and Unequal: The Kerner Commission and the Unraveling of American Liberalism* (New York: Basic Books, 2018), 1–3.

62. "An American Tragedy, 1967—Detroit," *Newsweek* 70, no. 6 (August 7, 1967): 18, 20–26, quote on 20; Gillon, *Separate and Unequal,* 3–5; Stephanie Steinberg, "Blind Pig Raid on 12th Street Lit Fire That Scarred Detroit for Decades," *Detroit News,* July 18, 2017; Elizabeth Hinton, *America on Fire: The Untold History of Police Violence and Black Rebellion since the 1960s* (New York: Norton, 2021).

63. Hinton, *America on Fire*; Johnson, "The President's Address to the Nation on Civil Disorders," July 27, 1967 https://www.presidency.ucsb.edu/documents/the-presidents-address-the-nation-civil-disorders.

64. *Report of the National Advisory Commission on Civil Disorder* (Washington, DC: US Government Printing Office, 1968), 15.

65. Stuart Schrader, *Badges without Borders: How Global Counterinsurgency Transformed American Policing* (Oakland: University of California Press, 2019), 192–213.

66. Rostow's memo is discussed in Schrader, *Badges without Borders,* 42–44; Rostow to Johnson, July 28, 1967, Riots (1), Box 32, Harry McPherson office files, LBJ Library.

67. Hinton, *America on Fire,* 11–12; Schrader, *Badges without Borders,* 197; "Transcript of Johnson's Statement on Signing Crime and Safety Bill," *New York Times,* June 20, 1968.

68. Jefferson Morley, *The Ghost: The Secret Life of CIA Spymaster James Jesus Angleton* (New York: St. Martin's, 2017), 185–186.

69. Wells, *The War Within,* 183–184, 311–312.

70. Thomas R. Johnson, *American Cryptology during the Cold War, 1945–1989, Book III: Retrenchment and Reform, 1973–1980,* United States Cryptologic History, National Security Agency, 1998, 84 https://www.nsa.gov/portals/75/documents/news-features/declassified-documents/cryptologic-histories/cold_war_iii.pdf.

71. Johnson, *American Cryptology during the Cold War, Book III,* 84–86.

72. SAC San Francisco to Director, FBI (Hoover) "Cointelpro New Left," September 7, 1968, FBI, The Vault, Cointelpro / New Left, San Francisco Files, Part 1.

73. Michael R. Fischbach, *Records of Dispossession: Palestinian Refugee Property and the Arab-Israeli Conflict* (New York: Columbia University Press, 2003); Osamah Khalil, "Pax Americana: The United States, the Palestinians, and the Peace Process, 1948–2008," *CR: The New Centennial Review* 8, no. 2: The Palestine Issue (2008): 1–41.

74. See Oren Barak, *The Lebanese Army: A National Institution in a Divided Society* (Albany: State University of New York Press, 2009); Khalil, "Pax Americana."

75. "Bayān al-'Āṣifah Raqm 1," January 1, 1965, WAFA: Palestinian News and Info Agency http://info.wafa.ps/ar_page.aspx?id=4925; Yezid Sayigh, *Armed Struggle and the Search for State: The Palestinian National Movement, 1949–1993* (Oxford: Oxford University Press, 1998), 80–108; "Intelligence Memorandum," December 2, 1966, Doc. 356, *FRUS, 1964–1968: Volume XVIII, Arab-Israeli Dispute, 1964–1967,* ed. Harriet Dashiell Schwar (Washington, DC: Government Printing Office, 2000).

76. Tom Segev, *1967: Israel, the War, and the Year That Transformed the Middle East* (New York: Metropolitan Books, 2007), 194–231.

77. Avi Shlaim, *The Iron Wall: Israel and the Arab World* (New York: Norton, 2001).

78. William Quandt, *Peace Process: American Diplomacy and the Arab-Israeli Conflict since 1967,* 3rd ed. (Berkeley: University of California Press; and Washington, DC: Brookings Institution, 2005).

79. Segev, *1967,* 240–241.

80. Segev, *1967,* 241–257, 364–384, 472.

81. Paul Chamberlin, *The Global Offensive: The United States, the Palestine Liberation Organization, and the Making of the Post–Cold War Order* (New York: Oxford University Press, 2012), 44–49, 70; Sayigh, *Armed Struggle and the Search for State,* 147; Khalil, "Pax Americana."

82. "Notes of Meeting," March 26, 1968, Doc. 157, *FRUS, 1964–1968, Volume VI: Vietnam, January–August 1968,* ed. Kent Sieg (Washington, DC: Government Printing Office, 2002).

83. Bunker telegram to Johnson, January 16, 1969, Doc. 285, *FRUS, 1964–1968, Volume VII: Vietnam, September 1968–January 1969,* ed. Kent Sieg (Washington, DC: Government Printing Office, 2003).

84. Laird memorandum to Nixon, March 13, 1969, Doc. 38, *FRUS, 1969–1976: Volume VI.*

85. Kissinger memorandum to Nixon, June 23, 1969, Doc. 87; Laird memorandum to Nixon, September 4, 1969, Doc. 114; and Kissinger memorandum to Nixon, October 30, 1969, Doc. 143, all in *FRUS, 1969–1976: Volume VI.*

86. Richard Nixon, "Address to the Nation on the War in Vietnam," November 3, 1969, transcript https://www.nixonlibrary.gov/sites/default/files/2018-08/silent majority_transcript.pdf, quote on 3.

87. Nixon, "Address to the Nation on the War in Vietnam," 3.

88. David L. Anderson, *Vietnamization: Politics, Strategy, Legacy* (London: Rowman and Littlefield, 2020), ch. 8. One outspoken critic was Richard Holbrooke; see Packer, *Our Man,* 166–167. See also Kissinger's criticism of Vietnamization: Henry Kissinger, *White House Years* (New York: Simon and Schuster, 1979), 477, 500.

89. Arafat quote in Avi Shlaim, *Lion of Jordan: The Life of King Hussein in War and Peace* (New York: Alfred A. Knopf, 2008), 325; Nigel Ashton, *King Hussein of Jordan: A Political Life* (New Haven: Yale University Press, 2008), 139–140.

90. Shlaim, *Lion of Jordan,* 320; Ashton, *King Hussein of Jordan,* 143–144.

91. Chamberlin, *The Global Offensive,* 108–121.

92. Nixon and Kissinger telephone conversation transcript, September 11, 1970, Doc. 226, *FRUS, 1969–1976: Volume XXIV, Middle East Region, 1969–1972,* ed. Linda W. Qaimmaqami and Adam M. Howard (Washington, DC: Government Printing Office, 2008); Chamberlin, *The Global Offensive,* 117.

93. James Reston, "The Impotence of Power," *New York Times,* September 11, 1970.

94. C. L. Sulzberger, "Foreign Affairs—Skyjack: Gnats and Sledges," *New York Times,* September 11, 1970.

95. Kissinger memorandum to Nixon, September 16, 1970, https://www.nixon library.gov/sites/default/files/virtuallibrary/documents/jan10/087.pdf.

96. Rogers to Brown, September 17, 1970, Doc. 252, *FRUS, 1969–1976: Volume XXIV.*

97. Shlaim, *Lion of Jordan,* 325–339.

98. Richard Nixon, "Address to the Nation on the Situation in Southeast Asia," April 30, 1970, American Presidency Project.

99. Lake, "Introduction," xvii.

2. NIXON'S WARS AND THE LONG 1970S

Epigraph: Richard Nixon, "Address to the Nation on the Situation in Southeast Asia," April 30, 1970.

1. See William G. Domhoff, *The Bohemian Grove and Other Retreats: A Study in Ruling Class Cohesiveness* (New York: Harper and Row, 1974); Alex Shoumatoff, "Bohemian Tragedy," *Vanity Fair,* April 1, 2009; Richard M. Nixon, *RN: The Memoirs of Richard Nixon* (New York: Grosset & Dunlap, 1978), 284.

2. "Address by Richard Nixon to the Bohemian Club," July 29, 1967, Doc. 2, *Foreign Relations of the United States* (hereafter *FRUS*), *1969–1976: Volume 1, Foundations of Foreign Policy, 1969–1972,* ed. Louis J. Smith and David H. Herschler (Washington, DC: Government Publishing Office, 2003).

3. "Address by Richard Nixon to the Bohemian Club."

4. "Address by Richard Nixon to the Bohemian Club."

5. Henry Kissinger, *White House Years* (New York: Simon and Schuster, 1979), 227; Nixon 1968 campaign commercial "Vietnam War," https://www.youtube.com /watch?v=5HBON-ZIyUE.

6. Rick Perlstein, *The Invisible Bridge: The Fall of Nixon and the Rise of Reagan* (New York: Simon and Schuster, 2014), 88.

7. John W. Finney, "Nixon and Reagan Ask War on Crime," *New York Times*, July 31, 1968; Richard M. Nixon, "Address Accepting the Presidential Nomination at the Republican National Convention in Miami Beach, Florida," August 8, 1968, American Presidency Project; Naomi Murakawa, *The First Civil Right: How Liberals Built Prison America* (New York: Oxford University Press, 2014).

8. Nixon-Agnew Victory Committee, "The First Civil Right," 1968, www .livingroomcandidate.org/commercials/1968/the-first-civil-right; and "Crime," 1968, www.livingroomcandidate.org/commercials/1968/crime, both in "The Living Room Candidate: Presidential Campaign Commercials 1952–2012," Museum of the Moving Image.

9. Tom Wells, *The War Within: America's Battle over Vietnam* (Berkeley: University of California Press, 1994).

10. Wells, *The War Within*, 406–408; Mark Rudd, *Underground: My Life with SDS and the Weathermen* (New York: HarperCollins, 2009).

11. Richard Nixon, "Remarks to Top Personnel at the Central Intelligence Agency," March 7, 1969, American Presidency Project; Seymour M. Hersh, *The Price of Power: Kissinger in the Nixon White House* (New York: Summit Books, 1983), 208–209.

12. Fred P. Graham, "FBI Files Tell of Surveillance of Students, Blacks, War Foes," *New York Times*, March 24, 1971, 1; Michelle Alexander, *The New Jim Crow: Mass Incarceration in the Age of Colorblindness* (New York: New Press, 2010), 53; Dan Berger, "Social Movements and Mass Incarceration: What Is to Be Done?" *Souls* 15, no. 1–2 (2013): 3–18; Joshua Bloom and Waldo E. Martin, *Black against Empire: A History of the Black Panther Party* (Berkeley: University of California Press, 2013).

13. Graham, "FBI Files Tell of Surveillance."

14. See Hersh, *The Price of Power*, 91–97, 209–210.

15. Hersh, *The Price of Power*, 84–86.

16. "Bayān Munazzamat Ailūl al-Aswad ḥawla mas'ūlīyatuhā 'an Maṣra' al-Sayyid Wasfī al-Tall" "Black September Statement Claims Responsibility for the Removal of Mr. Wasfi al-Tal in Egypt," November 28, 1971, *Al-Wathā'iq al-Filastiniyyah al-Arabiyah li-'Aām 1971* (Palestinian Arab Documents, 1971) (Beirut: Institute for Palestine Studies, 1974): 886; Osamah Khalil, "The Radical

Crescent: The United States, the Palestine Liberation Organisation, and the Lebanese Civil War, 1973–1978," *Diplomacy & Statecraft* 27, no. 3 (September 2016): 496–522.

17. Richard Nixon, "Remarks to Reporters about the Assault on Israeli Athletes at the Olympic Games in Munich, Germany," September 5, 1972, American Presidency Project; Paul Chamberlin, *The Global Offensive: The United States, the Palestine Liberation Organization, and the Making of the Post–Cold War Order* (New York: Oxford University Press, 2012): 140–141.

18. Conversation between Nixon and Kissinger, Doc. 93, Oval Office, September 6, 1972, *FRUS, 1969–1976, Volume E-1, Documents on Global Issues, 1969–1972*; Conversation between Nixon and Kissinger, Doc. 300, July 25, 1972 and Doc. 303, August 2, 1972, *FRUS, 1969–1976, Volume XXIII, Arab-Israeli Dispute, 1969–1972*; Ronen Bergman, *Rise and Kill First: The Secret History of Israel's Targeted Assassinations* (New York: Random House, 2019): 166–174, 215–224.

19. Rogers to Nixon, "Subject: Measures to Combat Terrorism," September 18, 1972, Doc. 103, *FRUS, 1969–1976, Volume E-1, Documents on Global Issues, 1969–1972*; Pamela Pennock, "From 1967 to Operation Boulder: The Erosion of Arab Americans' Civil Liberties in the 1970s," *Arab Studies Quarterly* 40, no. 1 (Winter 2018): 41–52, 44.

20. "U.S. Checks Arabs to Block Terror," *New York Times*, October 5, 1972; Pennock, "From 1967 to Operation Boulder," 44.

21. Khalil, "The Radical Crescent," 499.

22. Khalil, "The Radical Crescent," 500.

23. Khalil, "The Radical Crescent," 500.

24. Radley Balko, *Rise of the Warrior Cop* (New York: Public Affairs, 2013), 71.

25. Egil "Bud" Krogh interview, "Drug Wars: Part 1," October 9, 2000, *PBS Frontline* https://www.pbs.org/wgbh/pages/frontline/shows/drugs/interviews/krogh .html; Egil "Bud" Krogh, *Integrity: Good People, Bad Choices, and Life Lessons from the White House* (New York: Public Affairs, 2007), 18–19.

26. Nixon, "Special Message to the Congress on Control of Narcotics and Dangerous Drugs," July 14, 1969, American Presidency Project.

27. See Balko, *Rise of the Warrior Cop*, ch. 4.

28. Nick Kotz, "The Making of a Dark Horse, 1972: President Signs Drug-Control Bill, Sees Thousands of Lives Saved," *Washington Post*, October 28, 1970; Fred P. Graham, "Both Parties Press Crime as 1970 Campaign Issue," *New York Times*, January 4, 1970; Marjorie Hunter, "Congress Rushes Nixon's Crime Bills," *New York Times*, September 24, 1970; "Nixon Signs Drug Abuse Control Bill," *New York Times*, October 28, 1970.

29. The Federal Comprehensive Drug Abuse Prevention and Control Act of 1970, Public Law 91-513, October 27, 1970.

30. Charles Doyle, "RICO: A Brief Sketch," *Congressional Research Service*, Congressional Research Service, CRS Report 96-950, updated August 3, 2021, https://crsreports.congress.gov/product/pdf/RL/96-950/12.

31. James M. Naughton, "President Gives 'Highest Priority' to Drug Problem," *New York Times*, June 2, 1971; Carroll Kilpatrick, "Nixon Seeks National War on Drug Use," *Washington Post*, June 18, 1971; Richard Nixon, "Executive Order 1599: Establishing a Special Action Office for Drug Abuse Prevention," "Special Message to the Congress on Drug Abuse Prevention and Control," "Remarks About an Intensified Program for Drug Abuse Prevention and Control," June 17, 1971, American Presidency Project. See Jeremy Kuzmarov, *The Myth of the Addicted Army: Vietnam and the Modern War on Drugs* (Amherst: University of Massachusetts Press, 2009).

32. Mark Jacobson, "The Return of Superfly," *New York Magazine*, August 14, 2000 https://nymag.com/nymetro/news/people/features/3649/; and Mark Jacobson, "Lords of Dopetown," *New York Magazine*, October 29, 2007.

33. David Burnham, "$10-Million Heroin Stolen from a Police Office Vault," *New York Times*, December 15, 1972; Edward C. Burks, "Police Say That They Lost 24 More Pounds of Heroin," *New York Times*, December 16, 1972; Paul L. Montgomery, "12 in Police Narcotic Unit Charged with Corruption," *New York Times*, March 9, 1974.

34. Jacobson, "The Return of Superfly"; Victor S. Kaufman, "Trouble in the Golden Triangle: The United States, Taiwan, and the 93rd Nationalist Division," *China Quarterly* 166 (June 2001): 440–456; Bertil Lintner, "Heroin and Highland Insurgency in the Golden Triangle," in *War on Drugs: Studies in the Failure of U.S. Narcotics Policy*, ed. Alfred W. McCoy and Alan A. Block (Boulder, CO: Westview Press, 1992), 281–318.

35. Kaufman, "Trouble in the Golden Triangle."

36. Alfred W. McCoy, *The Politics of Heroin: CIA Complicity in the Global Drug Trade* (Brooklyn, NY: Lawrence Hill Books, 1991), 283–292; Tuan Shi-wen quoted in Lintner, "Heroin and Highland Insurgency," 288.

37. Lucas quoted in Jacobson, "The Return of Superfly."

38. Joseph E. Persico, *The Imperial Rockefeller: A Biography of Nelson A. Rockefeller* (New York: Simon and Schuster, 1982).

39. Richard Nixon, "Remarks during a Visit to New York City to Review Drug Abuse Law Enforcement Activities," March 20, 1972, American Presidency Project; Michael Javen Fortner, *Black Silent Majority: The Rockefeller Drug Laws and the Politics of Punishment* (Cambridge, MA: Harvard University Press, 2015), 182–183; M. A. Farber, "Opinion Remains Divided over Effect of State's New Drug Law," *New York Times*, August 31, 1973, 16.

40. Persico, *The Imperial Rockefeller*, 140–145; Farber, "Opinion Remains Divided"; Brian Mann, "The Drug Laws That Changed How We Punish," NPR

Morning Edition, February 14, 2013. Rockefeller quoted in Persico, *The Imperial Rockefeller,* 141; and Mann, "The Drug Laws That Changed How We Punish."

41. Farber, "Opinion Remains Divided"; Fortner, *Black Silent Majority,* 177–182.

42. Anthony Astrachan and Tim O'Brien, "Stiff N.Y. Law on Drug Use Takes Effect: Stiffest Anti-Drug Law Effective Today," *Washington Post,* September 1, 1973.

43. The 1973 laws were enacted in Chapters 276, 277, 278, 676, and 1051 of New York State Law. The laws were further amended in 1975 (Chapters 785 and 832) and 1976 (Chapter 424). See National Institute of Law Enforcement and Criminal Justice, Law Enforcement Assistance Administration, US Department of Justice, "The Nation's Toughest Drug Laws: Evaluating the New York Experience, Final Report of the Joint Committee on New York Drug Law Evaluation," March 1978 (Government Printing Office: Washington, DC), 3fn1.

44. "The Nation's Toughest Drug Law: Evaluating the New York Experience," Final Report of the Joint Committee on New York Drug Law Evaluation, National Institute of Law Enforcement and Criminal Justice, U.S. Department of Justice, March 1978, 7–11 https://www.ojp.gov/pdffiles1/Digitization/43315NCJRS.pdf.

45. "Background on New York's Draconian Rockefeller Drug Laws," Drug Policy Alliance, New York, undated https://www.almendron.com/tribuna/wp-content/uploads/2023/04/factsheet-ny-background-on-rdl-reforms.pdf. Similar findings in Fortner, *Black Silent Majority,* 258–259.

46. Mann, "The Drug Laws That Changed How We Punish"; Astrachan and O'Brien, "Stiff N.Y. Law On Drug Use Takes Effect." See also Ashley Nellis, "Mass Incarceration Trends," January 25, 2023 https://www.sentencingproject.org/reports/mass-incarceration-trends/; and "The Color of Justice: Racial and Ethnic Disparity in State Prisons," October 13. 2021, The Sentencing Project https://www.sentencingproject.org/reports/the-color-of-justice-racial-and-ethnic-disparity-in-state-prisons-the-sentencing-project/.

47. On Anslinger, see Johann Hari, *Chasing the Scream: The Search for the Truth about Addiction* (London: Bloomsbury, 2015); Kathleen Frydl, *The Drug Wars in America, 1940–1973* (New York, NY: Cambridge University Press, 2013); "Report of the U.S. Delegation to the Seventeenth Session of the UN Commission on Narcotic Drugs," August 15, 1962, Doc. 340, *FRUS, 1961–1963, Volume XXV, Organization of Foreign Policy; Information Policy; United Nations; Scientific Matters,* ed. Paul Claussen, Evan M. Duncan, and Jeffrey A. Soukup (Washington, DC: Government Publishing Office, 2001); William B. McAllister, "The Global Political Economy of Scheduling: The International–Historical Context of the Controlled Substances Act," *Drug and Alcohol Dependence* 76 (2004): 3–8.

48. McAllister, "The Global Political Economy of Scheduling"; David T. Courtwright, "The Controlled Substances Act: How a 'Big Tent' Reform Became a

Punitive Drug Law," *Drug and Alcohol Dependence* 76 (2004): 9–15; US Senate, Hearing Before the Committee on Foreign Relations, "Protocol Amending the Single Convention on Narcotic Drugs, 1961," June 27, 1972 (Washington, DC: Government Printing Office, 1972), 1–10.

49. "Nixon Plans to Unify Drug Enforcement Agencies," *New York Times*, March 29, 1973; Richard Nixon, "Executive Order 11727: Drug Law Enforcement," July 6, 1973, American Presidency Project; Lisa N. Sacco, "Drug Enforcement in the United States: History, Policy, and Trends," Congressional Research Service 7-5700, October 2, 2014 (Washington, DC: Government Printing Office).

50. Kate Doyle, "Operation Intercept: The Perils of Unilateralism," National Security Archive Briefing Book, April 13, 2003, https://nsarchive2.gwu.edu/NSAEBB/NSAEBB86/.

51. Moynihan to Mitchell, September 18, 1969, Doc. 143, *FRUS, 1969–1976, Volume E-1, Documents on Global Issues, 1969–1972*, ed. Susan K. Holly and William B. McAllister (Washington, DC: Government Publishing Office, 2005). Emphasis in original.

52. Evanthis Hatzivassiliou, "Nixon's Coup: Establishing the NATO Committee on the Challenges of Modern Society 1969–70," *International History Review* 38, no. 1 (2016): 88–108; Evanthis Hatzivassiliou, *The NATO Committee on the Challenges of Modern Society, 1969–75* (Cham, Switzerland: Palgrave Macmillan, 2017), 95–118.

53. Ryan Gingeras, *Heroin, Organized Crime, and the Making of Modern Turkey* (New York: Oxford University Press), 189–195.

54. Gingeras, *Heroin, Organized Crime*, 195–204.

55. Gingeras, *Heroin, Organized Crime*, 185.

56. "Narcotics, Marijuana, and Dangerous Drugs: Findings and Recommendations," Report of Special Presidential Task Force, June 6, 1969 https://nsarchive2.gwu.edu/NSAEBB/NSAEBB86/intercept01.pdf.

57. Dial Torgerson, "Checks at Border Cripple Tourism," *Los Angeles Times*, September 23, 1969.

58. McBride to Rogers, September 12, 1969 https://nsarchive2.gwu.edu/NSAEBB/NSAEBB86/intercept06.pdf; Whitehead to Krogh, "Proposed Major Program Issue on Marihuana Policy," September 29, 1969 https://nsarchive2.gwu.edu/NSAEBB/NSAEBB86/intercept09.pdf; Doyle, "Operation Intercept."

59. "Memorandum Prepared in the CIA," re: Mexico's Narcotics Problem, February 26, 1976, Doc. 92, *FRUS, 1969–1976, Volume E-11, Part 1, Documents on Mexico; Central America; and the Caribbean, 1973–1976*, ed. Halbert Jones (Washington, DC: Government Publishing Office, 2015).

60. Jeremy Kuzmarov, "From Counter-Insurgency to Narco-Insurgency: Vietnam and the International War on Drugs," *Journal of Policy History* 20, no. 3 (2008): 344–378, 346; Richard B. Craig, "La Campaña Permanente: Mexico's

Antidrug Campaign," *Journal of Interamerican Studies and World Affairs* 20, no. 2 (1978): 107–131, 107–110; Aileen Teague, "The United States, Mexico, and the Mutual Securitization of Drug Enforcement, 1969–1985," *Diplomatic History* 43, no. 5 (2019): 785–812, 795–799.

61. "Memorandum Prepared in the CIA," re: Mexico's Narcotics Problem, February 26, 1976; Peter Watt and Roberto Zepeda, *Drug War Mexico: Politics, Neoliberalism and Violence in the New Narcoeconomy* (London: Zed Books, 2012), 48–61; Oswaldo Zavala, *Drug Cartels Do Not Exist: Narcotrafficking in US and Mexican Culture* (Nashville, TN: Vanderbilt University Press, 2022), 3.

62. Ortiz telegram to Kissinger, "Views of the Uruguayan Military," March 19, 1973, Wikileaks Kissinger Cables https://wikileaks.org/plusd/cables/1973MONTEV 00838_b.html.

63. Paul Gootenberg, *Andean Cocaine: The Making of a Global Drug* (Chapel Hill: University of North Carolina Press, 2008), 303.

64. Francis E. Thoumi, *Illegal Drugs, Economy, and Society in the Andes* (Washington, DC: Woodrow Wilson Center Press and Baltimore: Johns Hopkins University Press, 2003), 80–83; Gootenberg, *Andean Cocaine*, 303–304.

65. Shlaudeman to Kissinger, "The 'Third World War' and South America," ARA Monthly Report (July): August 3, 1976, 1 https://nsarchive.gwu.edu/document /21756-document-03.

66. Shlaudeman "The 'Third World War' and South America."

67. Luis Roniger and Mario Sznajder, eds., *The Legacy of Human-Rights Violations in the Southern Cone: Argentina, Chile, and Uruguay* (New York: Oxford University Press, 1999).

68. Kyle Burke, *Revolutionaries for the Right: Anticommunist Internationalism and Paramilitary Warfare in the Cold War* (Chapel Hill: University of North Carolina Press, 2018), 70–71.

69. Thomas Borstelmann, *The Cold War and the Color Line: American Race Relations in the Global Arena* (Cambridge, MA: Harvard University Press, 2001), 223–224.

70. Eddie Michel, "Those Bothersome Rho-dents: Lyndon B. Johnson and the Rhodesian Information Office," *Safundi: The Journal of South African and American Studies* 19, no. 7 (2018): 227–245, 229–231.

71. See Michel, "Those Bothersome Rho-dents"; Josiah Brownell, *The Collapse of Rhodesia: Population Demographics and the Politics of Race* (London: I. B. Tauris, 2010).

72. Kissinger to Nixon, April 3, 1969, Doc. 5, *FRUS, 1969–1976, Volume XXVIII, Southern Africa*, ed. Myra F. Burton (Washington, DC: Government Publishing Office, 2011).

73. "Minutes of a National Security Council Meeting," December 17, 1969, Doc. 20, *FRUS, 1969–1976, Volume XXVIII*.

74. "Paper Prepared by the National Security Council Interdepartmental Group for Africa," December 9, 1969, Doc. 17, *FRUS, 1969–1976, Volume XXVIII*.

75. "Minutes of National Security Meeting," December 17, 1969.

76. "Minutes of National Security Meeting," December 17, 1969;

77. "Minutes of National Security Meeting," December 17, 1969; Anthony Lake, *The "Tar Baby" Option: American Policy toward Southern Rhodesia* (New York: Columbia University Press, 1976), 129.

78. Burke, *Revolutionaries for the Right*, 50–54; Borstelmann, *The Cold War and the Color Line*, 198–202.

79. "Intelligence Note Prepared in the Bureau of Intelligence and Research," re: USSR-Africa, August 11, 1970, Doc. 92, *FRUS, 1969–1976, Volume XXVIII*; Paul Moorcraft, *Total Onslaught: War and Revolution in Southern Africa since 1945* (Yorkshire: Pen and Sword Books, 2018), 222–229.

80. Borstelmann, *The Cold War and the Color Line*, 212–213, 237–241; Gerald Horne, *From the Barrel of a Gun: The United States and the War against Zimbabwe, 1965–1980* (Chapel Hill: University of North Carolina Press, 2001), 406; Robert C. Good, *U.D.I.: The International Politics of the Rhodesian Rebellion* (Princeton, NJ: Princeton University Press, 2015), 239.

81. Borstelmann, *The Cold War and the Color Line*, 236–237; "U.S. against the Charter," *New York Times*, November 12, 1971; Harry F. Byrd, "Should the U.S. Buy Rhodesian Chrome," *New York Times*, November 26, 1971.

82. Henry Kissinger, *Years of Renewal* (New York: Simon and Schuster, 1999), 809–825.

83. Kissinger, *Years of Renewal*, 809–825; David Binder, "Senate Votes to Cut Off Covert Aid for Angolans; Ford Predicts a 'Tragedy,'" *New York Times*, December 20, 1975; Ronald Walters, "The Clark Amendment: Analysis of U.S. Policy Choices in Angola," *The Black Scholar* 12, no. 4 (July/August 1981): 2–12; Julian Zelizer, *Arsenal of Democracy: The Politics of National Security—From World War II to the War on Terrorism* (New York: Basic Books, 2009), 263–264; "Memorandum of Conversation," December 18, 1975, Doc. 153, *FRUS, 1969–1976, Volume XXVIII*.

84. "Memorandum of Conversation," December 18, 1975, Doc. 153, *FRUS, 1969–1976, Volume XXVIII*.

85. Kissinger, *Years of Renewal*, 909.

86. Kissinger, *Years of Renewal*, 921–922.

87. "Editorial Note" (re: Kissinger Remarks on U.S. and Africa), April 27, 1976, Doc. 40, *FRUS, 1969–1976, Volume E-6, Documents on Africa, 1973–1976*, ed. Peter Samson and Laurie Van Hook (Washington, DC: Government Publishing Office, 2006). "Memorandum of Conversation," April 27, 1976, Doc. 195, *FRUS, 1969–1976, Vol. XXVIII*; "Memorandum of Conversation," April 21, 1976, Gerald R. Ford Library, National Security Adviser, Memoranda of Conversations, 1973–1977, Box 19.

88. Sargent, *A Superpower Transformed*, 252; Horne, *From the Barrel of a Gun*, 239–242.

89. "Memorandum of Conversation," April 11, 1969, Doc. 8; and "Memorandum of Conversation," April 1, 1969, Doc. 6; both in *FRUS, 1969–1976, Volume E–4, Documents on Iran and Iraq, 1969–1972*, ed. Monica Belmonte (Washington, DC: Government Publishing Office, 2006).

90. Helms to Kissinger, May 8, 1972, Doc. 190; and "Memorandum of Conversation," May 30, 1972, Doc. 200; both in *FRUS, 1969–1976, Volume E–4*.

91. David L. Phillips, *The Great Betrayal: How America Abandoned the Kurds and Lost the Middle East* (London: I. B. Tauris, 2019), 33–34.

92. Kissinger, *Years of Renewal*, 583, "Research Study RNAS-10," re: The Kurds of Iraq: Renewed Insurgency? May 31, 1972, Doc. 310, *FRUS, 1969–1976, Volume E–4*.

93. Phillips, *The Great Betrayal*, 36–39; Taylor Branch, "The Trial of the CIA," *New York Times*, September 12, 1976.

94. John Prados, *Safe for Democracy: The Secret Wars of the CIA* (Chicago: Ivan R. Dee, 2006), 431–438; Khalil, *America's Dream Palace*, ch. 7.

95. Phillips, *The Great Betrayal*, 34; Gerald Haines, "The Pike Committee Investigations and the CIA," *Studies in Intelligence* (1998–1999) https://www.cia.gov/static/CIA-Pike-Committee-Investigations.pdf; Kissinger, *Years of Renewal*, 596; William Safire, "Son of 'Secret Sellout,'" *New York Times*, February 12, 1976.

96. William Quandt, *Peace Process: American Diplomacy and the Arab-Israeli Conflict since 1967*, 3rd ed. (Berkeley: University of California Press; and Washington, DC: Brookings Institution, 2005), 159–169; Gerald R. Ford, *A Time to Heal: The Autobiography of Gerald R. Ford* (New York: Harper and Collins, 1979), 287; Yitzhak Rabin, *The Rabin Memoirs* (Boston: Little, Brown, 1979), 261–263.

97. See Khalil, "The Radical Crescent"; Kai Bird, *The Good Spy: The Life and Death of Robert Ames* (New York: Broadway, 2014); Jack O'Connell and Vernon Loeb, *King's Counsel: A Memoir of War, Espionage, and Diplomacy in the Middle East* (New York: Norton, 2011).

98. Fawwaz Traboulsi, *The History of Modern Lebanon* (New York: Pluto Press, 2007), 155.

99. Fatah is a reverse acronym in Arabic for the "Palestinian National Liberation Movement" or Harakat al-Tahrīr al-Watanī al-Filastinī.

100. "Palestinians in Lebanon: Troubled Past and Bleak Future," CIA Directorate of Intelligence, February 1983, CIA CREST https://www.cia.gov/readingroom/docs/CIA-RDP84S00558R000100080004-2.pdf.

101. Jonathan Marshall, *The Lebanese Connection: Corruption, Civil War, and the International Drug Traffic* (Stanford, CA: Stanford University Press, 2012), 144–148.

102. James Stocker, *Spheres of Intervention: US Foreign Policy and the Collapse of Lebanon, 1967–1976* (Ithaca, NY: Cornell University Press, 2016).

103. Khalil, "The Radical Crescent," 507, 511.

104. "Memorandum of Conversation," June 22, 1976, Doc. 290, *FRUS, 1969–1976, Volume XXVI, Arab-Israeli Dispute, 1974–1976,* ed. Adam M. Howard (Washington, DC: Government Publishing Office, 2011).

105. "Memorandum of Conversation," August 7, 1976, Doc. 292, *FRUS, 1969–1976, Volume XXVI.*

106. Patrick Seale, *Asad of Syria: The Struggle for the Middle East* (Berkeley: University of California Press, 1989); Khalil, "The Radical Crescent."

107. John K. Cooley, *Unholy Wars: Afghanistan, America, and International Terrorism,* 3rd ed. (London: Pluto Press, 2002), ch. 1; Mohamed Heikal, *Iran: The Untold Story* (New York: Pantheon Books, 1982), 115; Mahmood Mamdani, *Good Muslim, Bad Muslim: America, the Cold War, and the Roots of Terror* (New York: Random House, 2004), 83–85; Alexandre de Marenches, *Dans le Secret des Princes* (Paris: Editions Stock, 1986), 267–273.

108. "Study Prepared by the Ad Hoc Inter-Departmental Group for Africa," December 1976, Doc. 170, *FRUS, Volume E-6;* Odd Arne Westad, *The Global Cold War: Third World Interventions and the Making of Our Times* (Cambridge: Cambridge University Press, 2005), 273–275.

109. Mamdani, *Good Muslim, Bad Muslim,* 85–86; Westad, *The Global Cold War,* 275–277.

110. "Paper Prepared by the Policy Review Committee," undated, Doc. 10, *FRUS, 1977–1980, Volume XVII, Horn of Africa, 1977–1980, Part 1,* ed. Louise P. Woodroofe (Washington, DC: Government Publishing Office, 2016); Mamdani, *Good Muslim, Bad Muslim,* 84–85.

111. Mamdani, *Good Muslim, Bad Muslim,* 84–85; Heikal, *Iran,* 112–116.

112. Dan Baum, "Legalize It All," *Harper's Magazine,* April 2016.

3. CIVILIZATION'S THIN LINE AND THE FEAR OF DECLINE

Epigraph: Jimmy Carter, "Energy and the National Goals," July 15, 1979, American Presidency Project, University of California, Santa Barbara.

1. "Peace through Strength," Ronald Reagan campaign commercial, 1980 https://www.youtube.com/watch?v=_VXXwyl5GoA; emphasis in original; "Safire," Reagan-Bush Committee, 1980, Living Room Candidate, Museum of the Moving Image http://www.livingroomcandidate.org/commercials/1980/safire# 4074.

2. Natasha Zaretsky, *No Direction Home: The American Family and the Fear of National Decline, 1968–1980* (Chapel Hill: University of North Carolina Press, 2007), 233; Carter, "Energy and the National Goals."

3. Adam Clymer, "Poll Shows Carter Gaining Support on Afghan Moves, Slipping on Iran," *New York Times,* January 16, 1980; Jimmy Carter, "State of the Union Address, 1980," January 23, 1980.

4. Carter, "State of the Union"; Brzezinski to Carter, January 2, 1980, Doc. 127, *Foreign Relations of the United States* (hereafter *FRUS*), *1977–1980, Volume XII, Afghanistan,* ed. David Zierler (Washington, DC: Government Publishing Office, 2018). On the "Afghan trap" and the US breaking Soviet ciphers, Jonathan Haslam, *Russia's Cold War: From the October Revolution to the Fall of the Wall* (New Haven: Yale University Press, 2011): 318–327. On Soviet intentions and challenges, Vladislav M. Zubok, *A Failed Empire: The Soviet Union in the Cold War From Stalin to Gorbachev* (Chapel Hill, NC: University of North Carolina Press, 2007): 227–264; Yaacov Ro'i, *The Bleeding Wound: The Soviet War in Afghanistan and the Collapse of the Soviet System* (Stanford, CA: Stanford University Press, 2022): 9–40.

5. Hedrick Smith, "The Carter Doctrine," *New York Times,* January 23, 1980.

6. Thornton to Brzezinski, September 11, 1978, Doc. 29, *FRUS, 1977–1980, Volume XII.*

7. "Summary of Conclusions of a Special Coordination Committee Meeting," June 26, 1979, Doc. 53, *FRUS, 1977–1980, Volume XII.*

8. Blood to Vance, October 28, 1979, Doc. 78, *FRUS, 1977–1980, Volume XII*; Odd Arne Westad, *The Global Cold War: Third World Interventions and the Making of Our Times* (Cambridge: Cambridge University Press, 2005), 324–326.

9. Brzezinski quoted in Richard Burt, "U.S. Reappraises Persian Gulf Policies," *New York Times,* January 1, 1979.

10. "A Rhomboid of Rhetoric," *New York Times,* January 11, 1979; "The Crescent of Crisis," *Time Magazine,* January 15, 1979.

11. Ermarth to Brzezinski, January 2, 1980, Doc. 133, *FRUS, 1977–1980, Volume XII.*

12. Brzezinski to Carter, January 2, 1980, Doc. 134, *FRUS, 1977–1980, Volume XII.*

13. "Memorandum Prepared in the CIA," re: Afghan Exile Groups based in Pakistan, January 9, 1980, Doc. 153, *FRUS, 1977–1980, Volume XII*; Imtiaz H. Bokhari, "The War in Afghanistan: A Study of Insurgency and Counter-insurgency," *Strategic Studies* 5, no. 3 (Spring 1982): 19–47; Paul Thomas Chamberlin, *The Cold War's Killing Fields* (New York: HarperCollins, 2018), 446–448.

14. "Memorandum Prepared in the CIA," re: Afghan Exile Groups based in Pakistan; Bokhari, "The War in Afghanistan"; Chamberlin, *The Cold War's Killing Fields,* 446–448.

15. "Memorandum Prepared in the CIA," re: Afghan Exile Groups based in Pakistan; Mahmood Mamdani, *Good Muslim, Bad Muslim: America, the Cold War, and the Roots of Terror* (New York: Random House, 2004), 141; Bokhari, "The War in Afghanistan"; Chamberlin, *The Cold War's Killing Fields,* 447–448.

16. Casey quoted in Chamberlin, *The Cold War's Killing Fields,* 498–499.

17. Chamberlin, *The Cold War's Killing Fields,* 498–499; "U.S. Relations with the USSR," National Security Decision Directive 75, January 17, 1983, Ronald Reagan Presidential Library and Museum, Simi Valley, CA (hereafter Reagan Library) https://www.reaganlibrary.gov/public/archives/reference/scanned-nsdds/nsdd75.pdf.

18. John Prados, *Safe for Democracy: The Secret Wars of the CIA* (Chicago: Ivan R. Dee, 2006), 483; Mamdani, *Good Muslim, Bad Muslim,* 131–141.

19. "U.S. Policy, Programs, and Strategy in Afghanistan," National Security Decision Directive 166, March 27, 1985, Reagan Library https://www.reaganlibrary .gov/public/archives/reference/scanned-nsdds/nsdd166.pdf.

20. "Conventional Arms Transfer Policy," National Security Decision Directive 5, July 8, 1981, Reagan Library https://www.reaganlibrary.gov/public/archives /reference/scanned-nsdds/nsdd5.pdf.

21. "National Security Decision Directive on Cuba and Central America," National Security Decision Directive 17, January 4, 1982, Reagan Library https:// www.reaganlibrary.gov/public/archives/reference/scanned-nsdds/nsdd17.pdf.

22. Juan O. Tomayo, "U.S. Bankrolling Sandinistas' Foes," *Miami Herald,* December 19, 1982.

23. Pastora quoted in Liz Balmaseda, "Miami Is Nerve Center for Sandinista Foes," *Miami Herald,* November 26, 1982.

24. Sam Dillon, "U.S. Quadruples Its Latin Arms Sales," *Miami Herald,* November 28, 1982.

25. Tayacan, "Psychological Operations in Guerrilla Warfare," English translation October 15, 1984, Congressional Research Service https://www.cia.gov/reading room/docs/CIA-RDP86M00886R001300010029-9.pdf.

26. Bernard Weinraub, "Congress Renews Curbs on Actions against Nicaragua," *New York Times,* December 23, 1982; Julian Zelizer, *Arsenal of Democracy: The Politics of National Security—From World War II to the War on Terrorism* (New York: Basic Books, 2009), 315.

27. Ambassador John D. Negroponte, interview by Charles Stewart Kennedy, February 11, 2000, The Association for Diplomatic Studies and Training Foreign Affairs Oral History Project, transcript 2017, 96 https://adst.org/OH%20TOCs /Negroponte.John.D.pdf; Ginger Thompson and Gary Cohn, "Vietnam Experience Moved Negroponte," *Baltimore Sun,* June 18, 1995. Negroponte quoted in Thompson and Cohn.

28. "A Covert War," *Miami Herald,* December 8, 1982; Thompson and Cohn, "Vietnam Experience Moved Negroponte."

29. Negroponte interview, 101–102; Kyle Burke, *Revolutionaries for the Right: Anticommunist Internationalism and Paramilitary Warfare in the Cold War* (Chapel Hill: University of North Carolina Press, 2018), 140–143; Ginger Thompson and Gary Cohn, "A Carefully Crafted Deception," June 18, 1995; and "Hear No Evil, See No Evil, *Baltimore Sun,* June 19, 1995; Peter Kornbluth, ed. "The Negroponte Files," National Security Archive, April 12, 2005 https://nsarchive2.gwu.edu /NSAEBB/NSAEBB151/index.htm.

30. "Attorney General's Task Force on Violent Crime—Final Report," August 17, 1981, NCJ 78548, Office of Justice Programs, U.S. Department of Justice, iii–v https://www.ojp.gov/pdffiles1/Digitization/78548NCJRS.pdf.

31. "Attorney General's Task Force on Violent Crime—Final Report," 28–29. On Posse Comitatus, see Matthew Carlton Hammond, "The Posse Comitatus Act: A Principle in Need of Renewal," *Washington University Law Review* 75, no. 2 (January 1997), 954fn11. *Posse Comitatus* is defined as the "power of the county" and related to local law enforcement accepting assistance to maintain the peace or pursue wanted individuals.

32. "Attorney General's Task Force on Violent Crime—Final Report."

33. Public Law 97–86, "Department of Defense Authorization Act, 1982."

34. Ronald Reagan, "Remarks in New Orleans, Louisiana, at the Annual Meeting of the International Association of Chiefs of Police," September 28, 1981, American Presidency Project; "In Congress," *Washington Post,* December 25, 1981; Tom Wicker, "Reagan and Crime," *New York Times,* October 2, 1981.

35. Biography of Dr. Carlton Turner https://www.reaganlibrary.gov/archives/white-house-inventory/turner-carlton-e-files-1981-1987#; "U.S. Shifts Emphasis in New Drive on Drug Abuse," United Press International, October 6, 1982.

36. Radley Balko, *Rise of the Warrior Cop: The Militarization of America's Police Forces* (New York: Public Affairs, 2013), 141–143, Turner quote, 183.

37. "Marijuana Crop in Northern California Worth $400 Million," *Los Angeles Times,* April 24, 1983; Robert B. Gunnison, "In Remote California Region, Marijuana and Violence Thrive," *Philadelphia Inquirer,* October 30, 1983; Balko, *Rise of the Warrior Cop,* 147–148.

38. Ward Sinclair, "Drug Officials Fighting a Losing Battle," *Washington Post,* April 29, 1984; John Hurst, "Copter Forces Wage War on 'Pot' Growers," *Los Angeles Times,* October 14, 1984; Balko, *Rise of the Warrior Cop,* 147–148.

39. Dan Morain, "Judge Curtails Use of Copters in State's War on Marijuana," *Los Angeles Times,* October 19, 1984; Keane quoted in Hurst, "Copter Forces Wage War on 'Pot' Growers."

40. "Narcotics and National Security," National Security Decision Directive 221, April 8, 1986, Reagan Library https://www.reaganlibrary.gov/public/archives/reference/scanned-nsdds/nsdd221.pdf; Ronald Reagan, *The Reagan Diaries* (New York: HarperCollins, 2007), 561; Alison Teague, "The United States, Mexico, and the Mutual Securitization of Drug Enforcement, 1969–1985," *Diplomatic History* 43, no. 5 (2019): 785–812, 785.

41. Brad Heath, "Killed by a Cartel. Betrayed by His Own? US Reexamines Murder of Federal Agent Featured in 'Narcos,'" *USA Today,* February 27, 2020.

42. Howard Cohen, "How 'Miami Vice' Changed TV," *Miami Herald,* September 28, 2014; Michael Sherry, *The Punitive Turn in American Life: How the United States Learned to Fight Crime Like a War* (Chapel Hill, NC: The University of North Carolina Press, 2020), 100–101.

43. Wright quoted in Peter Kerr, "Anatomy of the Drug Issue: How, after Years, It Erupted," *New York Times,* November 17, 1986.

44. Kerr, "Anatomy of the Drug Issue"; Alfonse M. D'Amato, "Continuing the War on Drugs," *New York Times,* October 28, 1986.

45. Gerald M. Boyd, "Reagan Signs Anti-Drug Measure; 'Hopes for Drug-Free Generation,'" *New York Times,* October 27, 1986.

46. Boyd, "Reagan Signs Anti-Drug Measure"; Joel Brinkley, "Anti-Drug Law: Words, Deeds, Political Expediency," *New York Times,* October 27, 1986.

47. María Celia Toro, "The Internationalization of Police: The DEA in Mexico," *Journal of American History* 86, no. 2 (1999): 623–640, 624–625.

48. Toro, "The Internationalization of Police," 624–625; Christopher W. Sullivan, "User-Accountability Provisions in the Anti–Drug Abuse Act of 1988: Assaulting Civil Liberties in the War on Drugs," *Hastings Law Journal* 40 (1989): 1223–1251.

49. "High on Hot Air," editorial, *New Republic,* October 6, 1986; Adam Paul Weisman, "I Was a Drug-Hype Junkie: 48 Hours on Crock Street," *New Republic,* October 6, 1986.

50. Schumer quoted in Kerr, "Anatomy of the Drug Issue."

51. "Israel-United States: Memorandum of Understanding on Strategic Cooperation," November 30, 1981, *International Legal Materials* 20, no. 6 (November 1981): 1420–1423.

52. Osamah Khalil, "The Radical Crescent: The United States, the Palestine Liberation Organisation, and the Lebanese Civil War, 1973–1978," *Diplomacy and Statecraft* 27, no. 3 (September 2016): 496–522; John Boykin, *Cursed Is the Peacemaker: The American Diplomat versus the Israeli General, Beirut 1982* (Belmont, CA: Applegate Press, 2002).

53. Seth Anziska, *Preventing Palestine: A Political History from Camp David to Oslo* (Princeton, NJ: Princeton University Press, 2018); Osamah F. Khalil, "Cold War Twilight: The United States, the Soviet Union, and the Middle East in the American Imagination, 1981–1988," *Maghreb Review* 45, no. 3, 2020: 526–528.

54. Anziska, *Preventing Palestine,* 210–216.

55. Yezid Sayigh, *Armed Struggle and the Search for State: The Palestinian National Movement, 1949–1993* (Oxford: Oxford University Press, 1998), 539; Eqbal Ahmed and editors, "The 1982 Israeli Invasion of Lebanon: The Casualties," *Race and Class* 24, no. 4 (1983): 340–343.

56. Sayigh, *Armed Struggle and the Search for State,* 539; Khalil, "Cold War Twilight," 527–528; Eqbal Ahmed and editors, "The 1982 Israeli invasion of Lebanon," 343.

57. Anziska, *Preventing Palestine,* 210–216; Sayigh, *Armed Struggle and the Search for State,* 549–555; Ronald Reagan, "Address to the Nation Announcing the Formation of a New Multinational Force in Lebanon," September 20, 1982, Reagan Library.

58. Sayigh, *Armed Struggle and the Search for State,* 555–573; Khalil, "Cold War Twilight," 528–529.

59. Timothy Naftali, *Blind Spot: The Secret History of American Counterterrorism* (New York: Basic Books, 2005), 136–137; Chamberlin, *The Cold War's Killing Fields*, 505–508; Khalil, *America's Dream Palace*, 241–242.

60. Naftali, *Blind Spot*, 162–165; Aurelie Daher, *Hezbollah: Mobilisation and Power* (London: Oxford University Press, 2019), 52–53.

61. Jonathan Marshall, *The Lebanese Connection: Corruption, Civil War, and the International Drug Traffic* (Stanford, CA: Stanford University Press, 2012), 148–152.

62. "Combatting Terrorism," National Security Decision Directive 138, April 3, 1984, Reagan Library https://www.reaganlibrary.gov/public/archives/reference /scanned-nsdds/nsdd138.pdf.

63. "Combatting Terrorism," National Security Decision Directive 138.

64. Mahmoud Abbas, *Through Secret Channels: The Road to Oslo: Senior PLO Leader Abu Mazen's Revealing Story of the Negotiations with Israel* (Reading, UK: Garnet Publishing, 1995); Yevgeny Primakov, *Russia and the Arabs: Behind the Scenes in the Middle East from the Cold War to the Present* (New York: Basic Books, 2009); Lisa Stampnitzky, *Disciplining Terror: How Experts Invented 'Terrorism'* (Cambridge, UK: Cambridge University Press, 2014); Khalil, *America's Dream Palace*, ch. 7.

65. Elizabeth Bazan, "Assassination Ban and E.O. 12333: A Brief Summary," Congressional Research Service, January 4, 2002 https://irp.fas.org/crs/RS21037.pdf.

66. Christopher Simpson, *National Security Directives of the Reagan and Bush Administrations* (Boulder, CO: Westview Press, 1995), 365–366; Khalil, "Cold War Twilight," 528–530; Seymour Hersh, "The Vice President's Men," *London Review of Books,* January 24, 2019.

67. Simpson, *National Security Directives*, 366.

68. Bob Woodward, *Veil: The Secret Wars of the CIA, 1981–1987* (New York: Simon and Schuster, 1988): 453–456.

69. John Arquilla, *The Reagan Imprint: Ideas in American Foreign Policy from the Collapse of Communism to the War on Terror* (Chicago: Ivan R. Dee, 2006), 142.

70. "Managing Terrorist Incidents," National Security Decision Directive 30, April 10, 1982, Reagan Library https://www.reaganlibrary.gov/public/archives /reference/scanned-nsdds/nsdd30.pdf; "Terrorist Group Profiles," NCJ 115237, Office of Justice Programs, U.S. Department of Justice (Washington, DC: US Government Printing Office, 1988).

71. Bernard Gwertzman, "U.S. Policy Is Set on Terror Fight," *New York Times,* March 2, 1986; Hersh, "The Vice President's Men."

72. Counterterrorist Center, "The Abu Nidal Terror Network: Organization, State Sponsors, and Commercial Enterprise: A Reference Aid," July 1987, CIA Directorate of Intelligence https://www.cia.gov/readingroom/docs/THE%20ABU %20NIDAL%20TERROR%20NETW%5B14950297%5D.pdf; and "Abu Nidal Organization: A Reference Aid," February 1987, CIA Directorate of Intelligence

https://www.cia.gov/readingroom/docs/DOC_0005283775.pdf; Sayigh, *Armed Struggle and the Search for State,* 354–355.

73. Naftali, *Blind Spot,* 180–183; David C. Wills, *The First War on Terrorism: Counter-Terrorism Policy during the Reagan Administration* (Lanham, MD: Rowman and Littlefield, 2003), 176–177.

74. Harris quoted in Wills, *The First War on Terrorism,* 164–167.

75. Wills, *The First War on Terrorism,* 164–167; Jack Shaheen, *Reel Bad Arabs: How Hollywood Vilifies a People,* rev., updated ed. (Northampton, MA: Olive Branch Press, 2009), 91–92.

76. "Economic and Security Decisions for Libya," National Security Decision Directive 16, December 10, 1981 https://www.reaganlibrary.gov/public/archives/reference/scanned-nsdds/nsdd16.pdf; "Economic Decisions for Libya," National Security Decision Directive 27, March 9, 1982 https://www.reaganlibrary.gov/public/archives/reference/scanned-nsdds/nsdd27.pdf; both in Reagan Library.

77. "Acting against Libyan Support of International Terrorism," National Security Decision Directive 205 and Annex, January 8, 1986, Reagan Library https://www.reaganlibrary.gov/public/archives/reference/scanned-nsdds/nsdd205.pdf.

78. Wills, *The First War on Terrorism,* 187–211. After Qaddafi was overthrown and killed in 2011, there were indications that Hana Qaddafi survived the attack and had become a physician. See Chris Richardson, "Hana Qaddafi: Dictator's Daughter Survived Reagan's Bombs?" *Christian Science Monitor,* September 1, 2011.

79. Naftali, *Blind Spot,* 195–199; Khalil, "The Radical Crescent."

80. Naftali, *Blind Spot,* 195–199; Dewey Clarridge, *A Spy for All Seasons: My Life in the CIA* (New York: Scribner, 1997), 8–9; Mark Perry, *Eclipse: The Last Days of the CIA* (New York: William Morrow, 1992); "Document Suggests Abu Nidal Was behind the Slaying of Arafat Aide," *Washington Post,* July 23, 1991.

81. "Memorandum of Conversation," August 9, 1979, Doc. 36; Vance to Carter, October 23, 1979, Doc. 38; Griffith to Brzezinski, January 18, 1980, Doc. 42; all in *FRUS, 1977–1980, Volume XVI, Southern Africa,* ed. Myra F. Burton (Washington, DC: Government Publishing Office, 2016).

82. Paul Moorcraft, *Total Onslaught: War and Revolution in Southern Africa since 1945* (Yorkshire: Pen and Sword Military, 2018), 382–412.

83. Henry Allen, "Angola's Struggle from Within: Jonas Savimbi and the Search for Acceptance," *Washington Post,* December 12, 1981; Burke, *Revolutionaries for the Right,* 178–181.

84. Hyde and Webber quoted in Steven V. Roberts, "House Approves Foreign Aid Bill Opposing Marxists around the World," *New York Times,* July 12, 1985.

85. "United States Policy toward Angola," National Security Decision Directive 212, February 10, 1986, Reagan Library https://www.reaganlibrary.gov/public/archives/reference/scanned-nsdds/nsdd212.pdf.

86. "U.S. Policy toward South Africa," National Security Decision Directive 187, September 7, 1985, Reagan Library https://www.reaganlibrary.gov/public /archives/reference/scanned-nsdds/nsdd187.pdf.

87. Moorcraft, *Total Onslaught*, 189–193; Sasha Polakow-Suransky, *The Unspoken Alliance: Israel's Relationship with Apartheid South Africa* (New York: Random House, 2012).

88. Pieter Willem (P. W.) Botha, "Address at the Opening of the NP Natal Congress, Durban," August 15, 1985, PoliticsWeb (South Africa) https://www .politicsweb.co.za/politicsweb/action/media/downloadFile?media_fileid=1065.

89. Prados, *Safe for Democracy*, 503; Moorcraft, *Total Onslaught*, 200–220; John Battersby, "Savimbi Relishes Military Gains in His War against Angolan State," *Christian Science Monitor*, April 16, 1993.

90. Burke, *Revolutionaries for the Right*, 143–147.

91. James Rowley, "Vice President's Task Force Called a Flop," Associated Press, July 18, 1985.

92. "Drugs, Law Enforcement, and Foreign Policy: The Bahamas," US Senate Subcommittee on Terrorism, Narcotics, and International Operations of the Committee on Foreign Relations, May 27, 1987 https://fowlchicago.files.wordpress .com/2014/10/1989-kerry-report-volume-i.pdf.

93. Jesse Katz, "Deposed King of Crack: Now Free after 5 Years in Prison, This Master Marketer Was Key to the Drug's Spread in L.A.," *Los Angeles Times*, December 21, 1994.

94. "Remarks at a White House Meeting for Supporters of United States Assistance for the Nicaraguan Democratic Resistance," March 3, 1986, Reagan Library.

95. Ronald Reagan, "Address to the Nation on the Situation in Nicaragua," March 17, 1986, American Presidency Project.

96. James G. Blight, Janet M. Lang, Hussein Banai, Malcolm Byrne, and John Tirman, eds., *Becoming Enemies: U.S.-Iran Relations and the Iran-Iraq War, 1979–1988* (Lanham, MD: Rowman and Littlefield, 2012).

97. Reid G. Miller, "Hasenfus Hears Soldier Tell How He Shot Down Cargo Plane," Associated Press, November 1, 1986; Andrew Selsky, "American Says He's an Aviation Specialist," Associated Press, October 7, 1986; Prados, *Safe for Democracy*, 564.

98. "The Report of the Congressional Committees Investigating the Iran-Contra Affair: With Supplemental, Minority, and Additional Views," US House of Representatives Select Committee to Investigate Covert Arms Transactions with Iran, US Senate Select Committee on Secret Military Assistance to Iran and the Nicaraguan Opposition, 1987, 3–22, https://archive.org/details/reportofcongress 87unit/page/n21/mode/2up; Theodore Draper, *A Very Thin Line: The Iran-Contra Affair* (New York: Touchstone, 1991); Lawrence Walsh, "Final Report of the Independent Counsel for Iran/Contra Matters," August 4, 1993, vol. 1, ch. 28.

99. "The Report of the Congressional Committees Investigating the Iran-Contra Affair," 431; Sean Wilentz, *The Age of Reagan: A History, 1974–2008* (New York: Harper Collins, 2008), 60–61; Wilentz, "Mr. Cheney's Minority Report," *New York Times,* July 9, 2007; Khalil, *America's Dream Palace,* chs. 7–8.

100. Wilentz, "Mr. Cheney's Minority Report."

101. "Drugs, Law Enforcement, and Foreign Policy: The Bahamas," 1–4.

102. "Drugs, Law Enforcement, and Foreign Policy: The Bahamas," 1–4.

103. "Drugs, Law Enforcement, and Foreign Policy: A Report," December 1988, NCJ 131414, Office of Justice Programs, U.S. Department of Justice, 37–38, 41 https://www.ojp.gov/ncjrs/virtual-library/abstracts/drugs-law-enforcement-and-foreign-policy.

104. Gary Webb, *Dark Alliance: The CIA, the Contras, and the Crack Cocaine Explosion* (New York: Seven Stories Press, 1999); Ryan Devereaux, "How the CIA Watched Over the Destruction of Gary Webb," *The Intercept,* September 25, 2014.

105. "Statement of Richard Thornburgh, Attorney General of the United States, Committee on Foreign Relations, United States Senate, Concerning the United Nations Convention Against Illicit Traffic in Narcotic Drugs and Psychotropic Substances," Washington, DC, August 2, 1989, Dick Thornburgh Papers, University of Pittsburgh Digital Collections https://digital.library.pitt.edu/islandora/object/pitt%3Aais9830.13.01.0045#page/1/mode/1up.

106. "Statement of Richard Thornburgh," August 2, 1989.

107. Peter Schmeisser, "Is America in Decline?" *New York Times,* April 17, 1988; Paul Kennedy, *The Rise and Fall of the Great Powers* (New York: Random House, 1987), 489–498; Khalil, "Cold War Twilight," 533–535.

108. Kennedy, *The Rise and Fall of the Great Powers,* 499–505.

109. Schmeisser, "Is America in Decline?"; Dennis Hevesi, "'The Phone Rings All the Time,' Connecticut Q&A: Paul Kennedy," *New York Times,* April 3, 1988.

110. Schmeisser, "Is America in Decline?"

111. Daniel Patrick Moynihan, "Debunking the Myth of Decline," *New York Times,* June 19, 1988; James R. Schlesinger, "We Sometimes Forget . . . How Powerful This Nation Is," *New York Times,* June 19, 1988.

112. Paul Kennedy, "A Guide to Misinterpreters," *New York Times,* April 17, 1988.

113. Hedrick Smith, "Gorbachev's Shrewd Summitry," *New York Times Magazine,* December 6, 1987.

114. "Memorandum Prepared by the Deputy Director of Central Intelligence (Gates): Gorbachev's Gameplan: The Long View," November 24, 1987, Doc. 103, Attachment, *FRUS, 1981–1988, Volume VI, Soviet Union, October 1986–January 1989,* ed. James Graham Wilson (Washington, DC: Government Publishing Office, 2016); Khalil, "Cold War Twilight," 522–524.

115. Melvyn Leffler, *For the Soul of Mankind: The United States, the Soviet Union, and the Cold War* (New York: Hill and Wang, 2008); "Robert Gates Oral History," July 8–9, 2013, Miller Center, University of Virginia https://millercenter.org/the

-presidency/presidential-oral-histories/robert-gates-oral-history; James Graham Wilson, *The Triumph of Improvisation: Gorbachev's Adaptability, Reagan's Engagement and the End of the Cold War* (Ithaca, NY: Cornell University Press, 2014).

PART II. BADLANDS

1. David Zucchino, "In the Badlands of the City, Drugs Still Riding High," *Philadelphia Inquirer,* April 3, 1991, A1.

2. David Zucchino, "In Bush's Tire Tracks, Reason to Hope," *Philadelphia Inquirer,* May 13, 1992.

3. "Kids and Cocaine," *Newsweek,* March 17, 1986; "Kids Addicted to Crack," *Time Magazine,* May 13, 1991; "On Crack Street," *48 Hours,* CBS News, September 2, 1986; "Return to Crack Street," *48 Hours,* CBS News, September 14, 1989.

4. *New Jack City,* directed by Mario Van Peebles, 1991; *Scarface,* directed by Brian DePalma, 1983.

5. Frederic M. Thrasher, "Gangland," *Social Science* 1, no. 1 (1925): 1–3; Frederic M. Thrasher, *The Gang: A Study of 1,313 Gangs in Chicago* (Chicago: University of Chicago Press, 1927), 6–7, 15–17.

6. See "Chicago 'Beer Flat' Raids Put 250 in Police Cells," *New York Times,* May 21, 1928. An area in eastern Ohio was also known as the Badlands; see "Federal Deputy Is Slain at Steubenville; Life Had Been Threatened by Bootleggers," *New York Times,* August 8, 1937.

7. David Farber, *Crack: Rock Cocaine, Street Capitalism, and the Decade of Greed* (Cambridge: Cambridge University Press, 2019), 3–4, 41–45; Enid Logan, "The Wrong Race, Committing Crime, Doing Drugs, and Maladjusted for Motherhood: The Nation's Fury over 'Crack Babies,'" *Social Justice* 26, no. 1 (Spring 1999): 115–138; Susan Okie, "The Epidemic That Wasn't," *New York Times,* January 27, 2009; Elizabeth Hinton, *America on Fire: The Untold History of Police Violence and Black Rebellion since the 1960s* (New York: Norton, 2021), 233–238.

8. For example, see Barry Bearak with Eric Schmitt, "U.S.-Led Raids in Afghanistan Press Search for Qaeda Fighters," *New York Times,* May 2, 2002; Richard Marosi, "Mexico Arrests Shed Light on Migrant-Kidnapping Outfits," *Los Angeles Times,* July 18, 2010.

9. A. E. Scheidegger, S. A. Schumm, and R. W. Fairbridge, "Badlands," in *Encyclopedia of Geomorphology,* ed. Fairbridge, 43–49 (Berlin: Springer-Verlag, 1997).

4. THE LIMITS OF PRIMACY

Epigraph: George H. W. Bush, "Inaugural Address," January 20, 1989.

1. George H. W. Bush, "Remarks at the Community Welcome for Returning Troops in Sumter, South Carolina," March 17, 1991, American Presidency Project;

"President George H. W. Bush Thanks the Troops after the Gulf War," Shaw Air Force Base, Sumter, SC, March 17, 1991, News 19 WLTX https://www.youtube.com /watch?reload=9&v=T8620vZs7GQ (for a video of the event).

2. E. J. Dionne Jr., "Poll Shows Dukakis Leads Bush," *New York Times*, May 17, 1988; E. J. Dionne Jr., "Drugs as 1988 Issue: Filling a Vacuum," *New York Times*, May 24, 1988; David S. Broder and Richard Morin, "Dukakis Takes Early Lead over Bush," *Washington Post*, May 27, 1988. A May 1988 *New York Times*/CBS News Poll found that 16 percent of those polled believed drugs were America's "most important problem," the highest percentage of any issue. A *Washington Post*/ABC News Poll that same month reported that 26 percent of respondents believed drugs were "the most important issue facing this country today." The "federal budget deficit" and "economy" were tied for second with 8 percent each.

3. Richard Ben Cramer, *What It Takes: The Way to the White House* (New York: Random House, 1992); Adam Nagourney, "Bush '88 Rally Could Be Map for Trump '20," *New York Times*, August 23, 2020; Robert James Bidinotto, "Getting Away with Murder," *Reader's Digest*, July 1988, 57–63.

4. Keith Love, "Media Politics: Both Campaigns Launch Ads on Prison Furlough Issue," *Los Angeles Times* October 22, 1988; David T. Courtwright, "The Controlled Substances Act: How a 'Big Tent' Reform Became a Punitive Drug Law," *Drug and Alcohol Dependence* 76, no. 1 (2004): 9–15.

5. Michael Dukakis and George Bush Sr., Second Presidential Debate, October 13, 1988, *PBS News Hour* https://www.youtube.com/watch?v=hHCUvx 3tpnM.

6. "National Security Directive 13, re: "Cocaine Trafficking," June 7, 1989, George H. W. Bush Presidential Library and Museum, College Station, TX (hereafter Bush Library) https://bush41library.tamu.edu/files/nsd/nsd13.pdf; Michael Reid, "Peru and US Squabble over Base," *Christian Science Monitor*, November 7, 1989.

7. George H. W. Bush, "Address to the Nation on the National Drug Control Strategy," September 5, 1989, American Presidency Project; Tracy Thompson, "D.C. Student Is Given 10 Years in Drug Case," *Washington Post*, November 1, 1990.

8. Sporkin quoted in Thompson, "D.C. Student Is Given 10 Years in Drug Case."

9. Bush, "Address to the Nation on the National Drug Control Strategy," Waltraud Queiser Morales, "The War on Drugs: A New US National Security Doctrine?," *Third World Quarterly* 11, no. 3 (July 1989): 147–169.

10. Nathan James and Daniel H. Else, "The 'Militarization' of Law Enforcement and the Department of Defense's '1033 Program,'" CRS Insights, December 2, 2014 https://www.everycrsreport.com/files/20141202_IN10138_40db2a7b612093e71d 99daad7e6b8713f5334147.pdf; Abigail R. Hall and Christopher J. Coyne, "The Militarization of U.S. Domestic Policing," *Independent Review* 17, no. 4 (Spring

2013): 485–504; Brian Barrett, "The Pentagon's Hand-Me-Downs Helped Militarize Police. Here's How," *Wired*, June 2, 2020.

11. Reid, "Peru and US Squabble over Base"; Raphael F. Perl, "United States Andean Drug Policy: Background and Issues for Decisionmakers," *Journal of Interamerican Studies and World Affairs* 34, no. 3 (1992): 13–35.

12. Bush, "Address to the Nation on the National Drug Control Strategy."

13. Charles Mohr, "Drug Bill Passes, Finishing Business of 100th Congress," *New York Times*, October 23, 1988.

14. "Drug Control: Issues Surrounding Increased Use of the Military in Drug Interdiction," NSIAD 88-156, U.S. Government Accountability Office, April 29, 1988, 14–15, 17 https://www.gao.gov/assets/nsiad-88-156.pdf.

15. "Drug Control," Government Accountability Office; Richard Halloran, "In War on Drugs, Military Has Marginal Results," *New York Times*, May 30, 1988.

16. Donna Murch, "Crack in Los Angeles: Crisis, Militarization, and Black Response to the Late Twentieth-Century War on Drugs," *Journal of American History* 102, no. 1 (June 2015): 162–173.

17. Ruth Wilson Gilmore, *Golden Gulag: Prisons, Surplus, Crisis, and Opposition in Globalizing California* (Berkeley: University of California Press, 2007), 104–113.

18. DCI Counternarcotics Center, "International Narcotics Situation Report," May 1989, 4–6, CIA CREST https://www.cia.gov/readingroom/docs/CIA-RDP91 M01043R002200150004-9.pdf.

19. Francisco E. Thoumi, *Political Economy and Illegal Drugs in Colombia* (Boulder, CO: Lynne Rienner, 1995), 141, 221–228.

20. "A Review of the Drug Enforcement Administration's Use of Administrative Subpoenas to Collect or Exploit Bulk Data," Office of the Inspector General, U.S. Department of Justice, March 2019 https://oig.justice.gov/reports/2019/o1901.pdf; Brad Heath, "U.S. Secretly Tracked Billions of Calls for Decades," *USA Today*, April 8, 2015.

21. Heath, "U.S. Secretly Tracked Billions of Calls."

22. Heath, "U.S. Secretly Tracked Billions of Calls."

23. Stephen Engelberg, "C.I.A. Seeks Looser Rules on Killings during Coups," *New York Times*, October 16, 1989; and Stephen Engelberg, "White House Backs Call for C.I.A. Role in Coups," *New York Times*, October 17, 1989.

24. "Noriega Indictment Sparked by Wayward Cocaine Shipment with AM-US-Panama," Associated Press, February 27, 1988.

25. "Sense of the Community Memorandum: Economic Sanctions against Panama," September 7, 1988 https://www.cia.gov/readingroom/document/cia-rdp92 t00533r000100120015-2; and "Panama Sanctions," November 17, 1988, CIA CREST https://www.cia.gov/readingroom/docs/CIA-RDP90G01353R001500190001-9.pdf; Congressional Research Service, "The International Emergency Economic Powers Act: Origins, Evolution, and Use," CRS R45618, July 14, 2020 https://crsreports .congress.gov/product/pdf/R/R45618.

26. National Security Directive 21, re: "U.S. Policy towards Panama under Noriega after September 1," September 1, 1989, Bush Library https://bush41library .tamu.edu/files/nsd/nsd21.pdf.; Andrew Rosenthal, Stephen Engelberg, and Michael Gordon, "Panama Crisis: Disarray Hindered White House," *New York Times,* October 7, 1989.

27. Bernard Trainor, "Flaws in Panama Attack," *New York Times,* December 30, 1989; Larry Rohter, "Noriega Eludes U.S.," *New York Times,* December 24, 1989.

28. Cheney quoted in Stephen F. Hayes, *Cheney: The Untold Story of America's Most Powerful and Controversial Vice President* (New York: Harper Collins, 2007), 301.

29. National Security Directive 26, re: "U.S. Policy toward the Persian Gulf," October 2, 1989, Bush Library https://bush41library.tamu.edu/files/nsd/nsd26.pdf.

30. John Nixon, *Debriefing the President: The Interrogation of Saddam Hussein* (New York: Blue Rider Press, 2008).

31. Patrick Tyler, *A World of Trouble: The White House and the Middle East— From the Cold War to the War on Terror* (New York: Farrar, Straus Giroux, 2009).

32. Congressional Record, Senate, January 10, 1991, 476.

33. John Prados, *Safe for Democracy: The Secret Wars of the CIA* (Chicago: Ivan R. Dee, 2006), 597–598; Gareth R. V. Stansfield, *Iraqi Kurdistan: Political Development and Emergent Democracy* (London: Routledge, 2003).

34. Dick Cheney, *In My Time: A Personal and Political Memoir* (New York: Threshold, 2011), 335.

35. "Excerpts From Pentagon's Plan: 'Prevent the Re-Emergence of a New Rival,'" *New York Times,* March 8, 1992.

36. Memorandum, re: "FY 94-99 Defense Planning Guidance Sections for Comment, February 18, 1992," https://nsarchive2.gwu.edu/nukevault/ebb245/doc03 _full.pdf; and "Defense Planning Guidance, FY 1994–1999, Revised Draft for Scooter Libby," February 29, 1992 https://nsarchive2.gwu.edu/nukevault/ebb245/doc04.pdf.

37. Memorandum, re: "FY 94-99 Defense Planning Guidance Sections for Comment, February 18, 1992," 24–25; "Revised Draft for Scooter Libby," February 29, 1992, 19.

38. Walter S. Poole, *The Effort to Save Somalia, August 1992–March 1994,* Joint History Office, Office of the Chairman of the Joint Chiefs of Staff, 2005, 5–6 https://www.jcs.mil/Portals/36/Documents/History/Monographs/Somalia.pdf.

39. Brent Scowcroft Oral History Part II, Washington, DC, August 10–11, 2000, interview #2, George H. W. Bush Presidential History Project, Miller Center, University of Virginia, transcript https://s3.amazonaws.com/web.poh.transcripts /Scowcroft_Brent_08.10-11.2000.pdf.

40. John Chancellor, commentary (Somalia), *NBC Evening News,* December 3, 1992, Vanderbilt Television News Archive https://tvnews.vanderbilt.edu/broadcasts /584819.

41. George H. W. Bush, "Address to the Nation on the Situation in Somalia," December 4, 1992, American Presidency Project.

42. Samuel R. Berger Oral History, Charlottesville, VA, March 24–25, 2005, Clinton Presidential History Project, Miller Center, University of Virginia, transcript https://s3.amazonaws.com/web.poh.transcripts/ohp_2005_0324_berger.pdf; Anthony Lake Oral History (2002), Charlottesville, VA, May 21, 2002, Clinton Presidential History Project, Miller Center, University of Virginia, transcript https://s3.amazonaws.com/web.poh.transcripts/ohp_2002_0521_lake.pdf, quote 73.

43. Berger Oral History, March 24–25, 2005; Lewis to Christopher, "A Strategic Agenda for the First Year, and Beyond," February 16, 1993, State Department Freedom of Information Act Virtual Reading Room https://foia.state.gov/Search/Results.aspx?searchText=%20Strategic%20Agenda%20for%20the%20First%20Year,%20and%20Beyond&beginDate=19930201&endDate=19930301&publishedBeginDate=&publishedEndDate=&caseNumber=.

44. CIA Directorate of Intelligence, "Somalia: Dealing with Aideed," July 12, 1993, William J. Clinton Presidential Library and Museum, Little Rock, AK (hereafter Clinton Library) https://clinton.presidentiallibraries.us/items/show/49436; Anthony Lake Oral History, May 21, 2002.

45. Anthony Lake Oral History, May 21, 2002; Bill Clinton, *My Life* (New York: Knopf, 2004), ch. 35.

46. Robert C. Byrd, "The Perils of Peacekeeping," *New York Times,* August 19, 1993; Eric Schmitt, "U.S. Mission in Somalia: Seeking a Clear Rationale," *New York Times,* August 27, 1993.

47. Helen Dewar, "Senate Debates U.S. Role in Somalia," *Washington Post,* September 9, 1993; Helen Dewar and Barton Gellman, "Senate Asks Clinton to Get Approval for Continued Troop Deployment," *Washington Post,* September 10, 1993; Clifford Krauss, "Somalia, Sept. 5–11," *New York Times,* September 12, 1993; Poole, *The Effort to Save Somalia,* 56.

48. Poole, *The Effort to Save Somalia,* 56–58; *NBC Evening News*, October 5, 1993.

49. Anthony Lake Oral History, May 21, 2002; Poole, *The Effort to Save Somalia,* 57–67.

50. National Intelligence Estimate, "Yugoslavia Transformed," October 18, 1990, CIA FOIA Electronic Reading Room https://www.cia.gov/readingroom/document/5235e80c993294098d5174dd; Gregory F. Treverton and Renanah Miles, "Unheeded Warning of War: Why Policymakers Ignored the 1990 Yugoslavia Estimate," *Intelligence and National Security* 32, no. 4 (2017): 506–522.

51. NIE, "Yugoslavia Transformed"; Military History Office, US Army in Bosnia and Herzegovina: Military Operations, Army in Europe Pamphlet 525-100, October 7, 2003, 1–8 https://irp.fas.org/doddir/army/ae-pam-525-100.pdf.

52. Brent Scowcroft Oral History Part II, August 10–11, 2000.

53. Steve Crawshaw, "Burying Srebrenica," Amnesty International, July 9, 2015; Taylor Branch, *The Clinton Tapes: Wrestling History with the President* (New York: Simon and Schuster, 2009), 20–22; Clinton, *My Life,* ch. 32.

54. "Policy Statement: Bosnia" undated, National Security Council, European Affairs, Balkans Strategy Folder, Clinton Library, Digital Library https://clinton .presidentiallibraries.us/items/show/62556; Ivo H. Daalder, "Decision to Intervene: How the War in Bosnia Ended," Brookings Institution commentary, December 1, 1998.

55. Steve Coll, *Ghost Wars: The Secret History of the CIA, Afghanistan, and Bin Laden, from the Soviet Invasion to September 10, 2001* (New York: Penguin, 2004), 155; "Three Palestinians Are Killed in a Bomb Blast in Pakistan," Associated Press, November 25, 1989.

56. *Jihad* is frequently translated as "holy war." It also, however, refers to the internal struggle of a devout Muslim over questions of faith and devotion.

57. Coll, *Ghost Wars,* 60–66; Glenn Robinson, "The Four Waves of Global Jihad, 1979–2017," *Middle East Policy* 24, no. 3 (2017): 70–88, 73–74.

58. Coll, *Ghost Wars,* 154–157. *Takfiri* groups declare others, including Muslims, nonbelievers, or infidels. In contrast, Salafist movements advocate a return to a purer form of Islam, which is identified with the age of the Prophet Mohammad and the first three caliphs. It has become mistakenly identified with Salafi-jihadist movements and these are distinct and treated as such here. See Sabine Damir-Geils-dorf and Mira Menzfeld, "Methodological and Ethical Challenges in Empirical Approaches to Salafism," *Journal of Muslims in Europe* 9, no. 2 (2020): 135–149; Fawaz Gerges, *ISIS: A History* (Princeton, NJ: Princeton University Press, 2016).

59. Tyler, *A World of Trouble,* 379; Coll, *Ghost Wars,* 267–269.

60. Richard Aldrich, "America Used Islamists to Arm the Bosnian Muslims," *Guardian,* April 21, 2002; Arash Azizi, *The Shadow Commander: Soleimani, the U.S. and Iran's Global Ambitions* (New York: Oneworld, 2020), 223–224.

61. Clinton, *My Life,* 264, 440; Cees Wiebes, *Intelligence and the War in Bosnia, 1992–1995* (New Brunswick, NJ: Transaction, 2003), 207–208; Darryl Li, *The Universal Enemy: Jihad, Empire, and the Challenge of Solidarity* (Stanford, CA: Stanford University Press, 2020), 190–192.

62. "PLO Ties to Lebanon's Hizballah," Special Analysis, in National Daily Intelligence Report, November 30, 1987, 14–15, CIA CREST, General CIA Records https://www.cia.gov/readingroom/docs/CIA-RDP88T01422R000100230009-4.pdf; Osamah F. Khalil, "Cold War Twilight: The United States, the Soviet Union, and the Middle East in the American Imagination, 1981–1988," *Maghreb Review* 45, no. 3 (2020): 531–533.

63. "PLO Ties to Lebanon's Hizballah," Augustus Richard Norton, *Hezbollah: A Short History* (Princeton, NJ: Princeton University Press, 2007), 31–32.

64. "PLO Ties to Lebanon's Hizballah."

65. "Southern Lebanon: The Shia Crucible," March 19, 1986, Directorate of Intelligence, CIA CREST https://www.cia.gov/readingroom/docs/CIA-RDP86 T01017R000202090001-7.pdf; Khalil, "Cold War Twilight," 532–533.

66. Amal is described as "more moderate" than Hezbollah and as "Hezbollah's junior partner in the Shiite coalition" in Casey L. Addis, "Lebanon: Background and U.S. Relations," United States Congressional Research Service, Report R40054, February 1, 2011, 19.

67. Osamah Khalil, "Pax Americana: The United States, the Palestinians, and the Peace Process, 1948–2008," *CR: The New Centennial Review* 8, no. 2: The Palestine Issue (2008): 1–41; Osamah F. Khalil, *America's Dream Palace: Middle East Expertise and the Rise of the National Security State* (Cambridge, MA: Harvard University Press, 2016), ch. 7.

68. Clyde Haberman, "Lebanese Deploy to Bar Entry of Palestinians: Israel Expels 400 from Occupied Lands," *New York Times,* December 18, 1992; and Clyde Haberman, "400 Arabs Ousted by Israel Are Mired in Frozen Limbo," *New York Times,* December 19, 1992; Azzam Tamimi, *Hamas: Unwritten Chapters* (London: Hurst, 2009), 66–67.

69. Tamimi, *Hamas,* 66–67.

70. Tamimi, *Hamas,* 67–70.

71. John F. Hale, "The Making of the New Democrats," *Political Science Quarterly* 110, no. 2 (1995): 207–232; Michelle Alexander, *The New Jim Crow: Mass Incarceration in the Age of Colorblindness* (New York: New Press, 2010), 71.

72. Presidential Decision Directive 14, "U.S. Policy on International Counternarcotics in the Western Hemisphere," November 3, 1993, Clinton Library https:// clinton.presidentiallibraries.us/items/show/12742.

73. Joe Biden, speech on Senate floor, November 18, 1993 https://www.youtube .com/watch?v=3HY45DY2B8w; "Crime in the United States, 1991–2010," FBI, U.S. Department of Justice https://ucr.fbi.gov/crime-in-the-u.s/2010/crime-in-the -u.s.-2010/tables/10tbl01.xls; Steven R. Dozinger, ed. *The Real War on Crime: The Report of the National Criminal Justice Commission* (New York: HarperCollins, 1996), 2–10. The UCR and NCVS have different methodologies. The UCR relies on data provided by law enforcement at the time of the offense and so does not account for outcomes of incidents. UCR is also subject to inflation because crime incident records are issued for each individual involved; inflation is pronounced with crimes involving juveniles, as they are likely to be arrested in groups. The NCVS is an annual phone survey conducted by the Bureau of Justice Statistics (BJS) of a nationally representative sample of 160,000 persons age 12 or older, with individual households rotating every three years. Unlike the UCR, which is based on law enforcement incident reports, the NCVS collects information on crimes experienced by individuals and households, whether the incident was reported to law enforcement or not. Therefore, the NCVS includes crimes not reported to law enforcement but does not include homicide, arson, commercial crimes, and crimes against children under the age of 12. See "The Nation's Two Crime Measures," Crime in the U.S., 2015, FBI, U.S. Department of Justice, https://ucr.fbi.gov

/crime-in-the-u.s/2015/crime-in-the-u.s.-2015/resource-pages/nations_two_crime
_measures_final.

74. Oliver Roeder, Lauren-Brooke Eisen, and Julia Bowling, "What Caused the
Crime Decline?" Brennan Center for Justice, New York University School of Law,
2015, 3, 79.

75. "Past [Federal] Inmate Population Totals," Federal Bureau of Prisons https://
www.bop.gov/about/statistics/population_statistics.jsp#old_pops, updated August
10, 2013. FY 1994 prison population was 95,162 and increased to 214,149 in FY 2014.

76. Peter Wagner and Wendy Sawyer, "Mass Incarceration: The Whole Pie, 2018,"
Prison Policy Initiative, March 14, 2018 https://www.prisonpolicy.org/factsheets
/pie2018.pdf; Roeder, Eisen, and Bowling, "What Caused the Crime Decline?" 79.

77. Details about the Oklahoma City bombing and media coverage are from
Alia Malek, *A Country Called Amreeka* (New York: Free Press, 2009), 175–181;
Robert Dvorchak, "Day Care Disaster 'Beyond Comprehension,'" Associated Press,
April 27, 1995.

78. Liliana Segura, "Gutting Habeas Corpus," *The Intercept*, May 4, 2016
https://theintercept.com/2016/05/04/the-untold-story-of-bill-clintons-other-crime
-bill/; Klain to Reno and Rasco, November 22, 1994 https://www.documentcloud
.org/documents/2820704-RonKlain-November1994.html.

79. Presidential Decision Directive 39, "U.S. Policy on Counterterrorism," June
21, 1995, Clinton Library https://clinton.presidentiallibraries.us/items/show/12755.

80. David Johnston and Tim Weiner, "Seizing the Crime Issue, Clinton Blurs
Party Lines," *New York Times,* August 1, 1996.

81. William J. Clinton, "Statement on Signing the Antiterrorism and Effective
Death Penalty Act of 1996," April 24, 1996, *Public Papers of the Presidents of the
United States* (Washington, DC: Government Printing Office, 1996), 630–631.

82. Clinton, "Statement on Signing"; Lena Williams, "Law Aimed at Terrorists
Hits Legal Immigrants," *New York Times,* July 17, 1996.

83. Presidential Decision Directive 42, "International Organized Crime," October
21, 1995, Clinton Library https://clinton.presidentiallibraries.us/items/show/12756.

84. Joseph B. Treaster, "Effort to Curb Drug Flow May Be More Difficult,
Officials Say," *New York Times,* December 4, 1993; Executive Order 12978, "Block-
ing Assets and Prohibiting Transactions with Significant Narcotics Traffickers,"
October 21, 1995; "Summary of PDD 44, Heroin Control Policy," November 1995,
Federation of American Scientists https://irp.fas.org/offdocs/pdd44.htm.

85. On coca cultivation by year, see Colombia Reports Data https://colombia
reports.com/coca-cultivation-statistics/; Drug Enforcement Administration, "The
Cali Cartel: The New Kings of Cocaine, Drug Intelligence Report," November
1994, 1 https://www.ojp.gov/pdffiles1/Digitization/152436NCJRS.pdf; Clinton, *My
Life,* ch. 48; Executive Order 13099, "Prohibiting Transactions with Terrorists Who
Threaten to Disrupt the Middle East Peace Process," August 20, 1988, American

Presidency Project; Benjamin T. Smith, *The Dope: The Real History of the Mexican Drug Trade* (New York: W.W. Norton, 2021), 365–367; Oswaldo Zavala, *Drug Cartels Do Not Exist: Narcotrafficking in US and Mexican Culture* (Nashville, TN: Vanderbilt University Press, 2022), 3–4.

86. Smith, *The Dope*, 220, 368–369; Zavala, *Drug Cartels Do Not Exist*, 3–9.

87. AUC Profile, Colombia Reports.com https://colombiareports.com/auc/; Steven Dudley, *Walking Ghosts: Murder and Guerrilla Politics in Colombia* (New York: Routledge, 2006), 195–199.

88. Dudley, *Walking Ghosts*, 195–199.

89. Winifred Tate, *Drugs, Thugs, and Diplomats: U.S. Policymaking in Colombia* (Stanford: Stanford University Press, 2011), ch. 5; Michael Isikoff, Gregory Vistica, and Steven Ambrus, "Fighting the Other Drug War—Is a $1.3 Billion Colombia Aid Package Smart Policy?" *Newsweek*, April 3, 2000.

90. Tate, *Drugs, Thugs, and Diplomats*, ch. 5; Beers quoted in Diane Jean Schemo, "U.S. Seeks Sharp Increase in Funds to Fight Drugs in Colombia," *New York Times*, April 1, 1998.

91. Tate, *Drugs, Thugs, and Diplomats*, ch. 5.

92. Scott Wilson, "Colombia's Anti-Drug Plan Fuels Fight in Coca Country," *Washington Post*, October 14, 2000; Dudley, *Walking Ghosts*, 172–173.

93. Wilson, "Colombia's Anti-Drug Plan Fuels Fight in Coca Country."

94. Tate, *Drugs, Thugs, and Diplomats*, ch. 5; Congressional Research Service, "Colombia's Peace Process through 2016," R42982, December 31, 2016 https://crsreports.congress.gov/product/pdf/R/R42982/16.

95. Jim Hoagland, "Taking Cover in the Drug War," *Washington Post*, August 27, 2000; Anthony Lewis, "Abroad at Home: Into the Quagmire," *New York Times*, June 24, 2000.

96. Bernard Aronson, "Saving Colombia," *Washington Post*, June 29, 2000.

97. Clinton, *My Life*, 509–512; Berger Oral History, March 24–25, 2005.

98. John Barry, "A New Breed of Soldier," *Newsweek*, December 10, 2001.

99. Glenn E. Robinson, *Global Jihad: A Brief History* (Stanford, CA: Stanford University Press, 2021), 78–81; Walter Pincus, "Anti-U.S. Calls for Attacks Are Seen as Serious," *Washington Post*, February 25, 1998.

100. "Interview: Osama bin Laden," *ABC News Nightline*, June 10, 1998.

101. Branch, *The Clinton Tapes*, 689–690.

102. Berger Oral History, March 24–25, 2005; Executive Order 13099, "Prohibiting Transactions with Terrorists Who Threaten to Disrupt the Middle East Peace Process," August 20, 1998; Executive Order 12947, "Prohibiting Transactions with Terrorists Who Threaten to Disrupt the Middle East Peace Process," January 23, 1995, both in American Presidency Project.

103. Madeline K. Albright Oral History, Charlottesville, VA, August 30, 2006, Clinton Presidential History Project, Miller Center, University of Virginia,

transcript https://s3.amazonaws.com/web.poh.transcripts/ohp_2006_0830_albright .pdf, quote 51–52; Coll, *Ghost Wars*, 534–536.

104. "Algeria Seizes Islamic Leader, Curbs Rallies," Associated Press, January 23, 1992; Jacob Mundy, *Imaginative Geographies of Algerian Violence: Conflict Science, Conflict Management, Antipolitics* (Stanford, CA: Stanford University Press, 2015).

105. Coll, *Ghost Wars*, 537–538.

106. Ahmed Rashid, *Taliban: The Power of Militant Islam in Afghanistan and Beyond*, 3rd ed. (New Haven: Yale University Press, 2022), 17–29.

107. M. Kabir Mohabbat and Leah McInnis, *Delivering Osama: The Story of America's Secret Envoy* (Berlin: First Draft Publishing GmbH, 2020); Jeffrey St. Clair and Alexander Cockburn, "How Bush Was Offered Bin Laden and Blew It," *Counterpunch*, November 1, 2004.

108. Samuel Huntington, "Clash of Civilizations," *Foreign Affairs* 72 (1993): 22–49; Samuel Huntington, *The Clash of Civilizations and the Remaking of the World Order* (New York: Touchstone, 1996), 126–128, 554.

5. CONSTRUCTING GLOBAL TERRORISM AND THE LONG WAR FOR CIVILIZATION

Epigraph: George W. Bush, "Address to the Nation from Atlanta on Homeland Security," November 8, 2001.

1. Karl Rove, *Courage and Consequence: My Life as Conservative in the Fight* (New York: Threshold, 2010), 405–407; Bob Woodward, *Bush at War* (New York: Simon and Schuster, 2002), 94–95.

2. Dick Cheney, *In My Time: A Personal and Political Memoir* (New York: Threshold, 2011), 469–471.

3. R. W. Apple, Jr., "No Middle Ground Exists in the War on Terror," *New York Times*, September 13, 2001; George W. Bush, "Address Before a Joint Session of the Congress on the United States Response to the Terrorist Attacks of September 11," September 20, 2001, American Presidency Project.

4. "Authorization for Use of Military Force," Public Law 107–40, 107th Congress, September 18, 2001 https://www.congress.gov/107/plaws/publ40/PLAW -107publ40.pdf; Miles A. Pomper, "In for the Long Haul," *CQ Weekly*, September 15, 2001; Barbara Lee, "Why I Opposed the Resolution to Authorize Force," *San Francisco Chronicle*, September 23, 2001.

5. M. Kabir Mohabbat and L. McInnis, *Delivering Osama: The Story of America's Secret Envoy* (Berlin: First Draft Publishing GmbH, 2020); Jeffrey St. Clair and Alexander Cockburn, "How Bush Was Offered Bin Laden and Blew It," *Counterpunch*, November 1, 2004; "Bush Rejects Taliban Offer to Hand Bin Laden Over," *Guardian*, October 14, 2001; Carter Malkasian, *The American War in Afghanistan: A History* (New York: Oxford University Press, 2022), 54–60.

6. Bush quoted in Woodward, *Bush at War*, 108.

7. Rumsfeld to Feith, re: "U.S. Strategy in Afghanistan," Draft for Discussion, with edits by Rumsfeld, October 16, 2001 https://nsarchive.gwu.edu/sites/default /files/documents/qy3fic-1rilh/01.pdf; Bush quoted in Woodward, *Bush at War,* 108.

8. Feith's memorandum quoted in Gideon Rose, *How Wars End: Why We Always Fight the Last Battle* (New York: Simon and Schuster, 2010), 283 (emphasis in original); Rumsfeld to Feith, re: "Afghanistan," April 17, 2002 https://nsarchive.gwu .edu/sites/default/files/documents/qy3fic-cl4be/03.pdf.

9. National Security Presidential Directive 9, "Defeating the Terrorist Threat to the United States," October 25, 2001, courtesy of the Federation of American Scientists, Intelligence Resource Program https://irp.fas.org/offdocs/nspd/index .html; Leah Farrall, "How al Qaeda Works," *Foreign Affairs* 90, no. 2 (2011): 128–138.

10. Cheney, *In My Time,* 462.

11. George W. Bush, Executive Order 13224, "Blocking Property and Prohibiting Transactions with Persons Who Commit, Threaten to Commit, or Support Terrorism," September 23, 2001, American Presidency Project; Executive Order 13224, U.S. Department of State, Bureau of Counterterrorism https://www.state .gov/executive-order-13224/; UN Security Council Resolution 1390, January 16, 2002 https://documents-dds-ny.un.org/doc/UNDOC/GEN/N02/216/02/PDF /N0221602.pdf?OpenElement; John B. Taylor, *Global Financial Warriors: The Untold Story of International Finance in the Post-9/11 World* (New York: Norton, 2008).

12. Ron Suskind, *The One Percent Doctrine: Deep Inside America's Pursuit of Its Enemies since 9/11* (New York: Simon and Schuster, 2006), 86–87.

13. David Cole and James X. Dempsey, *Terrorism and the Constitution: Sacrificing Civil Liberties in the Name of National Security* (New York: New Press, 2006), 191–192. The Patriot Act's official name is "Uniting and Strengthening America by Providing Appropriate Tools Required to Intercept and Obstruct Terrorism," https://www.congress.gov/107/plaws/publ56/PLAW-107publ56.pdf.

14. Michael Chertoff Oral History, Washington, DC, January 31, 2012, George W. Bush Presidential History Project, Miller Center, University of Virginia, transcript https://s3.amazonaws.com/web.poh.transcripts/Chertoff _Michael.final2.pdf.

15. Chertoff Oral History.

16. Barton Gellman, *Angler: The Cheney Vice Presidency* (New York: Penguin, 2008), 131–139. Goldsmith quoted in "Cheney's Law," *PBS Frontline,* August 22, 2007 https://www.pbs.org/wgbh/pages/frontline/cheney/interviews/goldsmith.html.

17. Suskind, *The One Percent Doctrine,* 235; Joshua Foust, "Understanding the Strategic and Tactical Considerations of Drone Strikes," American Security Project, January 1, 2013.

18. Trevor Aaronson, *The Terror Factory: Inside the FBI's Manufactured War on Terrorism* (Brooklyn, NY: IG Publishing, 2013), 202–203.

19. Aaronson, *Terror Factory,* 202–203; Peter Bergen and Jennifer Rowland, "Drone Wars," *Washington Quarterly* 36, no. 3 (2013): 7–26; Cole and Dempsey, *Terrorism and the Constitution,* 232–235; US Department of Justice, "Report from the Field: The USA Patriot Act at Work," July 2004 https://www.justice.gov/archive /olp/pdf/patriot_report_from_the_field0704.pdf; "The Patriot Act: Justice Department Claims Success," Special Series: The Patriot Act, July 20, 2005, National Public Radio https://www.npr.org/2005/07/20/4756706/the-patriot-act -justice-department-claims-success.

20. Alfred W. McCoy, *A Question of Torture: CIA Interrogation, from the Cold War to the War on Terror* (New York: Metropolitan Books, 2006), 113–117.

21. "Extraordinary Rendition: A Backstory," *Guardian,* August 31, 2011.

22. *The Torture Memos: Rationalizing the Unthinkable,* ed. David Cole, (New York: New Press, 2009), 277–283; Jay Bybee to Alberto Gonzalez, "Re: Standards of Conduct for Interrogation under 18 U.S.C. §§ 2340–2340A," US Department of Justice, Office of Legal Counsel, August 1, 2002 https://nsarchive2.gwu.edu /NSAEBB/NSAEBB127/02.08.01.pdf.

23. Charles R. Church, "What Politics and the Media Still Get Wrong about Abu Zubaydah," *Lawfare* blog, August 1, 2018.

24. David Cole, "Introductory Commentary: The Torture Laws," in *The Torture Memos,* 13–18; Suskind, *The One Percent Doctrine,* 133–136.

25. Julian Borger, "Guantánamo: Psychologists Who Designed CIA Torture Program to Testify," *Guardian,* January 20, 2020.

26. Borger, "Guantánamo."

27. Bill Chappell, "Psychologists behind CIA 'Enhanced Interrogation' Program Settle Detainees' Lawsuit," NPR, August 17, 2017; James E. Mitchell and Bill Harlow, *Enhanced Interrogation: Inside the Minds and Motives of the Islamic Terrorists Trying to Destroy America* (New York: Crown, 2016).

28. Borger, "Guantánamo"; Chappell, "Psychologists behind CIA 'Enhanced Interrogation' Program"; Cheney, *In My Time,* 507.

29. Ryan Gallagher and Henrik Moltke, "The Wiretap Rooms," *The Intercept,* June 25, 2018; "AT&T Wiretap Whistleblower Fights Senate Deal," NPR *All Things Considered,* November 7, 2007; Michael V. Hayden Oral History, Washington, DC, November 20, 2012, George W. Bush Presidential History Project, Miller Center, University of Virginia, transcript https://s3.amazonaws.com/web.poh .transcripts/hayden_michael_2012_1120.pdf.

30. James Risen and Eric Lichtblau, "Bush Lets U.S. Spy on Callers without Courts: Secret Order to Widen Domestic Monitoring," *New York Times,* December 16, 2005; David Sanger, "In Address, Bush Says He Ordered Domestic Spying," *New York Times,* December 18, 2005; Cheney, *In My Time,* 494.

31. Cole and Dempsey, *Terrorism and the Constitution,* 104; Chertoff Oral History.

32. Murat Haner, Melissa M. Sloan, Justin T. Pickett, and Francis T. Cullen, "When Do Americans 'See Something, Say Something'? Experimental Evidence on the Willingness to Report Terrorist Activity," *Justice Quarterly* 39, no. 2 (2022): 1079–1103; Jacob N. Shapiro and Dara Kay Cohen, "Color Bind: Lessons from the Failed Homeland Security Advisory System," *International Security* 32, no. 2 (2007): 121–154; Muhammad Sankari, Hatem Abudayyeh, Sangi Ravichandran, and Andy Clarno, "Suspicious Activity Report and the Surveillance State: The Suppression of Dissent and the Criminalization of Arabs and Muslims in Illinois," Arab American Action Network, The Policing in Chicago Research Group at the University of Illinois, Chicago, May 2022 https://aaan.org/media/cerp-report/.

33. "FBI Charges Florida Professor with Terrorist Activities," *CNN.com*, February 20, 2003.

34. Florida Senate Debate, October 25, 2004, C-Span https://www.c-span.org /video/?184131-1/florida-senate-debate; Steve Bousquet, "Al-Arian Ads Stifle Real Issues in Race," *Tampa Bay Times*, October 16, 2004.

35. Julia Glick, "Al-Arian's Family Tells of Its Ordeal," *Herald Tribune*, December 16, 2005; Mike German, *Disrupt, Discredit, and Divide: How the New FBI Damages Democracy* (New York: New Press, 2019), 133–134, 141. Thanks to Abdullah al-Arian for clarifying aspects of the case.

36. In the first two months after September 11, the Immigration and Naturalization Service "detained, at least for questioning," 1,200 citizens and aliens across the country. However, the Department of Justice Public Affairs Office stopped publicly reporting cumulative totals of arrests after 1,200 "because the statistics became confusing." The FBI investigation led to arrests of 738 aliens between September 11, 2001, and August 2, 2002. See "The September 11 Detainees: A Review of the Treatment of Aliens Held on Immigration Charges in Connection with the Investigation of the September 11 Attacks," US Department of Justice, Office of the Inspector General, April 2003, 1–2, 15–23, https://irp.fas.org/agency /doj/oig/detainees.pdf.

37. Bob Woodward, *State of Denial* (New York: Simon and Schuster, 2006), 275–276; Chertoff Oral History; "The September 11 Detainees," U.S. Department of Justice, 15–26; Cole and Dempsey, *Terrorism and the Constitution*, 177–183; Mustafa Bayoumi, *How Does It Feel to Be a Problem? Being Young and Arab in America* (New York: Penguin, 2009), 266–267. For a defense of the administration's policies, see John Yoo, *War by Other Means: An Insider's Account of the War on Terror* (New York: Atlantic Monthly Press, 2006).

38. "The September 11 Detainees," U.S. Department of Justice, 1–6, 130–149.

39. Woodward, *Bush at War*, 112–113.

40. Rumsfeld quoted in Woodward, *Bush at War*, 112–113; Colin L. Powell and Richard L. Armitage Oral History, Alexandria, VA, March 28, 2017, George W. Bush Presidential History Project, Miller Center, University of Virginia, 26

https://s3.amazonaws.com/web.poh.transcripts/Powell_Colin+and+Armitage
_Richard.ARCHIVE.pdf.

41. Jeffrey St. Clair, *Grand Theft Pentagon: Tales of Corruption and Profiteering in the War on Terror* (Monroe, ME: Common Courage Press, 2005), 29–34.

42. Donald Rumsfeld, *Known and Unknown: A Memoir* (New York: Sentinel, 2011), 425.

43. Cheney, *In My Time,* 513–515.

44. "Memorandum for the President," Rumsfeld to Bush, re: "Strategic Thoughts," September 30, 2001, National Security Archive, https://nsarchive2.gwu .edu/NSAEBB/NSAEBB358a/doc13.pdf.

45. John Negroponte Oral History, Charlottesville, VA, September 14, 2012, George W. Bush Presidential History Project, Miller Center, University of Virginia, transcript https://s3.amazonaws.com/web.poh.transcripts/Negroponte.final3.pdf, quote 15. Emphasis in original.

46. Elisabeth Bumiller, "Red Faces in White House over '02 Analysis," *New York Times,* June 14, 2002; Alison Mitchell, "Republicans Wielding Iraq as an Issue in Senate Races in Conservative States," *New York Times,* September 18, 2002; Matt Bai, "Rove's Way," *New York Times,* October 20, 2002.

47. George W. Bush, "President Bush Delivers Graduation Speech at West Point," June 1, 2002 https://georgewbush-whitehouse.archives.gov/news/releases/2002/06 /20020601-3.html; George W. Bush, "The National Security Strategy of the United States of America," September 2002 https://apps.dtic.mil/sti/pdfs/ADA406411.pdf, 13–15; Osamah F. Khalil, *America's Dream Palace: Middle East Expertise and the Rise of the National Security State* (Cambridge, MA: Harvard University Press, 2016), ch. 8.

48. David Sanger and Carl Hulse, "Bush Appears to Soften Tone on Iraq Action," *New York Times,* October 2, 2002.

49. George W. Bush, "President Bush Outlines Iraqi Threat," speech delivered in Cincinnati, Ohio, October 7, 2002, transcript https://georgewbush-whitehouse .archives.gov/news/releases/2002/10/20021007-8.html; Alison Mitchell and Adam Nagourney, "G.O.P. Gains from War Talk but Does Not Talk about It," *New York Times,* September 21, 2002.

50. Carroll Doherty and Jocelyn Kiley, "A Look Back at How Fear and False Beliefs Bolstered U.S. Public Support for War in Iraq," Pew Research Center, March 14, 2023.

51. Khalil, *America's Dream Palace,* ch. 8; Eric Herring and Piers Robinson, "Report X Marks the Spot: The British Government's Deceptive Dossier on Iraq and WMD," *Political Science Quarterly* 129, no. 4 (2014): 551–583.

52. The Report of the Iraq Inquiry, Government of the United Kingdom, July 9, 2016 https://assets.publishing.service.gov.uk/government/uploads/system/uploads /attachment_data/file/535415/The_Report_of_the_Iraq_Inquiry_-_Volume_IV.pdf.

53. "Authorization of the use of United States Armed Forces against Iraq," Congressional Record, vol. 148, no. 132, Senate, October 9, 2002; David E.

Rosenbaum, "United Voice on Iraq Eludes Majority Leader," *New York Times,* October 4, 2002.

54. Mitchell and Nagourney, "G.O.P. Gains from War Talk"; Rove, *Courage and Consequence,* 453–455.

55. Roger Cohen, "Of Tricks and Trailers," *Washington Post,* June 5, 2003.

56. Stephen Engelberg, "New Evidence Adds Doubt to FBI's Case against Anthrax Suspect," ProPublica.org, October 10, 2011.

57. Negroponte Oral History; Powell and Armitage Oral History.

58. For example, see "The Secret History of ISIS," *PBS Frontline,* Season 2016, Episode 10.

59. George W. Bush, "Address to the Nation on Iraq from the U.S.S. *Abraham Lincoln,*" May 1, 2003, American Presidency Project; "USS *Abraham Lincoln:* History," http://www.uscarriers.net/cvn72history.htm.

60. L. Paul Bremer III Oral History, Charlottesville, VA, August 28–29, 2012, George W. Bush Presidential History Project, Miller Center, University of Virginia, transcript https://s3.amazonaws.com/web.poh.transcripts/Bremer_LPaul.final2.pdf; Ricardo S. Sanchez, *Wiser in Battle: A Soldier's Story* (New York: Harper Collins, 2008): 251–255, 309–322; Rajiv Chandrasekaran, *Imperial Life in the Emerald City: Inside Iraq's Green Zone* (New York: Alfred A. Knopf, 2006).

61. E. A. Torriero and Christine Spolar, "Pentagon Releases Grisly Photos to Prove Hussein Sons Are Dead," *Chicago Tribune,* July 25, 2003.

62. Mary Anne Weaver, "The Short, Violent Life of Abu Musab al-Zarqawi," *The Atlantic,* July/August 2006.

63. Weaver, "The Short, Violent Life of Abu Musab al-Zarqawi."

64. Daniel Byman, "An Autopsy of the Iraq Debacle: Policy Failure or Bridge Too Far?" *Security Studies* 17, no. 4 (2008): 599–643; Weaver, "The Short, Violent Life of Abu Musab al-Zarqawi."

65. Weaver, "The Short, Violent Life of Abu Musab al-Zarqawi"; James Dobbins, Seth G. Jones, Benjamin Runkle, and Siddharth Mohandas, *Occupying Iraq: A History of the Coalition Provisional Authority* (Santa Monica, CA: RAND Corporation 2009), 93–94; American Embassy, Amman to Secretary of State, Washington, DC, "Zarqawi's Hometown," November 18, 2004 https://wikileaks.org/plusd/cables/04AMMAN9226_a.html; Thomas Ricks, "Military Plays Up Role of Zarqawi," *Washington Post,* April 10, 2006.

66. Dobbins et al., *Occupying Iraq,* 318–319; Arash Azizi, *The Shadow Commander: Soleimani, the U.S. and Iran's Global Ambitions* (New York: Oneworld, 2020), 231–233.

67. John Kerry, Presidential Nomination Acceptance Speech, Democratic National Convention, July 29, 2004, Boston, C-Span https://www.c-span.org/video/?182721-3/john-kerry-accepts-2004-democratic-presidential-nomination.

68. "Bush Denounces TV Adverts Attacking Kerry," Associated Press, August 23, 2004; "Delegates Mock Kerry with 'Purple Heart' Bandages," *CNN,* September

1, 2004; George N. Dionisopoulos, "Incident on the Bay Hap River and the Guns of August: The 'Swift Boat Drama' and Counter-Narrative in the 2004 Election," *Communication Quarterly*, 57, 4 (2009): 487–511.

69. James E. Campbell, "Why Bush Won the Presidential Election of 2004: Incumbency, Ideology, Terrorism, and Turnout," *Political Science Quarterly* 120, no. 2 (2005): 219–241; "Kerry Wins Debate, but Little Change in Candidate Images," Pew Research Center, October 4, 2004; George W. Bush, interview with Tim Russert, February 7, 2004, *NBC News Meet the Press* https://www.nbcnews.com/id/wbna4179618.

70. "Kerry: U.S. 'Paying the Price' for Losing bin Laden," *CNN*, October 29, 2004; "Recorded Message from Osama bin Laden," Associated Press, October 31, 2004.

71. Seymour Hersh, *Chain of Command: The Road from 9/11 to Abu Ghraib* (New York: HarperCollins, 2004); Khalil, *America's Dream Palace,* ch. 6.

72. Hersh, *Chain of Command,* 56–68.

73. Hersh, *Chain of Command,* 52; Jamie Wilson, "Eight Years for US Soldier Who Abused Prisoners," *Guardian,* October 22, 2004. On prison violence, see Emily Widra, "No Escape: The Trauma of Witnessing Violence in Prison," Prison Policy Initiative, December 2, 2020; Kevin McCarthy, "Challenging Gladiator Fights in the CDCR," *UCLA Law Review Discourse,* May 10, 2021 https://www.ucla lawreview.org/challenging-gladiator-fights-in-the-cdcr/; Meghan Novisky and Robert Peralta, "Gladiator School: Returning Citizens' Experiences with Secondary Violence Exposure in Prison," *Victims & Offenders* 15, no. 5 (2020): 594–618.

74. Marc Sandalow, "Bush Claims Mandate, Sets 2nd-Term Goals," *San Francisco Chronicle,* November 5, 2004; Negroponte Oral History; Dana Priest and Anne Hull, "Soldiers Face Neglect, Frustration at Army's Top Medical Facility, *Washington Post,* February 18, 2007.

75. American Embassy, Baghdad to Secretary of State, Washington, DC, "USEB 154: 1st Marine Expeditionary Force Discusses Situation in Al Anbar Province," July 23, 2004; "Iraqi Shia Parties Not Embracing Sadr," August 15, 2004 https://search.wikileaks.org/plusd/cables/04BAGHDAD481_a.html; "Local Officials Share Views on al-Sadr's Future," August 27, 2004 https://search.wikileaks .org/plusd/cables/04BAGHDAD697_a.html.

76. Dobbins et al., *Occupying Iraq.*

77. American Embassy, Baghdad to Secretary of State, Washington, DC, "Baghdad Provincial Governor's Assassination Shakes Capital," January 4, 2005 https://search.wikileaks.org/plusd/cables/05BAGHDAD45_a.html; "Al-Anbar Governor Killed; Provincial Council Elects Replacement," June 4, 2005 https:// search.wikileaks.org/plusd/cables/05BAGHDAD2394_a.html; "Fallujah: Grass Roots Politics—Leaders Initiate Political and Security Meetings," June 20, 2005 https://search.wikileaks.org/plusd/cables/05BAGHDAD2611_a.html; "Key Sunni

Leader Envisions A Unity Government—Including Shia Islamists," December 12, 2005 https://search.wikileaks.org/plusd/cables/05BAGHDAD4959_a.html.

78. American Embassy, Baghdad to Secretary of State, Washington, DC, "Reports of Attacks Driving Families Out of Baghdad Communities," March 9, 2006 https://search.wikileaks.org/plusd/cables/06BAGHDAD768_a.html; "Militias and other Armed Groups in Iraq—Confronting the Sectarian Divide," March 13, 2006 https://search.wikileaks.org/plusd/cables/06BAGHDAD812_a.html.

79. David Kilcullen, "Countering Global Insurgency," *Journal of Strategic Studies* 28, no. 4 (2005): 597–617.

80. Negroponte Oral History; Curt Tanoff, "Iraq: Reconstruction Assistance," Congressional Research Service Report RL31833, August 7, 2009.

81. Negroponte Oral History.

82. Seymour Hersh, "Moving Targets," *New Yorker,* December 8, 2003; Sean D. Naylor, "Inside the Pentagon's Manhunting Machine," *The Atlantic,* August 28, 2015.

83. U.S. Department of the Army, Field Manual 3-24: "Counterinsurgency" (Washington, DC: Department of the Army, 2006); Khalil, *America's Dream Palace,* ch. 8.

84. George W. Bush, "Address to the Nation," January 10, 2007; Carter Malkasian, *Illusions of Victory: The Anbar Awakening and the Rise of the Islamic State* (New York: Oxford University Press, 2017); Terry Moran, Melinda Arons, and Katie Escherich, "Obama Won't 'Rubber Stamp' Military Decisions," *ABC News,* July 22, 2008.

85. Charles Enderlin, *Shattered Dreams: The Failure of the Peace Process in the Middle East, 1995 to 2002* (New York: Other Press, 2003); Ahron Bregman, *Cursed Victory: A History of Israel and the Occupied Territories* (London: Penguin, 2014).

86. Ron Suskind, *The Price of Loyalty: George W. Bush, the White House, and the Education of Paul O'Neill* (New York: Simon and Schuster, 2004), 70–72; Steven Mufson and Alan Sipress, "U.S. Was Set to Support Palestinian Statehood," *Washington Post,* October 2, 2001.

87. Melani McAlister, *Epic Encounters: Culture, Media, and U.S. Interests in the Middle East since 1945* (Berkeley: University of California Press, 2005); Martin Durham, "Evangelical Protestantism and Foreign Policy in the United States after September 11," *Patterns of Prejudice* 38, no. 2 (2004): 145–158; Stephen Walt and John Mearsheimer, *The Israel Lobby and U.S. Foreign Policy* (New York: Farrar, Straus and Giroux, 2007).

88. Bush quoted in Karen Hughes, *Ten Minutes from Normal* (New York: Penguin, 2005), 280; Osamah Khalil, "Pax Americana: The United States, the Palestinians, and the Peace Process, 1948–2008," *CR: The New Centennial Review* 8, no. 2: The Palestine Issue (2008): 1–41.

89. George W. Bush, "Remarks on the Middle East," June 24, 2002, American Presidency Project; Daniel E. Zoughbie, *Indecision Points: George W. Bush and the Israeli-Palestinian Conflict* (Cambridge, MA: MIT Press, 2014), 55–76.

90. American Consulate, Jerusalem to Secretary of State, Washington, DC, "Biographical Report: Gaza NSF Commander Jamal Kayyad," June 1, 2007 https://search.wikileaks.org/plusd/cables/07JERUSALEM1023_a.html.

91. Condoleezza Rice, *No Higher Honor: A Memoir of My Years in Washington* (New York: Random House, 2011), 415–418; "Bush Reaction to Palestinian Election Results," National Public Radio, *Talk of the Nation,* January 26, 2006.

92. Rice, *No Higher Honor,* 420; Khalil, "Pax Americana."

93. Aurelie Daher, *Hezbollah: Mobilisation and Power* (London: Oxford University Press, 2019), 89–94, 159; Khalil, *America's Dream Palace,* ch. 8.

94. Rebecca Leung, "Hezbollah: A-Team of Terrorists," CBS *60 Minutes,* April 18, 2003 https://www.cbsnews.com/news/hezbollah-a-team-of-terrorists/; Azizi, *The Shadow Commander,* 199–207; Adrian Levy and Catherine Scott-Clark, *The Exile: The Stunning Inside Story of Osama bin Laden and Al Qaeda in Flight* (New York: Bloomsbury, 2017).

95. Daher, *Hezbollah,* 183–199.

96. Daher, *Hezbollah,* 183–199; "Secretary Rice Holds a News Conference," *Washington Post,* July 21, 2006.

97. Rose, "The Gaza Bombshell"; American Consulate, Jerusalem to Secretary of State, Washington, DC, "Assessment of Fatah-Hamas Clashes and PASF Effectiveness," May 25, 2007, https://search.wikileaks.org/plusd/cables/07 JERUSALEM983_a.html; "Supporting Pro-Fatah NGO's in North Ramallah," June 8, 2007, https://search.wikileaks.org/plusd/cables/07JERUSALEM1105_a .html; "Fatah Leaders Pinning the Blame and Taking the Steps," June 19, 2007 https://search.wikileaks.org/plusd/cables/07JERUSALEM1267_a.html.

98. US Mission, UN New York to Secretary of State, Washington, DC, "Gaza: Security Council Meets to Discuss Humanitarian Situation," January 23, 2008 https://wikileaks.org/plusd/cables/08USUNNEWYORK64_a.html; American Embassy, Cairo to Secretary of State, Washington, DC, "Egypt-Gaza Border Update: January 27," January 27, 2008 https://wikileaks.org/plusd/cables/08CAIRO136_a.html.

99. American Embassy, Beirut, to Secretary of State, Washington, DC, "Lebanon: Theories about Mugnieh's Assassination," February 14, 2006 https://wikileaks.org/plusd/cables/08BEIRUT237_a.html.

100. American Embassy, Beirut, to Secretary of State, Washington, DC, "Lebanon: Hizballah Goes Fiber Optic," cable 08Beirut00523, April 16, 2008, http://wikileaks.fdn.fr/cable/2008/04/08BEIRUT523.html.

101. David Rivkin, Jr., and Lee A. Casey, "The Myth of Occupied Gaza," *Washington Post,* May 10, 2008.

102. For example, see Efraim Inbar and Eitan Shamir, "Mowing the Grass in Gaza," *Jerusalem Post,* July 22, 2014.

103. Rick Lyman, "White House Takes Step to Renew Ties to Hollywood," *New York Times,* November 10, 2001; Rick Lyman, "Hollywood Discusses War Effort," *New York Times,* November 11, 2001; George W. Bush Library, Staff Member Office

Files, Communications, White House Office of Brian Besanceney and Strategic Initiatives, White House Office of Chris Henick and Karl Rove, Box 1, Electronic and Textual Records.

104. Rove quoted in Lyman, "Hollywood Discusses War Effort."

105. Rick Lyman, "White House Sets Meeting with Film Executives to Discuss War on Terrorism," *New York Times,* November 7, 2001.

106. Jane Mayer, "Whatever It Takes," *New Yorker,* February 19, 2007.

107. Mayer, "Whatever It Takes."

108. Mayer, "Whatever It Takes"; Spencer Ackerman, "No Looking Back: The CIA Torture Report's Aftermath," *Guardian,* September 11, 2016; Michael Kaufman, "What Does the Pentagon See in 'Battle of Algiers,'" *New York Times,* September 7, 2003; Stuart Klawans, "Lessons of the Pentagon's Favorite Training Film," *New York Times,* January 4, 2004.

109. Rachel Gans-Boriskin and Russ Tisinger, "The Bushlet Administration: Terrorism and War on *The West Wing,*" *Journal of American Culture* 28, no. 1 (2005): 100–113; Andrew Davison "The 'Soft' Power of Hollywood Militainment: The Case of *The West Wing*'s Attack on Antalya, Turkey," *New Political Science* 28, no. 4 (2006): 467–487.

110. Marc Schneider, "President Uribe's Colombian Challenge," *The Observer,* June 8, 2002.

111. Juan Forero, "Rightist's Hard Line Appeals to War-Weary Colombians," *New York Times,* May 19, 2002; Juan Forero, "Colombia Voters Are Angry, and Rebels May Pay Price," *New York Times,* May 26, 2002.

112. American Embassy, Bogota to Secretary of State, Washington, DC, "Colombia National Police Presence in Conflictive Areas: Mission Accomplished," February 4, 2004 https://search.wikileaks.org/plusd/cables/04BOGOTA1187_a .html.

113. Maria Alejandra Silva, "Alvaro Uribe: The Most Dangerous Man in Colombian Politics," Council on Hemispheric Affairs, October 20, 2017 http:// www.coha.org/alvaro-uribe-the-most-dangerous-man-in-colombian-politics/; Adam Isacson, "The Human Rights Landscape in Colombia," testimony at the Hearing of the Tom Lantos Human Rights Commission "Creating Peace and Finding Justice in Colombia," United States Congress, October 24, 2013 https://www.wola.org /analysis/the-human-rights-landscape-in-colombia-adam-isacsons-testimony-before -the-tom-lantos-human-rights-commission/.

114. Isacson, "The Human Rights Landscape in Colombia," 4–5; June S. Beittel, "Colombia: Background, U.S. Relations, and Congressional Interest," Congressional Research Service November 28, 2012: 19–20 https://sgp.fas.org/crs/row/RL32250 .pdf#page=26.

115. "Colombia: Stop Abuses by Paramilitaries' Successor Groups," news release, Human Rights Watch, February 3, 2010 https://www.hrw.org/news/2010/02/03 /colombia-stop-abuses-paramilitaries-successor-groups.

116. Silva, "Alvaro Uribe: The Most Dangerous Man in Colombian Politics";
"Two Colombian Ex-Intelligence Officers Have Jail Terms Increased for Wiretap-
ping," *BBC Monitoring Americas,* May 26, 2014; Sara Schaefer Muñoz, "Colombia
Finds Former Security Head Guilty of Wiretapping," *Dow Jones Institutional News,*
February 27, 2015.

117. American Embassy, Bogota, to Secretary of State, Washington, DC, "Plan
Colombia Implementation Round-Up, June, 2005," partial extract, cable 05Bo-
gota6669, July 18, 2005 https://wikileaks.jcvignoli.com/cable_05BOGOTA6669;
Parker Asmann, "Asset Forfeiture in Latin America: A Moral Dilemma?" *InSight
Crime,* July 20, 2017 https://www.insightcrime.org/news/analysis/asset-forfeiture
-latin-america-moral-dilemma/.

118. Jim Wyss, "Plan Colombia: 15 Years Later Much Has Changed, but Some
Remains the Same," *Miami Herald,* February 2, 2016.

119. "Bush, Pakistan's Musharraf Pledge Unity against Terrorism," *CNN,*
November 10, 2001; Suskind, *The One Percent Doctrine,* 81–82.

120. Syed Irfan Raza, "A.Q. Khan Regrets 'Confession,'" *DAWN,* May 30, 2008.

121. American Embassy, Islamabad to Secretary of State, Washington, DC,
"Political Scenesetter for Visit by Pakistan Vice Chief of Army Staff," June 15, 2006
https://search.wikileaks.org/plusd/cables/06ISLAMABAD11311_a.html; "President
Musharraf Determined to Deal with Border Areas," November 8, 2006 https://
search.wikileaks.org/plusd/cables/06ISLAMABAD21879_a.html; and "2006
Country Reports on Terrorism—Pakistan," January 22, 2007 https://search.wiki
leaks.org/plusd/cables/07ISLAMABAD392_a.html.

122. American Embassy, Islamabad, to Secretary of State, Washington, DC,
Washington, "Political Scenesetter for Visit by Pakistan Vice Chief of Army Staff."

123. Suskind, *The One Percent Doctrine,* 82; Shah Mahmoud Hanifi, "Reflections
on the American War, Karzai, and Orientalism in Afghanistan," E-International
Relations, January 12, 2015; Coll, *Ghost Wars,* 285–287.

124. Bush, "State of the Union Address," January 10, 2002; Christoph Koettl,
"War Crimes in Afghanistan. Or: What You Don't Learn in Science Class,"
Amnesty International Human Rights Now Blog, July 17, 2009; Hanifi, "Reflec-
tions on the American War."

125. American Embassy, Kabul, to Secretary of State, Washington, DC, Washington, "PRT/Tarin Kowt—Taliban Remain Potent Threat in Southern Afghanistan," March 14, 2006 https://search.wikileaks.org/plusd/cables/06KABUL1103_a
.html.

126. Ronald E. Neumann, *Three Embassies, Four Wars: A Personal Memoir*
(Washington, DC: Association for Diplomatic Studies and Training, 2017), 43.

127. Rumsfeld to Feith and Wolfowitz, "Presence in Central Asia," December 17,
2001 https://nsarchive.gwu.edu/documents/Snowflakes.pdf#page=56 and Rumsfeld
to Franks and Myers, "Looking Ahead," December 27, 2001, National Security

Archive https://nsarchive.gwu.edu/documents/Snowflakes.pdf#page=57; Douglas Jehl, "Holy War Lured Saudis as Rulers Looked Away," *New York Times,* December 27, 2001.

128. George W. Bush, "President Bush Addresses the 89th Annual National Convention of the American Legion," Reno, NV, August 28, 2007.

129. "Presidential Approval Ratings: George W. Bush," 2001–2009, Gallup https://news.gallup.com/poll/116500/presidential-approval-ratings-george-bush.aspx; Phillip Swagel, "The Cost of the Financial Crisis: The Impact of the September 2008 Economic Collapse," Briefing Paper #18, PEW Financial Reform Project, 2009, Table 3, p. 16.

6. DARK LANDS AND THE GEOGRAPHY OF EMPIRE

Epigraph: Barack Obama, "Remarks by the President and First Lady on the End of the War in Iraq," December 14, 2011.

1. Christopher Rogers, "Civilian Harm and Conflict in Northwest Pakistan," Center for Civilians in Conflict, 2010, 62 https://civiliansinconflict.org/wp-content/uploads/2017/09/Pakistan_Report_2010_2013.pdf; "Counting Drone Strike Deaths," Columbia Law School, Human Rights Clinic, October 2012 https://scholarship.law.columbia.edu/human_rights_institute/51.

2. Barack Obama, *A Promised Land* (New York: Crown, 2020), 354.

3. Craig Whitlock, "In Confidential Documents, U.S. Officials Said Almost Everything They Did to End Opium Farming in Afghanistan Backfired," *Washington Post,* December 9, 2019; Afghan Opiate Trade Project, United Nations Office on Drugs and Crime https://www.unodc.org/unodc/en/data-and-analysis/aotp.html.

4. Whitlock, "In Confidential Documents."

5. Whitlock, "In Confidential Documents"; Sherard Cowper-Coles, *Cables from Kabul: The Inside Story of the West's Afghanistan Campaign* (London: Harper Press, 2011), 18–19.

6. Special Inspector General for Afghanistan Reconstruction, "Counternarcotics: Lessons from the U.S. Experience in Afghanistan," June 2018, viii https://www.sigar.mil/pdf/lessonslearned/SIGAR-18-52-LL.pdf#page=56.

7. Ashley Jackson, "Life Under the Taliban Shadow Government," Overseas Development Institute, Denmark, June 2018, 7–8 https://cdn.odi.org/media/documents/12269.pdf.

8. Dick Cheney, *In My Time: A Personal and Political Memoir* (New York: Threshold, 2011), 697; Diaa Hadid, "Once Ruled by Taliban, Residents of Pakistan's Swat Valley Say Army Should Leave," *National Public Radio,* June 2, 2018; American Embassy, Islamabad, to Secretary of State, Washington, DC, "FATA Implementation Plan Update (12/02/07)," cable 07Islamabad5140, December 5, 2007, https://wikileaks.jcvignoli.com/cable_07ISLAMABAD5140?hl=FATA%20

Implementation%20Plan%20Update%20(12/02/07); and American Embassy, Islamabad, to Secretary of State, Washington, DC, "Pakistan: Refocusing Security Assistance," January 8, 2008.

9. Jonathan Alter, *The Promise: President Obama, Year One* (New York: Simon and Schuster, 2010), 221–223.

10. Peter Baker, "Surgical Strikes Shape Afghanistan Debate," *New York Times,* October 6, 2009; Alter, *The Promise,* 589–605.

11. Bob Woodward, "McChrystal: More Forces or 'Mission Failure,'" *Washington Post,* September 21, 2009.

12. Alter, *The Promise,* ch. 21; Rajiv Chandrasekaran, *Little America: The War within the War for Afghanistan* (New York: Vintage, 2015), 50–54.

13. Special Investigator General for Afghanistan Reconstruction (SIGAR), Barnett Rubin (identity originally redacted), "Lessons Learned Record of Interview 07, Stabilization in Afghanistan: Strategy and Interventions of the U.S. Government," January 20, 2015 https://www.washingtonpost.com/graphics/2019 /investigations/afghanistan-papers/documents-database/?document=background _ll_01_xx_nyc_01202015; Department of State, SIGAR, "The U.S. Civilian Uplift in Afghanistan Has Cost Nearly $2 Billion, and State Should Continue to Strengthen Its Management and Oversight of the Funds Transferred to Other Agencies," September 8, 2011 https://www.sigar.mil/pdf/audits/2011-09-08audit -11-17.pdf.

14. Craig Whitlock, "U.S. Officials Failed to Devise a Clear Strategy for the War in Afghanistan, Confidential Documents Show," *Washington Post,* December 9, 2019.

15. Rubin, SIGAR, "Lessons Learned Record of Interview 07, Stabilization in Afghanistan," January 20, 2015; Alter, *The Promise,* 573.

16. Helene Cooper and Carlotta Gall, "Cables Depict a Roller-Coaster Trajectory for Karzai, from Exalted to Baffling," *New York Times,* December 3, 2010; Alter, *The Promise,* 597.

17. Whitlock, "U.S. Officials Failed."

18. ISAF's Mission Statement, in Gen. Stanley McChrystal, "Commander's Initial Assessment," August 30, 2009, page 2-2 https://nsarchive.gwu.edu/sites /default/files/documents/qy3fic-cl4be/15.pdf.

19. Obama, *A Promised Land,* 432–437; Whitlock, "U.S. Officials Failed."

20. Whitlock, "U.S. Officials Failed."

21. American Embassy, Kabul, to Secretary of State, Washington, DC, "Ex-Taliban Seek Mediation Role," July 31, 2008 https://www.theguardian.com /world/us-embassy-cables-documents/164257; "Ex-Taliban Propose Preliminary Negotiations," August 5, 2008, https://archive.org/details/08KABUL2065; and Secretary of State, Washington, DC, to Kabul, Riyadh, and Islamabad, "Saudi Negotiations with Taliban and Afghan Government," October 8, 2008.

22. Secretary of State, Washington, DC, to NATOEU, "U.S. Policy on Reconciliation in Afghanistan," November 8, 2008; American Embassy, Riyadh to CENTCOM, MacDill Air Force Base, Florida, "Saudi Arabia: Scenesetter for CENTCOM Commander Petraeus, October 8–9 Visit," November 4, 2008 https://search.wikileaks.org/plusd/cables/08RIYADH1659_a.html.

23. Lakhdar Brahimi and Thomas Pickering, "Settling the Afghan War," *New York Times,* March 23, 2001.

24. Daniel Byman, "Why Are We Losing in Afghanistan?" Brookings Institution commentary, August 22, 2017.

25. American Embassy, Islamabad, to Secretary of State, Washington, DC, "Pervez Musharraf Resigns," cable 08Islamabad2750_a, August 18, 2008 https://wikileaks.org/plusd/cables/08ISLAMABAD2750_a.html.

26. American Embassy, Islamabad, to Secretary of State, Washington, DC, "Focusing the U.S.-Pakistan Strategic Dialogue," cable 09Islamabad385, February 21, 2009, Section 7(C) https://wikileaks.org/plusd/cables/09ISLAMABAD385_a.html. Of the $2 billion, the majority was devoted to supporting coalition operations. Roughly $775 million was allocated for economic assistance, but 40 percent had not been delivered.

27. Islamabad to Washington, DC, "Focusing the U.S.-Pakistan Strategic Dialogue."

28. See Nicola Abé, "The Woes of an American Drone Operator," *Der Spiegel,* December 14, 2012 https://www.spiegel.de/international/world/pain-continues-after-war-for-american-drone-pilot-a-872726.html. On Hellfire missiles, see "AGM-114 Hellfire II Missile," Army Technology, January 21, 2020 https://www.army-technology.com/projects/hellfire-ii-missile/.

29. Database of Bureau of Investigative Journalism, London, notes that the number killed could be as high as 510. https://www.thebureauinvestigates.com/stories/2017-01-01/drone-wars-the-full-data. Bush quoted in both Bob Woodward, *Obama's Wars* (New York: Simon and Schuster, 2010), 25–26, 51; and Mark Mazzetti, *The Way of the Knife* (New York: Penguin, 2013), 266–267.

30. Michael V. Hayden Oral History, Washington, DC, November 20, 2012, George W. Bush Presidential History Project, Miller Center, University of Virginia, transcript, 7, 31 https://s3.amazonaws.com/web.poh.transcripts/hayden_michael_2012_1120.pdf. Woodward, *Obama's Wars,* 84–85.

31. Hayden Oral History, transcript, 32; Woodward, *Obama's Wars,* 85; Jo Becker and Scott Shane, "Secret 'Kill List' Proves a Test of Obama's Principles and Will," *New York Times,* May 29, 2012.

32. Alex Rubinstein, "Did the CIA Pressure Yemen to Release al-Qaeda Propagandist Anwar al-Awlaki?" RealAlexRubiSubstack, March 22, 2021 https://realalexrubi.substack.com/p/leaked-cia-pressured-yemen-to-release; Declan Leary, "'This Is My Person,' CIA Director Allegedly Said of Anwar al-Awlaki," *The*

American Conservative, March 22, 2021; Steve Lyttle, "American Samir Khan Killed in U.S. Attack in Yemen Along with Awlaki," *Miami Herald,* September 30, 2011; Becker and Shane, "Secret 'Kill List' Proves a Test of Obama's Principles."

33. American Civil Liberties Union, "Al-Aulaqi v. Panetta—Constitutional Challenge to Killing of Three U.S. Citizens," June 4, 2021 https://www.aclu.org /cases/al-aulaqi-v-panetta-constitutional-challenge-killing-three-us-citizens.

34. Abé, "The Woes of an American Drone Operator"; Woodward, *Obama's Wars,* 48.

35. Woodward, *Obama's Wars,* 167; American Embassy, Islamabad, to Secretary of State, Washington, DC, "Baitullah Mehsud Declares War," April 13, 2009 https://wikileaks.org/plusd/cables/09ISLAMABAD776_a.html.

36. American Embassy, Islamabad, to Secretary of State, Washington, DC, "Preparing for the Long Haul," April 27, 2009 https://wikileaks.org/plusd/cables /09ISLAMABAD888_a.html; US Consulate, Peshawar, to Secretary of State, Washington "Expected South Waziristan Operation Creates Displacement, Conflict," May 28, 2009 https://wikileaks.org/plusd/cables/09PESHAWAR114_a .html; "Pakistan Media Reaction 09ISLAMABAD 1266," August 10, 2009.

37. Greg Miller, "Plan for Hunting Terrorists Signals U.S. Intends to Keep Adding Names to Kill Lists," *Washington Post*, November 9, 2012; Becker and Shane, "Secret 'Kill List' Proves a Test of Obama's Principles."

38. Woodward, *Obama's Wars,* 171–174.

39. Jeremy Scahill and Ryan Deveraux, "Barack Obama's Secret Terrorist-Tracking System, by the Numbers," *The Intercept*, August 5, 2014 https://firstlook.org /theintercept/article/2014/08/05/watch-commander/; and Jeremy Scahill and Ryan Deveraux, "The Secret Government Rulebook for Labeling You a Terrorist," *The Intercept,* July 23, 2014 https://theintercept.com/2014/07/23/blacklisted/.

40. Scahill and Deveraux, "The Secret Government Rulebook."

41. Scahill and Deveraux, "The Secret Government Rulebook"; National Counterterrorism Center, "Directorate of Terrorist Identities (DTI) Strategic Accomplishments 2013," *The Intercept,* August 4, 2014, 2 https://theintercept.com /document/directorate-terrorist-identities-dti-strategic-accomplishments-2013/; "Acting DNI Grenell Announces Organizational Changes to National Counterterrorism Center," Office of the Director of National Intelligence, press release, May 15, 2020.

42. *Raza v. City of N.Y.*, 998 F. Supp. 2d 70 (E.D.N.Y. 2013), November 22, 2013; Matt Apuzzo and Adam Goldman, "With CIA Help, NYPD Moves Covertly in Muslim Areas," Associated Press, August 23, 2011.

43. Apuzzo and Goldman, "With CIA Help, NYPD Moves Covertly in Muslim Areas," Diala Shamas and Nermeen Arastu, "Mapping Muslims: NYPD Spying and Its Impact on American Muslims," Creating Law Enforcement Accountability & Responsibility Project, Muslim American Civil Liberties Coalition, and Asian

American Legal Defense and Education Fund, March 11, 2011, 7, 10 https://www .law.cuny.edu/wp-content/uploads/page-assets/academics/clinics/immigration/clear /Mapping-Muslims.pdf.

44. Shamas and Arastu, "Mapping Muslims," 12–25; "*Raza v. City of New York*: Policing and Surveillance," CUNY Clear, City University of New York Law School, n.d. https://www.cunyclear.org/raza-v-city-of-new-york.

45. Shamas and Arastu, "Mapping Muslims," 12–25.

46. Trevor Aaronson, *The Terror Network: Inside the FBI's Manufactured War on Terrorism* (Brooklyn, NY: Ig Publishing, 2013), 115–151; Michael R. Sisak and Jennifer Peltz, "Judge Orders Release of 3 of 'Newburgh Four' and Assails FBI's Role In a Post–9/11 Terror Sting," Associated Press, July 28, 2023.

47. Rowaida Abdelaziz, "Pervasive Surveillance Tactics Have Haunted Muslim Americans for Years," *Huffington Post*, December 16, 2020. A similar case involves Ahmed Chebil, "I Refused to Become an FBI Informant, and the Government Put Me on the No Fly List," ACLU.org, April 6, 2021.

48. Talal Ansari and Siraj Datoo, "Welcome to America—Now Spy on Your Friends," BuzzFeed News, January 28, 2016 https://www.buzzfeednews.com/article /talalansari/welcome-to-america-now-spy-on-your-friends; Trevor Aaronson, "How the FBI Recruits and Handles Its Army of Informants," *The Intercept* January 31, 2017 https://theintercept.com/annotation_sets/how-the-fbi-recruits-and-handles -its-army-of-informants/; Federal Bureau of Investigation Directorate of Intelligence, "FBI's Confidential Human Source Policy Guide," September 21, 2015 (via *The Intercept*) https://www.documentcloud.org/documents/3422065-CHS-FINAL -Redacted; Mazin Sidahmed, "How the FBI Coerced This Muslim Immigrant into Working as an Informant," *Documented*, December 22, 2020 https://documented ny.com/2020/12/22/how-the-fbi-coerced-this-muslim-immigrant-into-working-as -an-informant/.

49. Sheryl Stolberg, "Key Senators Reach Accord on Extending the Patriot Act," *New York Times,* February 10, 2006.

50. Ginger Thompson, "The Narco-Terror Trap," ProPublica.org, December 7, 2015, copublished with the *New Yorker*; and Ginger Thompson, "Trafficking in Terror," *New Yorker,* December 6, 2015; George W. Bush, "Remarks on Signing Legislation to Reauthorize Drug-Free Communities Programs," December 14, 2001.

51. Thompson, "The Narco-Terror Trap."

52. Subcommittee on the Middle East and South Asia, House Committee on Foreign Affairs, "Counternarcotics Strategy and Police Training in Afghanistan," Hearing before the 110th Cong. 5, October 4, 2007 (Washington, DC: Government Printing Office, 2008), 5–37.

53. Subcommittee on the Middle East and South Asia, 5–37; John E. Thomas, Jr., "Narco-Terrorism: Could the Legislative and Prosecutorial Responses Threaten Our Civil Liberties?" *Washington and Lee Law Review* 66, no. 4 (2009): 1881–1920.

54, "Member of Afghan Taliban Sentenced to Life in Prison in Nation's First Conviction on Narco-Terror Charges," US Department of Justice, December 22, 2008; "Taliban Man Convicted in U.S. For 'Narco-Terrorism,'" Reuters, May 15, 2008.

55. Rapporteur's summary of Michael Braun, "Drug Trafficking and Middle Eastern Terrorist Groups: A Growing Nexus?" lecture, July 18, 2018, in Matthew Levitt and Michael Jacobson, "Countering Transnational Threats: Terrorism, Narco-Trafficking, and WMD Proliferation," Policy Focus #92, 27–29, Washington Institute for Near East Policy, January 2009, 28.

56. William K. Rashbaum, "U.S. Charges 3 Malians in Drug Plot: Case Links Al Qaeda and Narcotics Trade," New York Times, December 19, 2009; "Two Malian Men Plead Guilty in Manhattan Federal Court to Conspiring to Provide Material Support to Terrorists," U.S. Attorney's Office for the Southern District of New York, press release, April 17, 2012; Thompson, "The Narco-Terror Trap."

57. "Overlooking Oversight," New York Times, June 5, 2011.

58. Lee Tien, "Peekaboo, I See You: Government Authority Intended for Terrorism Is Used for Other Purposes," Electronic Frontier Foundation, October 26, 2014.

59. Nathan James and Daniel H. Else, "The 'Militarization' of Law Enforcement and the Department of Defense's '1033 Program,'" CRS Insights, IN10138, December 2, 2014 https://www.everycrsreport.com/reports/IN10138.html; Radley Balko, Rise of the Warrior Cop: The Militarization of America's Police Forces (New York: Public Affairs, 2013), ch. 8.

60. James and Else, "The 'Militarization' of Law Enforcement"; Abigail R. Hall and Christopher J. Coyne, "The Militarization of U.S. Domestic Policing," Independent Review 17, no. 4 (2013): 485–504; Brian Barrett, "The Pentagon's Hand-Me-Downs Helped Militarize Police. Here's How," Wired, June 2, 2020.

61. Balko, Rise of the Warrior Cop, 243–247.

62. "The Cost of Kill/Capture: Impact of the Night Raid Surge on Afghan Civilians," Regional Policy Initiative on Afghanistan and Pakistan, Open Society Foundations, September 19, 2011; Mujib Mashal, "C.I.A.-led Afghan Forces Leave Grim Trail of Abuse," New York Times, December 31, 2018; "'They've Shot Many Like This': Abusive Night Raids by CIA-Backed Afghan Strike Forces," Human Rights Watch, October 31, 2019.

63. Balko, Rise of the Warrior Cop, 259–260.

64. Balko, Rise of the Warrior Cop, 253–259; Andrew Becker and G. W. Schulz, "Local Police Stockpile High-Tech, Combat-Ready Gear," Reveal news, Center for Investigative Reporting, December 21, 2011.

65. Kanya Bennett, "As We Remember the Militarized Response to the Ferguson Uprising, Trump Says Civilian Police Are Making 'Good Use' of Military Weapons," news and commentary, American Civil Liberties Union, August 8, 2017; Jonathan Topaz, "Cleaver: Ferguson Looks Like Fallujah," Politico, August 19,

2014; "War Comes Home: The Excessive Militarization of American Policing," report, American Civil Liberties Union, June 2014.

66. "DOD Excess Property: Enhanced Controls Needed for Access to Excess Controlled Property," GAO-17-532, US Government Accountability Office, July 18, 2017 https://www.gao.gov/products/gao-17-532.

67. US Senate, Committee on Armed Services, "Inquiry into the Treatment of Detainees in U.S. Custody" (Washington, DC: Government Printing Office, November 28, 2008), xii, xviii–xix.

68. Woodward, *Obama's Wars*, 88–90.

69. Laura Pitter, "After 16 Years, End Injustice at Guantanamo," Human Rights Watch, January 10, 2018; Laura Pitter and W. Paul Smith, "Another Blow for Justice in the Guantanamo Bay Military Commissions," Human Rights Watch, June 29, 2017; "Guantanamo Inmates Say They Were 'Sold,'" Associated Press, May 31, 2005; Mustafa Bayoumi, "Journey to Guantánamo: A Week in America's Notorious Penal Colony," *The Nation*, July 11, 2022; "This 9/11 Suspect and 'Torture Prop' Has Spent 20 Years in Guantánamo. Is He Nearing a Deal with the US?" *Guardian*, May 17, 2023.

70. Jose Rodriguez, Jr., *Hard Measures: How Aggressive CIA Actions after 9/11 Saved American Lives* (New York: Simon and Schuster, 2012); Rodriquez quoted in Mark Mazzetti and Charlie Savage, "No Criminal Charges Sought over CIA Tapes," *New York Times*, November 9, 2010.

71. *Zero Dark Thirty*, dir. Kathryn Bigelow, Sony Pictures, 2012; Jason Leopold and Ky Henderson, "Tequila, Painted Pearls, and Prada—How the CIA Helped Produce 'Zero Dark Thirty,'" *Vice News*, September 9, 2015; Alex Lubin, *Never-Ending War on Terror* (Oakland: University of California Press, 2021); Bayoumi, "This 9/11 Suspect and 'Torture Prop.'"

72. Mudd email quoted in the "Report of the Senate Select Committee on Intelligence: Committee Study of the Central Intelligence Agency's Detention and Interrogation Program," Senate Report 113-288, 113th Congress, 2nd Session, December 9, 2014, xvii–xviii, 195–196, 402–403 https://www.intelligence.senate.gov/sites/default/files/publications/CRPT-113srpt288.pdf.

73. David Jackson, "Obama: 'We Tortured Some Folks,'" *USA Today*, August 1, 2014.

74. "Report of the Senate Select Committee on Intelligence," vi, xi–xxiii, 4–8.

75. "Report of the Senate Select Committee on Intelligence," 8–19.

76. American Embassy, Mexico City, to Secretary of State, Washington, DC, "Anti-Drug Ops Extended to Eight States," March 2, 2007 https://wikileaks.org/plusd/cables/07MEXICO1068_a.html; and "Scenesetter for Under Secretary Karen Hughes Trip to Mexico, February 12–15, 2007," February 7, 2007 https://wikileaks.org/plusd/cables/07MEXICO571_a.html.

77. Mexico City to Washington, DC, "Anti-Drug Ops Extended to Eight States."

78. Mexico City to Washington, DC, "Anti-Drug Ops Extended to Eight States."

79. American Embassy, Bogota, to Secretary of State, Washington, DC, "United States, Colombia and Mexico Meeting Reinforces Counter-Narcotics Cooperation," October 18, 2007 https://wikileaks.org/plusd/cables/07BOGOTA7470_a.html; and American Embassy, London, to Secretary of State, Washington, DC, "ONDCP Director Walters Reviews Afghan and Other CN Issues with UK," April 4, 2007 https://wikileaks.org/plusd/cables/07LONDON1279_a.html.

80. American Embassy, Mexico City, to Washington, DC, "ONDCP Director Walters Meetings with Mexican Officials," April 13, 2007 https://wikileaks.org/plusd/cables/07MEXICO1854_a.html; Anabel Hernández, Narcoland: The Mexican Drug Lords and Their Godfathers (Brooklyn, NY: Verso, 2013), 333.

81. American Embassy, Mexico City, to Secretary of State, Washington, DC, "Concerns about Security, Human Rights Abuses Collide in Guerrero," December 19, 2007 https://wikileaks.org/plusd/cables/07MEXICO6219_a.html; "Narco-Killings Update," March 11, 2008 https://wikileaks.org/plusd/cables/08MEXICO713_a.html.

82. Marc Lacey, "Congress Trims Bush's Mexico Drug Plan," New York Times, May 23, 2008; American Embassy, Mexico City, to Secretary of State, Washington, DC, "Secretary Chertoff and GOM Officials Discuss Security Cooperation and Shared Challenges," July 24, 2008 https://wikileaks.org/plusd/cables/08MEXICO2276_a.html; and "Mexico Seeks to Turn the Page on Corruption," April 11, 2008 https://search.wikileaks.org/plusd/cables/08MEXICO1104_a.html.

83. American Embassy, Mexico City, to Secretary of State, Washington, DC, "The U.S.-Mexican Relationship: Meeting Challenges, Tapping Opportunities in 2009—Security and Reform," February 4, 2009 https://wikileaks.org/plusd/cables/09MEXICO283_a.html; Clare Ribando Seelke and Kristin Finklea, "U.S.-Mexican Security Cooperation: The Mérida Initiative and Beyond," Congressional Research Service, R41349, June 29, 2017 https://crsreports.congress.gov/product/pdf/R/R41349/55.

84. Seelke and Finklea, "U.S.-Mexican Security Cooperation," 9–12.

85. Calderón quoted in Eduardo Porter, "Numbers Tell of Failure in Drug War," New York Times, July 4, 2012; Oswaldo Zavala, Drug Cartels Do Not Exist: Narcotrafficking in US and Mexican Culture (Nashville, TN: Vanderbilt University Press, 2022), 46, 78–79; Randal C. Archibold and Damien Cave, "Mexico Election Signals New Tack in the Drug War," New York Times, June 11, 2012; Hernández, Narcoland, 240–241; "Cocaine Retail (Street) Prices," 1990–2010, United Nations Office on Drugs and Crime, https://www.unodc.org/unodc/secured/wdr/Cocaine_Heroin_Prices.pdf.

86. Hernández, Narcoland, 240–244; John Burnett, "Arrest of Genaro Garcia Luna Shocks Mexico," National Public Radio All Things Considered, December 15, 2019; American Embassy, Mexico City, to Secretary of State, Washington, DC, "The U.S.-Mexican Relationship: Meeting Challenges, Tapping Opportunities in

2009—Security and Reform," cable 09Mexico283_a, February 4, 2009 https://
wikileaks.org/plusd/cables/09MEXICO283_a.html.

    87. American Embassy, Mexico City, to Secretary of State, Washington, DC,
"Scenesetter for the Secretary's Visit to Mexico, March 25–26," March 19, 2009
https://wikileaks.org/plusd/cables/09MEXICO803_a.html; and "Scenesetter for
President Obama's Visit to Mexico City, April 16–17, 2009," April 14, 2009 https://
wikileaks.org/plusd/cables/09MEXICO1055_a.html.

    88. Michelle Shephard, "My Meeting with a Foreign Terrorist in Somalia,"
Toronto Star, March 10, 2017 https://www.thestar.com/news/world/my-meeting
-with-a-forgotten-terrorist-in-somalia/article_3a47e96b-cfbd-515b-830e-2ac601
a8e7e6.html; Mazzetti, *The Way of the Knife,* 138–139.

    89. "Hassan Dahir Aweys: Narrative Summary, ISIL (Da'esh) and Al-Qaida
Sanctions List," United Nations Security Council, March 28, 2011 https://www.un
.org/securitycouncil/sanctions/1267/aq_sanctions_list/summaries/individual/hassan
-dahir-aweys.

    90. Jeffrey Gettleman and Mark Mazzetti, "Somalia's Islamists and Ethiopia
Gird for a War," *New York Times,* December 14, 2006.

    91. Mark Mazzetti, "Pentagon Sees Covert Move in Somalia as Blueprint," *New
York Times,* January 13, 2007; American Embassy, Addis Ababa, to Secretary of
State, Washington, DC, "What Next for Ethiopia and Somalia? The View from
Addis Ababa," February 13, 2009.

    92. Hayden quoted in Mazzetti, *The Way of the Knife,* 242.

    93. American Embassy, Nairobi, to Secretary of State, Washington, DC, "A
Portrait of Al-Shabaab Recruitment in Kenya," 09Nairobi1171_a, June 11, 2009
https://wikileaks.org/plusd/cables/09NAIROBI1171_a.html.

    94. "A Portrait of Al-Shabaab Recruitment in Kenya," June 11, 2009.

    95. "A Portrait of Al-Shabaab Recruitment in Kenya," June 11, 2009. For the
history of Saudi support for Wahhabi missions and the split after the 1980s, see
David Commins, *The Mission and the Kingdom: Wahhabi Power behind the Saudi
Throne,* rev. ed. (London: I. B Tauris, 2016), 155–205.

    96. American Embassy, Addis Ababa, to Secretary of State, Washington, DC,
"Somalia: Time for Plan B," June 26, 2009.

    97. Amanda Sperber, "Somalis in Minnesota Question Counter-Extremism
Program Targeted at Muslims," *Guardian,* September 14, 2015.

    98. Jerome P. Bjelopera, "Countering Violent Extremism in the United States,"
Congressional Research Service R42553, February 19, 2014, 1 https://crsreports
.congress.gov/product/pdf/R/R42553/10; Mike German, *Disrupt, Discredit, and
Divide: How the New FBI Damages Democracy* (New York: New Press, 2019), 157.

    99. Bjelpora, "Countering Violent Extremism in the United States"; Vanessa
Taylor, "'Why Minneapolis'? How Deep Surveillance of Black Muslims Paved the
Way for George Floyd's Murder," *The Progressive,* June 8, 2020.

100. Michael Price, "Community Outreach or Intelligence Gathering?" Brennan Center for Justice, New York University School of Law, January 29, 2015, 1–3 https://www.brennancenter.org/media/415/download.

101. Nabihah Maqbool, "Defunding the Police Must Include Ending the Surveillance of Muslims," *The Intercept,* June 25, 2020; Sperber, "Somalis in Minnesota Question."

102. Greg Miller, "Under Obama, an Emerging Global Apparatus for Drone Killing," *Washington Post,* December 27, 2011; "Somalia: Reported US Covert Actions 2001–2016," Bureau for Investigative Journalism, London, archived at Airwars https://airwars.org/archives/bij-drone-war/drone-war/data/somalia-reported -us-covert-actions-2001-2017.

103. Mazzetti, *The Way of the Knife,* 246–247; Daniel Howden, "Terror in Nairobi: The Full Story behind al-Shabaab's Mall Attack," *Guardian,* October 4, 2013; Berouk Mesfin, "What Changes for al-Shabaab after the Death of Godane?" Institute for Security Studies, October 8, 2014.

104. Osamah Khalil, "The Counterrevolutionary Year: The Arab Spring, the Gulf Cooperation Council, and U.S. Foreign Policy in the Middle East," in *American Studies Encounters the Middle East,* ed. Alex Lubin and Marwan Kraidy, 286–301 (Chapel Hill: University of North Carolina Press, 2016).

105. Osamah F. Khalil, *America's Dream Palace: Middle East Expertise and the Rise of the National Security State* (Cambridge, MA: Harvard University Press, 2016), 282–286; Woodward, *Obama's Wars,* 83–86; Obama, *A Promised Land,* 644–650.

106. Khalil, "The Counterrevolutionary Year."

107. Barack Obama, "Remarks by the President on the Middle East and North Africa," May 19, 2011.

108. American Embassy, Tripoli, to Secretary of State, Washington, DC, "CODEL McCain Meets Muammar and Mauatassim al-Qadhafi," August 19, 2009; Richard Norton-Taylor, "MI6 Gets off Scot-Free over Rendition of Suspected Islamists to Libya," *Guardian,* June 9, 2016.

109. Jacob Mundy, *Libya* (Medford, MA: Polity Press, 2018), 72–77.

110. Mundy, *Libya,* 77–80; "Security Council Approves 'No-Fly Zone' over Libya," United Nations Security Council, Meetings Coverage, SC/10200, March 17, 2011 https://press.un.org/en/2011/sc10200.doc.htm.

111. Mundy, *Libya,* 81–85.

112. Jeffrey Goldberg, "The Obama Doctrine," *The Atlantic,* April 2016; Ian Black and Kim Wilsher, "Sarkozy Election Campaign Was Funded by Libya—Gaddafi Son," *Guardian,* March 16, 2011; "Rejoicing in Libya's Benghazi," *Al Jazeera English,* March 20, 2011; "Former French President Sarkozy Charged over Libyan Financing," *Al Jazeera English,* October 16, 2020; "Nicolas Sarkozy, Former President of France, Found Guilty of Corruption, Gets Prison Time," Associated Press, March 1, 2021.

113. Mundy, *Libya,* 131–134.

114. Obama, "Remarks on the Middle East and North Africa"; "Syria: Rampant Torture of Protesters," *Human Rights Watch,* April 15, 2011.

115. Obama, "Remarks on the Middle East and North Africa."

116. Patrick Cockburn, *The Rise of the Islamic State: ISIS and the New Sunni Revolution* (New York: Verso, 2015), ch. 4.

117. Steven Lee Meyers, "U.S. Joins Effort to Equip and Pay Rebels in Syria," *New York Times,* April 2, 2012; Sergio Peçanha, "An Arms Pipeline to Syrian Rebels," *New York Times,* March 24, 2013; Peter Baker, "Syria Exposes Split between Obama and Clinton," *New York Times,* October 4, 2015; Bill Law, "Smooth Operator: Qatar's Ex-PM Breaks His Silence," *Middle East Eye,* November 25, 2015.

118. Michael Gordon, "U.S. and Russia Reach a Deal on Dismantling Syria's Chemical Arms," *New York Times,* September 15, 2013. On internal deliberations over a response and the intelligence community's uncertain assessment, see Jeffrey Goldberg, "The Obama Doctrine," *The Atlantic,* April 2016.

119. Mark Mazzetti and Matt Apuzzo, "U.S. Relies Heavily on Saudi Money to Support Syrian Rebels," *New York Times,* January 23, 2016; Mark Mazzetti, Adam Goldman, and Michael S. Schmidt, "Under Trump, Shell of a Force in Syria Swiftly Lost C.I.A. Aid," *New York Times,* August 3, 2017.

120. "Nasrallah yaṣif 'Dāʿish' bi-al-Waḥsh alladhī yuhaddidu al-Urdun wa-Duwal al-Khalīj," (Nasrallah describes ISIS as a monster that threatens Jordan and the Gulf states) *France 24 Arabic,* August 15, 2014.

121. G. John Ikenberry, *Liberal Leviathan: The Origins, Crisis, and Transformation of the American World Order* (Princeton, NJ: Princeton University Press, 2011); Joseph Nye, Jr., *The Future of Power* (New York: Public Affairs, 2011); Josef Joffe, *The Myth of America's Decline: Politics, Economics, and a Half Century of False Prophecies* (New York: Liveright, 2013).

122. Fareed Zakaria, *The Post-American World* (New York: Norton, 2008); and *The Post-American World 2.0* (New York: Norton, 2012); Martin Jacques, *When China Rules the World: The End of the Western World and the Birth of a New Global Order* (New York: Penguin, 2009); Christopher Layne, "This Time It's Real: The End of Unipolarity and the *Pax Americana*," *International Studies Quarterly* 56, no. 1 (2012): 203–213.

123. Obama, *A Promised Land,* 439.

EPILOGUE

Epigraph: Donald J. Trump, Republican Leadership Summit, New Hampshire, April 18, 2015 https://www.c-span.org/video/?325374-10/donald-trump-hampshire-republican-leadership-summit.

1. Lt. General Michael Flynn, interview, *Breitbart News Daily,* August 26, 2016, https://soundcloud.com/breitbart/breitbart-news-daily-retired-lt-gen-michael

-t-flynn-august-26-2016; Andrew Kaczynski, "Michael Flynn Once Claimed Arabic Signs on Southern Border Guide 'Radicalized Muslims' into US," *CNN*, December 9, 2016.

2. Lt. General Michael Flynn, interview, August 26, 2016; Kaczynski, "Michael Flynn Once Claimed."

3. Osamah F. Khalil, "Between the Devil and the Deep Blue Sea," *The Hill. com*, June 2, 2014.

4. Jane Mayer, "The Reclusive Hedge-Fund Billionaire behind the Trump Presidency," *New Yorker,* March 17, 2017; Bethany Mandel, "The Monster Steve Bannon Created at Breitbart.com Was Not What Andrew Breitbart Wanted," *NBC News,* January 10, 2018.

5. A caliphate is a community of devout Muslims ruled by a caliph, or a rightful successor to the Prophet Mohammed. Baghdadi was the *nom de guerre* of Ibrahim ibn Awad Ibrahim Ali al-Badri al-Samarrai.

6. Fawaz Gerges, *ISIS: A History* (Princeton, NJ: Princeton University Press, 2017), 18–19; Patrick Cockburn, *The Rise of Islamic State: ISIS and the New Sunni Revolution,* updated ed. (London: Verso, 2015), ch. 2. In Arabic-language media and vernacular, ISIS is referred to as *Dā'ish or al-Dawlah al-Islāmīyah fī al-'Irāq wa-al-Shām.* Al-Sham is generally translated as "the Levant," but refers to "Greater Syria," including present-day Syria, Lebanon, Jordan, Israel-Palestine, and southern Turkey.

7. Gerges, *ISIS: A History,* 32–34, 144–146.

8. Gerges, *ISIS: A History,* 150–151; Cockburn, *The Rise of Islamic State,* ch. 5; Kenneth Katzman and Carla E. Humud, "Iraq: Politics and Governance," March 9, 2016, Congressional Research Service, RS21968, 16, https://www.refworld.org/docid /56e675014.html.

9. Gerges, *ISIS: A History,* 223–231; Cockburn, *The Rise of Islamic State,* ch. 6. Julani is the *nom de guerre* of Ahmad Husayn as-Sar.

10. Gerges, *ISIS: A History*, 234–235; Cockburn, *The Rise of Islamic State,* ch. 1.

11. Gerges, *ISIS: A History,* 21; Cockburn, *The Rise of Islamic State,* ch. 7; Erika Solomon, "The Rise and Fall of a US-Backed Rebel Commander in Syria," *Financial Times,* February 8, 2017.

12. Josh Dawsey, "'Whimpering, Screaming and Crying' 'A Beautiful Dog': Trump's Vivid Account of the Baghdadi Raid," *Washington Post,* October 27, 2019.

13. "Raqqa's Dirty Little Secret," *BBC,* November 13, 2017; "Syria: Dire Conditions for ISIS Suspects' Families," Human Rights Watch, July 23, 2019.

14. "Turkey/Syria: Civilians at Risk in Syria Operation," Human Rights Watch, October 11, 2019; Sam Magdy, "Turkey Deploys Extremists to Libya, Local Militias Say," Associated Press, February 5, 2020.

15. Katie Bo Williams, "In Syria, US Commanders Hold the Line—and Wait for Biden," *Defense One,* March 21, 2021; Phil Stewart, "Syria Mission Worth the Risk, Top U.S. General Says after Rare Visit," Reuters, March 5, 2023.

16. Gordon Lubold and Warren Strobel, "Secret U.S. Missile Aims to Kill Only Terrorists, Not Nearby Civilians," *Wall Street Journal,* March 9, 2019; Abu Mohammad al-Jolani, interview with Martin Smith, February 1 and February 14, 2021, Idlib, Syria, *Frontline* interviews, https://www.pbs.org/wgbh/frontline /interview/abu-mohammad-al-jolani/.

17. Gerges, *ISIS: A History,* 23.

18. Jacob Mundy, *Libya* (Medford, MA: Polity Press, 2018), ch. 4; "Statement from National Security Adviser Robert C. O'Brien Regarding Libya," Trump White House briefings, August 4, 2020; "Reuniting Libya, Divided Once More," commentary, International Crisis Group, May 25, 2022.

19. Gregory Johnsen, *The Last Refuge: Yemen, Al-Qaeda, and America's War in Arabia* (New York: Norton, 2013), 269–286.

20. Rod Norland, "Rebels in Yemen Say They Intend to Form a New Government," *New York Times,* February 7, 2015; Saeed al-Batati and Kareem Fahim, "Rebels Take Key Parts of Yemen's Third-Largest City," *New York Times,* March 23, 2015.

21. "Āṣifat al-ḥazm: Ladaynā adillah tudīn al-Ḥūthīyīn biqatl al-madanīyīn," (Operation Decisive Storm: We have evidence confirming that the Houthis kill civilians) Al-Arabiya, April 16, 2015; Mark Perry, "Lloyd Austin Isn't Who You Think He Is," *Foreign Policy,* December 16, 2020.

22. Gregory Johnsen, "The End of Yemen," commentary, Brookings Institution, March 25, 2021.

23. John Hudson, Missy Ryan, and Josh Dawsey, "On the Day U.S. Forces Killed Soleimani, They Targeted a Senior Iranian Official in Yemen," *Washington Post,* January 10, 2020.

24. Arash Azizi, *The Shadow Commander: Soleimani, the U.S. and Iran's Global Ambitions* (New York: Oneworld, 2020), 90–91, 180–181.

25. "US Launched Cyber Attack on Iranian Rockets and Missiles—Reports," Associated Press, June 22, 2019.

26. Patrick Cockburn, "The Drone Attacks in Saudi Arabia Have Changed the Nature of Global Warfare," *The Independent,* September 20, 2019; Alissa Rubin, "Was U.S. Wrong about Attack That Nearly Started a War with Iran," *New York Times,* February 6, 2020.

27. Mark Mazzetti, Helene Cooper, Julian E. Barnes, Alissa Rubin, and Eric Scmitt, "As Iran Reels, Trump Aides Clash over Escalating Military Showdown," *New York Times,* March 21, 2020; "Iran and China Sign 25-year Cooperation Agreement," Reuters, March 27, 2021.

28. Bernard Orr and Aziz El Yaakoubi, "Top Iranian, Saudi Envoys Meet in China in Restoration of Diplomatic Ties," Reuters, April 6, 2023.

29. "DEA and European Authorities Uncover Massive Hizballah Drug and Money Laundering Scheme," press release, United States Drug Enforcement Administration, February 1, 2016; Mimi Yagoub, "Hezbollah Laundering Money for

Colombia Cartel: DEA," InsightCrime.org, February 2, 2016; "Oficina de Envigado," InsightCrime.org, October 28, 2020; Emanuele Ottolenghi and John Hannah, "To Combat Illegal Immigration, Trump Should Target Latin America's Hezbollah-Narco Nexus," *Foreign Policy,* December 23, 2016; Roger F. Noriega and Jose R. Cardenas, "The Mounting Hezbollah Threat in Latin America," American Enterprise Institute, October 6, 2011; Matthew Levitt, *Hezbollah: The Global Footprint of Lebanon's Party of God* (Washington, DC: Georgetown University Press, 2013), 328.

30. "Nasrallah: Naktub Tārīkh al-Mintaqah . . . Lā Lubnān," (Nasrallah: We are writing the history of the region not only Lebanon) *Al Akhbar,* September 12, 2017; Josh Meyer, "The Secret Backstory of How Obama Let Hezbollah Off the Hook," *Politico,* December 20, 2017; John Fernandez, "The DEA's Targeting of Hezbollah's Global Criminal Support Network," Washington Institute, January 10, 2020; Erik Wemple, "Former Obama Officials Criticize Politico Story Alleging Weakness against Hezbollah," *Washington Post* blog, December 21, 2017; House Committee on Financial Services, Subcommittee on Monetary Policy and Trade, Subcommittee on Terrorism and Illicit Finance Hearing on Non-Nuclear Sanctions against Iran, April 4, 2017; House Foreign Affairs Committee, Subcommittee on The Western Hemisphere Hearing on the Kingpin Designation Act, November 8, 2017; "Saudi and UAE Ban Citizens from Travelling to Lebanon," *Al Jazeera,* February 24, 2016; "US Sanctions Lebanon-Based Firms, Person for Links to Hezbollah," *Al Jazeera,* September 17, 2020; "Lebanon's Gebran Bassil Hit by US Sanctions 'for Corruption,'" *BBC,* November 6, 2020; "US Treasury Sanctions 7 Lebanese Tied to Hezbollah Finances," Associated Press, May 11, 2021.

31. Maya Gebelly, "Arabs Bring Syria's Assad Back into Fold but Want Action on Drugs Trade," Reuters, May 10, 2023; "Xi, Assad Jointly Announce China-Syria Strategic Partnership," Xinhua News Agency (State Council, People's Republic of China), September 22, 2023.

32. Mark Harris, "Pentagon Testing Mass Surveillance Balloons across the US," *Guardian,* August 2, 2019.

33. Admiral Craig S. Faller, Commander, United States Southern Command, Posture Statement before the 116th Congress, Senate Armed Services Committee, February 7, 2019, https://www.southcom.mil/Media/Special-Coverage/SOUTH COMs-2019-Posture-Statement-to-Congress/.

34. American Embassy, Mexico City, to Secretary of State, Washington, DC "Setting the Record Straight on Zetas and U.S. Military Training," August 21, 2009; American Embassy, Guatemala City, to Secretary of State, Washington, DC "Rogue Elements of Guatemalan Military Selling Weapons to Narcos," June 8, 2009, Guadalupe Correa-Cabrera, *Los Zetas Inc.: Criminal Corporations, Energy, and Civil War in Mexico,* (Austin, TX: University of Texas Press, 2017): 15–23.

35. Anabel Hernández, *Narcoland: The Mexican Drug Lords and Their Godfathers* (Brooklyn, NY: Verso, 2013), 201–205; Ioan Grillo, "Special Report: Mexico's Zetas Rewrite Drug War in Blood," Reuters, May 23, 2012.

36. Hernández, *Narcoland*, 204, 301–302; Parker Asmann, "Mexico's Zetas: From Criminal Powerhouse to Fragmented Remnants," InSightCrime.org, April 6, 2018.

37. Vivian Salama, "Trump to Mexico: Take Care of 'Bad Hombres' or US Might," Associated Press, February 2, 2017; Chuck Rosenberg, "Trump's Incendiary Attacks on MS-13 and Immigrants Are Making It Harder to Fight Crime," *USA Today,* October 4, 2018.

38. Victor Garcia, "Sen. Graham: 'A Matter of Time' before Terrorist Takes Advantage of the Border Crisis," *Fox News,* July 23, 2019; Department of Justice, Eastern District of Virginia, "MS-13 Leader in El Salvador Charged with RICO and Terrorism Offenses," press release, United States Attorney's Office, Eastern District of Virginia, July 15, 2020; "Trump Administration Announces Arrests in 'Campaign to Destroy MS-13,'" PBS News, July 15, 2020.

39. Donald J. Trump, "Speech on National Security," Philadelphia, September 7, 2016, transcript https://thehill.com/blogs/pundits-blog/campaign/294817-transcript -of-donald-trumps-speech-on-national-security-in/.

40. Neta C. Crawford, "Afghanistan's Rising Civilian Death Toll Due to Airstrikes, 2017–2020," Costs of War Project, Boston University and Brown University, December 7, 2020.

41. "Trump in Yemen: New Airwars Study Shines Light on Opaque Campaign," Airwars.com, October 28, 2020; "Significant Drop in Civilian Harm during 2020 Indicates Covid Effect: Airwars Annual Report," Airwars.com, March 2, 2021; Stephanie Nebehay, "Possible War Crimes in Yemen Fueled by Arms Flows from West, Iran-U.N.," Reuters, September 15, 2020.

42. Nick Turse, "In the Least Wired Country on Earth, U.S. Military Asks Airstrike Victims to File Complaints Online," *The Intercept,* June 10, 2021; "Exception(s) to the Rule(s)," Center for Civilians in Conflict, November 19, 2020, https://civiliansinconflict.org/wp-content/uploads/2022/02/CIVIC_US_Report _Drones_Final.pdf; Josh Lederman and Courtney Kube, "Biden Sends Hundreds of U.S. Troops Back to Somalia to Fight Al-Shabab Extremists," *NBC News,* May 16, 2022; Omar Faruk and Cara Anna, "US Increases Military Support for Somalia against al-Shabab," Associated Press, March 1, 2023.

43. Bruce Riedel, "The Mess in Afghanistan," Brookings Institution commentary, March 4, 2020; Michael Phillips and Nancy Youssef, "Vets See Echoes of Vietnam in Afghanistan Withdrawal Plan," *Wall Street Journal,* April 27, 2021.

44. Human Rights Watch, "Economic Causes of Afghanistan's Humanitarian Crisis," August 4, 2022 https://www.hrw.org/news/2022/08/04/economic-causes -afghanistans-humanitarian-crisis; Dan Lamothe, "Mastermind of Kabul Airport Massacre Killed by Taliban, U.S. Says," *Washington Post,* April 25, 2023; White House, "Background Press Call by a Senior Administration Official on a U.S. Counterterrorism Operation," August 1, 2022; Samuel Lovett, Sarah Newey and

Ben Farmer, "How the Taliban Launched the 'Most Successful Counter-Narcotics Effort in Human History,'" *The Telegraph*, July 3, 2023.

45. Elissa Slotkin, *MSNBC Morning Joe*, January 8, 2021.

46. Charlie Savage, "F.B.I. Surveillance Cases Plummet amid Pandemic and Inquiry Fallout," *New York Times*, May 1, 2021; Rebecca Beitsch and Cristina Marcos, "New Report Highlights Severe Intelligence Failures on Jan. 6," *The Hill*, June 8, 2021.

47. Kathleen Belew, *Bring the War Home: The White Power Movement and Paramilitary America* (Cambridge, MA: Harvard University Press, 2018); Ben Makuch, "Department of Homeland Security Confirms Neo-Nazi Leader Used to Work for It," *Vice*, February 17, 2021.

48. Gen. H. R. McMaster, interview, *BBC News Hour*, August 12, 2021.

49. Nahal Toosi and Bryan Bender, "U.S. Cable Warns of Major Barriers to Tracking Ukraine Aid," *Politico*, December 14, 2022.

50. Neta C. Crawford, "United States Budgetary Costs and Obligations of Post–9/11 Wars through FY2020: $6.4 Trillion," Costs of War Project, Boston University and Brown University, November 13, 2019.

51. Betsy Pearl, "Ending the War on Drugs: By the Numbers," Center for American Progress, June 27, 2018.

52. See, among others, C. Peter Rydell and Susan S. Everingham, *Controlling Cocaine: Supply Versus Demand Programs* (Santa Monica, CA: RAND, 1994), https://www.rand.org/pubs/monograph_reports/MR331.html.

53. Frank G. Madsen, "International Narcotics Law Enforcement: A Study in Irrationality," *Journal of International Affairs* 66, no. 1 (2012): 123–141; "US Leads the World in Illegal Drug Use," *CBS News*, July 1, 2008; United Nations Office on Drugs and Crime, "World Drug Report, 2022, Executive Summary Policy Indications," 28–31, 63.

54. German Lopez, "America's Pandemic Failures," *New York Times*, August 18, 2022; Luis Eugenio Portela Fernandes de Souza, Marcia Caldas Castro, Eduardo Hage Carmo, and Maurício Polidoro, "The Global Failure of Facing the Pandemic," *Global Health Action* 15, no. 1 (2022): 1–4.

55. "War on Drugs," Report of the Global Commission on Drug Policy, June 2011, https://www.globalcommissionondrugs.org/wp-content/themes/gcdp_v1/pdf/Global_Commission_Report_English.pdf.

56. "Opioid Billionaires: The Deceptive Marketing of OxyContin," *ProPublica .org*, July 25, 2021.

57. "Kevin McCarthy Shares Shocking Facts about Fentanyl," *Fox News*, January 28, 2022; Philip Bump, "Why You're Hearing So Much about Fentanyl These Days," *Washington Post*, July 15, 2022; Michelle L. Price "GOP Steps Up Crime Message in Midterm's Final Stretch," Associated Press, October 7, 2022; Melanie Zanona and Kristin Wilson, "Exclusive: Kevin McCarthy Previews

Republicans' Plans for the Majority—Starting at the Border," *CNN*, November 7, 2022; Matt Welch, "The Republican Primary Consensus for Sending the Military into Mexico," *Reason,* May 24. 2023.

58. Pew Research Center, "Americans' Dismal Views of the Nation's Politics," September 19, 2023; Lydia Saad, "Historically Low Faith in U.S. Institutions Continues," Gallup, July 6, 2023; "Satisfaction with the United States," Gallup August 2023.

Acknowledgments

I have been thinking about this book for over three decades. I was an undergraduate at Temple University when I first heard the reference to "the Badlands" in the local media. It was not a straight line from there, but this book and I have benefited from the tangents and false starts.

This project would have been far more difficult without the digitization of archival sources. I am grateful to the archivists at the presidential libraries for making a range of documents available to researchers. I am also thankful for the tireless efforts of the National Security Archive at George Washington University to have documents released under the Freedom of Information Act. Special thanks go to Malcolm Byrne and the late John Prados for their commitment and example to other scholars. Online collections hosted by the Federation of American Scientists helped fill in important gaps in archival collections.

I am also grateful for the work of leading investigative journalists, especially Radley Balko, Seymour Hersh, Jeremy Scahill, Liliana Segura, and Nick Turse. This study benefited from their reporting and collections of leaked documents.

I am thankful for the excellent oral histories compiled by the Miller Center at the University of Virginia and the Association for Diplomatic Studies and Training's Foreign Affairs Oral History Program.

I benefited from the generosity of fellow scholars and friends. The research and writing of Kyle Burke, Jeremy Kuzmarov, Alfred McCoy, and Stuart Schrader informed this book. I am grateful to Daniel Sargent for his continuing guidance. I am indebted to Christopher Shaw, who was kind enough to review the manuscript in different stages and offered numerous thoughtful suggestions for improvement. Thanks to Yaman and Waseem Salahi for their insights and suggestions for this project. Thanks to Ervand Abrahamian, Paul Thomas Chamberlin, Nate Citino, Murat Dagli, Richard Immerman, Deepa Kumar, and Priya Satia for their support.

Special thanks to my colleagues at Syracuse: Susan Branson, Andrew Wender Cohen, Norman Kutcher, Ken Harper, Craige Champion, and David Bennett. Thanks to Mohammad Ebad Athar and Timothy Michael Collier for their assistance in support of the project. Syracuse's Maxwell School and History Department provided essential funding that helped with the book's completion. Thanks to Dean David Van Slyke, Associate Dean Carol Faulkner, the Frank and Helen Pellicone Faculty Scholar Program, and the Pigott Fund.

I presented aspects of this project at the annual Society for Historians of American Foreign Relations Conference and the Maghreb Studies Association Conference. Thanks to Mohamed Ben-Madani. Elements of Chapters 2 and 3 were examined in "The Radical Crescent: The United States, the Palestine Liberation Organisation, and the Lebanese Civil War, 1973–1978," *Diplomacy & Statecraft* 27, no. 3 (2016): 496–522. I explored some aspects of Chapters 3 and 4 in "Cold War Twilight: The United States, the Soviet Union, and the Middle East in the American Imagination," *Maghreb Review* 43, no. 5 (2020): 522–535. Thanks to the publishers for their consideration.

Special thanks to Joseph Stoll and the Syracuse University Cartographic Laboratory for creating the maps for this book. The maps were developed using OpenStreetMap (openstreetmap.org/copyright) as a data source and modified with my input. I consulted various sources in the creation of several maps here. Maps 2 and 9 benefited from reporting by *Al Jazeera* and the United Nations Relief and Works Agency; Maps 3 and 11 incorporate information from the United Nations Office on Drugs and Crime; Maps 5 and 10 drew on data collected by AirWars.org and the Bureau for Investigative Journalism; Map 6 benefited from Paul Moorcraft, *Total Onslaught: War and Revolution in Southern Africa Since 1945* (Yorkshire: Pen and Sword Books, 2018); Map 7 was informed by reporting in the *Philadelphia Inquirer*; Maps 8 and 12 drew on reports by *Insight Crime*; and Map 13 uses information from Gareth Stansfield and Mohammed Shareef, eds., *The Kurdish Question Revisited* (London: Hurst, 2017). Arabic transliterations are based on the *International Journal of Middle East Studies* standards, with some modifications for readability and common names. Any errors in the maps or transliterations are mine.

Andrew Kinney was a tireless advocate for this project. I am grateful for his support and encouragement throughout and will miss our Zoom calls. Special thanks to Emily Silk for adopting the book, to Julia Kirby for helping to improve it, and Jamie Armstrong and the Amnet ContentSource staff for overseeing production. Thanks to the anonymous reviewers for their feedback and suggestions.

My former professor and dear friend Howard Spodek passed away before this book was published. He was a constant source of encouragement and a wonderful example to future scholars. I am saddened that he won't be able to read this book and will miss him.

My wife, Dalal Yassine, has been exceptionally patient and supportive. She has helped this project in large and small ways that are too numerous to count. I am thankful for her keen insights and grace. My daughter, Laila, has been a great research assistant in support of this book. She was always eager to offer ideas for titles and cover designs (and encouraging me to finish so we could spend more time together). It has been a joy to watch her develop into a promising writer in her own right. This book is dedicated to them.

Index

Page numbers followed by *fig* indicate maps.

Abbas, Mahmoud, 217
Abizaid, John, 264
Abrams, Creighton, 44
Abu Ghraib prison, 208–209, 223, 257
Abu Nidal Organization (ANO), 121–123, 125
Acheson, Dean, 26, 79
Addington, David, 190
AEDPA. *see* Antiterrorism and Effective Death Penalty Act (AEDPA)
Afghanistan: Abu Ghraib prison and, 208–209, 223, 257; "Afghan Arabs," 102–103; Afghan National Security Forces (ANSF), 237, 240–241; Carter administration and, 99–103; drone strikes and, 191, 228*fig*, 233–234, 237, 243–247; Egyptian support and, 103; funding of anti-Soviet insurgency in, 100–104; Geneva Conventions and, 191–192; Islamic Alliance for the Liberation of Afghanistan, 102; Islamic Unity of Afghan Mujahideen, 102; Karzai government, 227–230, 235, 237, 261; map of, 228*fig*; National Islamic Front of Afghanistan, 102; night raids and, 255; Obama administration, 234–242, 261; opium economy and, 229–230, 234–236, 252; Pakistan and, 226–227; People's Democratic Party of Afghanistan, 100; Reagan administration and, 103–104, 139; Society of Islam (*Jamaat-i-Islami*) and, 102; Soviet invasion of, 99–101; Taliban and, 182, 212, 227, 229–230, 294; Trump administration and, 293–294; US withdrawal from, 294; Vietnamization and, 212–213
Afghan National Security Forces (ANSF), 237, 240–241
Agent Orange defoliant, 50
Aideed, Mohammad Farrah, 159–161
Akhtar Rahman, Abdur, 165
al-Arian, Sami, 195–196
al-Awlaki, Anwar, 244–245
al-Banna, Sabri (Abu Nidal), 121–122
Aldouri, Mohammed, 199
Alexander, Michelle, 56
Algeria, 16–18, 181, 269
al-Harethi, Qaed Salim Sinan, 191
Allende, Salvador, 76

Alliance for the Restoration of Peace and
    Counter-Terrorism (ARPCT), 264
al-Maliki, Nouri, 280–281
al-Qa'ida in Iraq (AQI), 204, 214
al-Qa'ida network: "Afghan Arabs" and,
    102–103; Algerian civil war and, 181;
    American use of torture and, 191–194;
    Azzam and, 164–165; bin Laden and, 2, 174,
    179, 180; Clinton administration and,
    179–183; drone strikes and, 243–247;
    formation of, 165–166; Global War on Terror
    and, 187; Lackawanna Six and, 191; Pakistan
    and, 227; Somalia and, 166; Taliban and,
    186–187; Terrorism Screening Database
    (TSDB) and, 248; UN Security Council
    Resolution 1390 and, 188; US embassy
    bombings, 180, 182; USS Cole attack and,
    181–182; World Islamic Front and, 179;
    Zarqawi and, 204–205
al-Shabaab, 264–268, 293
al-Shiraa, 133
al-Zawahiri, Ayman, 165, 186, 202, 227
American Civil Liberties Union (ACLU), 193,
    245, 258
American Enterprise Institute, 128, 134
American Friends of Vietnam (AFV), 7–8
American Gangster (Scott), 67
American Israel Public Affairs Committee
    (AIPAC), 215
American popular culture alignment with
    foreign policy and, 5, 221–224, 258, 298
Ames, Robert, 88, 118
Amin, Hafizullah, 100–101
Anderson, David, 45–46
Angleton, James Jesus, 37, 57
Angola, 81–82, 125–126, 127fig, 128–130,
    139
Anslinger, Harry, 71
anthrax, 189, 202
Anti-Drug Abuse Act (1986), 113, 134
Anti-Drug Abuse Law (1988), 147–149
Antiterrorism and Effective Death Penalty Act
    (AEDPA), 172–173
antiwar movement: Algeria and, 17; civil rights
    movement and, 34–35; COINTELPRO
    program and, 96; Continental US
    Intelligence Program break in and, 56–57;
    domestic surveillance and, 56–57; Iraq and,
    202; Johnson administration and, 54; killing
    students and, 50; Nixon administration and,
    54, 57; Nixon's anti-drug campaign and,
    61–64
Arab-Israeli (June 1967), 40, 41fig, 42–43, 60,
    90fig, 115

Arab-Israeli War (October 1973), 60
Arab League, 270, 290
Arafat, Yasir, 40, 46, 57, 59–60, 88–89, 117,
    122, 167, 215–216
Argov, Shlomo, 116
Arias, Oscar, 108
Armitage, Richard, 218
Army of the Republic of Vietnam (ARVN),
    43–44, 46, 49
Aronson, Bernard, 178
Asad, Hafiz al-, 60, 91–92, 117, 272–274
Ashcroft, John, 195
asset forfeiture, 63, 135–136, 226, 297
Atef, Mohammad, 191
Atkinson, Leslie "Ike," 64
Atta, Mohammad, 200
AUC (United Self Defense Forces of Colombia),
    174
Aweys, Hassan Dahir, 264
Azzam, Abdullah Yusuf, 164–165

Baader-Meinhof group, 58
Ba'th Party (Iraq), 85–86, 203
Ba'th Party (Syria), 91
Badlands (Philadelphia), 141, 142fig, 143
Baer, Robert, 192
Baghdadi, Abu Bakr al-, 280–283
Baker, James, 155, 163
Balko, Radley, 61, 255
Bannon, Steve, 279–280
Barak, Ehud, 215, 218
Barbary Pirates, 47–48
Barre, Mohammad Siad, 93, 157
Barrientos, René, 31
Barzani, Mustafa, 85–86
The Base group, 295
Bashir, Omar al-, 166
Battle of Algiers, The (Pontecorvo), 17–18, 223
Baum, Dan, 95–96
Beers, R. Rand, 175
Begin, Menachem, 116
Berger, Samuel "Sandy," 159, 179–181
Bias, Len, 113
Biden administration, 280, 283, 288–289
Biden, Joe, 2, 170, 237
Bigelow, Kathryn, 258
bin al-Shibh, Ramzi, 227
bin Laden, Osama: anti-Soviet activities in
    Afghanistan, 103; Clinton administration
    and, 179, 181–182; death of Azzam and, 165;
    election of 2004 and, 208; escape from
    Afghanistan and, 186, 227; fatwa of 1998,
    179; killing of, 1–2, 234; Saudi Arabia and,
    165–166; Taliban and, 182–183, 186; UN

Security Council Resolution 1390 and, 188; Zarqawi and, 204

Black Americans: Black Panther Party (BPP) and, 17, 56; California and, 150–151; Detroit riot (1967) and, 35–36; Newark riot (1967) and, 35; Rockefeller drug laws and, 69–70; surveillance and, 35, 39; 151 War on Crime and, 33–37; War on Drugs and, 95–96, 150–151

Black Panther Party (BPP), 17, 56

Black September Organization (BSO), 57–60

Blair, Dennis, 237

Blair, Tony, 200–201

Blood, Archer, 100

Boland, Edward, 106–107

Bolivia, 30–31, 148

Bordaberry, Juan Maria, 75

Bosnia and Herzegovina, 162, 162–164, 166

Botha, P. W., 129–130

Boutros-Ghali, Boutros, 158, 163

Boykin, William, 213

Braun, Michael, 253

Breitbart, Andrew, 279

Breitbart News, 278–280

Bremer, L. Paul, 203, 205

Brennan, John, 258–259

Brezhnev, Leonid, 101

Brown, Dean, 49, 91

Brown, Michael, 256

Brown, Pat, 54

Bruce, David, 8

Brzezinski, Zbigniew, 100–102

Buckley, William, 118

Bundy, McGeorge, 26

Bundy, William, 25–26

Bureau of Narcotics and Dangerous Drugs (BNDD), 63, 71–72

Burke, Arleigh, 9

Burma, 65

Bush, George H. W.: Bosnia and, 162; Iran-Contra affair and, 133; OpBat Task Force and, 131; Persian Gulf War and, 156; Terrorism Incident Working Group and, 121

Bush, George H. W., administration: Draft Defense Planning Guidance (1992), 156–157; drug policy of, 147–153; First Persian Gulf War and, 155–157; National Security Directive (NSD) 13 and, 147; NSD 21 and, 154; Panama and, 153–155; Somalia and, 157–159; Yugoslavia crisis, 162–164

Bush, George W.: bullhorn speech and, 185–186, 208, 231; drone strikes and, 243–244; Iraq War and, 198; "Mission Accomplished" speech of, 203; reelection of, 194, 206–208; torture and, 193

Bush, George W., administration: Abu Ghraib prison scandal and, 208–209, 223, 257; Afghanistan and, 186–187, 226–230; Africa Command (AFRICOM) and, 265; Algeria and, 181; anthrax attacks and, 189; bin Laden and, 183; Colombia and, 224–226; Department of Homeland Security (DHS) and, 194–195; domestic antiterrorism measures, 250–251; drone strikes and, 191, 233–234, 237, 243–244; drug policy and, 183, 230; EO 13224 and, 188; Hollywood and, 221–224, 298; Hurricane Katrina and, 214; Iraq War and, 197–206, 210–211, 231; mass surveillance and, 194, 250–251; Mexico and, 261–262; Middle East and, 214–221; NSPD 9 and, 187–188; secret bases and, 192; Taliban and, 186, 212, 239, 241; torture and, 191–194, 256–257; 2008 financial crisis and, 231–232; "unitary executive theory" and, 190; USA PATRIOT Act and, 189; Vietnam War service and, 206; War on Terror and, 186–190, 229–231

Bustani, Emile, 88

Byrd, Harry, Jr., 81–82

Byrd, Robert, 160

Cabinet Committee to Combat Terrorism, 59

Calderón, Felipe, 260–263

Calleo, David, 137

Camarena, Enrique "Kiki," 112

Cambodia, 29, 48–50, 54

Campaign Against Marijuana Production (CAMP), 110–112

Camp X-Ray, 209

Carlucci, Frank, 121

Carter, Jimmy: the Arab-Israeli conflict and, 95; Carter Doctrine and, 99–100; 1980 State of the Union address and, 99

Carter administration: Afghanistan and, 99–103; Angola and, 125–126; Arab-Israeli conflict and, 93, 95, 116; "arc of crisis" and, 101; Byrd Amendment and, 82; 1980 Presidential election and, 98–99; and Somalia, 93, 94*fig*, 95

Carver, George, 26

Casey, Lee A., 220–221

Casey, William, 103

Castor, Betty, 195–196

CBS News, 114–115

Center for Constitutional Rights, 245

Central Intelligence Agency (CIA): Abu Nidal Organization (ANO) and, 125; Afghanistan and, 103; Angola and, 82; bin Laden and, 181–182; Black September Organization

Central Intelligence Agency (CIA) (*continued*)
(BSO) and, 58–59; Bruce/Lovett report on,
8; cocaine trafficking and, 135; on Colombia,
151; Conus Intel operation, 38; Cuba and, 9;
Demographics Unit of, 248–249;
destabilization of Lebanon and, 118; domestic
political unrest and, 37–38; domestic
surveillance and, 56, 86–87; drone
assassinations in War on Terror, 191, 245;
Gorbachev and, 137; Guevara and, 31;
Honduras and, 108; Iran and, 8, 84, 87;
Iran-Contra scandal and, 132–133; Karzai
and, 228–229; Kuomintang (KMT) and, 65;
Mandela and, 130; on Mexico, 75; National
Security Council Directive 5412 and, 8;
Operation CHAOS, 37–38, 57; paramilitary
forces of, 120; Palestine Liberation
Organization (PLO) and, 88; Safari Club
agreement and, 92–93; Somalia and, 159,
265; Syria and, 273–274; tensions with US
military over Vietnamese insurgency and, 22;
torture program and, 191–193, 256–259;
Vietnamese National Police and, 25; *Zero
Dark Thirty* (Bigelow) and, 258–259
Chad, 123
Chancellor, John, 158
Cheney, Dick, 154–157, 188–190, 194, 197–198,
200
Chertoff, Michael, 189–190
Chile, 76
China, 82, 275, 288, 290
Christopher, Warren, 164
Church Commission (1975), 87, 120
CIA Appropriations Act (1975), 82–83
Citizens' Commission to Investigate the FBI, 56
Civil Operations and Revolutionary
Development Support (CORDS) program,
23–25, 31, 212
Clark Amendment, 126, 128
Clarke, Victoria, 198
Clarridge, Duane, 122
"Clash of Civilizations" (Huntington), 183
Cleaver, Eldridge, 17
Cleaver, Emanuel, 256
Clifford, Clark, 26, 116
Clinton, Bill, 160, 166, 169–170, 174, 180, 184
Clinton, Hillary, 273, 278
Clinton administration: al-Qaʻida network and,
179–183; anti-terrorism policies and,
171–173, 184; bin Laden and, 179, 181–182;
Bosnia crisis and, 163–164, 166; Colombia
and, 173–176; crime policies and, 170–172,
174; drug policies of, 170, 173–174; drug
policy and, 109; Executive Order 12978 and,

173; Executive Order 13099 and, 180; FARC
and, 174–178; habeas corpus petitions and,
109; Middle East and, 166–169, 215–216;
Oklahoma City bombing, 149, 171–172;
Presidential Decision Directive (PDD) 14
and, 170; Russia and, 179; Rwandan genocide
and, 161; Somalia and, 159–161
cocaine: Columbia and, 75, 226; Contras and,
108, 130–131; fallacies in approaches to, 301;
Mexico and, 75, 260–264; Plan Colombia
and, 174–178, 224–226; race and, 70. *See also*
crack cocaine; drugs; War on Drugs
Cohen, Roger, 202
Cohen, William, 156
Colby, William, 22, 24–25
Cold War: American Friends of Vietnam (AFV)
and, 7; American reception of Gorbachev
and, 138; American rhetoric around colonial
territories, 3; Congo and, 30; Cuban Missile
Crisis, 9; Huk insurgency and, 13–14;
Huntington on aftermath of, 183; NSA and,
38; Reagan administration and, 138–139;
student protest during, 55; triumphalism
after, 5; US domestic policy and, 5; War for
Civilization narrative and, 4. *See also
individual administrations*
Cole, David, 191
Colombia: Antiterrorism and Effective Death
Penalty Act (AEDPA), 173; asset forfeiture,
226; George H. W. Bush administration and,
148; George W. Bush administration and,
224–226; Clinton administration and,
173–176; drug trafficking and, 75–76;
Escobar and, 151, 173; FARC and, 174–178,
224–226; heroin and, 234; internal drug
policies of, 226; *Los Pepes* and, 174–175; mass
surveillance and, 225–226; Obama
administration and, 261, 277; United
Self-Defense Forces of Colombia, 225
Comprehensive Drug Abuse Prevention and
Control Act (1970), 63
Congo, 30
Congress: Anti-Drug Abuse Act (1986),
113–115; Cold War and, 106–107, 128–129,
297; Clinton administration and, 172–173;
Crime Bill and, 170, 172–173; Intelligence
Reform Act (2004), 195; International
Emergency Economic Powers Act (IEEPA),
173; Iran-Contra investigation and, 133–135;
Iraq War and, 201; Johnson administration
and, 33, 37; legislation around crime, drugs,
and terror, 297; narcoterrorism law and,
251–252, 297; Obama administration and,
276; post-September 11 vote authorization of

force, 186; Reagan administration and, 106–107, 113–114, 128–129; Senate Intelligence Committee Report on torture program, 194, 256–259; torture program investigations and, 256–259; Trump administration and, 295; USA PATRIOT Act and, 189, 251, 253, 295; War on Drugs and, 62–63, 71–72, 113–114; Watergate investigation and, 57, 72, 297
Contras, 104–108, 130–136
Controlled Substances Act (1970), 63
Convention on Psychotropic Substances (1971), 71
Costa Rica, 131
Cotes, Jorge Noguera, 226
Countering Violent Extremism (CVE) initiative, 266–267
COVID-19 pandemic, 288, 292, 301, 303
Cox, Donald L., 17
crack cocaine, 131, 143, 148, 150. See also cocaine; drugs; War on Drugs
crime: asset forfeiture and, 63, 135–136, 226, 297; Clinton administration and, 170–172; Controlled Substances Act (1970), 63; DC Court Reform and Criminal Procedure Act (1970), 62; death penalty and, 170; incarceration and drug convictions, 69–71; Johnson administration and, 33, 37; Law Enforcement Assistance Act (1965) and, 33; media coverage and, 170; militarization of police and, 148–150, 254–256; Nixon administration and, 54–55, 61–64; Nixon's linking of civil rights with, 55; Nixon's linking of drugs with, 62; Organized Crime Control Act (1970), 63; portrayal of as symptoms of American decline, 6; racialization of, 6, 37; Reagan administration and, 99, 108; RICO provisions and, 63; Rockefeller drug laws and, 67–72; student protests and, 54; Task Force on Violent Crime, 108–109; Uniform Crime Report (UCR) and, 33–34
criminal justice system: Abu Ghraib military police and, 209; asset forfeiture and, 63, 135–136, 297; death penalty and, 170–171; mass incarceration, 69–71, 151; minorities and, 151; "no knock" warrants, 62–63; police brutality, 35–36, 143–144, 184; police corruption, 96, 143–144; pretrial release, 62; prison culture, 209; prison funding, 114, 149, 171; prison mistreatment, 209; prison sentences, 148, 151, 171
Croatia, 162
Cromitie, James, 250

Crowther, Bosley, 17
Cuba, 9, 82–83, 120, 154, 191, 193
Cuban Missile Crisis, 9, 29, 38
cyberattacks, 287

D'Amato, Alfonse, 113
Daoud, Mohammad, 100
Dayan, Moshe, 42
Dayton Accords, 166, 178
DC Court Reform and Criminal Procedure Act (1970), 63
Dean, John, 61
Defense Authorization Act (1982), 109
de Gaulle, Charles de, 18
Delvalle, Eric Arturo, 154
Demirel, Süleyman, 73
Democratic National Convention (Charlotte, 2012), 2
Democratic National Convention (Chicago, 1968), 39
Department of Homeland Security, 189, 194–195, 255–256
DePuy, William, 26
Derwish, Kamel, 191
Detroit riots (1967), 35, 53
Díaz Ordaz, Gustavo, 74
Diem, Ngo Dinh, 12, 14, 19, 28
District of Columbia, 61–63
Dolgen, Jonathan, 221
domestic surveillance, 29, 38, 56–59, 86–87, 96, 194, 247–251, 298–299
Donovan, William "Will Bill," 7
Dostum, Abdul Rashid, 229
drone assassinations, 191, 233–234, 237, 243–247, 267–268, 298
Drug Enforcement Administration (DEA): budget of, 72; Chile and, 76; crack cocaine and, 148; establishment of, 71–72; international reach of, 72; Mexico and, 112, 174, 261; OpBat Task Force and, 131; Patriot Act and narcoterrorism, 251, 253–254, 276; Reagan administration and, 114–115; telephone records and (USTO program), 151–152
Drug Policy Alliance, 70
drugs: Afghanistan and, 229–230, 234–236, 252; alternative approaches to, 300–302; in American popular culture, 112–113; Badlands (Philadelphia) and, 141, 142fig, 143; border policy and, 109; Contras and, 132; Controlled Substances Act and, 63; crack cocaine, 131; decriminalization of, 300–301; heroin trade and, 64–65, 67; Mexico and, 74–75, 260–263, 290–292;

drugs (*continued*)
  militarization of efforts to combat, 109–110;
    Nixon administration and, 54, 61–64; Plan
    Colombia and, 174–178, 224–226; policy of
    George H. W. Bush administration and,
    147–153; returning soldiers from Vietnam
    and, 64; Rockefeller drug laws and, 67–72;
    Task Force on Violent Crime, 108–109;
    Vietnam War and, 64–65, 67. *See also* War on
    Drugs, *individual types*
Dukakis, Michael, 146–147
Dulles, Allen, 8–9, 14
Dulles, John Foster, 14

Eagleburger, Lawrence, 162–163
Egypt: Arab-Israel conflict and, 40, 42–43;
    Arab-Israeli War (June 1967), 40, 41*fig*,
    42–43; Arab-Israel War (1973) and, 60, 87;
    CIA covert operations in, 8–9; Egyptian
    Islamic Jihad, 103; Egypt-Israel Peace Treaty
    (1979), 95, 116; Mubarak and, 269; Obama
    administration and, 269; Palestine Liberation
    Organization (PLO) and, 43
Egyptian Islamic Jihad (EIJ), 103, 165, 179;
    Global War on Terror and, 188
Ehrlichman, John, 61–62, 95–96
Eikenberry, Karl, 238–239
Eilts, Hermann, 92
Eisenhower, Dwight, 8, 17
Ellsberg, Daniel, 26
Enders, Tom, 107
Enhanced Interrogation (Mitchell), 193
Enthoven, Alain, 23
Ermarth, Fritz, 101
Escobar, Pablo, 151, 173
Ethiopia: conflict with Somalia and, 93, 94*fig*,
    95; Obama-era intervention in Somalia,
    264–265

Fadlallah, Sayyid Muhammad Hussein, 120,
    167
Faller, Craig, 290
FARC, 174–178, 177*fig*
Fatah, 40, 43, 46, 57, 61, 89, 167, 215
fedayeen, 40, 43, 46–48
Federal Bureau of Investigation (FBI):
    antiterrorism measures and, 249–251; antiwar
    group break in of Continental US Intelligence
    Program and, 56–57; antiwar movement and,
    56; COINTELPROs of, 39, 56–57; domestic
    surveillance and, 56; Foreign Intelligence
    Surveillance Act (FISA) and, 295; National
    Counter-Terrorism Center, 195; Operation
    CHAOS (CIA) and, 38; paramilitary forces

of, 120; Terrorist Screening Center and, 195;
    Terrorist Threat Integration Center, 195;
    Uniform Crime Report (UCR), 33
Feinstein, Diane, 259
Feith, Douglas, 187
Fiers, Alan, Jr., 135
5412 Group, 8
Fleischer, Ari, 200
Floyd, George, 303
Flynn, Michael, 278–279
Ford administration, 75, 82–83, 119
Ford, Gerald, 83, 86, 96
Foreign Intelligence Surveillance Act (FISA),
    295
Fortner, Michael Javen, 69
France, 16–17, 92–93, 270–271
Frederick, Ivan, 209
Freedom House, 128
Free Syrian Army (FSA), 272–273
French Connection (Friedkin), 64
Friends of Rhodesian Independence, 80–81

Gailani, Sayed Ahmed, 102
gangs, 143, 150, 292
Gates, Robert, 138, 213, 215, 237, 240, 243
Gates, Thomas, Jr., 12
Gemayel, Bashir, 117
Geneva Accords (1954), 7, 14, 16
Geneva Conventions, 191–192
Germany: anxieties about American decline
    and, 136–137; Yugoslavia crisis and, 162
Global War on Terror: George W. Bush
    administration and, 186–188; Bush campaign
    for reelection, 199–200; Civil Operations and
    Rural Development Support (CORDS)
    program, 212; costs of, 296; DEA USTO
    program and, 152–153; domestic
    counterterrorism, 247–251; domestic
    extremists, 295; domestic surveillance and,
    29, 38, 56–57, 86–87, 194, 247–251,
    298–299; drone assassination program, 191,
    233–234, 237, 243–247, 267–268, 298;
    Geneva Conventions and, 191–192; Hollywood
    and, 221–224, 231, 297; immigration laws
    and, 196–197; Joint Special Operations
    Command (JSOC) and, 213; lessons from
    Nixon administration's war on crime, 62;
    mass surveillance, 194; militarization of police
    and, 149; Palestine and, 216; presentation of,
    3; racial profiling and, 248–249; Reagan
    administration policies and, 139–140; secret
    bases, 192; Somalia and, 264–265; targeting
    of financial networks and, 188; torture
    program and, 191–194, 223, 256–259, 298;

Vietnamization and, 212; as war for Civilization, 186, 199–200, 215, 231, 295–297; War on Crime and, 234, 247–251; War on Drugs and, 234, 251–254
Godane, Ahmad Abdi, 268
Golden Triangle (Southeast Asia), 64–65, 66fig, 67
Goldsmith, Jack, 190
Gonzalez, Alberto, 192, 250–251
Gorbachev, Mikhail, 136–138
Graham, Lindsey, 270, 292
Groupe Islamique Armé (GIA), 181
Guantanamo Bay base, 191, 193, 209, 256–259
guerilla warfare, 106
Guerrilla Warfare (Guevara), 106
Guevara, Ernesto "Che," 29–31

habeas corpus petitions, 109
Habib, Philip, 25–26, 116
Hadi, Abdu Rabbu Mansour, 285
Haftar, Khalifa, 285
Haig, Alexander, 123, 128
Halberstam, David, 26
Halperin, Morton, 29
Hamas: Clinton administration and, 180; Israel and, 168–169, 216–217; Global War on Terror and, 188, 201, 248–249; Hizbullah and, 219–220; Palestinian Authority and, 215–217
Hanifi, Shah Mahmoud, 229
Haqqani, Jalaluddin, 102–103
Hariri, Rafiq al-, 218–219
Hariri, Saad, 220
Harris, Lillian, 123
Hasenfus, Eugene, 132
Hassan II, King of Morocco, 95
Hawkins, Paula, 113
Hayden, Michael, 244, 265
Hekmatyar, Gulbuddin, 102
Helms, Richard, 37, 56
Henderson, Douglas, 31
Heritage Foundation, 128
heroin: Clinton administration and, 174; Controlled Substances Act and, 63; crack cocaine and, 150; fallacies in approaches to, 301; global trafficking of, 235fig; Golden Triangle drug trade and, 64–65, 67; Harlem heroin trade and, 64–65, 67; race and, 95–96; Rockefeller drug laws and, 67–70. *See also* drugs; War on Drugs
Hersh, Seymour, 56
Hinton, Elizabeth, 33, 36
Hizbullah: assassination attempt on Fadlallah and, 120; Biden administration and, 289;

George W. Bush administration and, 219–220; Clinton administration and, 166–169, 180; drug trafficking and, 119, 288–289; Future movement and, 220; insurgency during Iraq War and, 205; Iraq War and, 201; ISIS and, 274; Israel and, 217–219; in Lebanon, 118–119, 166–168, 219–220; Obama administration and, 288–289; Palestine Liberation Organization (PLO) and, 167–168; September 11 attacks and, 218; Syria and, 274; Terrorism Screening Database (TSDB) and, 248; Trump administration and, 289; UN Security Resolution 1559 and, 219; War on Terror and, 188, 218
Hoagland, Jim, 178
Holbrooke, Richard: Afghanistan and, 238–239; lessons from Vietnam and, 25–28, 239; Yugoslavia crisis and, 163–164
Hollywood, 13, 17–18, 221–224, 231, 298
Honduras, 105–108; cocaine trade and, 131; Contras and, 131; Reagan and, 131–132
Hoover, J. Edgar, 35, 56
Houthi movement (*Ansar Allah*), 285–287
Howe, John, 159–160
HTS. *see* Organization for the Liberation of Syria (*Hay'at Tahrir al-Sham*)
Huk insurgency, 13–14
Human Rights Watch, 255
Huntington, Samuel, 183
Hurtado, Maria Pilar del, 226
Husayn, Zayn al-Abidin Muhammad (Abu Zubaydah), 192–193
Hussain, Shahed, 250
Hussein, King of Jordan, 43, 46–49, 91, 117
Hussein, Saddam, 85, 155–156, 200
Hyde, Henry J., 128, 251

IEEPA. *see* International Emergency Economic Powers Act (IEEPA)
Iger, Bob, 222
Ikenberry, G. John, 275
Illegal Immigration and Reform and Immigrant Responsibility Act, 172
immigration, 172–173, 196–197, 278–279, 292
incarceration, 33, 56, 69–71, 151, 171, 184, 300, 301
Indonesia, 9, 32–33
Inspire, 244
Intelligence Reform Act (2004), 195
International Emergency Economic Powers Act (IEEPA), 173
Iran: Hizbullah and, 119, 132, 167, 217; insurgency during Iraq War and, 205;

Iran (*continued*)
  Iran-Contra affair, 132; ISIS and, 287; Joint
    Comprehensive Plan of Action, 282, 287,
    303; Nixon administration and, 84–87;
    NSDD 138 and, 120; Quds Force and, 287;
    Revolution (1979), 95; Trump administration
    and, 287–288; war with Iraq and, 132, 155,
    287
Iran-Contra scandal, 122, 130–136
Iraq: conflation of with September 11 attacks,
    197, 202; First Persian Gulf War, 155–157;
    ISIS in, 280, 286–287; Kurds, 85–87; map
    of, 206*fig*; Obama administration and, 269;
    State of Law Alliance, 280; Reagan
    administration and, 132; Syrian civil war
    and, 281; Trump administration and,
    287–288; war with Iran and, 132. *See also*
    Iraq War
Iraqi-Soviet Treaty of Friendship and
    Cooperation (1972), 85
Iraq War: al-Qa'ida in Iraq (AQI) and, 204,
    214; Blair and, 200–201; Bush
    administration and, 197–206; CENTCOM
    and, 198–199; Coalition Provisional
    Authority (CPA), 203, 205–206, 210;
    counterinsurgency strategy (COIN) and, 213;
    execution of, 202–206; Fallujah and, 210;
    Guantanamo Bay base and, 209; insurgency
    and, 204–205, 210–211, 213; Iraqi security
    forces and, 203; Israeli-Palestine relations
    and, 216; killing of Uday and Qusay Hussein
    and, 204; false link to al-Qa'ida and, 200;
    map of, 206*fig*; messaging and, 198; "Mission
    Accomplished" speech, 203; night raids and,
    255; sectarian violence and, 211–212, 214;
    Shi'a militias and, 211; "surge" tactic, 214;
    Vietnamization and, 212–213; weapons of
    mass destruction and, 200
ISIS. *see* Islamic State in Iraq and al-Sham (ISIS)
Islamic Courts Union (Somalia, ICU), 264
Islamic Party (Afghanistan, *Hizb-i-Islam*), 102
Islamic Salvation Front (ISF), 181
Islamic State in Iraq and al-Sham (ISIS): drone
    strikes and, 284; emergence of, 274; funding
    of, 281–282; international opposition to, 282;
    Libya and, 284–285; Mosul and, 280; Nusra
    Front (*Jabhat al-Nusra*) and, 281; Obama
    administration and, 280–282; state
    sponsorship of, 281–282; Syria and, 274;
    Syrian refugees and, 279; Turkey's October
    2019 invasion and, 283; Yemen and, 286
Islamic Unity of Afghan Mujahideen, 102
Israel: Amal and, 167–168; assassination attempt
    on Argov and, 116; Bush administration and,

215–221; Christian evangelicals and, 215;
    Egypt-Israel Peace Treaty (1979), 95, 116;
    First Palestinian *intifada* and, 168–169; Ford
    administration and, 87–88; Gaza and,
    220–221; Hizbullah and, 167–168; Johnson
    administration and, 39–40, 41*fig*, 42;
    Lebanon and, 115–117, 167–169; Likud Party
    and, 95, 214; Munich Olympics attack and,
    58; Oslo Accords and, 169, 217, 218;
    Palestine Liberation Organization (PLO)
    and, 91–92, 115–117, 168–169, 217; Reagan
    administration and, 115–116; Second
    Palestinian *intifada* and, 215–216; South
    Lebanon Army (SLA) and, 167; Trump
    administration and, 287–288; Vietnam War's
    influence on, 42
Izetbegović, Alija, 164, 166

Jackson, Henry, 95
Jackson, Keith, 148
January 6 riots, 294–295, 304
Japan, 136–137
Jessen, Bruce, 193
Jiang Jieshi, 65
Joffe, Josef, 275
Johnson, Lyndon B., 11–12, 19, 33, 36
Johnson administration: antiwar protests and,
    54; Arab-Israeli conflict and, 39–40, 42;
    Arab-Israeli War (June 1967) and, 40, 42;
    assessment of insurgency during pacification
    and, 22–24; Bolivia and, 30–31; CORDS/
    Phoenix Program/Project Phung Hoang and,
    23–25, 31; definition of Viet Cong
    infrastructure and, 23; domestic political
    unrest and, 35–37; domestic surveillance and,
    38–39, 56; emphasis on counterinsurgency in
    Vietnam under, 21; Holbrooke and, 27–28;
    Indonesia and, 31–33; Omnibus Crime
    Control and Safe Streets Act (1968), 37;
    Operation Minaret, 38; Tet Offensive (1968)
    and, 24, 26, 43; Vietnamization of the war,
    44–46; Vietnam Task Force, 26; War on
    Crime and, 33–39; War on Poverty, 33
Join the Caravan (Azzam), 164–165
Jones, Jim, 237
Jordan, 43, 46–49, 57, 88, 269, 272
Julani, Abu Mohammed al-, 281
Juppé, Alain, 270
Justice Department, 38, 108, 151–152, 195–196,
    252
"Just Say No" Anti-Drug Campaign, 114

Kael, Pauline, 17
Karamessines, Thomas, 37

Karzai, Hamid, 227–230, 239
Katzenbach, Nicholas, 29
Keane, Barry, 111
Kennan, George, 9
Kennedy, John F., 7–9, 13, 17
Kennedy, Paul, 136–137
Kennedy, Robert F., 9
Kennedy administration, 18–19, 21, 27–28, 38
Kenya, 265
Kerner Commission (National Advisory
  Commission on Civil Disorders), 36–37
Kerr, Malcolm, 118
Kerry, John, 134, 153, 206
Khalaf, Salah, 125
Khalilzad, Zalmay, 156, 211
Khan, Samir, 244–245
Khrushchev, Nikita, 9
Kilcullen, David, 212
Kill the Messenger, 135
King, Martin Luther, Jr., 34–35, 38
King, Rodney, 184
Kirkpatrick, Jeane, 137
Kissinger, Henry, 29, 45; on Angola, 82–83;
  Arab-Israel War (1973) and, 60; Arafat and,
  59–60, 91; change of African policy and,
  83–84; domestic surveillance and, 56–57;
  "grand strategy" approach for foreign policy
  and, 54; Iran and, 84; on Iraq, 86–87; Israel
  and, 58, 87–88; Israeli-Egyptian negotiations
  and, 87–88; Lebanon and, 88–89, 91–92;
  Negroponte and, 107; Nixon Doctrine and,
  96; Operation Condor and, 77; Palestine
  Liberation Organization (PLO) and, 47–48,
  60–61, 91–92; Rhodesia and, 78, 84; Sinai II
  agreement, 88; Vietnam's effect on American
  standing and, 53–54; Zambia and, 82–83
Klain, Ron, 172
Komer, Robert, 20–21, 27, 32
Korean War, 14
Kosovo, 163
Krogh, Egil "Bud," Jr., 61–62
Ku Klux Klan, 39, 81
Kuomintang (KMT), 65
Kurds, 85–87, 283, 284fig
Kuwait Iraq invasion of, 155
Kuzmarov, Jeremy, 64

Laird, Melvin, 24, 44, 85
Lake, Anthony, 25, 28–29, 49–51, 159–161
Lansdale, Edward, 9, 12–14
Lansing, Sherry, 221
Laos, 20, 50, 54
law enforcement: Anti-Drug Abuse Act (1986)
  and international reach of, 114; George W.

Bush administration, 183; Countering
  Violent Extremism (CVE) initiative and, 267;
  crack cocaine crisis and, 143–144;
  militarization of, 109, 148–150, 254–256,
  276; military support for, 150; minorities
  and, 70, 150; Reagan administration and,
  109–110; Special Weapons and Tactics
  (SWAT) teams, 254–255. See also criminal
  justice system
Law Enforcement Assistance Act (1965), 33
Law Enforcement Assistance Administration, 63
Layne, Christopher, 275
Lebanese National Movement (LNM), 91
Lebanon: Amal and, 167–168; Christian militias
  in, 91; civil war in, 91–92, 115–119, 218;
  expulsion of Palestine Liberation
  Organization (PLO) from Jordan and,
  48–49; Hariri assassination and, 218–219;
  Hizbullah and, 166–167, 289; Iran-Contra
  affair and, 132; Israel's 1982 invasion of,
  116–117; Israel's "security zone" in, 115,
  167–168; Israel's 2006 invasion of and, 219;
  Lebanese National Movement (LNM), 91;
  PLO and, 43, 48–49, 87–89, 90fig, 91–92,
  117; Reagan administration and, 116–119;
  Shatila refugee camp massacre, 117; South
  Lebanon Army (SLA) and, 167
Lee, Barbara, 186
Lewis, Anthony, 178
Lewis, John, 34
Lewis, Samuel, 159
Libya: Abu Nidal Organization (ANO) and,
  122–123, 125; American oil embargo and,
  124; Chad and, 123; collapse and, 284–285;
  Dawn coalition and, 286; "Day of Rage"
  protests, 270; drone strikes and, 271; ISIS
  and, 284–285; National Transitional Council
  (NTC) and, 270–271; NSDD 138 and, 120;
  Obama administration and, 269–272, 276;
  Panama and, 154; Reagan administration
  and, 122–125; Sandinistas and, 123
Lodge, Henry Cabot, Jr., 28, 32
López Obrador, Andrés Manuel, 290
Lovett, Robert, 8
Lucas, Frank, 64–65, 67
Luce, Henry, 7
Lumumba, Patrice, 30
Luna, García, 261, 263
lysergic acid diethylamide (LSD), 63

Magsaysay, Ramon, 14
Malaya, 14, 16, 18
Malbin, Michael, 134
Malcolm X, 38

Mandela, Nelson, 130
Marenches, Alexandre de, 93
marijuana, 63, 74, 95–96, 110–112, 169, 300.
    See also drugs; War on Drugs
Martinez, Mel, 195–196
Massoud, Ahmed Shah, 102, 181–182, 229
McCaffery, Barry, 176
McCain, John, 256, 270, 275
McCarthy, Kevin, 302
McChrystal, Stanley, 238, 240
McConnell, Mitch, 134
McGovern, George, 56
McKiernan, David D., 237
McMahon, Colleen, 250
McMaster, H. R., 295–296
McNamara, Robert, 21, 23
McRaven, William, 1
McVeigh, Timothy, 171–172
Mead, Walter Russell, 137
media: Badlands and, 141; break in at US Army
    Continental US Intelligence Program and, 56;
    crack cocaine and, 143, 150; crime coverage
    and, 170; DEA and, 114–115; domestic
    surveillance of journalists and, 38; on
    Gorbachev, 138; Holbrooke and, 27;
    Iran-Contra affair and, 133; Operation
    Boulder and, 59; Pentagon Papers and, 27;
    Plan Colombia and, 178; Rockefeller drug laws
    and, 69; Somalia coverage and, 161; War on
    Drugs and, 114–115. See also Hollywood
Medina Mora, Eduardo, 260–261
Meet the Press, 208
Mehsud, Baitullah, 245–246
Mengistu, Haile Mariam, 93
Mercer, Rebekah, 279
Mercer, Robert, 279
Mexico: corruption and, 261, 263; crack cocaine
    and, 131; DEA and, 112, 174, 261; drug
    trafficking organizations in, 174, 260, 262fig,
    290–292; Ford administration and, 75; Gulf
    Cartel, 291; heroin and, 234; human rights
    concerns and, 261–262; Kennedy
    administration and, 75; Mérida Initiative,
    261–263; Nixon's War on Drugs and, 74–75;
    Obama administration and, 260–264, 277;
    Reagan administration's War on Drugs and,
    112; Sinaloa Cartel, 263, 291; Trump
    administration and, 292; Los Zetas and,
    290–292
Miami Herald, 105, 107
Miami Vice (television show), 112–113
Military Cooperation with Civilian Law
    Enforcement Agencies Act (1982), 109
Military Police, 208–209

Miller, Geoffrey, 209
Milošević Slobodan, 179
Mitchell, James, 193
Mitchell, John, 61, 72, 74
Mitchell, Parren, 56
modernization theory, 13
Mohabbat, Kabir, 182
Mohammad, Khaled Sheikh, 193, 227
Mohammad, Khan, 252–253
Moreno, Bernardo, 226
Morocco, 269
Morris, Roger, 29
Moussaoui, Zacarias, 189–190
Moyers, Bill, 42
Moynihan, Daniel Patrick, 61, 72–73, 137
Mozambique, 81
MPLA. see Popular Movement for the Liberation
    of Angola (MPLA)
Mubarak, Hosni, 117, 269
Mudd, Phil, 258
Mughniyeh, Imad, 167, 220
Muhandis, Abu Mahdi Al-, 286–288
Munich Olympics attack, 58, 96
Musharraf, Pervez, 226–227, 242
My Lai massacre (1968), 25

naloxone, 300
Namibia, 126, 127fig, 128, 130, 139
Nasrallah, Hassan, 274, 289
Nasser, Gamal Abdel, 9, 16, 40, 42–43, 49, 88
National Advisory Commission on Civil
    Disorders. See Kerner Commission
National Crime Victimization Survey (NCVS),
    171
National Defense Authorization Act (1990,
    1991), 148–149, 254
National Front for the Liberation of Angola
    (FNLA), 82
National Institute of Law Enforcement and
    Criminal Justice, 70
National Islamic Front of Afghanistan (Mahaz-e
    Milli-ye Islami-ye Afghanistan), 102
National Liberation Army (ELN, Colombia),
    177, 224
National Liberation Front (NLF, Algeria),
    16–17
National Liberation Front (NLF, Vietnam),
    12–13
National Mobilization Committee to End the
    War in Vietnam (Mobe), 39
National Security Action Memorandum
    (NSAM) 124, 18
National Security Agency (NSA), 38, 56, 57,
    152–153, 194

National Security Council (NSC), 8, 10, 29, 57, 73, 79, 101, 132–133
National Union for the Total Independence of Angola (UNITA), 82, 126, 128–130
Native Americans, 2–3
Negroponte, John, 26, 107–108, 199, 202, 210
neoconservative movement, 134, 137, 214
Netanyahu, Benjamin, 218
Neto, Agostinho, 125–126
Neumann, Ronald, 229–230
New Jack City (Van Peebles), 143
New Republic, The, 115
Newsweek, 115
New Yorker, 223
New York Times, 35, 47–48, 56, 59, 82, 113–114, 133, 136, 160, 186, 257–258
Nicaragua, 104–108, 120, 131–132, 139, 154
Nicaraguan Democratic Force, 104
Nichols, Terry, 171
Nixon, Richard: antiwar movement and, 54–56; Arab-Israel War (October 1973) and, 60; Cambodia and, 29; campaign for reelection, 52–53; domestic surveillance and, 57, 96; Israel and, 58; Kurds and, 86; pardon of, 86; race and, 77–78; Rockefeller and, 68; South Africa and, 80; on Vietnamization, 45; Watergate investigation, 57, 72, 297
Nixon administration: Africa and, 77–84; antiwar movement and, 54–56, 95; Arab-Israeli War (October 1973) and, 60; Byrd Amendment and, 81–82; Cabinet Committee to Combat Terrorism, 59; Cambodia and, 29, 48–49, 54; Detroit riots and, 35, 53; domestic surveillance and, 56–59, 96; Drug Enforcement Administration (DEA) and, 71–72; drug policy and, 61–64; "grand strategy" approach for foreign policy and, 54; Iran and, 84–87; Jordanian Civil War and, 57; Laos and, 54; Middle East and, 46–49; Munich Olympics attacks and, 58; My Lai massacre (1968) investigation, 25; Nixon Doctrine, 45–46, 57; Operation Boulder, 58–59; race and, 96; Rhodesia and, 78–80; Vietnamization, 44–46; Vietnam War and, 44–46, 48–49, 96; War on Crime and, 34, 54–55; War on Drugs and, 61–64, 96
"no knock" warrants, 62–63
Noriega, Manuel, 153–155
North, Oliver, 133, 135
North Atlantic Treaty Organization (NATO): Afghan National Security Forces (ANSF) and, 240–241; Committee on the Challenges of Modern Society, 72–73; Kosovo and, 179;

Libya and, 269–272, 284; night raids and, 255; opium trade in Afghanistan and, 252; Ukraine and, 296; Yugoslavia crisis and, 163–164
Nusra Front (*Jabhat al-Nusra*), 272–274, 281, 283
Nye, Joseph, 275

Oakley, Robert, 160
Oath Keepers, 295
Obama, Barack, 1, 233, 237
Obama administration: Afghanistan and, 234–242; American decline narrative, 275–276; Benghazi consulate and, 271–272; Colombia and, 261, 277; Countering Violent Extremism (CVE) initiative and, 266–267; counternarcotics efforts in Afghanistan and, 234–236, 276–277; domestic counterterror efforts, 247–251, 276; domestic surveillance and, 254, 276; drone strikes and, 233–234, 237, 243–247, 267–268, 271, 277; Executive Order 13688 and, 256; Hizbullah and, 288–289; Hollywood and, 298; Iran and, 286; Iraq and, 277, 280–281; ISIS and, 280–282; Karzai government and, 237–239; Libya intervention and, 269–272, 276; Mexico and, 260–264, 277; Middle East and, 221, 268–275; militarization of law enforcement and, 256, 276–277; Pakistan and, 236, 242–243, 245–246; Project Colombia and, 234; Somalia and, 264–268; "surge" tactic and, 214, 237, 262; Syria and, 272–274, 276; torture program and, 256–259; 2008 financial crisis and, 275; Yemen and, 285–286
O'Connell, Jack, 88, 91
Office of National Drug Control Policy, 251
Oklahoma City bombing, 149, 171–173
Oman, 269
Omar, Mohammad, 186, 234, 236
Omnibus Crime Control and Safe Streets Act (1968), 37
O'Neill, Thomas P. "Tip," Jr., 113
Operation Bahamas, Turks, and Caicos (OpBat), 131
Operation Boulder, 58–59
Operation CHAOS (CIA), 37–38
Operation Condor, 75–76, 96
Operation Intercept, 74–75
Operation JMATE, 9
Operation Just Cause, 153
Operation Minaret (NSA), 38–39
Operation Mongoose, 9
Operation Neptune's Spear, 1–2

Operation Rolling Thunder, 11
Operation Shock and Awe (Buffalo, NY), 255
opioid epidemic, 302
Organization for the Liberation of Syria (*Hay'at Tahrir al-Sham*), 283–284
Organized Crime Control Act (1970), 63
Ortiz, Frank, 75–76
Oslo Accords, 169

Pahlavi, Mohammad Reza Shah, 84–86, 95
Pakistan: Bush administration and, 226–227, 236; casualties from Afghan War and, 227; drone strikes and, 228*fig*, 233–234, 237, 243–247; Federally Administered Tribal Areas (FATA), 236; internal unrest and, 227; Karzai government and, 227–228; map of, 228*fig*; Obama administration and, 236, 242–243, 245–246; Pakistani Taliban (*Tehrik-e-Taliban Pakistan*, TTP), 245–246; Taliban and, 182, 236, 242–243
Pakistani Taliban (*Tehrik-e-Taliban Pakistan*, TTP), 245–246
Palestine Liberation Organization (PLO), 43, 46–49; al-Banna and, 122, 125; BSO and, 57–60; internal tension in Lebanon and, 117; Israel's 1982 invasion of Lebanon and, 116–117; Lebanese para-state and, 88–89, 90*fig*, 91–92, 116; narcotics trafficking and, 89; Nixon administration and, 60–61; Oslo Accords and, 169, 217, 218; Qaddafi and, 123; Reagan administration and, 128; Soviet Union and, 119
Palestine War of 1948, 39–40
Palestinian Authority, Abbas and, 217; Arafat and, 215–216
Palestinian Islamic Jihad (PIJ), 180, 195; Fatah and, 215
Palestinian refugee camps, 39–40, 41*fig*, 42–43, 49, 89, 91, 167
Panama, 153–155
Panetta, Leon, 237, 273
Paris Peace Accords (1973), 45
Pastora, Eden (Comandante Cero), 105, 135
Pastrana, Andrés, 175–178
Patriot Act, 189–191, 194, 251–254, 295
Patriotic Union of Kurdistan, 86
Patterson, Anne, 242–243, 245–246
Pena Nieto, Enrique, 290
Pence, Mike, 252
People's Democratic Party of Afghanistan, 100
People's Liberation Army of Namibia (PLAN), 126
People's Movement for the Liberation of Angola (MPLA), 82

Peres, Shimon, 218
Peron, Isabelle, 76
Perot, Ross, 169
Perry, William, 171
Persian Gulf War, First, 143, 145, 155–157
Peru, 147–148
Petraeus, David, 213, 237, 273
Philadelphia Inquirer, 141
Philippines, 13–14, 18
Phillips, Rufus, 26
Phoenix Program/Project Phung Hoang (CORDS), 23–25, 31
Pike Committee (House Select Committee on Intelligence), 22, 87
PLAN. *see* People's Liberation Army of Namibia (PLAN)
Plan Colombia, 174–178, 224–226
Podhoretz, Norman, 137
Poindexter, John, 133
police brutality, 35–36, 143–144, 184
police corruption, 64–65, 96, 143–144
political activism: Cold War foreign policies and, 55; domestic surveillance and, 38, 50, 96; Nixon administration and, 54–55; Nixon's anti-drug campaign and, 61; "Port Huron Statement," 55; segregation and, 55; War on Drugs and, 96; Weathermen and, 55
Pompeo, Mike, 288
Pontecorvo, Gillo, 17
Popular Front for the Liberation of Palestine (PFLP), 46–47, 180
Popular Movement for the Liberation of Angola (MPLA), 126, 129
Posse Comitatus Act of 1878, 109–110
Powell, Colin: Iraq War and, 197–198, 202, 211; Somalia and, 159–161; Yugoslavia crisis and, 163
pretrial release, 62
prison culture, 209
prison funding, 114, 149, 171
prison sentences, 148, 151, 171
Prohibition, 143
Proud Boys, 295
Psychological Operations in Guerrilla Warfare, 106
Public Interest, The, 34

Qaddafi, Khamis, 271
Qaddafi, Muammar el-, 122–125, 269–272
Qaddafi, Mutassim, 270–271
Qaddafi, Seif al-Islam, 271
Qatar, 241, 272–273, 282, 286
Quiet American, The (Greene), 13
Qurayshi, Abu Ibrahim al-Hashimi al-, 283

Rabbani, Burhanuddin, 102
Rabin, Yitzhak, 87–88
Racketeer-influenced and Corrupt
    Organizations (RICO) provisions, 63
Rahman, Gul, 193
Ramparts magazine, 38
Razza v. City of New York, 249
Reagan, Nancy, 114
Reagan, Ronald, antiwar movement and, 54–55,
    84; law enforcement and, 108–110, 1980
    Presidential election and, 5, 98–99; Reagan
    Doctrine and, 128; Rhodesia and, 84; War
    on Drugs and, 110–113
Reagan administration: Afghanistan and,
    103–104; Anti-Drug Abuse Act (1986), 113;
    anti-Soviet propaganda and, 104; approach to
    crime of, 99, 108; assassination and, 120–121;
    Campaign Against Marijuana Production
    (CAMP), 110–112; Central America and,
    104–108; conservative organizations, 128;
    conventional arms sales and, 104, 106; covert
    actions in Honduras and Nicaragua,
    106–107; drug policy of, 99, 108–115,
    135–136; Iran-Contra scandal, 122,
    130–136; "Just Say No" Anti-Drug
    Campaign, 114; Libya and, 122–125; Middle
    East policy and, 115–119; NSDD 17, 105;
    NSDD 75 and, 103; NSDD 166 and, 104;
    NSDD 187 and, 129; NSDD 212 and,
    128–129; NSDD 221 and, 112; secret bases
    and, 192; southern Africa and, 125–126,
    127*fig*, 128–130; Task Force on Violent
    Crime and, 108–109; terrorism efforts and
    (NSDD 138), 119–120; Terrorism Incident
    Working Group, 121; Weinberger Doctrine
    and, 120–121
Redstone, Sumner, 221
Reno, Janet, 172
Reston, James, 47–48
Revolutionary Armed Forces of Colombia
    (FARC), 174–178, 177*fig*, 224–226
Rhodesia, 78–82, 84
Ribicoff, Abraham, 72
Rice, Condoleezza, 200, 211, 219, 241
Rise and Fall of the Great Powers, The (Kennedy),
    136–137
Rivkin, David B., Jr., 220–221
Rockefeller drug laws, 67–72
Rockefeller, Nelson: drug policy and, 67–69;
    political aspirations and, 68–69
Rodriguez, Felix, 31
Rodriguez, Jose, Jr., 257–258
Rogers, Don, 113
Rogers, William, 49, 59–60, 79–80, 84–85

Rohrabacher, Dana, 252
Roosevelt, Kermit "Kim," 75
Ross, Ricky, 131
Rostow, Walt Whitman, 13, 19–20, 31, 37
Rove, Karl, 199, 221–222
Rubin, Barnett, 239
Rudman, Warren, 134
Rumsfeld, Donald, 187, 197–199, 205, 211, 214,
    230–231
Rusk, Dean, 26–27
Russia, 273, 282, 296
Rwanda, 161

Sadat, Anwar al-, 60–61, 87–88, 92–93,
    103
Safari Club, 92–93, 95
Saleh, Ali Abdullah, 285–286
Sandinistas, 105–108
San Jose Mercury News, 136
Santa Lucia base, 147
Santarelli, Donald, 61
Sarkozy, Nicolas, 271
Saudi Arabia, 182, 230, 241, 272, 282, 286
Savimbi, Jonas, 126, 128, 130
Schlesinger, James, 137
Schrader, Stuart, 37
Schumer, Charles, 115
Schweich, Thomas, 252
Scowcroft, Brent, 158–159, 162–163
September 11 attacks, 103, 119, 144, 185–186,
    303. *See also* Global War on Terror
Serbia, 162–163
Sharon, Ariel, 116, 214–216
Sherry, Michael, 113
Shields, Vincent, 108
Shlaudeman, Harry, 76–77
Shultz, George, 120, 130
Siciliano, Rocco, 80
Singlaub, John, 132
Single Convention on Narcotic Drugs (1961),
    71, 299
Slotkin, Elissa, 294–295
Slovenia, 162
Smith, Benjamin, 174
Smith, Ian, 78
Smith, K. Wayne, 23
Smith, William French, 108
Soleimani, Qasem, 286–288
Somalia: airstrikes and, 293; Alliance for the
    Restoration of Peace and Counter-Terrorism
    (ARPCT), 264; al-Shabaab and, 264–268;
    civil war in, 157–158; conflict with Ethiopia
    and, 93, 94*fig*, 95; drone strikes and,
    267–268; famine, 157–158; Islamic Courts

Somalia (*continued*)
Union (ICU), 264; Obama administration and, 264–268; Somali National Alliance (SNA), 159–161; Transitional Federal Government (TFG), 264–266; Trump administration and, 293; US Somalia intervention and, 157–161
Somali National Alliance (SNA), 159–161
Somoza Debayle, Anastasio, 105
Sorkin, Aaron, 223
South Africa: African National Congress, 81; on American segregation, 81; Angola and, 126; apartheid, 30, 78, 81, 84, 128–130; civil unrest in, 129–130; Mandela and ANC and, 130; Namibia and, 126, 139; Nixon administration and, 78–80; Reagan administration, 126, 126*fig*, 128–129; Rhodesia and, 78, 81
South Lebanese Army (SLA), 167, 218
South West Africa People's Organization (SWAPO), 126
Soviet Union: Afghanistan and, 99–101; Angola and, 82; Arab-Israel War (1973) and, 60; Iranian Revolution and, 101; Iraq and, 85; June 1967 War and, 42; Namibia and, 126; Nixon administration and, 49; NSDD 138 and, 120; Reagan administration and, 103–104, 119–120, 138; Rhodesia and, 81–82; Safari Club agreement, 92–93; Somalia-Ethiopia conflict and, 93
Special Presidential Task Force Relating to Narcotics, Marihuana and Dangerous Drugs, 74
Special Weapons and Tactics (SWAT) teams, 254–255
Sporkin, Stanley, 148
Stalin, Joseph, 9–10
Stevens, Christopher, 271
Stolz, Richard, 259
Street Terrorism Enforcement and Prevention Act (CA, 1988), 150
Student Nonviolent Coordinating Committee (SNCC), 34
Students for a Democratic Society (SDS), 55
Suez War (1956), 16, 42
Suharto, 32–33
Sukarno, 9, 31–33
Sulzberger, C. L. "Cy," 48
Surnow, Joel, 222
Suskind, Ron, 189
Syria: Arab-Israeli (June 1967) War and, 40, 41*fig*, 42–43; Arab-Israeli War (October 1973) and, 60; CIA covert operations in, 9; drone strikes and, 284; foreign opposition groups, 274; Free Syrian Army (FSA) and, 272–273, 281, 283; ISIS and, 281–283; Lebanon and, 115; NSDD 138 and, 120; Nusra Front (*Jabhat al-Nusra*), 272–274, 281, 283; Obama administration, 272–274, 276; Organization for the Liberation of Syria (*Hay'at Tahrir al-Sham*), 283; refugees from, 279; sanctions and, 289–290; security service (*mukhabarat*), 272; Syrian Democratic Forces, 283

Taguba, Antonio, 209
Taliban: George W. Bush administration and, 186, 212, 239, 241; Clinton administration and, 182; drone strikes and, 245–246; as insurgency, 186–187, 236; Obama administration and, 235; opium cultivation and, 229–230, 234–236, 252; reemergence of, 227, 229–230; Trump administration and, 294
Tal, Wasfi al-, 57
Tandy, Karen, 261
Taraki, Nur Mohammad, 100
Tarnoff, Peter, 26
Task Force on Violent Crime, 108–109
Taylor, Maxwell: Bay of Pigs Review and, 9; Operation Mongoose and, 9
Tenet, George, 193, 202
terrorism, 58–59, 106, 119–121, 171–173. *See also* Global War on Terror
Terrorism Screening Database (TSDB), 247–248
Terrorist Identities Datamart Environment (TIDE), 248
Tet Offensive (1968), 22, 24, 26, 43
Thieu, Nguyen Van, 45
Thompson, Robert, 16
Thornburgh, Richard, 135–136
Thrasher, Frederic, 143
3 Percenters, 295
Tilton, John, 31–32
Time Magazine, 101, 115
Tito, Josip Broz, 162
Top Gun, 123
torture, 191–194, 223, 256–259, 298
Trump, Donald, 5, 276–277, 279–280
Trump administration: Afghanistan and, 293–294; Bannon and, 280; domestic antiterrorism measures, 251; domestic policy and, 292–293; foreign policy and, 293; Hizbullah and, 289; Iran and, 287–288; Iraq and, 287–288; ISIS and, 283, 293; Israel and, 287–288; January 6 riot, 294–295; Libya and, 286; Mexico and, 292; Middle East and, 293; Somalia and, 293; Syria and, 283; Yemen and, 286, 293

TTP (Pakistani Taliban, *Tehrik-e-Taliban Pakistan*), 245–246
Tuan Shi-wen, 67
Tunisia, 268–269
Tunney, John, 83
Turkey, 72–74, 271–273, 282–283, 286
Turner, Carlton, 110
Turse, Nick, 23
24 (television show), 222–223
2008 financial crisis, 5, 231–232, 275

Ugly American, The (Burdick), 13
Ukraine, 296
UNITA (National Union for the Total Independence of Angola), 82, 126, 128–130
United Arab Emirates, 182, 272, 282
United Kingdom, 14, 16, 84, 200–201, 234–235, 286
United Nations: Algeria and, 17; Clinton administration and, 159; Convention against Illicit Traffic in Narcotic Drugs and Psychotropic Substances, 135–136, 299; Guevara and, 29–30; Iraq War and, 200; Palestine Liberation Organization (PLO) and, 88; Somalia intervention and, 157–161; Yugoslavia crisis and, 162–164
United Self Defense Forces of Colombia (AUC), 174
United States: anxieties about decline of, 136–137, 275–276, 300; influence of international treatment of narcotics, 299; influence of international treatment of terrorism, 299; "radical Islam" narrative and, 278–279; segregation, 30; Syrian refugees and, 279. *See also individual administrations*; *individual people*
UN Security Council: Arab-Israeli War (June 1967), 60; Arab-Israeli War (October 1973), 60; Iraqi invasion of Kuwait and, 155–156; Iraq War and, 202; Libya and, 270; Namibia and, 126; Nixon administration and, 58; relationship to developing countries and, 158; Resolution 242 of, 60, 168; Resolution 338 of, 60; Resolution 1390 of, 188; Rhodesia and, 78; South Africa and, 126
Uribe Vélez, Álvaro, 224–225, 261
Uruguay, 75–76
US Agency for International Development (USAID), 235
USA PATRIOT Act, 189–191, 194, 251–254, 295
US Arms Export Control Act (1976), 83
US Coast Guard, 131, 150
US Defense Department, 85, 148, 156, 195, 274, 296

US military: Abu Ghraib prison and, 208–209; Africa Command (AFRICOM), 265; counterinsurgency strategy (COIN) and, 213; crime and drugs as justifications for domestic use of, 6; domestic surveillance and, 56–57; Lebanon and, 118; narcotics and, 302; Native American imagery and, 2; OpBat Task Force and, 131; political pressure on reporting in Vietnamese War, 23, 27; tensions with CIA over Vietnamese insurgency, 21–22; War for Civilization narrative and, 6. *See also individual operations*; *individual people*
US Military Assistance Command in Vietnam (MACV), 22, 44
US Navy, 150
US News and World Report, 115
USS *Cole*, 181
US Secret Service, 38
US Southern Command, 290
US State Department, 22, 73, 80, 85, 178

Valenti, Jack, 221
Valentine, Douglas, 24
Viet Minh, 13
Vietnam: "agroville" program and, 18; Diem and, 12; Johnson administration policies in, 20–21; Kennedy administration policies in, 14, 16, 18–19; Lansdale and, 14; Law 10/59 and, 12; map of, 15*fig*; National Liberation Front (NLF), 12–13; secure zones and, 18; South's civil defense units, 44; "Strategic Hamlet Program" and, 14, 16; Republic of Vietnam's National Police, 24–25
Vietnam Veterans Against the War, 207
Vietnam War: Acheson and, 79; Agent Orange defoliant and, 50; American antiwar movement, 35, 50, 54–55; American primacy and decline narrative, 5, 96; *The Battle of Algiers* and, 17; Bush-Kerry election and, 206–208; casualties from, 49; Civil Operations and Rural Development Support (CORDS) program/Phoenix Program/Project Phung Hoang, 23–25, 31, 212; civil rights groups and, 34–35; Golden Triangle heroin trade and, 64–65, 67; Guevara on, 31; Hamlet Evaluation System and, 21; Hollywood and, 298; influence of Algeria on, 17–18; Komer's reports about, 20–21; Kuomintang (KMT) and, 65, 67; My Lai massacre (1968), 25; Nixon administration and, 44–46, 48–49, 96; Paris Peace Accords (1973), 45; Pike Committee on, 22; political pressure to report effectiveness in counterinsurgency, 23; press and, 26;

Vietnam War (*continued*)
  returning soldiers and, 64; South Vietnamese
  "Civic Action Cadre" program, 21; Tet
  Offensive (1968), 22, 24, 28, 43;
  Vietnamization, 44–46
Violent Crime Control and Law Enforcement
  Act ("Crime Bill"), 170–171

Wag the Dog, 180
Walters, Vernon, 60–61, 93
War for Civilization rhetoric, 186, 199–200,
  215, 231, 295–298
War on Crime: antiterrorism measures and,
  247–251; Clinton administration, 170–172;
  costs of, 296; exportation of, 297; Johnson
  administration and, 33–39; Law Enforcement
  Assistance Act (1965), 33; militarization of
  police and, 148–150, 254–256; Nixon
  administration and, 54–55; Organized Crime
  Control Act (1970), 63; presentation of, 3;
  Reagan administration, 112, 139; tactics from
  Vietnam and, 50; Violent Crime Control and
  Law Enforcement Act ("Crime Bill"), 170–171
War on Drugs: in American popular culture,
  112–113; Andean Initiative, 148–149;
  Anti-Drug Abuse Law (1988), 147; antiwar
  movement and, 95–96; border policy and,
  109; George H. W. Bush administration and,
  147–153; George W. Bush administration
  and, 183, 224–226, 230; cartels and, 174;
  Clinton administration and, 170, 173–174;
  costs of, 296; counternarcotics efforts in
  Afghanistan, 234–236; criminal justice
  system and, 149; DEA collection of telephone
  records and (USTO program), 151–152;
  decriminalization policies vs., 301; domestic
  surveillance and, 251–254, 290; Drug
  Enforcement Administration (DEA) and,
  71–72, 174; Ehrlichman on, 95–96; George
  H. W. Bush campaign against Dukakis and,
  146–147; Hollywood and, 224; humanizing
  of, 300–301; institutionalization of, 4;
  international effects of, 71–77, 112; Latin
  America and, 75–76; Mexico and, 74–75,
  174, 260–263, 290–292; militarization and,
  148–150; "narcoterrorism and," 251–254,
  290; Nixon administration and, 61–64, 96;
  Panama and, 153–155; Plan Colombia and,

174–178, 224–226; presentation of, 3; race
  and, 95–96; racialization of, 6; Reagan
  administration, 109–115, 139; Rockefeller
  drug laws and, 67–72; Turkey and, 72–74;
  USA PATRIOT Act and, 251–254
War on Poverty, 33
Warsaw Pact, 138
Washington Post, 35, 57, 128, 220; on bin Laden,
  179
Waters, Maxine, 135
Watts, William, 29
Weather Underground, 55, 57
Webb, Gary, 135
Weber, Vin, 128
Webster, William, 153
Weinberger, Casper, 120
Weinberger Doctrine, 120–121
Western Somali Liberation Front, 93
West Wing, The (television show), 223
Wheeler, Earle, 21, 44
white supremacism, 80–81, 171–172
Wicker, Tom, 110
Wilson, Harold, 78
Wilson, James Q., 33–34, 105
Wire, The (television show), 224
Wisner, Frank, 26
Wolfowitz, Paul, 156; on Iraq, 197
Woodward, Bob, 238
Wood, William, 235
World Bank, 234–235
Wright, Jim, 113

Yamamoto, Donald, 265
Yassin, Sheikh Ahmed, 216
Yemen, 285–286, 293
Yoo, John, 190
Younge, Sammy, Jr., 34
Yugoslavia, 162

Zaire, 83
Zakaria, Fareed, 275
Zambia, 82–83
Zardari, Asif Ali, 243–244
Zarqawi, Abu Musab al-, 204–205, 214
Zenawi, Meles, 264
Zero Dark Thirty (Bigelow), 258–259
Zia ul-Huq, Mohammed, 165
Zimbabwe African People's Union, 81